VOLUME 639

JANUARY 2012

THE ANNALS

of The American Academy of Political
and Social Science

Gender and Race Inequality in Management: Critical Issues, New Evidence

Special Editor:

MATT L. HUFFMAN
University of California, Irvine

Los Angeles | London | New Delhi
Singapore | Washington DC

Origin and Purpose. The Academy was organized December 14, 1889, to promote the progress of political and social science, especially through publications and meetings. The Academy does not take sides in controverted questions, but seeks to gather and present reliable information to assist the public in forming an intelligent and accurate judgment.

Meetings. The Academy occasionally holds a meeting in the spring extending over two days.

Publications. THE ANNALS of The American Academy of Political and Social Science is the bimonthly publication of the Academy. Each issue contains articles on some prominent social or political problem, written at the invitation of the editors. These volumes constitute important reference works on the topics with which they deal, and they are extensively cited by authorities throughout the United States and abroad.

Membership. Each member of the Academy receives THE ANNALS and may attend the meetings of the Academy. Membership is open only to individuals. Annual dues: $94.00 for the regular paperbound edition (clothbound, $134.00). Members may also purchase single issues of THE ANNALS for $35 each (clothbound, $48). Student memberships are available for $52.00.

Subscriptions. THE ANNALS of The American Academy of Political and Social Science (ISSN 0002-7162) (J295) is published bimonthly—in January, March, May, July, September, and November—by SAGE Publications, 2455 Teller Road, Thousand Oaks, CA 91320. Periodicals postage paid at Thousand Oaks, California, and at additional mailing offices. POSTMASTER: Send address changes to The Annals of The American Academy of Political and Social Science, c/o SAGE Publications, 2455 Teller Road, Thousand Oaks, CA 91320. Institutions may subscribe to THE ANNALS at the annual rate: $827 (clothbound, $933). Single issues of THE ANNALS may be obtained by individuals who are not members of the Academy for $106 each (clothbound, $155). Single issues of THE ANNALS have proven to be excellent supplementary texts for classroom use. Direct inquiries regarding adoptions to THE ANNALS c/o SAGE Publications (address below).

All correspondence concerning membership in the Academy, dues renewals, inquiries about membership status, and/or purchase of single issues of THE ANNALS should be sent to THE ANNALS c/o SAGE Publications, 2455 Teller Road, Thousand Oaks, CA 91320. Telephone: (800) 818-SAGE (7243) and (805) 499-0721; Fax/Order line: (805) 375-1700; e-mail: journals@sagepub.com. *Please note that orders under $30 must be prepaid.* For all customers outside the Americas, please visit http://www.sagepub.co.uk/customerCare.nav for information.

Printed on acid-free paper

THE ANNALS

© 2012 by The American Academy of Political and Social Science

Editorial Office: 202 S. 36th Street, Philadelphia, PA 19104-3806
For information about membership* (individuals only) and subscriptions (institutions), address:
SAGE Publications
2455 Teller Road
Thousand Oaks, CA 91320

For SAGE Publications: Allison Leung (Production) and Lori Hart (Marketing)

From India and South Asia,
write to:
SAGE PUBLICATIONS INDIA Pvt Ltd
B-42 Panchsheel Enclave, P.O. Box 4109
New Delhi 110 017
INDIA

From Europe, the Middle East,
and Africa, write to:
SAGE PUBLICATIONS LTD
1 Oliver's Yard, 55 City Road
London EC1Y 1SP
UNITED KINGDOM

*Please note that members of the Academy receive THE ANNALS with their membership.
International Standard Serial Number ISSN 0002-7162
International Standard Book Number ISBN 978-1-4522-4085-5 (Vol. 639, 2012) paper
International Standard Book Number ISBN 978-1-4522-4084-8 (Vol. 639, 2012) cloth
Manufactured in the United States of America. First printing, January 2012.

Please visit http://ann.sagepub.com and under the "More about this journal" menu on the right-hand side, click on the Abstracting/Indexing link to view a full list of databases in which this journal is indexed.

Information about membership rates, institutional subscriptions, and back issue prices may be found on the facing page.

Advertising. Current rates and specifications may be obtained by writing to The Annals Advertising and Promotion Manager at the Thousand Oaks office (address above). Acceptance of advertising in this journal in no way implies endorsement of the advertised product or service by SAGE or the journal's affiliated society(ies) or the journal editor(s). No endorsement is intended or implied. SAGE reserves the right to reject any advertising it deems as inappropriate for this journal.

Claims. Claims for undelivered copies must be made no later than six months following month of publication. The publisher will supply replacement issues when losses have been sustained in transit and when the reserve stock will permit.

Change of Address. Six weeks' advance notice must be given when notifying of change of address. Please send the old address label along with the new address to the SAGE office address above to ensure proper identification. Please specify the name of the journal.

THE ANNALS

OF THE AMERICAN ACADEMY OF POLITICAL AND SOCIAL SCIENCE

Volume 639   January 2012

IN THIS ISSUE:

*Gender and Race Inequality in Management:
Critical Issues, New Evidence*

Special Editor: MATT L. HUFFMAN

FORTHCOMING

Advancing Reasoned Action Theory: New Populations, New Behaviors, New Understandings
Special Editor: MICHAEL HENNESSY

Immigration and the Changing Neighborhood Dynamics of Crime in American Cities
Special Editors: JOHN MACDONALD AND ROBERT SAMPSON

Keywords: gender; race; management; inequality

Gender, Race, and Management

By
MATT L. HUFFMAN

Inequality scholars need no convincing about the importance of managerial occupations. Differential access to managerial jobs is one of inequality's linchpins, as these positions secure higher average wages and other rewards for their incumbents than do other jobs. Besides spawning an expansive academic literature, the question of access to managerial jobs for protected groups has also been the focus of countless gender and race discrimination lawsuits, has formed the basis of numerous government reports (e.g., U.S. Government Accountability Office 2010), and, made the "glass ceiling" a household term.

The past few decades have witnessed provocative trends regarding women and racial/ethnic minorities in management. For women, their overall representation in managerial occupations has markedly improved, although there is mounting empirical evidence of the slowing of managerial gender integration (Cohen, Huffman, and Knauer 2009). Therefore, changes in women's managerial representation can be viewed in the context of the possible stall in progress toward gender equality that has captured some scholars' attention recently (e.g., Cotter, Hermsen, and Vanneman 2004; England 2010). Research on the gender stall points to an ebbing of progress toward gender equality on a number of key indicators, including labor force participation among female managers (Percheski 2008) and wages

Matt L. Huffman is an associate professor of sociology at the University of California, Irvine. In addition to gender and racial inequality within and across organizations, his work examines changes in access to managerial positions for women and racial minorities and the consequences of those changes for other workers. His recent work appears in the American Sociological Review *and* Administrative Science Quarterly.

DOI: 10.1177/0002716211422035

ANNALS, *AAPSS*, 639, January, 2012

(Cohen, Huffman, and Knauer 2009). Despite increasing interest—and at times lively debate—regarding the gender stall, management trends have yet to be fully considered, which is one way that the importance of the research appearing in this volume is underscored. Finally, given profound changes in workplace diversity, we are sorely in need of new and innovative studies regarding the processes that lead to racial and ethnic disparities in high-status occupations and managerial careers.

It is obvious that the issues addressed in this volume of *The Annals of the American Academy of Political and Social Science* are not waning in importance. As the relative size of various groups change, the demographic composition of workplaces shifts, reviving old debates and bringing new challenges to those with an interest in managing—or studying—workplace diversity. This volume comprises a collection of articles that represent some of the most innovative and creative work relating to gender, race, and management. While the articles are diverse in their methodological approaches and theoretical orientations, they are united by their rigor and insightfulness regarding the fundamental issues they address. For example, the article by William T. Bielby examines racial inequality in the financial securities industry, analyzing the case of African American stockbrokers (now "financial consultants" or "financial advisers") employed in one of the nation's largest financial services firms. His detailed and provocative analysis considers the applicability of the minority vulnerability thesis—usually used to account for racial gaps in career stability (see Wilson and McBrier 2005)—to racial wage disparities. Financial consultants provide a fascinating lens through which to view inequality-generating processes, because their compensation is determined mathematically as part of an output-based, pay-for-performance system. As such, one might assume that meritocracy would reign supreme and workers would not be subject to the kinds, or degree, of ascription that underlies inequality in other lines of work. Bielby convincingly demonstrates that this is not the case. Instead of operating meritocratically, barriers to racial equality are common, including those that affect wage trajectories early in the careers of workers, producing cumulative disadvantage over the career. Bielby concludes with several lessons for management, which are especially insightful given that the processes that contribute to inequality in the case he studies are in some ways less obvious than those seen in other employment contexts.

Susan T. Fiske's important article extends her prior work on the Stereotype Content Model (e.g., Fiske et al. 2002; Fiske, Cuddy, and Glick 2007), showing the role of ambivalent prejudices and how they are relevant to both out-group members in management positions and those interested in managing diversity. Her case studies (ambivalent sexism, heterosexism, racism, anti-immigrant biases, ageism, and classism) cogently demonstrate how the Stereotype Content Model matters for the management of diversity and issues that vary across protected groups. Fiske closes with several crucial insights about how ambivalent prejudices can be managed in contemporary workplaces, given, among other realities, that not all prejudices are alike, biases leading to inequality are often subtle and unexamined rather than overt, and emotional prejudices are the root cause of discrimination. Finally, she suggests that strategies at the level of the organization should focus on the status and interdependence structures that foster stereotypes and prejudices.

The article by Jeffery W. Lucas and Amy R. Baxter provides a lucid summary and analysis of theory and research on power, status, and influence—particularly how the concepts are treated in sociology's group processes tradition—and discusses these concepts' relevance for organizational diversity. Although it is clear that workplace diversity is increasing, gains for underrepresented groups are not extending to upper-level management positions. And although research supports the contention that diversity is positively related to outcomes that may benefit an organization (for example, innovation and creativity), Lucas and Baxter show how status processes and disparities in power and influence pose significant challenges for underrepresented groups, even when efforts to avoid discrimination are undertaken. Their comprehensive treatment of social psychological concepts that are central for understanding, among other things, the microlevel bases of inequality in organizations leads them to some provocative yet practical solutions to some of the challenges associated with increasing workplace diversity.

Lauren A. Rivera's piece brings critical qualitative evidence to the fundamental question of how to design diversity programs that are more than mere "window dressings" that project a façade of effectiveness. Rivera's article is extremely important because although diversity management is a burgeoning field, we know little about how diversity programs actually work—or fail to work—on the ground, in real organizational contexts. By gleaning and analyzing detailed ethnographic and interview data from a professional service firm (which she notes to be a "contemporary gateway into the American managerial elite"), Rivera reports a strong divergence in how race and gender impact the hiring process, implying that a "one-size-fits-all" approach to diversity programs is ill-advised. Additionally, and in line with prior research (e.g., Kalev, Dobbin, and Kelly 2006), she finds that authority may be an indispensable part of effective diversity practices. The importance of authority is shown in one of her key findings, which highlights pronounced status and structural divides between individuals responsible for overseeing diversity recruitment and those who actually wield the authority to make hiring decisions. This disconnect, along with pervasive cultural beliefs held by decision-makers that devalue diversity while positing that university prestige is an essential sign of merit, is identified as a major obstacle that limits diversity programs' effectiveness.

The article by Fiona M. Kay and Elizabeth H. Gorman investigates racial/ethnic differences in access to high-status positions in large U.S. law firms. Specifically, they examine the role of formal developmental practices and cultural values in shaping the representation of African Americans, Latinos, and Asian Americans among law firm partners. What is important is that they find that the commonsense notion that organizational attempts to improve nonmanagerial workers' social connections and technical and interpersonal skills through cultural values and formal practices is misguided. In fact, some practices are associated with a *reduction* in protected groups' representation among firm partners. To the extent that those who create and manage diversity and employee-development programs rely blindly on commonsense notions of what works to increase diversity, the goal of racial integration in work organizations will not be well served. In fact, as Kay and Gorman lucidly demonstrate, some programs and policies that appear perfectly justifiable on paper may actually represent a step backward.

The article by Heather A. Haveman and Lauren S. Beresford provides a not-so-subtle reminder of the importance of culture in shaping managerial careers. Responding to supply-side, investment accounts that stress choices made by individuals regarding education, training, and occupational aspirations, Haveman and Beresford argue that taken-for-granted cultural expectations and gender stereotypes are what underlie the supply-side differences we observe. Thus, what appear to be gendered "choices" that create and maintain gender differences in managerial careers are often not choices at all. Rather, Haveman and Beresford persuasively argue for the primacy of widely held assumptions about who is best suited to lead, who is mathematically inclined, and who should shoulder the housework and child care responsibilities. These beliefs and stereotypes, they argue, are the driving forces behind observed gender differences in women's educational attainment, job preferences, and work experiences. As such, models that purport to explain the vertical gender gap in management must address these factors.

The compelling piece by George Wilson yields valuable insights into racial differences in predictors of women's mobility into upper-tier occupational categories and addresses notable shortcomings in the literature. His dynamic analysis of the Panel Study of Income Dynamics is rife with important findings. For example, his results support and simultaneously extend the particularistic mobility thesis, which posits a racial continuum in the factors underlying the timing and determinants of mobility into upper-tier occupations. Specifically, mobility among white women not only occurs the quickest, but is relatively unstructured by the same factors that limit the mobility opportunities for black women. The forms of disadvantage that depress the mobility chances for blacks operate similarly among Latinas, although less strongly, which places them in an intermediate position. Wilson engages questions that are fundamental to stratification researchers while also providing a much-needed focus on how traditional stratification variables intersect with race/ethnicity to produce unique labor market advantages and disadvantages with respect to mobility into highly paid occupations.

In his article, Ryan A. Smith provides new, important findings regarding two major sources of inequality by race and gender. Using data from the Multi-City Study of Urban Inequality (MCSUI), Smith tests hypotheses drawn from the glass ceiling and the glass escalator hypotheses. Although there is no shortage of tests of the glass ceiling hypothesis and debates about its meaning and proper specification (e.g., Cotter et al. 2001; Wright, Baxter, and Birkelund 1995), those interested in the glass escalator (see Williams 1992) might feel shortchanged. Of course, both theories are salient for understanding inequality in organizational hierarchies, which makes Smith's empirical findings especially noteworthy. Smith finds that wage inequality between white men and other groups is largely constant across levels of authority and, as such, is not more pronounced at higher levels. However, Smith's data allow him to address variation in supervisory effects. Specifically, he reports that in settings where workers report to female and minority supervisors, nearly all groups increasingly fall behind white men in terms of relative wages. This marks important new evidence regarding the glass escalator. Smith's other findings regarding employer benefits are equally engaging and nuanced.

Fidan Ana Kurtulus and Donald Tomaskovic-Devey engage an important but thorny empirical question: To what extent do female managers influence patterns of inequality in U.S. workplaces? Specifically, they analyze panel data (covering 1990 to 2003) from the Equal Employment Opportunity Commission that includes more than twenty thousand large private-sector firms representing all states and industries. Using a fixed effects regression model, which allows for stringent tests of within-firm change, they demonstrate that female top managers exert a significant positive influence on the representation of women in lower-level managerial ranks of U.S. firms. Furthermore, they find, as does some prior research on this topic (e.g., Huffman, Cohen, and Pearlman 2010), that the female manager effect has waned over time. In addition to this primary finding, the importance of this article lies in its attention to potential racial and ethnic differences in the managerial gender composition effect. Their finding—that the representation of black, Hispanic, and Asian female top managers is also positively related to the subsequent representation of black, Hispanic, and Asian women at the lower levels of management—fills a gaping hole in the literature. As research addressing potential ripple effects of the changing gender and race composition of management grows, this article is sure to figure prominently.

David J. Maume's article, based on detailed analyses of the 1997 and 2002 National Study of the Changing Workforce (NSCW) surveys, also provides critical insights into racial dynamics in management. His article focuses on, among other provocative issues, the largely neglected question of whether minority status shapes wages and working conditions among managers and the subordinates who report to them. Maume's findings also provide an important assessment of progress in eliminating racial ascription in entry into management, by testing whether racial gaps in managerial rewards and working conditions have decreased. Although there is some evidence for this optimistic view of racial progress, the story is in some ways not a pretty one, and far from simple. The story remains complex and nuanced and perhaps even less sanguine when Maume discusses the potential for minority managers to foster the careers of minority subordinates. Here, bottom-up ascription proves prominent, leading to minority bosses' supervising minority workers while being largely ghettoized in what amount to glorified administrative jobs.

Adding to this line of inquiry, Kevin Stainback and Soyoung Kwon inject important and timely cross-national evidence into debates about whether female organizational leaders significantly impact inequality among those who work below them. That is, they return to the question of whether female leaders act as "agents of change" or merely "cogs in the machine," exerting no effect on inequality. Offering a detailed analysis of longitudinal data from the 2005 Korean Workplace Panel Survey, they find some support for the "agents of change" perspective. Specifically, they report lower levels of gender segregation in organizations where women hold a larger share of the managerial positions. In addition, and marking a weighty innovation, Stainback and Kwon are able to distinguish the effects of female managers from female supervisors (something I have unfortunately been unable to do in my own recent work). The effects for female supervisors are less clear-cut: at lower levels of representation, female supervisors are associated with lower levels of gender segregation, which is consistent with the "agents of change" expectation. However, when women hold approximately one-third of supervisory positions, segregation increases as female representation rises among supervisors. They attribute this provocative result to "bottom-up ascription," where women in supervisory positions are most likely to direct other female workers instead of men (see Elliott and Smith 2004).

Sheryl L. Skaggs and Julie A. Kmec analyze a unique establishment-level dataset on hospitals to test predictions about the effects of external institutional and legal pressures, as well as internal pressures, on the representation of nonwhites among health care professionals. As such, this article marks a rich contribution to scholarship that addresses the effects of organizational environments on processes that exacerbate or reduce ascriptive inequality in organizations and shape diversity. Their findings clearly delineate the internal and external factors that increase the racial and ethnic diversity among health care professionals. Notably, their findings highlight the potential effect of the racial/ethnic composition of a hospital's existing managerial workforce on the racial/ethnic makeup of its health care professionals. The result is clear and important: diversity within the top ranks of organizations tends to "trickle down" to shape the demographic composition of other parts of the workforce.

Taekjin Shin's piece addresses the important topic of inequality at the top of corporate hierarchies; specifically, Shin breaks new ground by examining the gender gap in executive compensation. Using underutilized compensation data from Standard and Poor's ExecuComp dataset, Shin draws from theories of in-group bias and demographic similarity effects to hypothesize that women serving on compensation committees are less likely than men to assess the competence and leadership of female executives negatively. As a result, women on the compensation committee are predicted to offer more valuable compensation packages to female executives than to their male counterparts. The results from Shin's models support this view by showing a negative relationship between the size of the gender compensation gap and the proportion of women on the compensation committee. This article importantly addresses the "critical mass" issue regarding the potential effect of women's representation in powerful positions (e.g., Konrad and Kramer 2006). This issue has not often been subjected to the kind of rigorous analysis that Shin provides.

In closing, let me offer a disclaimer: any attempt to briefly summarize the engaging and provocative articles that constitute this volume will not do them justice. I can only hope that this introduction will provide the motivation to read further, as these thought-provoking and expertly crafted articles signify cutting-edge research on gender, race, and management by prominent scholars who represent diverse disciplines and methodological approaches. As such, anyone interested in this volume's theme will ignore them at their own peril.

References

Cohen, Philip N., Matt L. Huffman, and Stefanie Knauer. 2009. Stalled progress? Gender segregation and wage inequality among managers, 1980–2000. *Work and Occupations* 36:318–42.

Cotter, David A., Joan M. Hermsen, Seth Ovadia, and Reeve Vanneman. 2001. The glass ceiling effect. *Social Forces* 80:655–81.

Cotter, David A., Joan M. Hermsen, and Reeve Vanneman. 2004. *Gender inequality at work.* New York, NY: Russell Sage Foundation and Population Reference Bureau.

Elliott, James R., and Ryan A. Smith. 2004. Race, gender and workplace power. *American Sociological Review* 69:365–86.

England, Paula. 2010. The gender revolution: Uneven and stalled. *Gender & Society* 24:149–66.

Fiske, Susan T., Amy J. C. Cuddy, and Peter Glick. 2007. Universal dimensions of social perception: Warmth and competence. *Trends in Cognitive Science* 11:77–83.

Fiske, Susan T., Amy J. C. Cuddy, Peter Glick, and Jun Xu. 2002. A model of (often mixed) stereotype content: Competence and warmth respectively follow from perceived status and competition. *Journal of Personality and Social Psychology* 82:878–902.

Huffman, Matt L., Philip N. Cohen, and Jessica Pearlman. 2010. Engendering change: Organizational dynamics and workplace gender desegregation, 1975–2005. *Administrative Science Quarterly* 55:255–77.

Kalev, Alexandra, Frank Dobbin, and Erin Kelly. 2006. Best practices or best guesses? Assessing the efficacy of corporate affirmative action and diversity policies. *American Sociological Review* 71:589–617.

Konrad, Alison M., and Vicki W. Kramer. December 2006. How many women do boards need? *Harvard Business Review.* Available from http://hbr.org/2006/12/how-many-women-do-boards-need/ar/1.

Percheski, Christine. 2008. Opting out? Cohort differences in professional women's employment rates from 1960 to 2005. *American Sociological Review* 73:497–517.

U.S. Government Accountability Office (GAO). 2010. Women in management: Analysis of female managers' representation, characteristics, and pay. GAO-10-892R. Washington, DC: GAO.

Williams, Christine L. 1992. The glass escalator: Hidden advantages for men in the "female" professions. *Social Problems* 39:253–66.

Wilson, George, and Debra McBrier. 2005. Race and loss of privilege: African American/white differences in the determinants of layoffs from upper-tier occupations. *Sociological Forum* 20:301–21.

Wright, Erik Olin, Janeen Baxter, and Gunn Elisabeth Birkelund. 1995. The gender gap in workplace authority: A cross-national study. *American Sociological Review* 60:407–35.

Minority Vulnerability in Privileged Occupations: Why Do African American Financial Advisers Earn Less than Whites in a Large Financial Services Firm?

By
WILLIAM T. BIELBY

Building on recent work on contemporary forms of bias in meritocratic personnel systems, the author assesses sources of racial disadvantage in an output-based pay-for-performance system for compensating financial advisers in a large financial services firm. Using data from expert reports submitted in racial discrimination litigation, the author shows how racial differences in access to white wealth, limits on African Americans' full participation in broker teams, racialized approaches to multicultural marketing, and diffuse lines of authority for diversity and nondiscrimination created racial barriers that were sustained and amplified by a cumulative advantage system for allocating productivity-enhancing resources. The author concludes with a discussion of management strategies for minimizing minority vulnerability in privileged professions and the challenges faced when the sources of bias are neither unconscious nor unintended but are instead located at least in part in racially segregated social relations and power differences among professionals who hold formally equivalent positions in a company's job structure.

Keywords: meritocracy; racial bias; cumulative advantage; opportunity hoarding; racialized jobs; accountability structures; discrimination

The Significance of Race in Privileged Occupations

In a recent essay published in *Daedalus*, William Julius Wilson (2011) reflected on the hundreds of published studies undertaken to test the provocative thesis of his landmark book *The Declining Significance of Race* (1980). The essay defended his claim that changes in politics

William T. Bielby is a professor of sociology at the University of Illinois, Chicago, and a distinguished research scholar in the University of Arizona's Department of Sociology. His current research is on racial and gender bias in discretionary employment systems and on the use of social science research in Title VII litigation.

DOI: 10.1177/0002716211422338

and the economy during and immediately following the civil rights era of the 1960s mainly benefited middle-class African Americans and that hardly any of the consequences of profound institutional changes of that era accrued to blacks who compose the overwhelming majority of the urban poor. But in the essay he also conceded that his optimistic assessment of continuing income gains of younger well-educated African Americans and declining racial disparities in socioeconomic attainments was wrong. Reviewing quantitative studies of black/white earnings inequality, he noted that the expansion of the racial gap in earnings coincided with both a decline in public support for affirmative action and a retreat from antidiscrimination enforcement by government agencies. In light of these findings, Wilson (2011) acknowledged that, were he writing the book today, he "would place greater emphasis not only on the role of the public sector in accounting for black occupational mobility, but also on the importance of sustained public support for anti-discrimination programs, including affirmative action, to ensure that the gains continue or, at the least, are not reversed" (p. 63).

In *The Declining Significance of Race* and related works, William Julius Wilson attributed gains of highly educated African Americans since the mid-1960s to the expansion of the service sector of the economy, increased opportunities in the public sector, and the impact of affirmative action and other antidiscrimination efforts launched during the civil rights era. He was mostly silent on the nature of opportunities and barriers faced by African Americans employed in the private corporate sector. His essay and other recent writings do not address the issue in any depth, but his revised stance is at least consistent with the conclusions of a large body of research on the precariousness of the socioeconomic advances of the African American middle class. Important research by Sharon Collins and other sociologists shows that African Americans in mid- to upper-level corporate positions tend to be channeled into jobs dealing with minority concerns and constituencies with limited opportunities for further advancement (Collins 1997, 2005; Spalter-Roth and Deitch 1999). A series of studies by George Wilson and colleagues indicate that their careers are often undermined by layoff decisions rooted in cognitive bias but legitimated in terms of meritocratic ideologies of efficiency and business necessity (G. Wilson and Roscigno 2010; G. Wilson and McBrier 2005). Synthesizing this line of empirical studies with conceptual models of social closure, cognitive bias, and statistical discrimination, George Wilson developed his "minority vulnerability thesis" as a framework for understanding racial disparities in career stability in mid- to upper-level jobs. In a succinct statement of his thesis as applied to job layoffs from "upper-tier" occupations, G. Wilson and McBrier write,

> Studies comprising the minority vulnerability thesis document how employers in work settings characterized by meritocratic ideologies make layoff decisions that reinforce existing patterns of racial exclusion. Accordingly, race-based patterns of layoffs are a manifestation of "modern racial prejudice," which is characterized as situational, ostensibly nonracial, and institutional in nature. In general, the minority vulnerability thesis posits that dynamics ranging from perceived need to conform to existing norms of racial

exclusion in order to maintain a stable workforce and steady customer/client base to cognitive distortions inherent in "self-serving attributional bias" and "statistical discrimination" arising from stereotypes result in layoffs that are not discriminatory in intent but serve to disproportionately exclude racial minorities from top-level positions. (2005, 304)

The thesis also maintains "that at privileged levels of the American occupational structure African Americans' placement in racially delineated jobs and the constraints on their ability to demonstrate the 'right stuff' for favorable performance evaluations result in a set of race-specific determinants of layoffs" (p. 304). While developed to account for racial disparities in layoffs, the minority vulnerability thesis should apply in the same way to access to top-level positions, pay, and other career outcomes for African Americans in white-dominated corporate settings.

Assessing the Minority Vulnerability Thesis Applied to Financial Advisers in the Financial Services Industry

In this article, I assess whether and how the minority vulnerability thesis applies to earnings disparities by race in the financial securities industry—specifically, to the experience of African American stockbrokers (now usually referred to as "financial consultants" or "financial advisers") in the brokerage division of one of the country's largest financial services firms. It is a substantively interesting case for several reasons. First, it is an occupation with an output-based pay-for-performance system—compensation is determined by a fixed mathematical formula applied to the commissions flowing to the firm from the business that brokers do with their clients. On one hand, compared to other lucrative jobs in financial services, such as investment banking or branch management, individuals concerned about racial bias in subjective evaluations of their contributions might perceive that they will be evaluated more fairly in an area of the business in which pay is seemingly determined solely by objective measures (Roth 2004, 630–31). On the other hand, an important recent line of research and theorizing suggests that it is precisely this kind of meritocratic evaluation system that is vulnerable to contemporary forms of racial and gender bias (G. Wilson and Roscigno 2010; Castilla 2008; Castilla and Benard 2010). As Castilla and Benard note, "Meritocracy as a cultural value can serve as an 'environmental trigger' or be part of a 'tool kit' of habits that unleashes individual cognitive biases" (2010, 544).

Second, the provision of brokerage and financial services typically requires a high level of trust between broker and client, which can reinforce homophily in client preferences. Stated bluntly, all else equal, affluent white clients of a financial services firm may be more comfortable with and prefer to do business with a white financial adviser than with an African American. Relatedly, because there is substantially more wealth in the white community than in the African American community (Oliver and Shapiro 2006) and because social networks tend to be highly segregated by race (McPherson, Smith-Lovin, and Brashears 2006), African American stockbrokers who "build their book" by tapping into those networks may be at a disadvantage relative to their white counterparts. Should these prove to be significant factors creating disadvantages to earnings parity between African American and white financial advisers, it would raise difficult questions about how policies and practices inside the firm reproduce or counter institutionalized racism in the larger society.

Third, while the minority vulnerability thesis was developed to understand the precariousness of minorities in upper-tier jobs generally, specific mechanisms can and do vary by organizational context. As Stainback, Tomaskovic-Devey, and Skaggs observe (2010, 242), an adequate organizational perspective on inequality needs to be "built at the intersection of (a) organizational structure, logic, and practice; (b) the relative power of actors within workplaces; and (c) the organization's institutional and competitive environment." The case of African American stockbrokers moves the study of minorities in positions of privilege out of the realm of management (the focus of almost all extant research) to one of highly compensated professionals. And in particular, in the brokers' world, considerable power resides in the hands of brokers' most successful coworkers. Indeed, the "rainmaker" brokers who work alongside them may have as much, if not more, influence over the circumstances of their employment as do the managers who occupy formal positions of authority above them in the organizational hierarchy. As a result, this is a case in which processes of social closure and opportunity hoarding by coworkers of formally equal status are likely to be particularly visible, providing an opportunity to bring empirical evidence to bear on processes that are often inaccessible in studies of persons of color in the higher ranks of large corporations.

Below, I first describe the organizational setting and data on which my analysis is based and the methods used to analyze the data. Then I describe the company's compensation system and the pattern of earnings disparities between African American and white brokers. I then present my analysis of the factors that account for the pattern of racial disparity in earnings at this large financial services firm and conclude with implications for managerial interventions to reduce bias in privileged occupations.

Data and Methods

The data for my case study come from the publicly available expert witness reports generated in employment discrimination litigation against a large financial services firm. I served as an expert for the plaintiffs in the class certification stage of the litigation, analyzing company materials to determine whether there were systematic features of the company's policies and practices that created barriers to career advancement for African Americans relative to whites employed as stockbrokers at the company. At this company brokers have the official title of "financial adviser"; throughout I use that term, "FA," and "broker" interchangeably.

In preparing my initial expert report, I had access to deposition testimony given in 2006 and 2007 by the company's managers and executives, who were responsible for designing, implementing, and overseeing the company's personnel policies and practices, and by those who make personnel decisions affecting the careers of the company's employees. Among them were the company's CEO and the top executives responsible for the company's brokerage division, for human resources, and for diversity and equal employment opportunity. I also had access to hundreds of thousands of pages of documents relating to the company's personnel practices from 2001 through the first quarter of 2007; these documents were indexed and provided to me in computer-searchable format. For my initial report, I also had access to the statistical report prepared by the labor economists retained by the plaintiffs. All quotes from and citations of deposition testimony and company documents that appear in this article, as well as all statistics reported here, also appear in one of the publicly available expert reports. Confidentiality restrictions prohibit me from citing or quoting from other case materials that do not appear in the public record.

The company submitted expert reports from eight individuals: a labor economist, a sociologist who presented a report on racial disparities in wealth and social networks, a sociologist who addressed some technical sampling issues, an industrial psychologist, a diversity consultant, a marketing specialist, and a psychologist and a sociologist who opined on the methods used in my report. Three of those reports are not public, but the ones most relevant to the issues addressed in this article are public.

To do my analysis, I first reviewed the testimony of executives designated by the company to testify on its behalf about its compensation system, EEO and diversity practices, and the like, as well as documents describing those policies and practices.[1] I then reviewed testimony from other company managers ("fact witnesses") who had knowledge of the company's policies and practices based on their personal experiences and observations as employees of the firm. As central concepts and themes emerged from this review, I conducted automated searches of the document database for key words and phrases.[2] Next, I returned to the database of manager depositions, doing a similar search across deposition transcripts for key words and phrases, further refining concepts and themes. These searches were repeated again once the statistical results of the plaintiffs' statistical experts were made available to me; in this stage of the analysis, I focused specifically on evaluating potential explanations for patterns of statistical disparities in compensation by race. I followed a similar procedure upon receiving the reports of the defendant's experts—first reading the reports and the deposition testimony of the experts, then searching the databases of testimony by company managers and company documents to refine my analysis.

This case study is not simply an exercise in inductive "grounded theory" in which themes emerge from the data unguided by prior theorization, hypotheses, and conceptualization (Martin and Turner 1986; Charmaz 2006). The litigation context imposes a structure not just on the form of the data (e.g., sworn testimony, official documents, expert reports, and the like) but also on the narrative themes embedded in the testimony of each side's witnesses. As in any lawsuit, each side had its own "theories of the case." For example, the plaintiffs maintained that a "success breeds success" compensation system amplified the impact of racial bias in the course of financial advisers' careers, while the company maintained that African Americans entering the industry faced challenges in accessing networks of wealthy individuals and thus suffered earnings disadvantages despite being treated the same as whites. These themes shaped questions posed to witnesses in depositions, and they were the focus of expert reports submitted by each side. I view this as a strength of the data and of the case study, because the legal issues at stake overlap with the questions of central interest to sociologists that I described above. While I take into account that deposition testimony by company employees and by experts takes place within an adversarial process, I also note that it is given under oath and subject to cross-examination (and in the case of experts, subject to rebuttal reports and testimony). The potential bias due to self-serving statements is not unique to research based on data generated by litigation; any reactive research method, from qualitative approaches such as participant observation to quantitative survey research, must take into account the possibility of biases due to social desirability concerns and similar processes (Nielsen, Myrick, and Weinberg 2011).

Throughout the article I refer to the firm as "Grand Financial" ("GF"), instead of its real name. This is not done to keep the name of the company anonymous; it is identified in the references to expert reports cited herein. I do so because the focus of this article is on substantive sociological issues relating to the minority vulnerability thesis, not whether this particular company should be held liable for systematic and unlawful discrimination.

Grand Financial's Compensation System and Patterns of Racial Disparities in Earnings

From 2001 through 2006, African American financial advisers at Grand Financial earned on average approximately one-third to 40 percent less than their white counterparts, with the size of the disparity depending on years of experience as a financial adviser in the industry. The pattern for 2006, based on a (log) earnings regression analysis with linear and quadratic controls for experience, is reported in Figure 1, and the pattern is virtually identical in each of the prior years (Madden and Vekker 2008).

Similar to all large brokerage firms, GF has a commission-based pay system for FAs. FAs' pay is linked to "production credits" or "production"—the payout earned on the fees generated by client transactions. The specific factors in the mathematical formula for commission and their weighting is adjusted from year

FIGURE 1
Earnings by Race and Years in Industry

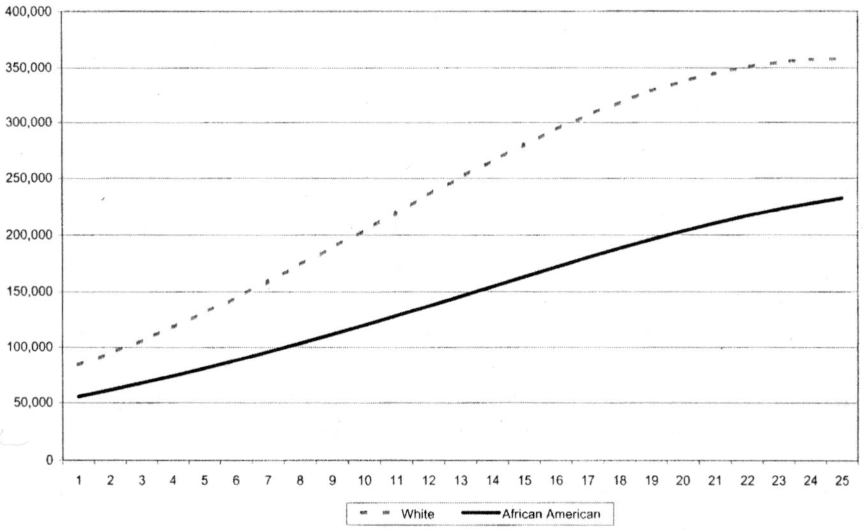

SOURCE: Madden and Vekker (2008).

to year, but, consistently across years FAs were compensated by the amount of business they generated from their retail and institutional clients.

Especially important for the analysis reported here is that for any given level of industry experience, the payout rate on production increases with the FA's level of production. In addition, for a variety of training programs, resources, and opportunities, eligibility is based on an FA's production. As a result, those who become the highest producers and are paid on production at the highest rate also have the greatest capacity to improve their effectiveness as a result of the company's support. In short, compensation is awarded according to a cumulative advantage system, and as a result, factors that produce even small disparities between individuals have a cumulative impact and generate growing disparities over time (Merton 1988; DiPrete and Eirich 2006).

What Accounts for the Pattern of Black/White Disparities in Earnings at Grand Financial?

Cumulative advantage, "supply side" differences, and earnings disparities

A cumulative advantage system is not inherently discriminatory, so long as disparities are attributable to individual differences in productivity and have not emerged as a result of differential, discriminatory treatment by the organization. On the other hand, when organizational policies and practices give one group an advantage over the other, even if it is just a mild benefit or "tailwind" favoring the advantaged group, small discriminatory disparities grow into large ones. Furthermore, any racial differences in the skills or other personal attributes affecting a broker's productivity (and thus compensation) that exist prior to employment at the company will be magnified during the course of the brokers' careers in a cumulative advantage system.

GF executives testified at length about the skills required to be a successful FA, about their knowledge regarding whether African Americans hired by the company had a deficiency in relevant skills, and about their understanding of the reasons for the disparities by race in production credits and earnings. There was widespread agreement that technical and relationship-building skills are viewed as key to becoming a successful FA, with the latter becoming increasingly important as the industry has moved toward an emphasis on financial planning and away from revenues generated from trading (Bielby 2008, 14). The industrial psychologist retained by GF testified that the traits needed to succeed financially as an FA include having an "entrepreneurial spirit" and job-related experience, along with the ability to gain the trust of potential clients, take risks, and face rejection. He also emphasized that FAs "be able to interact well with other people," "possess strong oral communication skills," and "be able to listen actively and respond appropriately to verbal and non-verbal cues" (Outtz 2008, 12–17; Bielby 2009, 12). Overall, there appeared to be a consensus among those who testified on behalf of the company that these skills and personality traits do not vary by race in any significant way in the company's FA workforce (Bielby 2008, 14–15; 2009, 12).

If human capital differences between African American and white FAs are negligible, might there be differences by race in social capital? There are, of course, substantial differences in wealth between African American and white households (Oliver and Shapiro 2006), which reflect a legacy of institutionalized racism, contemporary discrimination in housing and credit markets, and racial differences in types of investments and returns (Conley 2001; Keister 2004). As a result, for any successful stockbroker, a majority of retail clients will almost certainly be from white households. The idea that there was a cost to African American FAs in accessing social networks of wealthy individuals was a strong theme running through the testimony of company officials. For example, the CEO of GF from 2003 to 2007 (who happens to be African American) testified that it was his belief that because of the challenge of "crossing cultural boundaries," it was more difficult for an African American FA to generate commissions than for an FA who is not African American (Bielby 2008, 15).[3] Also, based on interviews with 111 successful white FAs, the company's industrial psychology expert asserted that relying on social networks and personal referrals was an important mechanism used by brokers to develop their business early in their careers (Bielby 2009, 3–4, 7–9).

If it is indeed the case that African American FAs are disadvantaged by pre-hire deficits in social capital, which are at least indirectly due to societal racial discrimination, they are likely to be somewhat less successful at the very start of their careers with the company. And since the cumulative advantage principle applies to the allocation of many productivity-enhancing resources, beginning with broker training and continuing throughout their careers with the company, small to modest differences in earnings by race early on will become magnified over time (Bielby 2009, 4). They are also likely to affect the ability of African American FAs to join broker teams, an issue I address in the following section.

Social isolation, access to broker teams, and opportunity hoarding

African Americans constitute about 2 percent of those employed as FAs or FA trainees at GF, and excluding trainees the figure is 1.3 percent to 1.4 percent in each year from 2001 through 2006 (Saad 2008, 52–53; Bielby 2009, 8–9). More than 85 percent of the company's offices had no African American FAs. In 2006, only 97 of GF's offices employed African American FAs; none were employed at the other 578 offices. And among those offices that did employ African Americans as FAs in that year, most employed just one African American. At year-end 2006, 69 offices employed one African American FA, another 18 offices employed two, and just 10 offices employed three or more African Americans. Similar patterns hold for the five prior years (Bielby 2008, 5–6). In short, African American FAs and FA trainees at the company were literally few and far between. Less than a fourth of the company's offices hired any African American FAs over the period from 2001 through 2006. A newly hired African American trainee was unlikely to have another African American trainee peer, and he or she was likely to be hired in an office that had no African American FAs or at most token African American representation. And if an African American FA was working in an office that employed African Americans in other positions, they were four times more likely to be in service positions than in management roles (in 2006, 6.7 percent of the company's U.S. workforce was African American, including 13.3 percent of those in service jobs and 3.3 percent of those categorized as "officials and managers" [Bielby 2008, 7–12]).

Social science research shows that African Americans and other persons of color in predominantly white work settings receive less support in the form of mentorship and professional development and are more likely to be socially isolated and excluded from informal workplace social networks than their white peers (Cox and Nkomo 1991; Ibarra 1995; Mehra, Kidruff, and Brass 1998; James 2000; Bacharach, Bamberger, and Vashdi 2005). This had important consequences for African American participation in broker teams at GF. Teams are a kind of partnership among FAs, and they were actively promoted by the company. GF had formal teaming policies and a corporate department for supporting teams; the percentage of FAs on teams increased from 20 percent in 2000 to more than 40 percent for each year from 2003 through 2006. Under a team arrangement, multiple FAs pooled at least a third of their production under a single pool number, with a prearranged percentage split of the production being allocated to the individual team. Teams could range from simple 50/50 partnerships between a pair of FAs to a

TABLE 1
Racial Disparities in Participation on Broker Teams

| | Percentage of Financial Advisers (FAs) on Multiple-FA Teams | |
Year	Non–African American FAs	African American FAs
2000	20.4	4.8
2001	30.5	6.7
2002	35.8	14.1
2003	41.2	20.3
2004	41.9	16.8
2005	41.7	12.6
2006	41.6	11.6

SOURCE: Bielby (2008, 23).

larger and more structured arrangement in which a team head oversaw multiple FAs who covered particular clients and specialties. Internal company documents showed that brokers who were part of teams were more successful than those working alone, especially for FAs who were in the early years of their careers with the company. The executive responsible for managing the FA workforce testified that among the benefits experienced by an FA from being on a team were improvements in client service, client acquisition, production, assets under management, and "lifestyle advantage" (coverage by another team member when the FA is away from the office [Bielby 2008, 19–22]).

African Americans participated on teams at GF at a much lower rate than did other FAs. For example, in 2006, just 11.6 percent of African American FAs were on broker teams, compared to 41.6 percent of non–African American FAs (see Table 1). The social science research cited above is useful for understanding factors contributing to African Americans' consistently low participation on teams. If African Americans tend to be isolated and excluded from informal social networks, and if, through the operation of cumulative advantage mechanisms, African American FAs are generating fewer production credits than non-African Americans and are perceived to be less productive, they are less likely to be invited to join established teams. This is especially likely to be true for an African American FA if the existing and newly formed teams in his or her office consist exclusively of FAs who are not African Americans. And, of course, this is true by definition for the many African American FAs employed in offices with no other African Americans in those positions.

Racial isolation in an organizational context in which the dominant group forms tight social networks that have control over resources creates what sociologist Charles Tilly defines as "opportunity hoarding" (1998, 2003). He describes the term as follows:

> If members of a network acquire access to a resource that is valuable, renewable, subject to monopoly, supportive of network activities, and enhanced by the network's modus operandi, network members regularly hoard access to the resource, creating beliefs and practices that sustain their control. If that network is categorically bounded, opportunity hoarding thereby contributes to the maintenance of categorical inequality. (1998, 154)

Applied to GF, teams represent the network, inherited accounts (accounts of departing FAs that are distributed to team members who stay with the firm) represent the renewable resource that is supportive of the network, and race is the categorical boundary.

The transfer of accounts to fellow team members by FAs who are leaving the firm is an important mechanism of opportunity hoarding. Formally, every account is an asset of the firm, not of the FA who services it, but substantively, successful FAs often assert and transfer ownership rights to their accounts when they antici-pate leaving the firm. As part of the settlement of class-action gender discrimina-tion litigation in 1998, the firm implemented a formal National Accounts Distribution Policy that was designed to limit discretion and in-group favoritism in the distribution of accounts. In addition to specifying the criteria for eligibility to receive account distributions and for ranking eligible FAs within an office, the policies in place for each year specified the circumstances in which managers had discretion to depart from the ranking system (Bielby 2008, 26–28).

The policies in place from 2001 through 2006 put African American FAs at a disadvantage in a number of ways. For example, the policies made it possible for remaining members of a team to inherit the accounts of a departing member, regardless of their rankings on the criteria established by the policy. Indeed, the policy implemented in 2000 states that management has discretion to give prefer-ence to team members, based on the premise that they are more familiar with a client than are other FAs. Because African American FAs are substantially less likely than other FAs to be on teams, GF's policy and practice regarding account distribution had a disparate impact on African Americans. In one internal com-pany document from 2006, a senior vice president expressed concern that $3.5 billion in assets were transferred FA-to-FA outside the redistribution policy specified by the company's ranking system. And because inherited accounts allow FAs to qualify for other resources—including additional inherited accounts—this disadvantage to FAs locked out from this kind of "regifting" is cumulative (Bielby 2008, 28–32).

Multicultural marketing and racialized jobs

In fall 2001, GF's brokerage division launched its multicultural marketing function, and from its inception it was expected to "partner" with diversity efforts throughout the firm. In March 2003, the company's CEO announced that the head of that function would "assume responsibility for coordinating diversity activities throughout the firm" (Bielby 2008, 36–38). Race/identity matching was an explicit principle in selecting the heads of each of the multicultural marketing groups: an African American was selected to head the African American group, a South Asian to head the South Asian group, and so on. The head of the multicultural marketing function testified that race-matching was used in part because "communities are usually more likely to embrace one of their own" (Bielby 2008, 39).

The assignment of minority professionals to racialized jobs is sometimes part of an explicit diversity strategy, what management scholars have called the "access-and-legitimacy" paradigm in which "organizations have pushed for access to—and legitimacy with—a more diverse clientele by matching the demographics of the organization to those of critical consumer or constituent groups" (Thomas and Ely 1996, 83). In other words, the minority employee provides the organization with both access to and legitimacy with a minority constituency. However, strategies like this can create barriers to career advancement for minority employees. Management scholars David Thomas and Robin Ely note that while the strategy can lead to increases in diversity in some instances, it is "perhaps more notable for its limitations," especially being "too quick to push staff with niche capabilities into differentiated pigeonholes without trying to understand what those capabilities really are and how they could be integrated into the company's mainstream work" (Thomas and Ely 1996, 83). Consistent with the research of Sharon Collins (1997), Thomas and Ely add that the access-and-legitimacy approach can lead to disaffection among minority employees, who feel exploited when they see their opportunities limited to niche markets, especially if the company later redirects its focus away from the niche area, thereby undermining opportunities for minorities to be successful outside their niche (84–85).

The merging of diversity and multicultural marketing functions did indeed lead to the perception among African American FAs at GF that they were being "pigeonholed" into racialized jobs. For example, in fall 2005, the company conducted a research study of brokers and managers who participated actively in servicing the African American market. Among the findings in a November 2005 internal company report titled "A Qualitative Research Study of the African American Market among GF FAs and GF Managers" is the following:

> Advisors and managers criticized always trying to fit an African American client with an African American advisor, especially when an advisor leaves the business. Because of the high turnover of African American advisors, this often results in a client being paired with 2 or 3 advisors just because they are African Americans. Ultimately, this "shuffling" results in the client becoming frustrated and requesting a white advisor, because they feel they will provide a more stable relationship.

Overall, African American FAs received mixed messages from the company, with resources devoted to racialized approaches to multicultural marketing on one hand and occasional emphasis on the importance of having a (racially) "diversified book" on the other (Bielby 2008, 38–39).

Racialization of the FA position was also institutionalized through the company's "virtual teams" initiative in 2003. In a virtual team, FAs in different offices work together on a specific client relationship. These arrangements existed throughout the FA workforce as a way of building on complementary skills that existed among FAs in different offices in the same region. However, when applied to the company's African American multicultural marketing efforts, the virtual team concept was used in a way that likely reinforced the typecasting of African American FAs.

The presence of African Americans on these teams was viewed as a way of gaining access to and legitimacy in communities of color. This rationale was stated explicitly in company documents, as in this example, from a document prepared for the July 2005 African American Financial Advisor Symposium:

> We believe it is paramount that diverse FA teams are able to access key and influential local organizations that are tied in with the key business and business owners. By positioning the firm as corporate members of these "key" organizations and associations, diverse FA teams gain access to these groups that might otherwise be difficult to penetrate. By "branding" [the company] at annual recognition dinners, symposiums and events AAFA teams become recognized as leaders in their communities.

And from the same document: "Diverse FA teams . . . raise the profile of [GF] in diverse communities that previously have been under penetrated but represent significant business opportunities." One of the benefits of virtual teams as part of multicultural marketing, according to this document, is that diverse virtual teams can bring business from "nontraditional markets (e.g. athletes, entertainers, casino operators, et al.)" (Bielby 2008, 40–41).

In short, GF saw its African American FA workforce as central to its effort to penetrate minority markets, and it linked that racialized marketing effort to its company-wide diversity policy. As suggested by research on the topic, this approach led to racialized jobs and constrained opportunities for African Americans, and the company's policies and practices along these lines were perceived as such by African American FAs.

Ambiguous and diffuse lines of authority regarding nondiscrimination

As research by Frank Dobbin and Alexandra Kalev has shown, diversity training programs and similar workplace interventions typically have little impact on discriminatory workplace barriers and often do more harm than good (Kalev, Dobbin, and Kelly 2006; Dobbin 2009). Their research on the rate at which women and persons of color move into management shows that "structures that embed accountability, authority, and expertise (affirmative action plans, diversity committees and taskforces, diversity managers and departments)" are the most effective way to address discriminatory barriers (Kalev, Dobbin and Kelly 2006, 611). Related research by Lauren Edelman demonstrates that changes made in response to litigation or Equal Employment Opportunity Commission (EEOC) regulatory enforcement sometimes have measurable impacts on reducing discriminatory barriers, but often they are just "window dressing," adopted mainly because they create the appearance of compliance with the law (Edelman 1992). As she notes,

"Organizations may strategically seek to create compliance structures merely as symbolic gestures by 'decoupling' those structures from core organizational activities. Organizations may, for example, create affirmative action officer positions but give the officer little or no autonomy or authority or create grievance procedures that are hard to access and known to provide little relief" (Edelman 2005, 345–46).

Prior to the settlement of a high-profile gender discrimination lawsuit in 1998, GF, similar to other large firms in the industry, had little in the way of accountability structures related to diversity and nondiscrimination. The company did little in the way of monitoring disparities by gender and race in the career outcomes among its brokers and managers, and accountability for equal employment opportunity was minimal. As part of the settlement, the company agreed to abandon mandatory arbitration in bias cases, enhance and extend its diversity programs, and establish firmwide guidelines for distribution of the accounts of departing FAs. In the wake of the settlement, the company adopted a range of diversity-related programs and initiatives on both a company-wide basis and within its brokerage division, including diversity advisory boards and offices, FA training and mentorship programs, diversity training for managers, minority symposia, focus groups, surveys, exit interviews, and diversity "dashboards" and similar tools and reports for tracking disparities by gender and minority status of FAs (Bielby 2008, 54).

These programs and initiatives differed in their sponsorship, resources, focus, continuity, and duration, but what is common to all is that they were implemented in a context of ambiguous, unstable, and diffuse structures of responsibility and authority. For example, according to the company's 2003 Affirmative Action Plan, the company's CEO had overall responsibility for affirmative action results, with responsibility and accountability at the corporate level delegated to the senior vice president of human resources. In a statement that same year, the CEO proclaimed that besides him and the top human resources executive, responsibility for diversity was to be shared by all members of the executive team (Bielby 2008, 55–56). Yet the individual who was the company's vice chair and head of its brokerage division testified in 2007 that he did not know if the company had an affirmative action plan, and other senior executives gave similar testimony. The person who headed the human resources function for the brokerage division for two years starting in 2003 testified that she had never seen an affirmative action plan, had never viewed an underutilization report, and had no responsibility for doing so. She and the head of the multicultural marketing function had conflicting views about whether the multicultural marketing function had been assigned and had assumed responsibility for issues relating to the diversity of the FA workforce. In March 2003, the company distributed to all employees an announcement that the multicultural marketing function would "continue to identify recruitment, retention and development programs for diverse professionals"; but the function's head testified that at the time she felt she didn't have the mandate, support, or structure to take on that responsibility (Bielby 2008, 55–59).

Throughout 2005 and 2006, the company was still grappling with the issue of whether "ownership" for diversity programs should be "nested down in the business" or be centralized within the multicultural marketing function (or elsewhere). In June 2006, around the same time that stories appeared in the *Wall Street Journal* and *New York Times* about the race discrimination litigation, the company announced the establishment of an Office of Diversity in its brokerage division (Bielby 2008, 59–64). A "Diversity Strategy Update" memo, issued by that office in fall 2006, noted that due to "the large decentralized nature of [the brokerage division], senior management determined that in order to increase our effectiveness, we needed to create a centralized function with the appropriate infrastructure to drive our diversity strategy and address the unique challenges that exist in our business" (Bielby 2008, 64). By early 2007, although the Office of Diversity was still in its formative stages, internal documents indicate that it was developing a template for designing and implementing meaningful and effective accountability structures. Unfortunately, the documents and testimony available to me through the race discrimination litigation end as of April 2007, and the company was acquired by one of the country's largest banks shortly after the financial crisis of October 2008 and no longer exists as an independent corporate entity. As a result, it is impossible to know whether accountability structures could have and would have been implemented in a way that overcame the ambiguous, diffuse, and decoupled lines of responsibility and authority for diversity and equal employment opportunity that have characterized the company's brokerage division for more than a decade and whether those interventions would have any measurable impact on the cumulative advantage system that created racial disparities in earnings between African American and white brokers.

Discussion: African American Vulnerability in the Financial Services Sector

On its surface, the output-based, pay-for-performance system used to compensate financial advisers in the brokerage divisions of large financial services firms would seem to approach the ideal of a pure meritocracy in which the factors influencing pay are objective and transparent, with little room for the kind of discretion and subjectivity that often leads to bias against persons of color (Bielby 2007). But the analysis of how that system worked at GF shows that a quarter-century after the publication of *The Declining Significance of Race* (W. J. Wilson 1980), highly educated African Americans occupying some of the most lucrative jobs in the financial services industry faced barriers to achieving earnings parity with their white counterparts, encountered those barriers early in their careers, and found themselves falling further behind over the course of their careers. This pattern is consistent with recent research by Heywood and Parent (2009), whose study, using Panel Study of Income Dynamics data, shows that for individuals compensated in performance pay systems, the black/white difference in earnings is greatest at the upper end of the earnings distribution, whereas the opposite is true in other kinds of pay systems. The GF case reveals the mechanisms through which this comes about in an output-based performance pay system. First, differential access to white wealth alone in the context of a cumulative advantage system for allocating productivity-enhancing resources would be sufficient to generate this pattern. Second, simply the belief by branch managers that newly recruited African American FAs would have difficulty building a book because of racially segregated social networks, coupled with a racialized approach to multicultural marketing, would be sufficient to generate this pattern, even in the absence of any racial disparity in access to wealth. Third, white FAs who share this belief, or who believe simply that all else being equal their wealthiest white clients have a preference for working with white advisers over African American advisers, have an incentive to avoid bringing African American advisers onto their teams. The kind of opportunity hoarding that is facilitated by team membership only adds to the pressures toward homophily and social closure.

Finally, as noted above, compared to time-based compensation, output-based performance pay is usually viewed as inherently meritocratic, rendering bias invisible to all but those who perceive that they are being treated unfairly. Performance-based pay and the meritocracy that accompanies it are not simply technical features of a compensation system; meritocracy can also be a cultural framework. As Light, Roscigno, and Kalev note, "Formal meritocratic procedures and rhetoric can become an institutionalized cloak for ongoing ascriptive bias—a legitimating discourse, where managers, employers, and judges exchange symbols of meritocracy for equality. . . . When formal procedures are in place, managers (and judges) are more apt to believe the structure is unbiased and that unequal outcomes therefore reflect differences in merit" (2011, 43). The results reported here show one way that racialized practices become embedded in a performance pay system and how cumulative advantage and social closure processes can generate what Castilla and Benard (2010) have defined (and experimentally validated) as the "paradox of meritocracy effect."

Conclusion: Lessons for Management

African Americans who seek to work as financial advisers may in fact encounter obstacles to acquiring wealthy clients that are not faced by their white counterparts. But if they do, legally and ethically companies do not have the option to deny employment to African Americans because of the racial preferences of their customers. To avoid the pattern of racial disparities in earnings observed at GF, firms need to proactively manage the distribution of productivity-enhancing resources so as to avoid reproducing institutionalized racism from the outside and perpetuating sources of racial bias arising from the inside. For example, at GF, prior to litigation there was no awareness or acknowledgment of potential racial bias arising from the team formation process. Company executives at GF steadfastly maintained that the process by which teams were formed was analogous to the formation of marriages among consenting adults and that it was not the company policy to force "arranged marriages" (Bielby 2008, 24). Yet at the same time, it took a hands-off, racially neutral approach to teams, the company actively managed the racial composition of business units and positions dealing with minority markets. The cultural frame of meritocracy provided a rationale to the former and the rhetoric of diversity legitimated the latter. Had both aspects of the company's human resource management of its FA workforce been subject to the oversight and authority of an accountability structure tasked with ensuring racial equity and nondiscrimination, the link between these two practices and the racialized nature and consequences of each could have been identified and remedied, with the company accepting responsibility for desegregating broker teams while developing and disseminating a rationale for multicultural marketing not based on the typecasting of its broker workforce.

The case of stockbrokers in the financial services industry also suggests that "unconscious" or "implicit" bias may play only a minor role in creating and sustaining minority vulnerability in privileged occupations. While cognitive bias figures into the kind of typecasting that channels African Americans into roles dealing with minority markets (Jost et al. 2009; Bielby 2007), the maintenance of categorical inequality through opportunity hoarding (e.g., through the gifting of accounts to team members) is a deliberate form of collective action intended to maintain the privileged position of successful white brokers. As a result, the introduction of formal procedures that limit discretion and subjectivity are likely to be of limited efficacy, because they will be viewed (perhaps accurately) as a threat to the power of those who benefit from the status quo. At GF, this was visible in the form of active resistance by some of the company's most successful FAs to changes in the formal account distribution policies that were introduced specifically to direct more accounts to women and minorities (Bielby 2008, 67–69). Adequate interventions require not only monitoring and oversight to ensure effective implementation but also recognition that they are altering relational aspects of work that are embedded in hierarchical structures of power (Light, Roscigno, and Kalev 2011). And in the case of the financial services industry, the challenge is likely to be even more formidable because the source of power of successful white brokers is not in visible formal authority, which is amenable to restructuring of lines of authority and responsibility, but instead in patterns of social relations among individuals with formally equivalent positions. Moreover, top company executives are likely to believe both the rhetoric of meritocracy that legitimizes existing arrangements and fear that alienating brokers with the most clout will damage the firm because those brokers can leave for a competing firm and take their accounts with them.

Finally, industry executives should recognize that African American financial advisers are not naïve regarding the realities of race in the financial services industry; nor do they enter their careers expecting to have a marginalized status due to the challenges of "crossing cultural boundaries." As documented by Karyn Lacy and others, many middle-class African Americans successfully engage in forms of "boundary work," moving with relative ease between the cultural milieu of white-dominated corporate environments and segregated social spaces outside of the workplace (Lacy 2004; Lamont and Fleming 2005; Thomas and Gabarro 1999). FAs have considerable autonomy in choosing methods and techniques for client development, and they can and do choose those that work best for themselves (Outtz 2008, 18–20). By recognizing, encouraging, and supporting diversity in approaches to building a book at career entry, companies can actively support methods that that have proven successful for African Americans, rather than assuming that from the start African American FAs face nearly insurmountable barriers to applying their talents as effectively as do their white peers.

In sum, the case study of GF shows how the minority vulnerability thesis applies to African Americans in a privileged profession and offers insights on how to establish racial parity in an industry that relies on an output-based performance pay system. The merit-based rhetoric of such systems legitimates arrangements that structurally advantage whites over African Americans. A racialized approach to multicultural marketing is race-conscious in ways that disadvantage African Americans, and human resources systems that fail to assess the structural sources of that bias are race-neutral in name only, allowing the vulnerabilities faced by African Americans to persist and grow over time. Diversity programs and accountability structures need to be built on a premise that not all racial bias is simply cognitive, unconscious, and unintentional, and that effective interventions will require addressing head-on sources of resistance that are embedded in racially segregated social relations and power differences among professionals who are formally identical in their locations in the firm's job structure.

Notes

1. Under Federal Rules of Civil Procedure Rule 30(b)(6), a party to a lawsuit can request that a corporation testify on a specific issue, and the corporation designates an individual knowledgeable on that issue to testify on its behalf. The 30(b)(6) deponent's testimony represents the knowledge of the corporation. In contrast, the testimony of a "fact witness" represents that individual's personal knowledge of facts relevant to the case.

2. Documents were made available to me in the form of a LexisNexis Concordance database, which includes a software package that allows for sophisticated Boolean searches.

3. In support of this proposition, the company offered an expert report by sociologist Roberto Fernandez, who presented an analysis of data from the Survey of Income and Program Participation, documenting racial disparities in wealth, and from the General Social Survey, documenting racial segregation in social networks (Fernandez 2008; Bielby 2009, 3–6). The company also submitted the report of a labor economist who conducted a spatial analysis purporting to show that African American FAs were much less likely than whites to do business with clients who live in wealthy white neighborhoods, although the findings of that report were vigorously disputed by the plaintiffs' experts (Saad 2008, 23–27; Bielby 2009, 3–5, 15; Madden and Vekker 2009, 26–34).

References

Bacharach, Samuel B., Peter A. Bamberger, and Dana Vashdi. 2005. Diversity and homophily at work: Supportive relations among white and African-American peers. *Academy of Management Journal* 48:619–44.

Bielby, William T. 2007. Promoting racial diversity at work: Challenges and solutions. In *Diversity at work*, ed. Arthur P. Brief, 53–86. New York, NY: Cambridge University Press.

Bielby, William T. 25 June 2008. Expert report of William T. Bielby. In *George McReynolds et al. v. Merrill Lynch, Pierce, Fenner & Smith, Incorporated*. Available from www.merrillclassaction.com/pdfs/DrBielbyExpRep.pdf (accessed 17 May 2011).

Bielby, William T. 3 February 2009. Expert rebuttal report of William T. Bielby. In *George McReynolds et al. v. Merrill Lynch, Pierce, Fenner & Smith, Incorporated*. Available from www.merrillclassaction.com/pdfs/DrBielbyExpRebuttalRep.pdf (accessed 17 May 2011).

Castilla, Emilio J. 2008. Gender, race, and meritocracy in organizational careers. *American Journal of Sociology* 113:1479–526.

Castilla, Emilio J., and Stephan Benard. 2010. The paradox of meritocracy in organizations. *Administrative Science Quarterly* 55:543–76.

Charmaz, Kathy. 2006. *Constructing grounded theory: A practical guide through qualitative analysis*. Thousand Oaks, CA: Sage.

Collins, Sharon. 1997. *Black corporate executives: The making and breaking of a black middle class*. Philadelphia, PA: Temple University Press.

Collins, Sharon. 2005. Occupational mobility among African-Americans: Assimilation or resegregation. In *Handbook on employment discrimination research: Rights and realities*, eds. Robert L. Nelson and Laura Beth Nielsen, 187–98. Boston, MA: Kluwer Academic.

Conley, Dalton. 2001. Decomposing the black-white wealth gap: The role of parental resources, inheritance, and investment dynamics. *Sociological Inquiry* 71:39–66.

Cox, Taylor H., and Stella M. Nkomo. 1991. A race and gender-group analysis of the early career experience of MBAs. *Work and Occupations* 18:436–46.

DiPrete, Thomas A., and Gregory M. Eirich. 2006. Cumulative advantage as a mechanism for inequality: A review of theoretical and empirical developments. *Annual Review of Sociology* 32:271–97.

Dobbin, Frank. 2009. *Inventing equal opportunity*. Princeton, NJ: Princeton University Press.

Edelman, Lauren B. 1992. Legal ambiguity and symbolic structures: Organizational mediation of civil rights law. *American Journal of Sociology* 97:1531–76.

Edelman, Lauren B. 2005. Law at work: The endogenous construction of civil rights. In *Handbook on employment discrimination research: Rights and realities*, eds. Robert L. Nelson and Laura Beth Nielsen, 337–52. Boston, MA: Kluwer Academic.

Fernandez, Roberto M. 13 November 2008. Report of Roberto M. Fernandez. In *George McReynolds et al. v. Merrill Lynch, Pierce, Fenner & Smith, Incorporated*. Available from www.merrillclassaction.com (accessed 17 May 2011).

Heywood, John S., and Daniel Parent. 2009. Performance pay and the white-black wage gap. Compensation Research Initiative Paper 17. Available from http://digitalcommons.ilr.cornell.edu/cri/17 (accessed 5 May 2011).

Ibarra, Herminia. 1995. Race, opportunity, and diversity of social circles in managerial networks. *Academy of Management Journal* 38:673–703.

James, Erika Hayes. 2000. Race-related differences in promotions and support: Underlying effects of human and social capital. *Organization Science* 11:493–508.

Jost, John T., Laurie A. Rudman, Irene V. Blair, Dana R. Carney, Nilanjana Dasgupta, Jack Glaser, and Curtis D. Hardin. 2009. The existence of implicit bias is beyond reasonable doubt: A refutation of ideological and methodological objections and executive summary of ten studies that no manager should ignore. *Research in Organizational Behavior* 29:39–69.

Kalev, Alexandra, Frank Dobbin, and Erin Kelly. 2006. Best practices or best guesses? Assessing the efficacy of corporate affirmative action and diversity policies. *American Sociological Review* 71:589–617.

Keister, Lisa A. 2004. Race, family structure, and wealth: The effect of childhood family on adult asset ownership. *Sociological Perspectives* 47:161–87.

Lacy, Karyn R. 2004. Black spaces, black places: Strategic assimilation and identity construction in middle-class suburbia. *Ethnic and Racial Studies* 27:908–30.

Lamont, Michèle, and Crystal Fleming. 2005. Everyday anti-racism: Competence and religion in the cultural repertoire of the African-American elite. *Du Bois Review* 2:29–43.

Light, Ryan, Vincent J. Roscigno, and Alexandra Kalev. 2011. Racial discrimination, interpretation, and legitimation at work. *The Annals of the American Academy of Political and Social Science* 634:39–59.

Madden, Janice Fanning, and Alexander Vekker. 5 June 2008. Evaluating whether employment outcomes for brokers and broker trainees at Merrill Lynch are racially neutral. Expert report of Janice Fanning Madden and Alexander Vekker. In *George McReynolds et al. v. Merrill Lynch, Pierce, Fenner & Smith, Incorporated.* Available from www.merrillclassaction.com/pdfs/DrsMaddenVekkerExpRep.pdf (accessed 17 May 2011).

Madden, Janice Fanning, and Alexander Vekker. 23 February 2009. Rebuttal report: Evaluating whether employment outcomes for brokers and broker trainees at Merrill Lynch are racially neutral. In *George McReynolds et al. v. Merrill Lynch, Pierce, Fenner & Smith, Incorporated.* Available from http://merrillclassaction.com/pdfs/DrsMaddenVekkerExpRebuttalRep.pdf (accessed 17 May 2011).

Martin, Patricia Yancey, and Barry A. Turner. 1986. Grounded theory and organizational research. *Journal of Applied Behavioral Science* 22:141–57.

McPherson, J. Miller, Lynn Smith-Lovin, and Matthew E. Brashears. 2006. Social isolation in America: Changes in core discussion networks over two decades. *American Sociological Review* 74:670–81.

Mehra, Ajay, Martin Kilduff, and Donald J. Brass. 1998. At the margins: A distinctiveness approach to the social identity and social networks of underrepresented groups. *Academy of Management Journal* 41:441–52.

Merton, Robert K. 1988. The Matthew effect in science, II: Cumulative advantage and the symbolism of intellectual property. *Isis* 79:606–23.

Nielsen, Laura Beth, Amy Myrick, and Jill Weinberg. 2011. Social science in *Wal-Mart Stores v. Dukes:* A reply to the ASA's missed opportunity to promote sound science in court by Mitchell, Monahan, and Walker. Available from http://ssrn.com/abstract_id=1844550.

Oliver, Melvin L., and Thomas M. Shapiro. 2006. *Black wealth/white wealth: A new perspective on racial inequality.* New York, NY: Routledge.

Outtz, James L. 14 November 2008. Expert report of James L. Outtz, Ph.D., regarding class certification issues. In *George McReynolds et al. v. Merrill Lynch, Pierce, Fenner & Smith, Incorporated.* Available from www.merrillclassaction.com (accessed 17 May 2011).

Roth, Louise Marie. 2004. Bringing clients back in: Homophily preferences and inequality on Wall Street. *Sociological Quarterly* 45:613–35.

Saad, Ali. 14 November 2008. Expert report of Ali Saad, Ph.D., regarding class certification issues. In *George McReynolds et al. v. Merrill Lynch, Pierce, Fenner & Smith, Incorporated.* Available from www.merrillclassaction.com (accessed 17 May 2011).

Spalter-Roth, Roberta, and Cynthia Deitch. 1999. I don't feel right sized, I feel out-of-work sized: Gender, race, ethnicity, and the unequal costs of displacement. *Work and Occupations* 26:446–82.

Stainback, Kevin, Donald Tomaskovic-Devey, and Sheryl Skaggs. 2010. Organizational approaches to inequality: Inertia, relative power, and environments. *Annual Review of Sociology* 36:225–47.

Thomas, David A., and Robin J. Ely. 1996. Making differences matter: A new paradigm for managing diversity. *Harvard Business Review* 74 (September-October): 79–90.

Thomas, David A., and John J. Gabarro. 1999. *Breaking through: The making of minority executives in corporate America.* Cambridge, MA: Harvard Business School Press.

Tilly, Charles. 1998. *Durable inequality.* Berkeley: University of California Press.

Tilly, Charles. 2003. Changing forms of inequality. *Sociological Theory* 21:31–36.

Wilson, George, and Debra McBrier. 2005. Race and loss of privilege: African American/white differences in the determinants of layoffs from upper-tier occupations. *Sociological Forum* 20:301–21.

Wilson, George, and Vincent J. Roscigno. 2010. Race and downward mobility from privileged occupations: African American/white dynamics across the early work-career. *Social Science Research* 39:67–77.

Wilson, William Julius. 1980. *The declining significance of race: Blacks and changing American institutions.* 2nd ed. Chicago, IL: University of Chicago Press.

Wilson, William Julius. 2011. The declining significance of race: Revisited and revised. *Daedalus* 140 (2): 55–69.

Managing Ambivalent Prejudices: Smart-but-Cold and Warm-but-Dumb Stereotypes

By
SUSAN T. FISKE

Not all biases are equivalent, and not all biases are uniformly negative. Two fundamental dimensions differentiate stereotyped groups in cultures across the globe: status predicts perceived competence, and cooperation predicts perceived warmth. Crossing the competence and warmth dimensions, two combinations produce ambivalent prejudices: pitied groups (often traditional women or older people) appear warm but incompetent, and envied groups (often nontraditional women or outsider entrepreneurs) appear competent but cold. Case studies in ambivalent sexism, heterosexism, racism, anti-immigrant biases, ageism, and classism illustrate both the dynamics and the management of these complex but knowable prejudices.

Keywords: stereotypes; prejudice; discrimination; race; gender; age; class

A middle-aged white man walks into an office . . . what is your mental image? People assume a lot, right away, sizing each other up, in an instant. Social categories such as gender, race, and age immediately impinge on impressions, whether we like it or not. In today's global management context, immigrant status, nationality, and social class rapidly shape impressions as well. Beyond these first-millisecond impressions, social categories condition what ensues. First impressions do count. More and more, organizations are expected to know that decision-makers and peers cannot help automatically noticing social categories. What is more, people often act on these categories, unaware of their influence. Decades of research establish these realities (Macrae and Bodenhausen 2000; Fiske 1998).

Susan T. Fiske is Eugene Higgins Professor of Psychology, Princeton University, and author of Envy Up, Scorn Down: How Status Divides Us *(Russell Sage Foundation 2011), supported by a Guggenheim and a Russell Sage Foundation Visiting Scholar award. She also wrote* Social Cognition *(McGraw-Hill 2008) and edits the* Annual Review of Psychology *and the* Handbook of Social Psychology.

DOI: 10.1177/0002716211418444

Evolution argues for the utility of this rapid category-based social judgment. People have to know whom to approach or avoid and for what purposes. Evolution also argues that just a few fundamental principles describe how people understand each other. Knowing these dimensions organizes and informs what may otherwise seem an arbitrary and overwhelming miscellany of group images that could affect diversity management. This article describes two fundamental, apparently universal, dimensions of out-group images, which situate race, gender, and other categories in a larger societal map that predicts stereotypic beliefs, emotional prejudices, and discriminatory tendencies. A novel contribution of this framework is the concept of ambivalent images, applied here particularly to gender bias, heterosexism, racism, anti-immigrant biases, ageism, and classism. Another novel contribution demonstrates the primacy of warmth and trust over sheer status and power, what might be termed a focus on relational capital in management.

Universal Dimensions of Social Cognition

When people encounter an individual or group, they first need to know the "Other's" intentions, for good or ill. Whether someone walks into your office, approaches you in a dark alley, or sits next to you in public, you need to know immediately whether that Other is benign or harmful. Our ancestors had the same dilemma, and modern citizens especially have the same problem in reaction to new immigrant groups. People have intentions, which set them apart from inanimate objects and help to predict what they will do. The Stereotype Content Model (SCM) calls this first dimension perceived warmth, which includes apparent trustworthiness, friendliness, and sociability (Fiske et al. 2002; Fiske, Cuddy, and Glick 2007). People infer warm (or cold) intent from respectively cooperative or competitive structural relationships between individuals or groups. That is, those groups who cooperate appear warm and trustworthy; those who compete appear cold and untrustworthy, even exploitative. These links are robust (Cuddy, Fiske, and Glick 2008).

Knowing a stranger's intentions solves only part of the dilemma, because one must know the Other's capability to enact those intentions. An incompetent foe poses less threat and an incompetent friend offers less benefit than their more competent counterparts. People infer this competence (capability, skill) from apparent status (prestige, economic success) (Cuddy, Fiske, and Glick 2008; Kervyn, Fiske, and Yzerbyt n.d.-b). People all over the world believe in meritocracy (status = competence) to a surprising degree.

Most prior descriptions of group images have focused mainly on either status characteristics (Berger, Cohen, and Zelditch 1972; Ridgeway 1991) or on cooperation-competition (Sherif and Sherif 1953). Combining these two dimensions also goes beyond standard dichotomous in-group/out-group designations (Tajfel 1981). These dimensions emerge from multidimensional scaling (Kervyn, Fiske, and Yzerbyt n.d.-a); in representative and convenience samples; in surveys,

FIGURE 1

Stereotype Content Model's Clusters of Groups and Emotional Prejudices

	Low Competence, Low Status	High Competence, High Status
High Warmth, Cooperative	Older people, disabled people, traditional women (Pity, sympathy)	In-group, allies, reference groups: e.g., middle class, white, Christian, heterosexual (Pride, admiration)
Low Warmth, Competitive	Poor people, welfare recipients, homeless people, immigrants (Disgust, contempt)	Rich people, female professionals, lesbians, feminists, Asians, Jews (Envy, jealousy)

experiments, and neuroimaging data; and across countries and time (see Cuddy, Fiske, and Glick 2008).

The quadrants reveal systematic clusters that map a society's images of its groups. As Figure 1 shows, at a cultural level, societal in-groups, allies, and reference groups might include American defaults, such as middle class, white, Christian, and heterosexual. Even those not identified with these groups recognize their hegemony and rate their cultural image as being both warm and competent. A source of pride and admiration, they are viewed as relatively high status and cooperating with society's goals and values. People willingly help them and associate with them (Cuddy, Fiske, and Glick 2007).

Society's most extreme out-groups, stereotyped as neither warm nor competent, include poor people and immigrants (all over the world) as well as homeless people and drug addicts (in the United States). Even members of these groups know where they stand in society. Triggering disgust and contempt, they are viewed as extremely low-status and as undermining the values of society. In the current context, note that poor blacks and poor whites, as well as welfare recipients, land here. These groups, opposite to the collective in-groups, are also viewed unambivalently. They allegedly lack both typically human qualities such as sociability and uniquely human qualities such as autonomy, so people effectively dehumanize them, according to self-report and neuroimaging data (Harris and Fiske 2006). People avoid, neglect, and demean them, devaluing their lives relative to those of others (Cikara et al. 2010) and may even attack them (Cuddy, Fiske, and Glick 2007). Not often the purview of white-collar management concerns, these groups enter into blue-collar management concerns, for example, for entry-level service and maintenance work.

Ambivalent Out-Groups

Under the radar, more subtle, unexamined prejudices target groups that elicit mixed biases. Ambivalent out-groups fall into two types, with particular relevance to out-group members in management positions. Mixed out-groups include, first, those seen as nice but incompetent. All over the world, across samples, this includes older people and (where mentioned) people with disabilities. Traditional women land here, in many samples, as do Irish and Italian immigrants in the United States—they all are liked but not especially respected. Recipients of pity and sympathy, they are viewed as low-status but harmless and nice, not exactly management material. Note that pity is an ambivalent emotion, in that it implies a subjectively benign attitude that depends on the target remaining subordinate; that is, pity is paternalistic. These groups receive help, even overhelping, which demonstrably undermines performance (Gilbert and Silvera 1996), as we will see, but people also avoid them socially (Cuddy, Fiske, and Glick 2007). In essence, this inattention is scorn (Fiske 2011). Given the strength of informal networks (Podolny and Baron 1997), social neglect is not trivial in the workplace.

The complementary type of ambivalence identifies other out-groups as competent but cold. All over the world, this includes rich people and ethnicities often seen as outsider entrepreneurs (e.g., Asians and Jews). Nontraditional women land here (female professionals, feminists, lesbians), as do minority professionals and gay professionals. Targets of envy and resentment, these groups are admitted to be high-status but not "one of us," not on our side (Fiske 2011). Describing resentment of elites, this form of envy explains *Schadenfreude* (glee at their misfortunes). People are obliged to associate with these groups because they control resources, but they may attack and sabotage them when they can get away with it (Cuddy, Fiske, and Glick 2007; Rudman and Phelan 2008).

The Big Picture

Why does this SCM matter to managing diversity? Not all bias is the same; prejudice is not one-size-fits-all. Ambivalent prejudices are especially hard to detect because they contain mixed beliefs, mixed feelings, and mixed behaviors. Subjectively positive regard (liking or respect) combines with negative reactions (disliking or disrespect). Indeed, such mixed feelings are more common than not. Given information positive on one of the fundamental dimensions, people assume the other is negative, a kind of compensation effect (Kervyn et al. 2009). This helps to justify inequality, with societal beliefs that the poor are happy or the rich are heartless. Consistent with this system-justification view, more income inequality predicts more ambivalent out-group images across twenty countries (Durante et al. n.d.).

Across cultures, the SCM maps societal theories of ethnic, gender, and other social group positions, revealing cultural variations. For example, East Asian samples do not self-promote the in-groups to the high-warmth/high-competence position of Western samples' in-groups, instead preferring a more neutral self-image in keeping with cultural modesty norms (Cuddy et al. 2009). Nevertheless, East Asia's rich people, poor people, old people, and immigrants land in the same clusters as in Western samples.

The SCM is not just an artifact of modern multicultural, global societies. It yields descriptively valid data for qualitative analyses of articles from Italian Fascists (Durante, Volpato, and Fiske 2009) and from 1930s American college students, revealing patterns of stereotype change and continuity over time (Bergsieker et al. n.d.). Related dimensions have appeared in prior analyses of interpersonal space (Peeters 2001; Rosenberg, Nelson, and Vivekananthan 1968; Wojciszke, Abele, and Baryla 2009) and attitudinal space (Osgood, Suci, and Tannenbaum 1957; see Fiske, Cuddy, and Glick [2007] for a conceptual comparison and Kervyn and Fiske [n.d.] for an empirical comparison).

Given the apparent universality of the warmth and competence dimensions, they potentially aid understanding the perceived fit between a group's status or power and its role in an organization. Some organizational roles emphasize status and competence, and groups stereotypically high on these dimensions might seem to fit better. Other organizational roles might require more relational capital, and groups stereotypically high on cooperation, trustworthiness, and warmth might seem to fit well there. Bias can masquerade as perceived lack of fit.

Case Studies

Different management dilemmas accompany different groups, but the SCM provides a systematic window into each group's unique challenges. The conceptual framework provides practical angles on predictable clusters of groups. Consider gender, sexuality, race/ethnicity, immigrant status, age, and social class.

Ambivalent sexism. Early theories of sexism focused on antifemale sentiments and hostility toward women (e.g., Spence, Helmreich, and Stapp 1973; but presciently, especially competent ones, Spence and Helmreich 1972). This negative framing bumped into the women-are-wonderful effect, showing that women are liked better than men (Eagly, Mladinic, and Otto 1991). Noting these apparent contradictions, a new approach analyzed the relationships between men and women, identifying the unique intergroup combination of societal dominance (by men), common to many in-group/out-group relations, with the intimate interdependence, unique to male-female relations. Ambivalent sexism reflects this duality (Glick and Fiske 1996, 2007). Hostile sexism (HS) targets nontraditional women who threaten male dominance in various ways: female professionals, intellectuals, and trades-women compete for men's traditional roles; lesbians and vamps reject heterosexual intimacy; and feminists challenge male power. These women are stereotyped as threateningly capable but not nice. In contrast to hostile sexism, subjectively benevolent sexism (BS) protects women who adhere to traditional roles, interdependence, and power relations. These include housewives, secretaries, and "typical" women (Eckes 2002), all viewed as nice but dumb. These two forms of sexism represent ambivalent polarities; one viewing women as warm but incompetent (BS), the other viewing women as competent but not warm (HS).

BS paternalizes compliant women by promising protection and help, but this weakens their autonomy and ability. Benevolent sexist treatment ("all the men will always help you") distracts women with self-doubt and undermines their performance (Dardenne, Dumont, and Bollier 2007; Dumont, Sarlet, and Dardenne 2010), making them devalue their task competence (Barreto et al. 2010). BS disarms women's recognition of and resistance to sexism: protective paternalism suffuses women's experience (Fields, Swan, and Kloos 2010), making them less likely to notice it and to identify it as harmful despite its ill effects (Bosson, Pinel, and Vandello 2010).

BS doubtless helps to explain the working-mother wage penalty of about 5 percent, controlling for all other relevant variables (Benard, Paik, and Correll 2008; Budig and England 2001). Women workers with children seem warmer but less competent than other employees, whereas working fathers gain in warmth without losing competence (Cuddy, Fiske, and Glick 2004). Working mothers are seen as less worth hiring, training, and promoting, even controlling for all else. Women by default are viewed through a caregiver lens, according to the gender-role-congruity theory (Eagly and Karau 2002). Managers worry more about women's work-life conflicts than about men's (Hoobler, Wayne, and Lemmon 2009), with women in traditional roles especially paying the price. Women are traditionally lower-status, so they get greater scrutiny in hiring and at work; thus, mothers get less leeway to juggle than fathers do (Correll, Benard, and Paik 2007). BS would help to explain this by the subjectively benign concern about whether the working mother "can handle" everything.

As noted, ambivalent sexism teaches that there are two kinds of women. In the workplace, the nontraditional women suffer the better-known kind of sexism—hostility. Subtypes of women seen as competent but cold include, as just listed, career women, feminists, intellectual women, vamps, and lesbians (Eckes 2002). HS views women as competitors in the workplace and even in the bedroom. In the world of societal empowerment (CEO roles, government positions) and advancement (education, basic rights), countries with higher HS fail to empower and advance women as a group (Glick et al. 2000). In the workplace, HS predicts negative stereotypes of career women (Glick et al. 1997). Consistent with being threatened by female professionals, prescriptive gender stereotypes (implicit beliefs that women should be nice and low-status) predict backlash against agentic (i.e., competent) women (Rudman and Glick 2001; Rudman and Phelan 2008). Agentic, effective women are perceived as highly competent but cold, compared with equally agentic men; what is more, social skills suddenly loom larger than competence in hiring agentic women, unlike all other job candidates (Phelan, Moss-Racusin, and Rudman 2008).

Gender stereotypes are especially sticky because they are prescriptive. Descriptive stereotypes say what a group does; prescriptive ones say what a group should do. When intergroup relations are also interdependent, prescriptive stereotypes flourish. Gender stereotypes are heavily prescriptive (Burgess and Borgida 1999; Fiske and Stevens 1993; Heilman 2001), specifying that traditional women are preferable to nontraditional women, or at least liked better.

Overall, in managing gender issues, organizations must monitor two contrasting kinds of bias against women: the protective but demeaning benevolence, and the threatened but dangerous hostility. Ambivalence strikes again.

A note on heterosexism. Warmth and competence likewise describe types of bias toward gay men (Clausell and Fiske 2005). The more effeminate stereotypic subtypes seem well-intentioned but effectual, whereas the gay-professional subtypes (e.g., artists) seem competent but not warm. Whereas most heterosexism research documents fiercely negative attitudes toward gay men (e.g., Hegarty and Pratto 2001; Herek 2000), understanding some of the ambivalent subtypes may mitigate some of the management issues. For example, although straight-acting gay men are most accepted, and leather-biker gays are despised, at least the stereotypically effeminate gays are liked and the gay professionals are respected. The costs come on the compensating negative dimension. That is, gay men who seem feminine may be disrespected, and openly gay men who seem professional may appear cold.

Racism. In modern times, racism reflects more ambivalence than it did a century ago. Ambivalent racism pits hostile (antiblack) sentiments against subjectively sympathetic but paternalistic (problack) sentiments (Katz and Hass 1988). Ambivalent racism depicts two contrasting reactions by whites toward blacks.

"Problack" attitudes blame black disadvantage on discrimination, segregation, and lack of opportunities. This pole of attitude ambivalence links to humanitarian-egalitarian values of kindness, prosociality, equality, and recognizing the power of circumstances. Both correlational studies and priming experiments show this link (Katz and Hass 1988).

In itself, consistent with the SCM, this subjectively problack attitude is ambivalent because it focuses on black disadvantage (disrespecting them all as victims) but also sympathizes with their plight (liking them). However, it fails to acknowledge black resilience, black progress, and the sizable proportion of black Americans who succeed. Thus, it fits the SCM pity quadrant, rather than the admiration-pride quadrant. Pity is an ambivalent emotion, and liking but disrespecting is intrinsically ambivalent.

In contrast, hostile antiblack racism resembles old-fashioned, unambivalent racism, claiming that black people are unambitious, disorganized, free-riding, and do not value education (Katz and Hass 1988). This hostility links to work-ethic beliefs, in both correlational and priming studies: believing that people have excess leisure, that failure reflects a lack of effort, and that work shows strength of character. This hostility harbors no ambivalence, only resentment.

Nevertheless, this work-ethic kind of antiblack racism might allow for more flexibility than a potentially worse genetic-essentialist form of hostile racism. In theory, the perceived work-ethic kind of racism would respond differently to unemployed black people than to professional, successful black people. Indeed, examining American cultural subtypes of black Americans, racial stereotypes do split poor blacks (viewed as neither competent nor warm) from black professionals (competent and almost as warm as the in-groups) (Cuddy, Fiske, and Glick 2007). Even black Americans split their own subtypes by social class (Fiske et al. 2009). The black middle class receives the most admiration.

Thus, the main evidence for racial ambivalence so far provides only a loose fit to the SCM. Black Americans land in two unambivalent but opposite quadrants of SCM space, low on both dimensions or high on both. Black Americans are viewed ambivalently mainly to the extent that white Americans simultaneously harbor a more subjectively positive and a more hostile attitude, which can flip from one polarity to the other, depending on individual differences in beliefs and on situational cues (Katz and Hass 1988).

Another version of ambivalent racial polarity, however, appears in aversive racism (Dovidio and Gaertner 2004). Well-intentioned whites express overtly positive verbal, explicit beliefs about their own egalitarian treatment of black Americans. But whites simultaneously harbor negative, nonverbal, implicit reactions that are detectable not only by researchers (Dovidio, Kawakami, and Gaertner 2002) but also by their black interaction partners (Shelton 2003; Shelton and Richesen 2006).

The implications for managing race are that nonblack managers and employees need to be aware of this ambivalent duality and its subtlety. The bad news is that people typically resist this feedback. The good news is that when whites do try hard to be nonracist, their black partners like them better (Shelton 2003).

Immigrant status. Ethnic stereotypes are accidents of immigration, according to the SCM. Groups emigrate as systematic subsets of their national populations, depending on political, economic, and cultural push factors. Sometimes more privileged, educated segments emigrate, and sometimes less educated physical laborers emigrate. For example, when Chinese immigrants to the United States arrived to build the railroads, their stereotypes revolved around their peasant status in their home country and their work roles here. After later waves of highly educated, technically trained Chinese immigrants arrived, their ethnicity's stereotype contrasted dramatically with the earlier one. Who happens to come and what jobs await them together generalize in observers' minds to describe the entire ethnicity. (Social role theory makes a similar argument about gender differences and stereotypes [Eagly 1987].) People observe who fills which roles, not without some accuracy, but then they erroneously assume that the roles reflect the predispositions, traits, and abilities of their occupants' ethnic categories.

Generic immigrants are among the most disliked and disrespected groups in the SCM space, across nations. In the United States, unspecified immigrants are stereotyped as lacking both warmth and competence (Cuddy, Fiske, and Glick 2007), and other countries agree (Cuddy et al. 2009; Durante et al. n.d.). Participants report disgust and contempt, active harm (attacks), and passive harm (neglect) by society—a dire situation.

A closer look shows why. Immigrant stereotypes depend entirely on ethnicity (Lee and Fiske 2006). The only types of immigrants who seem low on both warmth and competence are Latino and African immigrants; all the others receive at least one positive evaluation. Immigrants who are Mexicans, South Americans, Africans, or undocumented rate unambivalently low, and they are associated with farm workers. In contrast, generic European immigrants rate as equal to Americans on both dimensions, and Canadian immigrants rate higher than both, all associated with the middle class. These high-high and low-low immigrant clusters represent the two polarities of immigrant images.

Other immigrants fit the SCM ambivalent clusters: East Asian immigrants seem competent but not warm and are associated with the tech industry. Chinese, Japanese, Korean, and generic Asians land here. Indians are the Asian exception, falling in the in-group cluster—shared language may contribute to this.

The other ambivalent cluster for immigrants contains only Italian and Irish immigrants—last century's waves now seen as harmless and familiar, warm but not highly competent. Within the European Union countries' mutual stereotypes, these nationalities are viewed the same way (Cuddy et al. 2009). (Within the EU, Germans and the British are seen as competent but cold.)

For immigrants, the most obvious bridges to acceptance ought to be documentation, language, and generational longevity. Indeed, generic documented immigrants and third-generation immigrants land in the in-group cluster. English-speaking ethnicities (Canadians, Irish, Indians) fare better than non-native English speakers (Latinos, East Asians). Nevertheless, ethnicity trumps documentation and generational longevity, with these factors improving the perceptions of specific groups but usually leaving them within the same cluster as their generic ethnicity (Fiske and Lee forthcoming). Unfortunately, factors under a group's control, such as documentation, language, and generations of residence, do not trump ethnicity, although they help. These features, however, can mitigate anti-immigrant sentiment (whose default is negative, but some is ambivalent) as managers confront these issues.

Ageism. Another management challenge—a protected category like gender and race but also like immigration status, and a shifting one that people occupy differently throughout the life course—age is understudied as a basis of prejudice (North and Fiske n.d.-a). The default descriptive stereotype of older people, all over the world, is that they are warm but incompetent (Cuddy and Fiske 2002; Cuddy et al. 2009; Durante et al. n.d.). Even in rural China, older people are viewed as pitifully incompetent, though well intentioned (Chen and Fiske n.d.). The elder stereotype resists change (Cuddy, Norton, and Fiske 2005); attempts to make an older person seem more competent do not succeed well at changing competence, though they do inversely affect warmth ratings. This experimental vignette result fits the contact literature's finding that young-old contact programs rarely work to improve ageist bias (North and Fiske n.d.-a).

One reason for the stickiness of the old-age stereotype may be its prescriptive as well as its descriptive nature. As noted, gender stereotypes are prescriptive because of men's and women's intimate interdependence. People not only have both genders in their families, but also many age categories, all of which are interdependent. This interdependence underlies intergenerational resentments over resources (North and Fiske n.d.-b), as follows.

Consider intergenerational relations as a movie-ticket line, with younger people at the back; ahead of them are middle-aged people, and older people stand at the front. If the older people take too long with the resources of the ticket-seller's attention, those behind them become impatient. This resembles tensions over orderly succession for higher-status positions at work or for family wealth and possessions at home. In this case, the older people enjoy an enviable position, seen as high-status, though perhaps cold and unfeeling for actively rejecting the needs of those behind them. If the older people at the front of the line use up all the tickets (at a senior discount), other tensions may result over their unwarranted consumption of shared resources. These selfish older people are ignoring the needs of others, more passively in this case, so perhaps they are not so much enviable as contemptible in their exploitation of their turn. Finally, if the senior citizens are buying tickets to a seemingly age-inappropriate movie, the younger audience members may resent the invasion of their generational identity.

Moving beyond analogies, intergenerational tensions over resources, identity, and consumption do predict ageist prejudice uniquely targeting older people and uniquely held by younger people (North and Fiske n.d.-b). Each of these dimensions constitutes a component of ageist reactions to vignettes in which an older person either adheres to or violates ageist prescriptions regarding orderly succession, unfair consumption, and age-inappropriate identity. Each dimension also constitutes a piece of a reliable ageism scale.

From a management perspective, this suggests that patterns of ageism differ depending on the older person's perceived response to ageist prescriptions. Just as nontraditional women incur a penalty for challenging the low-competence, high-warmth default roles for women, so do nontraditional elders forfeit the same cluster that entails sympathy and pity. Violating prescriptive stereotypes incurs costs on both perceived warmth and competence as well as on younger people's willingness to interact with older people.

Classism. Although social class is not a protected category in the workplace, class divides are increasing in the United States, with ill effects on well-being (Wilkinson and Pickett 2009) that relate to work. Increased inequality decreases social mobility (Blanden, Gregg, and Machin 2005; Solon 2002), trust (Uslaner 2002; Kawachi et al. 1997; Wilkinson and Pickett 2009), education (Wilkinson and Pickett 2009), happiness, and well-being (Alesina, Di Tella, and MacCulloch 2004). As noted earlier, societies with more inequality recruit SCM's ambivalent clusters to a reliably greater degree, consistent with a system-justifying function of stereotypes (Durante et al. n.d.).

Social class divides manifest in daily interactions (Fiske 2011; Fiske and Markus forthcoming), undermining the feeling of fit when people from working-class backgrounds or identities navigate the resource-rich contexts of privilege in the professions, higher education, and even elementary school. Of course, sociologists have long considered social class (e.g., Lareau and Conley 2010), but a social psychological angle identifies the face-to-face mechanisms that sustain social class divides.

Starting with elementary school, working-class parents encounter the world of middle-class teachers with some differing assumptions that may undermine their advocacy for their children (Lareau and Calarco forthcoming). For example, middle-class parents often view education as growing their children, allowing them to blossom, whereas working-class parents view education as disciplining their unruly little animals, turning them into responsible adults (Kusserow forthcoming). Working-class children's collaborative storytelling styles (e.g., interdependent, call and response) do not fit middle-class educational settings, which are relentlessly individualistic (Miller and Sperry forthcoming).

As adults, individuals with a working-class background or identity encounter crucial gateway interactions: college and employment interviews, networking at school and at work, and daily workplace interactions; where middle-class models are more likely to succeed, providing access to the resources for social mobility (Ridgeway and Fisk forthcoming; Stephens, Fryberg, and Markus forthcoming). The cues are often subtle and unexamined nonverbal signals (Kraus, Rheinschmidt, and Piff forthcoming) or unexamined affiliative and competence beliefs about different social class groups (Fiske et al. forthcoming). These signals and beliefs produce feelings of being a misfit and mistrust in cross-class interactions. Mistrust between those of different class backgrounds, fostered by institutional experiences and stereotyped beliefs, can foster inequality through everyday interactions.

How Does This Relate to Management?

In hiring, training, and promotion, first impressions shape subsequent impressions. Even as decision-makers gain additional information, the new information is anchored in the initial impressions, for better or worse (Fiske 1998; Macrae and Bodenhausen 2000). Individuating information—beyond the initial demographic categories of gender, sexuality, race, immigrant status, age, and class—does not eliminate the problem. For effective management of these prejudices, the takeaway messages are as follows:

- Not all prejudices are alike; they vary in perceived warmth and competence, creating predictable clusters of stereotypes, emotional prejudices, and discriminatory tendencies.

- Managing a specific group's dilemma should work to counteract its stereo-typically weak dimension, for example, warmth for Asians, competence for older people.
- Emotions drive behavior, and emotional prejudices are the proximal causes of discrimination.
- Antecedents, indicators, and consequences of bias will differ by specific out-group.
- Often these biases are subtle and unexamined, not the overt biases of the past century.
- Organization-level management strategies suggest a focus on the anteced-ents (status and interdependence structures) that predict stereotypes and prejudices.
- Societal levels of management suggest that growing income inequality (sta-tus divides) and political polarization (failures to cooperate) worsen these destructive dynamics.
- Constructive contact between groups (involving cooperation, equal-status in the setting, important goals and authority sanctions) especially improves emotional prejudices (Pettigrew and Tropp 2006).

In addition to worrying about status divides that result from inequality, we also need to worry about affiliative divides that affect relational capital. Both warmth and competence determine success.

References

Alesina, Alberto, Rafael Di Tella, and Robert MacCulloch. 2004. Inequality and happiness: Are Europeans and Americans different? *Journal of Public Economics* 88:2009–42.

Barreto, Manuela, Naomi Ellemers, Laura Piebinga, and Miguel Moya. 2010. How nice of us and how dumb of me: The effect of exposure to benevolent sexism on women's task and relational self-descriptions. *Sex Roles* 62 (7–8): 532–44.

Benard, Stephen, In Paik, and Shelley J. Correll. 2008. Cognitive bias and the motherhood penalty. *Hastings Law Journal* 59:1359–87.

Berger, Joseph, Bernard P. Cohen, and Morris Zelditch. 1972. Status characteristics and social interaction. *American Sociological Review* 37 (3): 241–55.

Bergsieker, Hilary B., Lisa M. Leslie, Vanessa S. Constantine, and Susan T. Fiske. n.d. *Stereotyping by omission: Eliminate the negative, accentuate the positive*. Manuscript under review.

Blanden, Jo, Paul Gregg, and Stephen Machin. 2005. *Intergenerational mobility in Europe and North America*. London: Centre for Economic Performance, London School of Economics.

Bosson, Jennifer K., Elizabeth C. Pinel, and Joseph A. Vandello. 2010. The emotional impact of ambivalent sexism: Forecasts versus real experiences. *Sex Roles* 62 (7–8): 520–31.

Budig, Michelle J., and Paula England. 2001. The wage penalty for motherhood. *American Sociological Review* 66 (2): 204–25.

Burgess, Diana, and Eugene Borgida. 1999. Who women are, who women should be: Descriptive and prescriptive gender stereotyping in sex discrimination. *Psychology, Public Policy, and Law* 5 (3): 665–92.

Chen, Zhixia, and Susan T. Fiske. n.d. [Unpublished data].

Cikara, Mina, Rachel A. Farnsworth, Lasana T. Harris, and Susan T. Fiske. 2010. On the wrong side of the trolley track: Neural correlates of relative social valuation. *Social Cognitive and Affective Neuroscience* 5:404–13.

Clausell, Eric, and Susan T. Fiske. 2005. When do the parts add up to the whole? Ambivalent stereotype content for gay male subgroups. *Social Cognition* 23:157–76.

Correll, Shelley J., Stephen Benard, and In Paik. 2007. Getting a job: Is there a motherhood penalty? *American Journal of Sociology* 112:1297–1338.

Cuddy, Amy J. C., and Susan T. Fiske. 2002. Doddering, but dear: Process, content, and function in stereotyping of older persons. In *Ageism*, ed. Todd D. Nelson, 3–26. Cambridge, MA: MIT Press.

Cuddy, Amy J. C., Susan T. Fiske, and Peter Glick. 2004. When professionals become mothers, warmth doesn't cut the ice. *Journal of Social Issues* 60:701–18.

Cuddy, Amy J. C., Susan T. Fiske, and Peter Glick. 2007. The BIAS map: Behaviors from intergroup affect and stereotypes. *Journal of Personality and Social Psychology* 92:631–48.

Cuddy, Amy J. C., Susan T. Fiske, and Peter Glick. 2008. Competence and warmth as universal trait dimensions of interpersonal and intergroup perception: The Stereotype Content Model and the BIAS Map. In *Advances in experimental social psychology*, ed. Mark P. Zanna, 61–149. New York, NY: Academic Press.

Cuddy, Amy J. C., Susan T. Fiske, Virginia S. Y. Kwan, Peter Glick, Stephanie Demoulin, Jacques-Philippe Leyens, Michael Harris Bond, Jean-Claude Croizet, Naomi Ellemers, Ed Sleebos, et al. 2009. Stereotype content model across cultures: Towards universal similarities and some differences. *British Journal of Social Psychology* 48:1–33.

Cuddy, Amy J. C., Michael I. Norton, and Susan T. Fiske. 2005. This old stereotype: The pervasiveness and persistence of the elderly stereotype. *Journal of Social Issues* 61:265–83.

Dardenne, Benoit, Muriel Dumont, and Thierry Bollier. 2007. Insidious dangers of benevolent sexism: Consequences for women's performance. *Journal of Personality and Social Psychology* 93 (5): 764–79.

Dovidio, John F., and Samuel L. Gaertner. 2004. Aversive racism. In *Advances in experimental social psychology*, ed. Mark P. Zanna, 1–52. San Diego, CA: Academic Press.

Dovidio, John F., Kerry Kawakami, and Samuel L. Gaertner. 2002. Implicit and explicit prejudice and interracial interaction. *Journal of Personality and Social Psychology* 82 (1): 62–68.

Dumont, Muriel, Marie Sarlet, and Benoit Dardenne. 2010. Be too kind to a woman, she'll feel incompetent: Benevolent sexism shifts self-construal and autobiographical memories toward incompetence. *Sex Roles* 62 (7–8): 545–53.

Durante, Federica, Susan T. Fiske, Nicolas Kervyn, Amy J. C. Cuddy, Adebowale (Debo) Akande, Fiona Kate Barlow, Janine Bosak, Ed Cairns, Claire Doherty, Dora Capozza, et al. n.d. *Nations' income inequality predicts ambivalence in stereotype content: How societies mind the gap.* Manuscript under review.

Durante, Federica, Chiara Volpato, and Susan T. Fiske. 2009. Using the Stereotype Content Model to examine group depictions in fascism: An archival approach. *European Journal of Social Psychology* 39:1–19.

Eagly, Alice H. 1987. *Sex differences in social behavior: A social-role interpretation.* Hillsdale, NJ: Erlbaum.

Eagly, Alice H., and Steven J. Karau. 2002. Role congruity theory of prejudice toward female leaders. *Psychological Review* 109:573–98.

Eagly, Alice H., Antonio Mladinic, and Stacey Otto. 1991. Are women evaluated more favorably than men? An analysis of attitudes, beliefs, and emotions. *Psychology of Women Quarterly* 15 (2): 203–16.

Eckes, Thomas. 2002. Paternalistic and envious gender stereotypes: Testing predictions from the stereotype content model. *Sex Roles* 47 (3–4): 99–114.

Fields, Alice M., Suzanne Swan, and Bret Kloos. 2010. "What it means to be a woman": Ambivalent sexism in female college students' experiences and attitudes. *Sex Roles* 62 (7–8): 554–67.

Fiske, Susan T. 1998. Stereotyping, prejudice, and discrimination. In *Handbook of social psychology*, 4th ed., eds. Daniel T. Gilbert, Susan T. Fiske, and Gardner Lindzey, 357–411. New York, NY: McGraw-Hill.

Fiske, Susan T. 2011. *Envy up, scorn down: How status divides us.* New York, NY: Russell Sage Foundation.

Fiske, Susan T., Hilary Bergsieker, Ann-Marie Russell, and Lyle Williams. 2009. Images of black Americans: Then, "them" and now, "Obama!" *DuBois Review: Social Science Research on Race* 6:83–101.

Fiske, Susan T., Amy J. C. Cuddy, and Peter Glick. 2007. Universal dimensions of social perception: Warmth and competence. *Trends in Cognitive Science* 11:77–83.

Fiske, Susan T., Amy J. C. Cuddy, Peter Glick, and Jun Xu. 2002. A model of (often mixed) stereotype content: Competence and warmth respectively follow from perceived status and competition. *Journal of Personality and Social Psychology* 82:878–902.

Fiske, Susan T., and Tiane L. Lee. Forthcoming. Xenophobia and how to fight it: Immigrants as the quintessential "other." In *Social categories in everyday experience*, eds. Shaun Wiley, Tracey Revenson, and Gina Philogene. Washington, DC: American Psychological Association.

Fiske, Susan T., and Hazel Rose Markus. Forthcoming. *Facing social class: Social psychology of social class.* New York, NY: Russell Sage Foundation.

Fiske, Susan T., Miguel Moya, Ann Marie Russell, and Courtney Bearns. Forthcoming. The secret handshake: Trust in cross-class encounters. In *Facing social class: Social psychology of social class*, eds. Susan T. Fiske and Hazel Rose Markus. New York, NY: Russell Sage Foundation.

Fiske, Susan T., and Laura E. Stevens. 1993. What's so special about sex? Gender stereotyping and discrimination. In *Gender issues in contemporary society: Applied social psychology annual*, eds. Stuart Oskamp and Mark Costanzo, 173–96. Thousand Oaks, CA: Sage.

Gilbert, Daniel T., and David H. Silvera. 1996. Overhelping. *Journal of Personality and Social Psychology* 70 (4): 678–90.

Glick, Peter, Jeffrey Diebold, Barbara Bailey-Werner, and Lin Zhu. 1997. The two faces of Adam: Ambivalent sexism and polarized attitudes toward women. *Personality and Social Psychology Bulletin* 23 (12): 1323–34.

Glick, Peter, and Susan T. Fiske. 1996. The Ambivalent Sexism Inventory: Differentiating hostile and benevolent sexism. *Journal of Personality and Social Psychology* 70:491–512.

Glick, Peter, and Susan T. Fiske. 2007. Sex discrimination: The psychological approach. In *Sex discrimination in the workplace: Multidisciplinary approaches*, eds. Faye J. Crosby, Margaret S. Stockdale, and S. Ann Ropp. 155–88. Malden, MA: Blackwell.

Glick, Peter, Susan T. Fiske, Antonio Mladinic, José L. Saiz, Dominic Abrams, Barbara Masser, Bolanle Adetoun, Johnstone E. Osagie, Adebowale Akande, Amos Alao, et al. 2000. Beyond prejudice as simple antipathy: Hostile and benevolent sexism across cultures. *Journal of Personality and Social Psychology* 79:763–75.

Harris, Lasana T., and Susan T. Fiske. 2006. Dehumanizing the lowest of the low: Neuro-imaging responses to extreme outgroups. *Psychological Science* 17:847–53.

Hegarty, Peter, and Felicia Pratto. 2001. Sexual orientation beliefs: Their relationship to anti-gay attitudes and biological determinist arguments. *Journal of Homosexuality* 41 (1): 121–35.

Heilman, Madeline E. 2001. Description and prescription: How gender stereotypes prevent women's ascent up the organizational ladder. *Journal of Social Issues* 57 (4): 657–74.

Herek, Gregory M. 2000. The psychology of sexual prejudice. *Current Directions in Psychological Science* 9 (1): 19–22.

Hoobler, Jenny M., Sandy A. Wayne, and Grace Lemmon. 2009. Bosses' perceptions of family-work conflict and women's promotability: Glass ceiling effects. *Academy of Management Journal* 52 (5): 939–57.

Katz, Irwin, and R. Glen Hass. 1988. Racial ambivalence and American value conflict: Correlational and priming studies of dual cognitive structures. *Journal of Personality and Social Psychology* 55:893–905.

Kawachi, Ichiro, Bruce P. Kennedy, Kimberly Lochner, and Deborah Prothrow-Stith. 1997. Social capital, income inequality, and mortality. *American Journal of Public Health* 87:1491–98.

Kervyn, Nicolas, and Susan T. Fiske. n.d. *The Stereotype Content Model and Osgood's Semantic Differential: Reconciling warmth and competence with evaluation, potency, and activity.* Manuscript under review.

Kervyn, Nicolas, Susan T. Fiske, and Vincent Yzerbyt. n.d.-a. *Mapping social perception: Testing the stereotype content model with a multidimensional approach.* Manuscript under review.

Kervyn, Nicolas, Susan T. Fiske, and Vincent Yzerbyt. n.d.-b. *Why is the primary dimension of social cognition so hard to predict? Symbolic and realistic threats together predict warmth in the stereotype content model.* Manuscript under review.

Kervyn, Nicolas, Vincent Y. Yzerbyt, Charles M. Judd, and Ana Nunes. 2009. A question of compensation: The social life of the fundamental dimensions of social perception. *Journal of Personality and Social Psychology* 96 (4): 828–42.

Kraus, Michael W., Michelle L. Rheinschmidt, and Paul K. Piff. Forthcoming. The intersection of resources and rank: Signaling social class in face-to-face encounters. In *Facing social class: Social psychology of social class*, eds. Susan T. Fiske and Hazel Rose Markus. New York, NY: Russell Sage Foundation.

Kusserow, Adrie. Forthcoming. When hard and soft clash: Class-based individualisms in Manhattan and Queens. In *Facing social class: Social psychology of social class*, eds. Susan T. Fiske and Hazel Rose Markus. New York, NY: Russell Sage Foundation.

Lareau, Annette, and Jessica McCrory Calarco. Forthcoming. Class, cultural capital, and institutions: The case of families and schools. In *Facing social class: Social psychology of social class*, eds. Susan T. Fiske and Hazel Rose Markus. New York, NY: Russell Sage Foundation.

Lareau, Annette, and Dalton Conley. 2010. *Social class: How does it work?* New York, NY: Russell Sage Foundation.

Lee, Tiane L., and Susan T. Fiske. 2006. Not an out-group, but not yet an in-group: Immigrants in the stereotype content model. *International Journal of Intercultural Relations* 30:751–68.

Macrae, C. Neil, and Galen V. Bodenhausen. 2000. Social cognition: Thinking categorically about others. *Annual Review of Psychology* 51:93–120.

Miller, Peggy J., and Douglas E. Sperry. Forthcoming. Déjà vu: Contesting language deficiency again. In *Facing social class: Social psychology of social class*, eds. Susan T. Fiske and Hazel Rose Markus. New York, NY: Russell Sage Foundation.

North, Michael S., and Susan T. Fiske. n.d.-a. *An inconvenienced youth: Ageism as intergenerational tensions over resources*. Manuscript under review.

North, Michael S., and Susan T. Fiske. n.d.-b. *The young and the ageist: Intergenerational tensions over succession, identity, and consumption*. Manuscript under review.

Osgood, Charles E., George J. Suci, and Percy H. Tannenbaum. 1957. *The measurement of meaning*. Urbana: University of Illinois Press.

Peeters, Guido. 2001. In search for a social-behavioral approach-avoidance dimension associated with evaluative trait meanings. *Psychologica Belgica* 41 (4): 187–203.

Pettigrew, Thomas F., and Linda R. Tropp. 2006. A meta-analytic test of intergroup contact theory. *Journal of Personality and Social Psychology* 90 (5): 751–83.

Phelan, Julie E., Corinne A. Moss-Racusin, and Laurie A. Rudman. 2008. Competent yet out in the cold: Shifting criteria for hiring reflect backlash toward agentic women. *Psychology of Women Quarterly* 32 (4): 406–13.

Podolny, Joel M., and James N. Baron. 1997. Resources and relationships: Social networks and mobility in the workplace. *American Sociological Review* 62 (5): 673–93.

Ridgeway, Cecilia L. 1991. The social construction of status value: Gender and other nominal characteristics. *Social Forces* 70 (2): 367–86.

Ridgeway, Cecilia L., and Susan T. Fiske. Forthcoming. Class rules, status dynamics, and "gateway" interactions. In *Facing social class: Social psychology of social class*, eds. Susan T. Fiske and Hazel Rose Markus. New York, NY: Russell Sage Foundation.

Rosenberg, Seymour, Carnot Nelson, and P. S. Vivekananthan. 1968. A multidimensional approach to the structure of personality impressions. *Journal of Personality and Social Psychology* 9 (4): 283–94.

Rudman, Laurie A., and Peter Glick. 2001. Prescriptive gender stereotypes and backlash toward agentic women. *Journal of Social Issues* 57 (4): 743–62.

Rudman, Laurie A., and Julie E. Phelan. 2008. Backlash effects for disconfirming gender stereotypes in organizations. In *Research in organizational behavior*, eds. Arthur P. Brief and Barry M. Staw, 61–79. New York, NY: Elsevier.

Shelton, J. Nicole. 2003. Interpersonal concerns in social encounters between majority and minority group members. *Group Processes and Intergroup Relations* 6 (2): 171–85.

Shelton, J. Nicole, and Jennifer A. Richeson. 2006. Interracial interactions: A relational approach. In *Advances in experimental social psychology*, ed. Mark P. Zanna, 121–81. San Diego, CA: Academic Press.

Sherif, Muzafer, and Carolyn W. Sherif. 1953. *Groups in harmony and tension: An integration of studies of intergroup relations*. Oxford: Harper.

Solon, Gary. 2002. Cross-country differences in intergenerational earnings mobility. *Journal of Economic Perspectives* 16:59–66.

Spence, Janet T., and Robert Helmreich. 1972. Who likes competent women? Competence, sex role congruence of interests, and subjects' attitudes toward women as determinants of interpersonal attraction. *Journal of Applied Social Psychology* 2 (3): 197–213.

Spence, Janet T., Robert Helmreich, and Joy Stapp. 1973. A short version of the Attitudes toward Women Scale (AWS). *Bulletin of the Psychonomic Society* 2 (4): 219–20.

Stephens, Nicole M., Stephanie A. Fryberg, and Hazel Rose Markus. Forthcoming. It's your choice: How the middle class model of independence disadvantages working class Americans. In *Facing social class: Social psychology of social class*, eds. Susan T. Fiske and Hazel Rose Markus. New York, NY: Russell Sage Foundation.

Tajfel, Henri. 1981. *Human groups and social categories*. New York, NY: Cambridge University Press.

Uslaner, Eric M. 2002. *The moral foundations of trust*. Cambridge: Cambridge University Press.

Wilkinson, Richard G., and Kate E. Pickett. 2009. Income inequality and social dysfunction. *Annual Review of Sociology* 35:493–511.

Wojciszke, Bogdan, Andrea E. Abele, and Wiesław Baryla. 2009. Two dimensions of interpersonal attitudes: Liking depends on communion, respect depends on agency. *European Journal of Social Psychology* 39 (6): 973–90.

Power, Influence, and Diversity in Organizations

This article summarizes literatures on power, status, and influence in sociology's group processes tradition and applies them to issues of diversity in organizations. Power—defined as the ability to impose one's will even against resistance from others—results primarily from position in a social structure. Influence—defined as compelling behavior change without threat of punishment or promise of reward—results largely from the respect and esteem in which one is held by others. Research identifies status as a foundation of influence differences in groups and indicates that members of disadvantaged status groups, such as women and minorities, will have decreased influence and face challenges in acquiring and using power. The literature also suggests solutions to these challenges, including self-presentation strategies of group motivation and institutional arrangements that support women and minority group members in powerful leadership positions.

Keywords: power; status; influence; leadership; management; diversity

By
JEFFREY W. LUCAS
and
AMY R. BAXTER

Reflecting the changing demographics of American society, organizations in the United States are becoming increasingly diverse places to work. Women, for the first time in history, make up half of the U.S. workforce, up from about 35 percent of the workforce 40 years ago (U.S. Department of Labor 2009). If demographic trends continue, nonwhites will make up half the U.S. workforce by 2050 (Toossi 2006). At the same time, this increasing diversity is not extending to high-level management positions. In fact, women and minority group members lost ground overall in representation in Fortune 500 corporate boards between 2004

Jeffrey W. Lucas is an associate professor of sociology at the University of Maryland. He carries out basic experimental research on group processes, particularly status, power, and leadership.

Amy R. Baxter is a PhD candidate in the Department of Sociology at the University of Maryland. Her current research is experimental work focusing on factors that contribute to the wage and promotion gap between women and men.

DOI: 10.1177/0002716211420231

and 2010 (Lang et al. 2011). Despite composing only about one-third of the U.S. workforce, white men hold more than 75 percent of board seats and 95 percent of board chair positions in Fortune 500 corporations (Lang et al. 2011).

A consequence of inequalities in access to corporate leadership positions is that it is harder for persons in certain social groups to exercise their will in organizations. In this way, the experiences of women, persons of color, and members of other disadvantaged groups in organizations are shaped in significant ways by processes of power and influence. This article summarizes bodies of theory and research on power, status, and influence—particularly as the concepts are treated in sociology's group processes tradition—and discusses their relevance to issues of management and diversity in organizations.

Power, status, and influence are concepts with multiple treatments, both colloquially and in academic literatures. Meanings and uses of the concept *power*, for example, vary considerably across academic disciplines and subdisciplines. The philosopher Bertrand Russell identified power as the most important element in the development of any society and its study as the central aim of all social sciences (Russell 1938). Summarizing the literature on a concept of such breadth presents obvious challenges. The concepts of *status* and *influence* have similarly varied meanings and treatments. It would be impossible to survey the full range of treatments of power, status, and influence, and we make no effort to do so. Rather, we draw from basic research that has defined the concepts in narrow and consistent ways.

In colloquial language, power and influence are often viewed as more or less the same thing: the ability to affect the behavior of others in some intended way. Alternatively, power and influence are sometimes seen as two parts of the same process—power as a *capacity* to change behavior and influence as the *practice* of using power to effect behavior change (French and Raven 1959). According to Wrong (1979), *power* and *influence* are used synonymously because of the absence of a verb form for the term *power*. We do not argue that these treatments of the concepts are incorrect. Rather, we focus on research that identifies the concepts more narrowly and as clearly distinct. Power, as defined in the group processes perspective, is the ability to get what one wants even in the face of resistance (Markovsky, Willer, and Patton 1987; Weber 1978). Influence is the ability to get what one wants even in the absence of fear of punishment or promise of reward (Rashotte and Webster 2005). The theory and research we review is consistent with these treatments of the concepts. For other treatments, see Kelly (1994) on power and Manz (1986) on influence.

We first define and discuss the concept of influence. Group processes treatments of influence address it primarily as an outcome of status, another concept narrowly defined in the tradition. We discuss theory and research on status in groups, work that has clear relevance to issues of diversity in organizations. We then discuss theory and research on power in networks. We close with a discussion of how the concepts relate to each other and what the power and influence literatures together can tell us about managing diversity in work organizations.

Influence in Groups

Power, as typically conceived, is a capacity (Salancik and Pfeffer 1977). It is the ability to get things done if one chooses. When power is used to get people to do things, power is often defined as influence (Dahl 1957). Group processes research, in contrast, treats influence as clearly distinct from power use. Influence occurs when people perform actions because they have been convinced they are the right actions to take, not because someone with power told them to do them (Sell et al. 2004). Consider a supervisor who directs subordinates to fill boxes in a factory. The subordinates do what the supervisor says because she has power over them. In contrast, consider a minister who asks members of her congregation to volunteer to fill boxes for a charity drive. If the members of the congregation volunteer to fill the boxes, they have been influenced. The minister has little or no power to direct the behavior of the members of the congregation, but they do what she wants without promise of reward or fear of punishment. They have been convinced that the activity is the right thing to do.

As we discuss, power is principally the result of a position in a social structure (Emerson 1972). The factory supervisor has power because her position gives her the ability to discipline subordinates who do not comply and reward subordinates who are especially compliant. Influence results less from social structure than from status (the respect and esteem in which a person is held by others) (Wagner and Berger 1993). Below we discuss the most well-developed and widely studied theoretical account of status processes in groups.

Expectation states and status characteristics theories

Status is a position in a group based on esteem or respect (Berger, Cohen, and Zelditch 1972; Berger et al. 1977). Although status has a number of outcomes, influence is perhaps its most fundamental. Those with higher status in groups have more influence over group decisions than do those with lower status. Expectation states and status characteristics theory, which resides in sociology's group processes tradition, explains the processes by which groups set up and maintain status hierarchies (Berger, Wagner, and Zelditch 1985; Berger and Webster 2006).

Dating to the 1950s, research currently finds that, initially, status-undifferentiated task groups organize themselves into hierarchies of prestige (Bales 1950). The most complete theoretical account of these processes is the expectation states program of Berger and colleagues. Status characteristics theory (SCT) (Berger et al. 1977; Berger, Wagner, and Zelditch 1985) links characteristics of an individual such as gender and race to that person's rank in a status hierarchy based on the esteem in which the person is held by self and others. The theory proposes that members of a task group form expectations about each other's competence to contribute to group goals based on each person's status characteristics. Individuals expected to contribute more are more highly valued by the group and held in higher esteem (Webster and Driskell 1978).

Two scope conditions limit the domain of SCT—task orientation and collective orientation (Berger et al. 1977). Task orientation means that the group is formed for the purpose of solving some problem. Collective orientation means that group members consider it necessary to take into account the input of every group member in solving the problem or performing the task. For all groups that meet its scope conditions, the theory makes predictions about the process through which observable status characteristics lead to behavioral inequalities. Many groups in organizational settings satisfy these scope conditions—a group choosing which candidate to hire for an open position, a committee determining an incentive system, a team deciding which direction to go on a project, and so on. Additionally, research has extended the scope of the theory to include individual performances when individuals anticipate that those performances will have implications for future group interaction (Lovaglia et al. 1998).

Research on status processes in groups has produced several consistent findings. According to SCT, group members (often outside their conscious awareness) develop expectations for their own performances and those of other group members. In the theory, these expectations develop based on status characteristics, which are characteristics around which expectations and beliefs come to be organized (Berger et al. 1977). Examples of status characteristics include race, gender, education, and task expertise (Webster and Hysom 1998). Individuals in categories of status characteristics that produce higher expectations for performance than those of other group members are held in higher esteem and have higher positions in the group's status order (Bienenstock and Bianchi 2004). One consequence of the status order is that high-status group members are expected to make more competent contributions to the group. In this way, the status order of the group becomes self-fulfilling, with the contributions of high-status members evaluated as more competent regardless of their objective merit (Walker and Simpson 2000).

SCT specifies two types of status characteristics. For both, one category is considered to be more socially desirable and highly valued than another (Simpson and Walker 2002). A status characteristic is specific if it carries expectations for competence in a narrow range of situations. Computer programming skills is a specific characteristic because it leads to expectations for competence only in limited settings. A characteristic is diffuse if it carries with it expectations for competence in a wide variety of situations. Age, gender, race, and social class are examples of diffuse characteristics. In the theory, both types of status characteristics contribute to determining group members' relative status by altering expectations for competence that members hold for one another (Berger et al. 1977). Diffuse status characteristics, however, have a distinct moral component, with high status on the characteristics being viewed as broadly superior to low status on the characteristics (Berger, Rosenholtz, and Zelditch 1980).

In SCT, status characteristics produce rank in a status hierarchy through a chain of four logically connected assumptions (Webster and Foschi 1988). First, the theory assumes that any characteristic will become salient (i.e., stand out) to group members if it is known or believed to be related to the task or if it differentiates among the members of the group. Second, the burden-of-proof assumption states that all salient characteristics will be treated as relevant (i.e., used to develop performance expectations) by group members unless specifically disassociated from the task. Therefore, in a mixed-sex group in which gender operates as a status characteristic, the theory assumes that gender will be treated as relevant by group members unless it is specifically demonstrated that gender is not indicative of ability to perform the group's task. In other words, the burden of proof lies with showing group members that a characteristic is *not* relevant to the group's task (Berger et al. 1977).

The theory's third assumption is the formation of aggregated expectation states. In simple terms, this assumption holds that when group members are confronted with more than one relevant characteristic, they act as if they combine the expectations associated with each characteristic in developing an overall performance expectation. The fourth assumption in the link between status characteristics and a group's status order is the basic expectation assumption. According to this assumption, a member's rank in the group's status hierarchy will be a direct function of the group's expectations for that member's performance. With this assumption, the status order of the group will be determined by the aggregated expectation states that each group member has for herself and other group members.

Dozens of studies over the past four decades have supported the principles of SCT (for a review, see Kalkhoff and Thye 2006). Research in the theory is primarily carried out in a standard experimental setting. The setting involves participants at computer terminals being told information about partners on computers in different rooms. The participants and partners then complete a task together in which the partner has opportunities to influence the participant. Partners in these studies are often fictitious, with experimental conditions determining the partner's characteristics. Partner influence is treated as an indicator of status. If, for example, participants with male partners were influenced more than participants with female partners, it would provide evidence that gender acts as a status characteristic that advantages men.

Status orders in groups, then, reflect status characteristics of group members, such as gender and race. Research has identified a number of outcomes of status processes, including that high-status group members perform more in the group (e.g., talk more during group interactions), have more opportunities to perform (e.g., have their opinions solicited more often), and have their performances evaluated more highly (e.g., get more positive feedback on their suggestions) than low-status group members (Berger, Rosenholtz, and Zelditch 1980). The principal behavioral outcome of status is influence; those of higher status play a bigger role in determining decisions in the group and its members than do those of lower status (Berger et al. 1977).

A key element of status is that it is relative. Corporate CEOs, for example, do not have high status in and of themselves, but only in relation to persons in other, less prestigious positions. It is this relational aspect of status that makes it a group process. Furthermore, the processes by which individuals set up and maintain status hierarchies in groups are largely nonconscious (Berger, Wagner, and Zelditch 1985). Individuals tend not to consciously choose to defer to men more than women, for example, but they do so in a large number of settings (Ridgeway 1993). And status orders tend to be self-reinforcing; high-status group members are evaluated more highly because they are high-status. The self-reinforcing nature of status orders, combined with the fact that status processes tend to operate below conscious awareness, makes status hierarchies very resistant to change. For example, research has found that status orders in an organization's work groups tend to match the status characteristics of group members even when those groups have been in place for extended periods of time (B. Cohen and Zhou 1991).

Gender, race, and status

Substantial evidence indicates that gender and race operate as status characteristics in American society. Despite our society becoming increasingly diverse by race and ethnicity, contributions from European Americans are still valued more highly than those from members of other racial and ethnic groups (Lovaglia et al. 1998). And despite girls and women now outperforming boys and men on nearly all indicators at every level of education (Freeman 2004), men remain higher status than women (Ridgeway and Correll 2000). Based on the indicators of status discussed above—opportunities to perform, performances, performance evaluations, and influence—the contributions of men and European Americans are overvalued, whereas contributions from women and minority group members tend to be devalued or ignored.

Gender is a diffuse characteristic because it carries expectations for performance in a wide range of situations (Ridgeway 2004; Wagner and Berger 1997). Studies repeatedly indicate that gender acts as a status characteristic in the United States, with men expected to perform better than women on many important tasks (Berger, Rosenholtz, and Zelditch 1980; Carli 1991; Pugh and Wahrman 1983). Research shows that men have more influence than women on tasks that would appear to be gender-neutral and that men tend to receive higher evaluations for their performances than do women, despite the objective merit of those performances (Eagley, Makhijani, and Klonsky 1992).

Status research additionally finds that women tend to resist taking leadership positions and that when women do attain leadership based on their own merits, their positions are often not seen as legitimate (Ridgeway and Berger 1986). For example, in an experimental study in which a confederate took leadership of a group by acting in a competent and assertive manner, group members responded more negatively to female than to male leaders (Butler and Geis 1990). This study and others indicate that women are not viewed as legitimate occupants of leadership positions (Johnson, Clay-Warner, and Funk 1996; Lucas 2003). Reflecting these differences—although more women graduate from college now than men, and although women make up roughly half of the U.S. workforce—only about 3 percent of Fortune 500 CEOs are women (CNN Money 2010).

Similar to gender, race is a diffuse status characteristic. In the United States, contributions from European Americans are valued more highly than those from members of other racial (and ethnic) groups (Berger, Rosenholtz, and Zelditch 1980; Webster and Driskell 1978). For example, employers often rate black workers and applicants lower than white workers and applicants in various ways (Bobo and Fox 2003). In one experimental study, members of racial minorities, in comparison to whites, had to demonstrate higher levels of competence before participants deemed them to have the ability to successfully carry out a task (Biernat and Kobrynowicz 1997). And survey research finds that, controlling for factors other than race, people of color receive lower ratings as leaders than whites (Knight et al. 2003). In organizational hiring, perceptions of qualifications interact with race in ways that disadvantage applicants of color (Moss and Tilly 1996). In all of these ways, race/ethnicity is a status characteristic that advantages European Americans relative to persons in other racial and ethnic groups.

Much of the research in the status characteristics and expectation states tradition has attended to issues of overcoming status disadvantages. The goal of this work is to identify how to create situations in which the contributions of all group members, irrespective of standing on status characteristics, receive proper recognition. We discuss this work below.

Overcoming status disadvantage

As can be seen from the discussion on status processes above, women and minority group members (as well as others in low-status categories of status characteristics) face disadvantages that can limit advancement in organizations. Even in the presence of efforts to avoid discrimination in selections for management positions, for example, status processes can lead to candidates from majority groups being more qualified for promotions (Lovaglia et al. 2006). Because of the self-reinforcing nature of status processes, we should expect men and European Americans, when being considered for promotions, to have higher performance evaluations from supervisors, higher ratings from coworkers, and histories of more influence in comparison to otherwise similarly qualified women and non–European Americans. Status research has indicated strategies, resulting both from efforts of a person in a disadvantaged social category and from more structural approaches, that can successfully overcome status inequality.

According to the principle of aggregated expectations in SCT, individuals act as though they combine the expectations associated with all of each person's status characteristics when developing performance expectations for self and others (Berger, Rosenholtz, and Zelditch 1980). Note that some status characteristics are largely or wholly out of a person's control, whereas others can be changed. To gain status, individuals can change their standings on status characteristics within their control. Increasing educational credentials, for example, typically leads to

)eyond any directly job-related benefits of the acquired knowledge. : value of an MBA degree over that of a bachelor's degree far exceeds ar investment required to complete it. In 2001, after accounting for tuiu.. _ d lost compensation while a student, the cash-in-hand value of an MBA was $550,000 (Davies and Cline 2005). Appearance is another important status characteristic, with more attractive people accorded higher status than less attractive people (Umberson and Hughes 1987). How people dress also alters expectations for their performance in groups, ultimately affecting how much influence they have (Bunderson 2003).

Research has identified one self-presentation strategy that is particularly effective for increasing influence in groups, a strategy especially useful for women and minority group members (Ridgeway 1982). Individuals typically assume that high-status group members are more oriented toward the interests of the group than are low-status group members, whom people are more likely to assume are more selfishly motivated (Wagner and Berger 1997). This is one reason why high-status persons tend to be leaders in groups; people assume that high-status persons have the interests of the group in mind (Lucas and Lovaglia 2006). Research shows that presenting one's contributions as motivated by the interests of the group works to increase status for persons in disadvantaged status categories (Ridgeway 1982; Shackelford, Wood, and Worchel 1996). In other words, women and minority group members can increase their standing in groups by making it clear that their recommendations and performances are carried out with the best interests of the group in mind.

There are additional structural changes that can counteract status processes that disadvantage women and minority group members. Cohen and colleagues, in a series of studies in educational settings, found that racial and ethnic minorities attained status as high as majority group members when all group members were trained to recognize the expertise and contributions of minority group members (e.g., E. Cohen and Lotan 1995). This research suggests that fostering an environment in which individuals are encouraged to give proper recognition to performances from all group members can work toward reducing status inequalities.

Other research shows that changing institutional arrangements in an organization can successfully alter influence patterns that disadvantage individuals with low states of diffuse status characteristics. Institutional theory proposes that legitimacy concerns drive much organizational action and that organizations adopt practices that are taken for granted or institutionalized in their environments (Troyer and Silver 1999). Lucas (2003) found that when a group structure with women in leadership positions was institutionalized, women as leaders were as influential as men as leaders. This indicates that strong institutional support for arrangements in which women and minority group members hold leadership positions can go a long way toward reducing the resistance they face when in such positions.

Theory and research on status in groups demonstrate how status processes work to disadvantage persons in social categories accorded low status. In particular, men and European Americans are more influential in U.S. culture and have their contributions valued more highly than women and minority group members. One consequence of these differences is inequality in access to powerful positions.

Power and Social Structure

As discussed above, influence stems largely from the respect and esteem in which a person is held by others. Power, in contrast, results primarily from a position in a social structure (D. Willer, Lovaglia, and Markovsky 1997). In theory and research in the group processes tradition, power is treated principally as a feature of social networks (Cook et al. 1983). Like status, power is relative in that one can have it only in relation to others. For this reason, power is treated as a feature of an interconnected group of people, typically a group in which resources are contested (D. Willer 1999).

Power in networks

In traditional treatments of the term, power was studied as an attribute of individual people (Gibb 1969). In particular, the goal of research on power was to determine what traits, resources, or attributes confer power (Wolfinger 1960). An early insight in group processes approaches to power was the understanding that power rests in relationships between people, not in people themselves (Emerson 1962). For this reason, power is treated as a feature of network organization.

Power is the ability to get what one wants even when others resist (Lovaglia 1999). Treatments of power in disciplines other than group processes often focus on typologies of power. For example, social psychologists often draw from French and Raven's (1959) classic five bases of power: expert power, legitimate power, referent power, coercive power, and reward power. Group processes work focuses more narrowly on the capacity to get what one wants; in French and Raven's parlance, power in the group processes perspective is a capacity to engage in coercive power. This narrow treatment of power has facilitated research on the concept and led to a number of insights, most important of which is that power results from a position in a social structure. Unlike status, which is grounded in feelings of respect (and is very similar to French and Raven's referent power), power is a result of one's structural position. Typically, formal rules, such as those that give authority to supervisors in an organization, grant power to control the behavior of others.

There are a number of features of social structure that might confer power, and much of the group processes research has focused on identifying what characteristics of networks give power to some positions versus others. A line of research in this tradition involves studies that connect experimental participants in networks in which they compete for resources (Markovsky, Willer, and Patton 1987; Lawler, Thye, and Yoon 2008; Molm, Collett, and Schaefer 2007). Some argue that central locations in networks are an important basis of power; from this perspective, positions acquire power when others must go through them to acquire resources (e.g., Pfeffer 1992). Ultimately, experimental research on power in networks has identified that it is the ability to exclude actors from resources they desire, as opposed to centrality or some other feature of network organization, that primarily confers power in networks (Markovsky, Willer, and Patton 1987). If a person controls access to resources, that person will have power. Such power can be seen in human resources departments that have power beyond what their positions in the organizational structure alone indicate. They control resources that are valuable to persons in the organization.

Research over the past few decades has produced several important insights on power. One such insight is that to have power is to use power (Emerson 1972). Even if those with power would choose not to use it, they sometimes must. Organizational structures, for example, grant managers power to determine bonus distributions to subordinates, and the managers must use the power in determining allocations. In the same way, supervisors must submit performance evaluations of subordinates, discipline subordinates who underperform, and so on. Additionally, those with power need not intend to use that power for it nevertheless to have dramatic effects (Bonacich 2002). For example, consider a manager who intends to foster a collaborative atmosphere by giving equal bonuses to subordinates. Despite the manager's intentions, subordinates might well undermine the collaborative environment by undercutting each other to win favor with the manager.

Power and influence, then, are distinct in group processes approaches. One way the distinction is discussed is that power changes behavior without changing attitudes, whereas influence is a change in attitudes that produces a change in behavior. According to Zelditch (1992), the distinction between power and influence is that power involves sanctions, whereas influence persuades an actor to carry out actions because she believes such actions are in her own best interests. Similarly, Parsons (1963) sees power as involving positive and negative sanctions in contrast to influence, which has an effect on the attitudes and opinions of others. In this way, influence has advantages that power use does not. Also, whereas group members, at a minimum, act as though they agree on the status order (which leads to influence) in a group (Ridgeway and Smith-Lovin 1989), positions of power are usually highly contested. An outcome that power and influence share is getting what one wants. Power leads to other outcomes as well, and we discuss these below.

Outcomes of power

The use of power has two primary outcomes. One is that those with power get their way, typically including the accumulation of valued resources. The second is that those without power come to resent those who use power (Walker et al. 2000). This resentment occurs whether people are threatened with punishment for undesirable behavior or promised rewards for desirable behavior (D. Willer, Lovaglia, and Markovsky 1997). Both rewards and punishments compel people to do things they would not do if the rewards or punishments were not in place. Using power to compel action is also inefficient, requiring a great deal of energy on the part of the power holder to always have rewards and punishments in place to gain compliance. From a leadership perspective, if leaders initiate action only through the use of power, then followers will stop carrying out actions that the leader desires as soon as the incentives are removed. A consequence of creating resentment is that it leads to a loss of status (D. Willer, Lovaglia, and Markovsky 1997).

Power also has a number of effects on those who hold it. One is that the more powerful are more likely to take action than the less powerful (Guinote 2007). One experimental study had participants first write about an experience in which they felt powerful or powerless (Galinsky, Gruenfeld, and Magee 2003). This activity had the effect of "priming" power for those who wrote about experiences of being powerful. When participants subsequently started a study task, they discovered that they were very close to an annoying tabletop fan. The research found that twice as many participants in the high-power group moved the fan compared to participants in the low-power group (about 80 percent compared to about 40 percent). Individuals with more power are also more likely to take risks (Anderson and Galinsky 2006). Another "priming" study, for example, found that participants in the high-power group were about three times as likely as those in the low-power group to be the first to offer help to a stranger in distress (Galinsky, Jordan, and Sivanathan 2008).

Power, then, tends to lead to an orientation toward action, including risky action. It also appears to lead persons to be less likely to consider the nuances of situations. For example, the more powerful are less likely to consider the perspectives of others (Galinsky et al. 2006). Power also makes individuals more likely to objectify others (Georgesen and Harris 2000). And power tends to make people greedier and less likely to distribute rewards to others (Anderson and Berdahl 2002).

In addition to differences in how powerful people act toward others and in varied situations, power also affects how people view themselves. Power makes people more confident and aware of their own points of view (Brinol et al. 2007; Weick and Guinote 2008). They become more focused on potential rewards, particularly for themselves, that situations might produce (Keltner, Gruenfeld, and Anderson 2003). High-powered people also rely less on group norms and more on their individual motives to govern their behavior, and their actions tend to be more variable than those of low-power group members (Brauer 2005). Power is also found to make people more likely to engage in moral hypocrisy, applying strict moral standards to others but not practicing them themselves (Lammers and Stapel 2009).

In sum, those in power generally accumulate valued resources and gain compliance from others. However, leading with power breeds resentment and is inefficient. Powerful people are also more oriented toward taking action, particularly action that benefits them, and they are less likely to consider the perspectives of others.

Additionally, powerful people are in tune with their own perspectives but neverthe-less more likely to engage in moral hypocrisy than are less powerful people.

Gender, race, and power

Just as U.S. organizations exist in a culture in which women and minority group members are accorded lower status than others, persons in disadvantaged groups in our society face challenges in both reaching powerful positions and exercising power once in those positions. In particular, status processes influence who gets access to powerful positions and how the use of power is interpreted by others.

Selections and elections to powerful positions in the United States happen based on perceptions of competence. When making a promotion decision in a work organization, for example, the selection is made based on who will be most able to competently carry out the job. As can be seen from the discussion of sta-tus processes in groups, such competency expectations are developed largely based on status characteristics. Thus, those in disadvantaged status categories, such as women and minority group members, are less likely to have access to powerful positions than are those in advantaged status categories.

Once in positions of power, those with low states of diffuse status characteristics are often seen as illegitimate occupants of their positions. For example, people tend to resist directives from women and minority group members in positions of authority (Eagly, Makhijani, and Klonsky 1992). A consequence of this resistance is that their power comes into question. When power is viewed as legitimate, those with power need not carry out any actions to demonstrate that they are powerful (Brass and Burkhardt 1993). When power is viewed as illegitimate, however, those with power feel threatened (Rodríguez-Bailón, Moya, and Yzerbyt 2000). The result is often that women and minority group members in positions of authority feel that they must use their power to show that they have it (Bruins, Ellemers, and De Gilder 1999). Such behaviors likely gain compliance, but because power use creates resentment, they also pose problems. By using their power this way, women and minority group members likely lose further status.

Power, Status, and Diversity

We have summarized the literature on the concepts of power, status, and influ-ence as they are treated in sociology's group processes tradition. We now discuss how the concepts interrelate, paying particular attention to implications for diversity. Although the group processes tradition treats power and status as dis-tinct, each can be used in strategic ways to increase the other.

Relationships between power and status

Curiously, power and status tend to vary together. Positions high in power (corporate CEOs, for example) are also typically high in status, and positions low in power (mailroom clerks, for example) are also typically low in status. This is counterintuitive when considering that the use of power, because of the resentment it produces, decreases status (Lovaglia et al. 2005). Why is it then that power and status tend to align? In part it is because power activity is often hidden, and people in organizations often do not understand well the power structures of those organizations (Walker et al. 2000). Additionally, those with power typically operate restraint when using that power. In a classic treatment, Emerson (1962) famously noted that to use power is to lose it. Although having power also sometimes requires its use, those with power can retain positions of high status if they use the power with restraint.

Warren Buffett has managed to maintain a position of extraordinarily high status while at the same time accumulating one of the largest fortunes in the world (Shell 2008). Buffett likely accomplished this in part through his reputation for using his power with restraint. Buffett is notorious for his resistance to marketing his name as a brand; he maintains a modest lifestyle and holds to a management principle that those under him should be allowed to operate with as much freedom as possible (Schroeder 2009). Donald Trump, in contrast, attaches his moniker to seemingly everything he can, makes ostentatious claims about his wealth, and is perhaps most closely associated with his trademark phrase "You're fired!" Such strategies have almost certainly increased Trump's power, but they seem to have cost him social status. Parodies of Trump abound, and many treated his entries into the national political scene as a joke (Hertzberg 2011). In addition to maintaining status through restraint in the use of power, there are a number of ways that power can be used to gain status.

The foundation of status differences is expectations that people have for competent contributions to social groups. The foundation of power differences, in contrast, is positions in social structures rather than respect or personal ability. Those with power accumulate resources, however, and if we consistently see one person accumulating more resources than others, we are likely to assume that that person is more competent than those others (Stewart and Moore 1992). Thus, one way power translates to status is that people assume those using power are competent because they see the powerful persons accumulating valued resources or otherwise getting their way.

Another way that power can be used to gain status is to use the resources that come with power to "purchase" status. Adjusting for inflation, John D. Rockefeller is considered the wealthiest person in history (CNN Money 2006). Rockefeller used his power as head of Standard Oil to ruthless effect, gaining near complete control of the oil industry in the United States. Once he was powerful, however, Rockefeller cultivated a reputation for being generous with the proceeds of his activities. Late in life, Rockefeller was widely known to keep his pockets filled with coins, giving out dimes to adults and nickels to children he encountered in his daily life (Fox 2006). These gifts reflected a minuscule portion of his wealth, which was over $1 billion at his death, but the activity seems to have worked to increase his status.

A third way that power can translate into status is through strategic image control. For example, one way to sidestep the resentment that the use of power produces is to use power on a marginalized out-group while maintaining or gaining influence over the majority in-group (R. Willer, Troyer, and Lovaglia 2005). Also, in contrast to those with high status, who are typically viewed as having the interests of the group in mind, those with power are often presumed by others to be self-interested and greedy (Lovaglia, Willer, and Troyer 2003). By engaging in strategic philanthropy, powerful persons can counter expectations of greed and in fact enhance their status with others who admire their perceived restraint and compassion. The status positions of Buffett and Rockefeller, for example, likely benefited from the substantial portions of their fortunes they gave away.

Power, then, can be used in various ways to gain status. It is easier, however, to use status to gain power. Power is a natural outgrowth of status. Status arises principally out of expectations for competence. The reason that status naturally leads to power is that selections or elections to powerful positions are typically made based on perceptions of competence. As mentioned above, persons who are perceived to be the most competent candidates hold leadership positions in organizations. Thus, those who are higher in status, persons who may or may not be the most competent candidates, are typically rewarded with powerful positions. In this way, status processes make it more difficult for persons in disadvantaged status groups to attain powerful positions in organizations.

Status also leads to power because we perceive resources held by high-status others to be more valuable than resources held by low-status others. In a series of experiments, Thye (2000) found that participants were willing to give more of their own resources in exchange for resources that high-status partners held than for resources held by low-status partners. At the time of this writing, a short social note handwritten by Albert Einstein, a person much higher in status than he was in power, is listed on eBay for a price of $25,000. Einstein's status gives value to items he possessed. People will trade money for autographs from high-status individuals, giving a resource they value a great deal for a resource relatively insignificant to the high-status person. Status, then, naturally leads to power.

Power, influence, and leadership

Leadership, like power, status, and influence, is a concept that has been subject to a limitless number of treatments. At its most basic level, however, we can say that leadership is about getting people to do things. If people are carrying out actions they would otherwise perform in any case, then there is no need for a leader. Because power and influence are fundamental ways to get people to do things, theory and research on the concepts have clear relevance to issues of leadership.

As discussed, a key feature of power is that it produces public compliance without private acceptance. In other words, power use changes behavior but not attitudes. Research finds that when leaders use power to reward and punish, it creates both resentment and resistance to the leader's directives (D. Willer, Lovaglia, and Markovsky 1997). In contrast, people willingly follow high-status leaders out of respect and honor. They are influenced, changing both behavior and attitudes.

Unlike positions of power that are often fiercely contested, high status once attained is relatively easy to maintain. This is because of the self-fulfilling nature of status orders; high-status persons receive higher evaluations because they are high-status and in turn maintain their positions. The advantage of leaders compelling behavior with influence rather than power is that because it changes attitudes, influence aligns the personal goals of followers with organizational goals (Parsons 1963; Zelditch 1992). With power, a leader communicates which behaviors followers should carry out. With influence, in contrast, a leader can convey a vision of the group's mission and then encourage followers to use their abilities to further that mission.

Leadership research finds that effective leaders have power but use it sparingly (Rashotte 2006). Instead, they rely on the benefits of leading with influence. A limitation to this approach is that persons in groups accorded low social status do not have the reserves of influence from which to draw in compelling behavior. For this reason, we should expect persons in disadvantaged social groups to encounter difficulties when in leadership positions. Research supports this expectation. Despite typically utilizing leadership styles that can have advantages over those more characteristic of men, women often receive unfair evaluations of their leadership and are given less authority on the job (Eagly and Carli 2003) Other studies find that black leaders are rated more negatively than white leaders, suggesting that they are not seen as legitimate in their leadership positions (Knight et al. 2003). Research also indicates that women suffer a penalty from negative reactions to their success at stereotypically male tasks (Heilman et al. 2004).

Research does indicate methods whereby persons in low-status social categories can increase their influence. We have discussed two, presenting contributions as group motivated and increasing standing on other status characteristics, such as education. Additionally, those who build consistent records of success gain status and influence. And being assertive increases status and influence (Lee and Ofshe 1981). Assertiveness may backfire (see, for example, Butler and Geis 1990), but when the alternative is having contributions ignored, as is often the case for women and minority group members, being assertive will tend to result in higher influence than will a more passive approach.

Power, status, and social identity

Power and status are fundamental ways by which people organize themselves in groups. Dividing into groups is perhaps the most fundamental organizing feature of people. Research finds that people tend to view themselves and others in terms of group memberships and that such categorizations have powerful effects on impressions we develop (Tajfel 1981).

According to social identity theory, we have as many social identities as groups to which we see ourselves belonging. When social identities become salient, they tell us who we are, how we should behave, and how we should treat others. We perceive members of our in-groups in in-group stereotypical ways and as similar to ourselves. We perceive members of out-groups in out-group stereotypical and discriminatory ways. Furthermore, we are motivated to view members of our in-groups in favorable ways. As a result, we engage in strategies to protect our in-groups (Tajfel 1986).

Work on social identities has implications for issues of diversity in organizations. One implication is that in-group membership confers influence much like status does. Research finds that persons perceived to be in-group members have more influence than persons perceived to be out-group members and also that group membership combines with status characteristics in affecting performance expectations (Kalkhoff and Barnum 2000).

A key to understanding social identity processes is understanding which memberships are most salient to people when they are evaluating themselves and others. If membership in categories of diffuse status characteristics such as gender and race are most salient, we would expect these characteristics to powerfully drive evaluations and behavior. If membership in the organization is the most salient identity, we might expect it to have the effect of lessening impacts of diffuse status characteristics. Research on social identities indicates that this is likely not the case.

When the salience of a group membership is high, members of the group become especially socially attracted to other members whom they see as prototypical representations of the group (Hogg and Terry 2000). By this process, members least resembling the prototype become marginalized. Like status processes, these stereotype-producing processes emerge without conscious thought but nevertheless become embedded over time (Bargh and Chartrand 1999). They result in minority group members facing devaluation and discrimination because they are not seen as prototypical group members. Additionally, groups favor as leaders individuals whom they see as best representing prototypes of their groups (Hogg 2001).

In-group membership, like high status in groups, brings with it substantial benefits. According to social identity theory, group members look more favorably upon and distribute more rewards to those whom they perceive to be in-group members. Additionally, prototypical group members have more opportunities to perform and tend to receive higher performance evaluations from superiors (Rowe 1981). And in-group members gain status as other group members defer to them at higher rates (DiTomaso, Post, and Parks-Yancy 2007).

Research on social identities indicates that these processes of identification and categorization interact in important ways with processes of power and status, although these connections are little researched. In particular, prototypical or majority group members are advantaged in ways similar to high-status members in groups, receiving higher evaluations for their performances, gaining higher rates of deference, and being more likely to be selected to leadership positions than individuals not viewed as prototypical representations of the group.

Conclusion

Diverse workforces provide substantial benefits to organizations. Studies generally find that increased diversity on any number of dimensions, including race and gender, is associated with innovation, creativity, and performance in organizations (Horwitz and Horwitz 2007; Somech and Drach-Zahavy 2011). For these reasons and others, the effective management of organizations requires efforts to increase diversity. At the same time, processes of influence and power pose challenges for managing a diverse workplace.

Research on status processes in groups shows them to be a major determining factor in access to powerful positions, and the same research shows how status characteristics shape expectations of people in various social groups, albeit in often nonconscious ways. We focused primarily on gender and race as status characteristics, but status research has identified others as well, including age, height, beauty, wealth, education, and occupation. Different status characteristics lead to different performance expectations, which in turn lead to differences in influence.

Organizations in the United States are becoming more diverse. Major efforts are of course in place to manage diversity in organizations, but they may not adequately account for processes that make status orders so stable and resistant to change. For example, efforts to increase diverse representation in powerful leadership positions will be limited in their effectiveness if status processes that disadvantage members of certain social groups remain. Persons in low-status social groups are evaluated as less effective when in powerful positions, have their power viewed as illegitimate, have to use their power more to show that they have it, and suffer status loss from the use of power.

Power, the ability to exercise one's will even against resistance from others, derives from a position in a social structure. In particular, it rests on the ability to exclude others from resources they desire. Research indicates a number of outcomes of power, including being more likely to take action, being more self-interested, being more risky, and being less likely to take others' perspectives. The use of power also leads to resentment among those who have had power used against them. As a result, there are significant advantages to using influence rather than power to compel behavior. As discussed, however, members of some groups are more likely to have influence from which to draw.

The group processes literature, particularly research on status in groups, indicates viable solutions to these challenges of diversity. Members of disadvantaged status groups can increase their influence by moving to more highly valued categories on status characteristics within their control, acting assertively, and presenting their contributions as motivated by the best interests of the group. Management in organizations can also adopt strategies to train group members to value contributions from all group members and institutionalize environments in which members of status-disadvantaged groups hold leadership positions. Additionally, research on power, status, and influence in groups, which to date has been primarily concerned with understanding the formation and consequences of hierarchy processes in groups, would benefit from greater attention to applying knowledge gained on the processes to the challenges of managing diversity in organizations.

References

Anderson, Cameron, and Jennifer L. Berdahl. 2002. The experience of power: Examining the effects of power on approach and inhibition tendencies. *Journal of Personality and Social Psychology* 83: 1362–77.

Anderson, Cameron, and Adam D. Galinsky. 2006. Power, optimism, and risk-taking. *European Journal of Social Psychology* 36:511–36.

Bales, Robert F. 1950. *Interaction process analysis: A method for the study of small groups*. Chicago, IL: University of Chicago Press.

Bargh, John A., and Tanya L. Chartrand. 1999. The unbearable automaticity of being. *American Psychologist* 54:462–79.

Berger, Joseph, Bernard P. Cohen, and Morris Zelditch. 1972. *Status characteristics and social interaction*. New York, NY: Elsevier.

Berger, Joseph, M. Hamit Fisek, Robert Z. Norman, and Morris Zelditch Jr. 1977. *Status characteristics and social interaction*. New York, NY: Elsevier.

Berger, Joseph, Susan J. Rosenholtz, and Morris Zelditch Jr. 1980. Status organizing processes. *Annual Review of Sociology* 6:470–508.

Berger, Joseph, David G. Wagner, and Morris Zelditch Jr. 1985. Expectation states theory: Review and assessment. In *Status, rewards, and influence*, eds. Joseph Berger and Morris Zelditch Jr., 1–72. San Francisco, CA: Jossey-Bass.

Berger, Joseph, and Murray Webster Jr. 2006. Expectations, status, and behavior. In *Contemporary social psychological theories*, ed. Peter J. Burke, 268–300. Stanford, CA: Stanford University Press.

Bienenstock, Elisa Jayne, and Alison J. Bianchi. 2004. Activating performance expectations and status difference through gift exchange: Experimental results. *Social Psychology Quarterly* 67:310–18.

Biernat, Monica R., and D. Kobrynowicz. 1997. Gender- and race-based standards of competence: Lower minimum standards but higher ability standards for devalued groups. *Journal of Personality and Social Psychology* 72:544–57.

Bobo, Lawrence D., and Cybelle Fox. 2003. Race, racism, and discrimination: Bridging problems, methods and theory in social psychological research. *Social Psychology Quarterly* 66:319–32.

Bonacich, Phillip. 2002. The strength of weak power: A simulation study of network evolution. In *The growth of social knowledge: Theory, simulation, and empirical research in group processes*, eds. Jacek Szmatka, Michael J. Lovaglia, and Kynga Wysienska. Westport, CT: Praeger.

Brass, Daniel J., and Marlene E. Burkhardt. 1993. Potential power and power use: An investigation of structure and behavior. *Academy of Management Journal* 36:441–70.

Brauer, M. 2005. Reactions to norm transgressions in powerful and powerless groups. Paper presented at the meeting of the Society of Personality and Social Psychology, New Orleans, LA.

Brinol, Pablo, Carmen Valle, Derek D. Rucker, and A. Becerra. 2007. The effects of message recipients' power before and after persuasion: A self-validation analysis. *Journal of Personality and Social Psychology* 93:1040–53.

Bruins, Jan, Naomi Ellemers, and Dick De Gilder. 1999. Power use and differential competence as determinants of subordinates' evaluative and behavioural responses in simulated organizations. *European Journal of Social Psychology* 29:843–70.

Bunderson, J. Stuart. 2003. Recognizing and utilizing expertise in work groups: A status characteristics perspective. *Administrative Science Quarterly* 48:557–91.

Butler, Dore, and Florence L. Geis. 1990. Nonverbal affect responses to male and female leaders: Implications for leadership. *Journal of Personality and Social Psychology* 58:48–59.

Carli, Linda L. 1991. Gender, status, and influence. *Advances in Group Processes: Theory and Research* 8:89–113.

CNN Money. 2006. The richest Americans in the almanac of American wealth. Available from http://money.cnn.com.

CNN Money. 2010. Fortune 500 women CEOs. Available from http://money.cnn.com.

Cohen, Bernard P., and Xuegueng Zhou. 1991. Status processes in enduring work groups. *American Sociological Review* 56:179–88.

Cohen, Elizabeth G., and Rachel A. Lotan. 1995. Producing equal-status interaction in the heterogeneous classroom. *American Educational Research Journal* 32:99–120.

Cook, Karen S., Richard M. Emerson, Mary R. Gillmore, and Toshio Yamagishi. 1983. The distribution of power in exchange networks: Theory and experimental results. *American Journal of Sociology* 89:275–305.

Dahl, Robert A. 1957. The concept of power. *Behavioral Science* 2:201–15.

Davies, Antony, and Thomas W. Cline. January/February 2005. The ROI on the MBA. *BizEd*, 42–45.

DiTomaso, Nancy, Corinne Post, and Rochelle Parks-Yancy. 2007. Workforce diversity and inequality: Power, status, and numbers. *Annual Review of Sociology* 33:473–501.

Eagly, Alice H., and Linda L. Carli. 2003. The female leadership advantage: An evaluation of the evidence. *Leadership Quarterly* 14:807–34.

Eagly, Alice H., Arjun Makhijani, and Bruce G. Klonsky. 1992. Gender and the evaluation of leaders: A meta-analysis. *Psychological Bulletin* 111:3–22.

Emerson, Richard M. 1962. Power-dependence relations. *American Sociological Review* 27:21–41.

Emerson, Richard M. 1972. Exchange theory, part II: Exchange relations and networks. In *Sociological theories in progress*, vol. 2, eds. Joseph Berger, Morris Zelditch Jr., and Bo Anderson. Boston, MA: Houghton-Mifflin.

Fox, Don W. 2006. Doing the right thing—Fiscal law tips: Dealing with conferences, coins, and the use of government resources. *Entrepreneur*. Available from www.entrepreneur.com.

Freeman, Catherine. 2004. *Trends in educational equity for girls and women: 2004*. Washington, DC: U.S. Department of Education, National Center for Education Statistics.

French, John R. P., Jr., and Bertram Raven. 1959. The bases of social power. In *Studies in social power*, ed. Dorwin Cartwright, 150–67. Ann Arbor: University of Michigan Press.

Galinsky, Adam D., Deborah H. Gruenfeld, and Joe C. Magee. 2003. From power to action. *Journal of Personality and Social Psychology* 85:453–66.

Galinsky, Adam D., Jennifer Jordan, and Niro Sivanathan. 2008. Harnessing power to capture leadership. In *Leadership at the crossroads*, ed. Joanna B. Cuilla. Westport, CT: Praeger.

Galinsky, Adam D., Joe C. Magee, M. Ena Inesi, and Deborah H. Gruenfeld. 2006. Power and perspectives not taken. *Psychological Science* 17:1068–74.

Georgesen, John C., and Monica J. Harris. 2000. The balance of power: Interpersonal consequences of differential power and expectations. *Personality and Social Psychology Bulletin* 26:1239–57.

Gibb, Cecil A. 1969. Leadership. In *Handbook of social psychology*, vol. 4, 2nd ed., eds. Gardner Lindzey and Elliot Aronson. Reading, MA: Addison-Wesley.

Guinote, Ana. 2007. Power and goal pursuit. *Personality and Social Psychology Bulletin* 33:1076–87.

Heilman, Madeline E., Aaron S. Wallen, Daniella Fuchs, and Melinda M. Tamkins. 2004. Penalties for success: Reactions to women who succeed at male gender-typed tasks. *Journal of Applied Psychology* 89:416–27.

Hertzberg, Hendrik. 2 May 2011. Trumpery. *New Yorker* 87:21–22.

Hogg, Michael A. 2001. A social identity theory of leadership. *Personality and Social Psychology Review* 5:184–200.

Hogg, Michael A., and Deborah J. Terry. 2000. Social identity and self-categorization processes in organizational contexts. *Academy of Management Review* 25:121–40.

Horwitz, Sujin K., and Irwin B. Horwitz. 2007. The effects of team diversity on team outcomes: A meta-analytic review of team demography. *Journal of Management* 33:987–1015.

Johnson, Cathryn, Jody Clay-Warner, and Stephanie J. Funk. 1996. Effects of authority structures and gender on interaction in same-sex task groups. *Social Psychology Quarterly* 59:221–36.

Kalkhoff, Will, and Christopher Barnum. 2000. The effects of status-organizing and social identity processes on patterns of social influence. *Social Psychology Quarterly* 63:95–115.

Kalkhoff, Will, and Shane R. Thye. 2006. Expectation states theory and research: New observations from meta-analysis. *Sociological Methods and Research* 35:219–49.

Kelly, Michael, ed. 1994. *Critique and power: Recasting the Foucault/Habermas debate.* Cambridge, MA: MIT Press.

Keltner, Dacher, Deborah H. Gruenfeld, and Cameron Anderson. 2003. Power, approach, and inhibition. *Psychological Review* 110:265–285.

Knight, Jennifer L., Michelle R. Hebl, Jessica B. Foster, and Laura M. Mannix. 2003. Out of role? Out of luck: The influence of race and leadership status on performance appraisals. *Journal of Leadership and Organizational Studies* 9:85–93.

Lammers, Joris, and Diederik A. Stapel. 2009. How power influences moral thinking. *Journal of Personality and Social Psychology* 97:279–89.

Lang, Ilene, Arnold W. Donald, Carlos F. Orta, and J. D. Hokoyama. 2011. *Missing pieces: Women and minorities on Fortune 500 boards.* 2010 Alliance for Board Diversity Census. New York, NY: Catalyst.

Lawler, Edward J., Shane R. Thye, and Jeongkoo Yoon. 2008. Social exchange and micro social order. *American Sociological Review* 73:519–42.

Lee, Margaret T., and Richard Ofshe. 1981. The impact of behavioral style and status characteristics on social influence: A test of two competing theories. *Social Psychology Quarterly* 44:73–82.

Lovaglia, Michael J. 1999. Understanding network exchange theory. *Advances in Group Processes* 16:31–59.

Lovaglia, Michael J., Jeffrey W. Lucas, Jeffrey A. Houser, Shane R. Thye, and Barry Markovsky. 1998. Status processes and mental ability test scores. *American Journal of Sociology* 104:195–228.

Lovaglia, Michael J., Jeffrey W. Lucas, Christabel L. Rogalin, and Abigail Darwin. 2006. Power, status, and leadership in diverse organizations: From basic research to program development. In *Advances in group processes*, vol. 23, eds. Shane R. Thye and Edward Lawler, 183–206. Bingley, UK: Emerald Group Publishing Limited.

Lovaglia, Michael J., Elizabeth A. Mannix, Charles D. Samuelson, Jane Sell, and Rick K. Wilson. 2005. Conflict, power, and status in groups. In *Theories of small groups: Interdisciplinary perspectives*, eds. Marshall Scott Poole and Andrea B. Hollingshead, 139–84. Thousand Oaks, CA: Sage.

Lovaglia, Michael J., Robb Willer, and Lisa Troyer. 2003. Power, status, and collective action. In *Advances in group processes*, vol. 20, eds. Shane R. Thye and Edward Lawler, 105–31. Bingley, UK: Emerald Group Publishing Limited.

Lucas, Jeffrey W. 2003. Status processes and the institutionalization of women as leaders. *American Sociological Review* 68:464–80.

Lucas, Jeffrey W., and Michael J. Lovaglia. 2006. Legitimation and institutionalization as trust-building: Reducing resistance to power and influence in organizations. *Advances in Group Processes* 23:229–52.

Manz, Charles C. 1986. Self-leadership: Toward an expanded theory of self-influence processes in organizations. *Academy of Management Review* 11:585–600.

Markovsky, Barry, David Willer, and Travis Patton. 1987. Power relations in exchange networks. *American Sociological Review* 53:220–36.

Molm, Linda D., Jessica L. Collett, and David R. Schaefer. 2007. Building solidarity through generalized exchange: A theory of reciprocity. *American Journal of Sociology* 113:205–42.

Moss, Philip, and Chris Tilly. 1996. Soft skills and race: An investigation of black men's employment problems. *Work and Occupations* 23:252–76.

Parsons, Talcott. 1963. On the concept of influence. *Public Opinion Quarterly* 27:37–62.

Pfeffer, Jeffrey. 1992. *Managing with power: Politics and influence in organizations.* Boston, MA: Harvard Business School Press.

Pugh, M. D., and Ralph Wahrman. 1983. Neutralizing sexism in mixed-sex groups: Do women have to be better than men? *American Journal of Sociology* 88:746–62.

Rashotte, Lisa Slattery. 2006. Social influence. In *The Blackwell encyclopedia of sociology*, eds. George Ritzer and J. Michael Ryan, 4426–29. Oxford, UK: Blackwell.

Rashotte, Lisa Slattery, and Murray Webster Jr. 2005. Gender status beliefs. *Social Science Research* 34:618–33.

Ridgeway, Cecilia L. 1982. Status in groups: The importance of motivation. *American Sociological Review* 47:76–88.

Ridgeway, Cecelia L. 1993. Gender, status, and the social psychology of expectations. In *Theory on gender/ feminism on theory*, ed. Paula England, 175–97. New York, NY: Aldine.

Ridgeway, Cecilia L. 2004. Gender, status and leadership. *Journal of Social Issues* 57:637–55.

Ridgeway, Cecilia L., and Joseph Berger. 1986. Expectations, legitimation, and dominance behavior in task groups. *American Sociological Review* 51:603–17.

Ridgeway, Cecilia L., and Shelley J. Correll. 2000. Limiting inequality through interaction: The end(s) of gender. *Contemporary Sociology* 29:110–20.

Ridgeway, Cecilia L., and Lynn Smith-Lovin. 1989. The gender system and interaction. *Annual Review of Sociology* 25:191–216.

Rodríguez-Bailón, Rosa, Miguel Moya, and Vincent Yzerbyt. 2000. Why do superiors attend to negative stereotypic information about their subordinates? Effects of power legitimacy on social perception. *European Journal of Social Psychology* 30:651–71.

Rowe, Mary. 1981. The minutiae of discrimination: The need for support. In *Outsiders on the inside: Women and organizations*, eds. Barbara L. Forisha and Barbara H. Goldman, 155–77. Englewood Cliffs, NJ: Prentice Hall.

Russell, Bertrand. 1938. *Power: A new social analysis*. New York, NY: Norton.

Salancik, Gerald R., and Jeffrey Pfeffer. 1977. Who gets power—and how they hold onto it: A strategic contingency model of power. *Organizational Dynamics* 5:3–21.

Schroeder, Alice. 2009. *Warren Buffett and the business of life*. New York, NY: Random House.

Sell, Jane, Michael J. Lovaglia, Elizabeth A. Mannix, Charles D. Samuelson, and Rick K. Wilson. 2004. Investigating conflict, power, and status within and among groups. *Small Groups Research* 35: 44–72.

Shackelford, Susan, Wendy Wood, and Stephen Worchel. 1996. Behavioral styles and the influences of women in mixed-sex groups. *Social Psychology Quarterly* 59:284–93.

Shell, Adam. 2008. Warren Buffett hones rock-star stats. *USA Today*. Available from www.usatoday.com.

Simpson, Brent, and Henry A. Walker. 2002. Status characteristics and performance expectations: A reformulation. *Sociological Theory* 20:24–40.

Somech, Anit, and Anat Drach-Zahavy. 2011. Translating team creativity to innovation implementation: The role of team composition and climate for innovation. *Journal of Management* 37:1–25.

Stewart, Penni A., and James C. Moore. 1992. Wage disparities and performance expectations. *Social Psychology Quarterly* 55:78–85.

Tajfel, Henri. 1981. *Human groups and social categories*. Cambridge: Cambridge University Press.

Tajfel, Henri. 1986. The social identity theory of intergroup behavior. In *The social psychology of intergroup relations*, ed. Stephen A. Worchel and William G. Austin, 7–24. Chicago, IL: Nelson Hall.

Thye, Shane R. 2000. A status value theory of power in exchange relations. *American Sociological Review* 65:407–32.

Toossi, Mitra. 2006. A new look at long-term labor force projections to 2050. *Monthly Labor Review* (November): 19–39.

Troyer, Lisa, and Steven D. Silver. 1999. Institutional logics and group environments: Toward an open systems perspective on group processes. In *Advances in group processes*, vol. 16, eds. Shane R. Thye, Edward J. Lawler, Michael W. Macey, and Henry A. Walker, 219–52. Greenwich, CT: JAI.

Umberson, Debra, and Michael Hughes. 1987. The impact of physical attractiveness on achievement and psychological well-being. *Social Psychology Quarterly* 50:227–36.

U.S. Department of Labor. 2009. *Quick stats on women workers, 2009*. Available from www.dol.gov/wb/ stats/main.htm.

Wagner, David G., and Joseph Berger. 1993. Status characteristics theory: The growth of a program. In *Theoretical research programs: Studies in the growth of theory*, eds. Joseph Berger and Morris Zelditch, 23–63. Stanford, CA: Stanford University Press.

Wagner, David G., and Joseph Berger. 1997. Gender and interpersonal task behaviors: Status expectation accounts. *Sociological Perspectives* 40:1–32.

Walker, Henry A., and Brent Simpson. 2000. Equating characteristics and status-organizing processes. *Social Psychology Quarterly* 63:175–85.

Walker, Henry A., Shane R. Thye, Brent Simpson, Michael J. Lovaglia, and Barry Markovsky. 2000. Network exchange theory: Recent developments and new directions. *Social Psychology Quarterly* 63:324–37.

Weber, Max. 1978. *Economy and society*, eds. Guenther Roth and Klaus Wittich. Berkeley: University of California Press.

Webster, Murray, Jr., and James E. Driskell. 1978. Status generalization: A review and some new data. *American Sociological Review* 43:220–36.

Webster, Murray, and Martha Foschi, eds. 1988. *Status generalization: New theory and research*. Stanford, CA: Stanford University Press.

Webster, Murray, Jr., and Stuart Hysom. 1998. Creating status characteristics. *American Sociological Review* 63:351–78.

Weick, Mario, and Ana Guinote. 2008. When subjective experiences matter: Power increases reliance on the ease of retrieval. *Journal of Personality and Social Psychology* 94:956–70.

Willer, David. 1999. *Network exchange theory*. Westport, CT: Praeger.

Willer, David, Michael J. Lovaglia, and Barry Markovsky. 1997. Power and influence: A theoretical bridge. *Social Forces* 76:571–603.

Willer, Robb, Lisa Troyer, and Michael J. Lovaglia. 2005. Influence over observers of structural power: An experimental investigation. *Sociological Quarterly* 46:263–77.

Wolfinger, Raymond E. 1960. Reputation and reality in the study of community power. *American Sociological Review* 25:636–44.

Wrong, Dennis H. 1979. *Power: Its forms, bases, and uses*. New York, NY: Harper & Row.

Zelditch, Morris, Jr. 1992. Interpersonal power. In *Encyclopedia of sociology*, eds. Edgar F. Borgotta and Marie L. Borgotta, 994–101. New York, NY: Macmillan.

Diversity within Reach: Recruitment versus Hiring in Elite Firms

Despite the popularity of diversity management, there is little consensus on how to design diversity practices that work. In this article, the author provides an inside look into one type of diversity practice: diversity recruitment. Drawing on qualitative evidence from hiring in elite law firms, investment banks, and management consulting firms, the author analyzes what diversity recruitment looks like in these firms in theory and in practice. The author finds that although these firms tend to have the ingredients for success on paper, in practice the presence of structural and status divides between those responsible for overseeing diversity recruitment and those making hiring decisions, alongside widespread cultural beliefs among decision-makers that diversity is not a valid criterion of evaluation, stymies firms' efforts to diversify. The author's findings highlight that to be successful in translating diversity programs into results, those charged with overseeing diversity programs need not only formal organizational authority but also sufficient informal power and status to wield influence.

Keywords: diversity; inequality; race; gender; hiring; culture; elites

By
LAUREN A. RIVERA

Over the past 20 years, sociologists have become increasingly interested in understanding not only what causes ascriptive inequalities in organizations but also how best to craft policies and practices to ameliorate them. Despite the fact that "diversity management" is now a mainstream field of scholarly research and professional practice (Dobbin 2009), there is surprisingly little consensus on how to design diversity practices that work (Paluck and Green 2009).

Lauren A. Rivera is an assistant professor of management and organizations and sociology (by courtesy) at Northwestern University. Her research, which resides at the cusp of cultural sociology, social psychology, and social stratification, investigates how microlevel processes of interpersonal evaluation relate to broader inequalities in real-life, organizational settings. Her research has been published in American Sociological Review, Research in Social Stratification and Mobility, *and* Qualitative Sociology. *Prior to her academic career, she worked as a management consultant.*

DOI: 10.1177/0002716211421112

iologists have argued that diversity programs are largely impres-
activities designed to appease courts, clients, and customers
from on-the-ground practice (e.g., Edelman 1992), others
ersity programs can result in concrete gains for women and
Reskin 1998). Still others have found that diversity programs can
potentially exacerbate inequalities in firms by making ascription a more salient
basis of evaluation and generating backlash among whites and males who disproportionately hold positions of power in organizations (Kidder et al. 2004).
Analyzing the mechanisms underlying the relative effectiveness or ineffectiveness
of diversity programs can provide scholars and policymakers with critical insights
necessary to successfully reduce gender and racial inequalities in organizations.
Although relevant to many types of employment, understanding this issue is particularly important with respect to access to managerial and professional tracks
because, despite significant educational and labor market gains over the past half
century, women and racial minorities remain significantly underrepresented in
positions of high pay, prestige, and authority in organizations and across industries
(see Cohen and Huffman 2007; Huffman and Cohen 2004).

One factor that seems to play a large role in the effectiveness of diversity practices is the nature of the specific program(s) adopted. Analyzing federal,
establishment-level data from the Equal Employment Opportunity Commission
over a 31-year period, Kalev, Dobbin, and Kelly (2006) find that initiatives aimed
at establishing oversight for diversity (e.g., diversity councils, diversity staff)
resulted in significant inroads for women and minorities in managerial positions,
while those aimed at reducing stereotyping or individual bias, including the widespread practice of diversity training, yielded virtually no benefit. From these
results, Kalev, Dobbin, and Kelly suggest that authority is a crucial component of
successful diversity practices. In particular, they argue that establishing responsibility for diversity through developing accountability structures and appoint-
ing specialists specifically tasked with managing diversity can significantly
improve the effectiveness of diversity practices.

Although such research makes great progress in illuminating which types of
programs tend to increase opportunities for women and minorities in managerial and professional tracks, how diversity practices actually work to challenge or
reinforce existing social inequalities in firms remains less clear. To fully understand how specific programs can help or hinder diversity, it is necessary to study
not only the aggregate effects of adoption but also (1) the content of particular
programs and (2) what staff tasked with overseeing and executing diversity programs actually do.

In this article, I provide an inside look into diversity recruitment—a type of
diversity practice generally considered to be effective in reducing organizational
inequalities (Edelman and Petterson 1999; Reskin 1998)—in elite professional
service firms. Drawing on interview and ethnographic evidence from recruitment and hiring in elite law firms, investment banks, and management consulting
firms, I analyze what diversity recruitment looks like in these firms in theory
and in practice. Examining these programs in depth can provide more nuanced

understandings of what diversity recruitment initiatives and staff actually do that challenges or reproduces ascriptive inequalities in organizations.

I find that although elite professional service firms tend to have the ingredients for success on paper—they typically are federal contractors, have adopted targeted diversity recruitment programs, have full- or part-time diversity staff, create diversity goals, and track diversity statistics for applicants versus hires, all of which have been associated with greater program effectiveness—they face significant obstacles in increasing the representation of racial minorities among new hires. I identify two key barriers inhibiting the effectiveness of diversity recruitment programs in these firms: (1) structural and status divides between those responsible for overseeing diversity recruitment versus those who have the power and authority to make actual hiring decisions and (2) widespread cultural beliefs among decision-makers that university prestige is an essential signal of merit but that diversity is not. My findings highlight that to be successful in translating diversity recruitment programs into hiring results, those charged with overseeing diversity programs need not only formal organizational authority (Kalev, Dobbin, and Kelly 2006) but also sufficient power and informal status to be influential in decision-making.

Case Selection

Elite professional service firms represent an exciting case in which to study diversity recruitment. First, despite stereotypes of these firms as being predominantly white and male, most have adopted targeted diversity recruitment programs that, given the relative success of these firms in increasing the representation of women in new hire classes in recent years, are often heralded as "best practices" among diversity professionals.[1] Yet despite their success in bringing more women into firms, these firms still struggle to increase the racial diversity of new hires; blacks and Latinos remain particularly underrepresented. As such, these firms represent a fruitful case in which to study both the potential successes and limitations of diversity recruitment.

Second, positions in these firms are highly coveted and provide unparalleled access to financial and symbolic rewards for recent college and professional school graduates. Starting salaries in these firms represent the top 10 percent of household incomes in the United States and are often two or more times the amounts earned by graduates from the same schools entering other fields (Guren and Sherman 2008; Zimmerman 2009). Thus, understanding how these firms hire can reveal important insights about entry into the upper echelons of the U.S. income distribution, which have disproportionately driven American economic inequality in recent decades (Saez 2008).

Third, although elite professional service firms engage in lateral hiring, the bulk of managers in these organizations are promoted from within. Consequently, analyzing their initial hiring processes provides unique opportunities to understand not only who receives the unparalleled starting salaries offered in the short term but also who ultimately is eligible to rise to the top of these firms. Even among those who leave—given that "doing time" within these firms is increasingly required for senior positions not only within corporations but also within the government and nonprofit sectors (Kalfayan 2009)—these firms can be thought of as contemporary gateways to the broader American managerial elite. Analyzing their hiring processes can inform debates about the role of gender and race in modern-day elite formation and reproduction (Zweigenhaft and Domhoff 1998).

Finally, these firms share strong similarities in their recruitment and hiring processes.[2] Firms solicit the bulk of new hires through annual, formalized recruitment programs, operated in tandem with university career service offices. Firms seek to create incoming classes of new employees, who enter the firm and undergo intensive on-the-job training and professional socialization together. Firms identify "target" universities where they recruit, most commonly through national prestige rankings. At these campuses, any student may apply. Competition is largely closed, however, to students who do not attend a prestigious school (Rivera 2011b). After an initial resume screen,[3] most commonly on the basis of educational prestige, a basic grade floor, and participation in extracurricular activities, firms choose a subgroup of applicants for first-round interviews, where applicants meet with one or two professionals for a period of 20 to 45 minutes. At each campus, firms typically interview dozens of candidates back-to-back. It is crucial to note that candidates are interviewed by professionals—rather than human resource (HR) representatives—who have undergone minimal training in interviewing and could potentially work closely with the candidate if hired. Applicants who receive favorable evaluations subsequently participate in a final round of three to six back-to-back interviews either on campus or in office. Recruiting committees typically weigh interviews more than resumes in final offer decisions.

Methods

To analyze diversity recruitment in elite professional service firms, I conducted both interviews and participant observation.

Interviews

From 2006 through 2008, I conducted 120 interviews with professionals involved in undergraduate and graduate hiring decisions in top-tier firms[4] (40 per industry). Participants included hiring partners, managing directors, and midlevel employees who conduct interviews and screen resumes, as well as HR and diversity managers. I recruited participants through stratified sampling from public directories of recruiting contacts, university alumni directories, and multisited referral chains. As elite populations are often difficult to access, referrals and my university and prior corporate affiliations were helpful in gaining consent and building rapport with participants. Interviews lasted between 40 and 90 minutes, took place at the time and location of the participant's choosing, and were tape-recorded and transcribed word-for-word with participant consent. Given that the bulk of firms are headquartered in Manhattan, I temporarily relocated to New York to facilitate data collection. Following Lamont's (2009) protocol for probing evaluative criteria, I asked evaluators specific questions about the qualities they look for and about candidates they recently interviewed whom they believed were well suited or malsuited for the job. As qualitative research is a social endeavor, it is possible that my identity influenced the tone of interviews. I am an Ivy League–educated female from a mixed ethnoreligious background, which may have primed respondents to emphasize high-status cultural practices (which they did) and favor diversity (which they did not).

Participant observation. From 2006 through 2007, I conducted fieldwork within the recruiting department of an elite professional service firm, which I refer to by the pseudonym Holt Halliday, or simply Holt, over a period of nine months. I was brought on through a personal connection as an unpaid recruiting intern to help to execute recruitment events. In exchange, Holt granted me permission to observe its hiring process for research purposes. During this period, I shadowed HR staff and evaluators through full-time and summer associate recruitment from an elite professional school. Due to institutional review board restrictions and Holt's request, I was unable to sit in on interviews. However, I attended recruitment events, interacted with candidates in Holt's hotel hospitality suite before and after interviews, debriefed evaluators on candidates after interviews, and sat in on group deliberations where candidates were discussed and ultimately selected. In addition to informing my interview protocol, such observation was crucial because it may have revealed patterns outside the awareness of individual evaluators, which is important given that employers do not necessarily do what they say (Pager and Quillian 2005). Although I gained entrée to only one firm, given the similarities in evaluative criteria among firms, the observational data obtained represents a launching point for understanding basic features of recruitment and assessment.

In addition, to understand how firms solicit new hires, market their strengths and recruitment process to prospective applicants, and publicly articulate the qualities they seek in candidates, I observed nearly every recruitment presentation hosted by these firms at local universities in a large, northeastern city over a period of six months. I located these events through advertisements in student newspapers and through career service offices' on-campus recruitment schedules. I also attended several diversity job fairs. During this time, I presented myself as a graduate student who was interested in learning about summer opportunities. I took detailed field notes about how firms presented themselves and their hiring procedures to students as well as about informal conversations I had with firm representatives and prospective applicants.

Data analysis

I coded interview transcripts and field notes for criteria and mechanisms of candidate evaluation. In accordance with the analytical strategy of grounded theory (Charmaz 2001), I developed coding categories inductively and refined them in tandem with data analysis. In primary coding rounds, I coded mentions of any criteria or mechanism that participants used to evaluate candidates. In inductive fashion, I did not set out to analyze diversity or diversity recruitment. However, after noticing a strong disconnect between how firms publicly discussed diversity in information sessions and brochures versus how participants discussed its role in the hiring process, I developed secondary codes referring to the role of diversity in evaluation. Codes included the content of diversity programs, participants' opinions of these programs, participants' reports about the role of diversity in hiring, how firms used (or did not use) diversity in candidate evaluation, and recruiters' overall opinions about the state of diversity in their firm and industry, being mindful to distinguish between discussions of diversity of gender, race, and experience. I quantified and compared frequencies of coding categories using the data analysis software ATLAS-ti.

Diversity within Reach[5]

As federal contractors, the elite professional service firms under study are required to demonstrate that they are taking "affirmative action" to increase their representations of qualified women and minorities (Dobbin 2009). Indeed, compared to many other types of white-collar, high-prestige employers in the United States, these firms devote significant monetary and human resources to attracting and retaining diverse talent. Many have diversity councils and full- or part-time diversity staff, and nearly all participate in targeted recruiting programs aimed at increasing the demographic diversity of applicant pools. Indeed, these firms have been fairly successful at diversifying their junior and midlevel ranks,[6] particularly compared to the virtually all-white, all-male professional service firms of the past (Heinz et al. 2005; Roth 2006).

Most firms set explicit but informal goals of matching the gender and race composition of typical graduating classes at the elite universities from which they recruit. Conversations with industry experts and HR professionals suggested that in elite law firms, women typically compose roughly half of newly minted JD hires. Consulting firms tend to be equally split between men and women at the undergraduate level and tend to be roughly 30 to 40 percent female among new MBA hires. Investment banks tend to be the least gender diverse. The representation of women varies by division, but generally undergraduate hires tend to be 30 to 40 percent female, and MBA hires are typically 15 to 25 percent female. Although new hire classes are more diverse than what one might expect given the historic reputations of these firms, progress has been lopsided. In general, firms' efforts to increase the representation of women among new hires have been successful. In fact, women are no longer considered to be "diversity candidates" in law firms or in many consulting firms. Investment banks, on the other hand, consistently struggle to meet their gender targets.

Progress in terms of race has been much slower; blacks and Latinos remain particularly underrepresented among new hires compared to elite university graduates and the population at large. The dearth of black and Latino hires was a sore spot for many of the employers I spoke to, not only because of the threat of compliance reviews but also because, in the elite professional services world, a firm's "diversity numbers," as they were called, were described as a key performance indicator that clients, competitors, and, increasingly, job candidates use to ascertain the overall quality and prestige of a firm.[7]

I argue that two factors serve as important barriers to firms' abilities to successfully diversify racially beyond a basic threshold: (1) the perception that diversity is a problem of the pipeline rather than one of a biased hiring process, yet firms define the pipeline in a manner that excludes the majority of nonwhite graduates nationally; and (2) structural, status, and ideological divides between those charged with overseeing diversity recruitment and those who have the actual power to make hiring decisions.

The golden pipeline

Perhaps unsurprisingly, the majority of participants believed that their hiring processes were gender- and race-neutral. When asked to discuss why firms experienced particular difficulty attracting blacks and Latinos, participants typically perceived the problem to be "in the pipeline." HR staff and decision-making professionals repeatedly emphasized how the problem of diversity lay in the fact that there were simply "not enough" qualified blacks or Latinos for their firm to hire. Diana (white, female), who was her firm's hiring partner, explained the lack of racial minorities in her firm as a "numbers game." She explained,

> It's just the numbers that are coming out of law school. It's the law school admissions percentage numbers. We can only take who goes to law school. There just aren't many diversity candidates to go around. When you get like someone who has done really well who was a diversity candidate, I mean the firms just go nuts. It's like a Supreme Court clerk.

However, employers typically defined the pipeline very narrowly, frequently restricting competition to students at elite "target" (top five to fifteen) or, preferably, superelite "core" (top four) universities. As I discuss elsewhere (see Rivera 2011b), firms typically do so out of perceptions of efficiency and the widespread belief that the prestige of one's educational credentials is a crucial indicator of an individual's intellectual, social, and moral worth. However, given that racial minorities are often concentrated in less prestigious universities, particularly at the professional school level,[8] conceptualizing the pipeline in this manner serves to exclude a large percentage of potentially high-performing diversity candidates nationally. Dash (Indian, male), a partner who helped oversee recruitment for his consulting firm, described how deeper structural barriers beyond his firm's control limited the number of minorities in the applicant pool:

> I don't think it's an issue with the process, it's a whole value chain that starts with high school education to undergrad and graduate school admissions—by the time we actually go to campus, we don't have as many candidates as we'd like to pick and choose from. We get very slim pickings.

Several firms were aware that defining the pool in such a narrow fashion had the potential to thwart attempts to diversify. Two investment banks represented in the research reported including historically black universities Spelman and Morehouse in their list of "targets." In addition, one law firm reported granting an interview to the top student at any law school, regardless of its prestige. However, such firms were in the minority.

Within this restricted view of the pipeline, employers discussed how many eligible minorities at elite schools were simply not interested in professional service careers. In addition, a surprisingly high number of HR staff openly discussed how they believed that many of those who were interested were not qualified. Law firm hiring manager Evelyn (white, female), who was charged with diversity recruitment for her firm, described this discrepancy:

> It's very difficult to find diverse candidates who actually can also fit the bill of a good candidate. What we often find is that the diverse candidates have the low grades or low campus involvement. So everybody is clamoring for the students who are diverse and have grades that are either acceptable or really exceptional.

As such, within the artificially narrow pipeline of minority students at elite schools, the pool of qualified candidates is believed to be even narrower. Moreover, decision-making professionals who did the bulk of resume screening and interviewing in these firms were adamant about what they called not "lowering the bar" or modifying metrics used to assess majority candidates. Lowering the bar included relaxing institutional prestige requirements. Banker Fernando (Hispanic, male) explained: "There is no willingness to jeopardize some quality of a candidate over a category of gender, ethnicity or something like that. . . . People are not willing to hire someone substandard because of that reason as opposed to just waiting for the right candidate."

Thus, although participants perceived the problem to be in the pipeline, they constructed the pipeline in a manner that excluded a large proportion of diversity candidates nationwide. The career services director of a top MBA program I spoke with about my research summarized how firms' narrow conception of the pipeline can constrain diversity:

> Firms are scrambling for diversity. They want gender diversity, racial diversity, you name it, and [they] go to great lengths to attract diverse applicants. They are all fighting for the same tiny piece of the pie. But they are focusing on that slice rather than expanding it, which is the real problem.

Of course, not all participants agreed with their firms' hefty emphasis on institutional prestige. Individuals who themselves came from lower-status institutions—who were often HR managers and diversity staff—were most likely to be opposed to it. However, these individuals often lacked the power or status to take substantive action to expand the slice of the pie their firm considered. For example, HR manager Abby (white, female), who was charged with diversity recruitment for her law firm, expressed strong skepticism about her firm's refusal to recruit at second- and third-tier schools. When I asked if she had ever tried to expand her firm's on-campus list, she shrugged: "It's not my choice. The recruitment committee [composed of partners and associates] decides. I can make suggestions, like I think we should go to [local law school] because their diversity numbers are good, but my hands are tied."

Targeting diversity

Given that employers typically conceptualize the problem of diversity as a problem in the pipeline, they have crafted diversity recruitment programs aimed at increasing the diversity of the applicant pool rather than reducing bias within the decision-making process itself. Banker Finn (white, male), who was actively involved in diversity recruitment and was on the diversity committee at his bank, stated:

> You can't lower the bar so . . . we just recruit harder. You can find a lot of those great candidates that meet the same level of, I guess intelligence and excitement as your run-of-the-mill white males. There's just fewer of them, so you've got to work harder to find them. . . . We never hire someone because of their race or their gender or anything. It's more about getting the best people through the door, right. But there's a smaller pool of talent within those areas, so they get more attention.

Outreach. Firms gave diversity candidates "more attention" through participation in national and regional diversity job fairs, which were open to diverse students regardless of the prestige of their educational credentials. Fairs were organized by a variety of commercial (e.g., Vault.com), nonprofit (e.g., Reaching Out), and student organizations. At these fairs, which were typically held at a hotel or conference center, employers paid to have a booth where applicants could speak informally with representatives, drop their resumes, and, in some cases, participate in a preliminary interview.

As part of the ethnographic portion of my research, I attended several of these events. In between panels advising students how to craft a compelling cover letter or refine their interview skills and keynote speakers articulating their own vision of the promise of diversity, the main attraction was typically the employer expo, where representatives from each participating firm were available to speak directly with candidates in a large ballroom at designated booths. Students were typically given a list of employers upon registering for the job fair.

At each logo-laden table typically huddled one to four firm representatives, usually a combination of HR staff and visibly diverse professionals. Sprinkled atop tables were treasure troves of freebies, alongside stacks of high-gloss brochures of varying thickness outlining the firm's commitment to diversity, as evidenced by its list of outreach activities (such as participation in the diversity fairs) and testimonials from conspicuously diverse yet highly pedigreed employees. Finally, tables sported one or more clipboards, where participants could list their name, school, and e-mail address, should they want to be kept abreast of recruiting developments.

At some fairs, participants could register in advance for one-on-one interviews that would be conducted at a particular time, typically in an area away from the firm's booth, either in a separate interview room or hotel room. At all fairs, however, students were strongly encouraged to bring their resumes and speak directly with firm representatives. If a representative had a sufficiently positive impression of a candidate, he or she could ask for his or her resume. If the impression was stellar, he or she could pull him or her aside for a more formal interview. Students typically ebbed and flowed between tables. The most prestigious firms typically had lines of students waiting to speak with representatives or sign up for their e-mail lists.

At job fairs, the mood among firm representatives was typically light and energetic; the mood among candidates, tense. These events were high-stakes for students who did not attend elite schools—this was, for many, what they believed was their only shot at getting a Big Firm job. They often traveled long distances at their own expense for this opportunity.

Whereas candidates tended to approach diversity job fairs as legitimate opportunities to get in the door, HR staff, who were typically responsible for overseeing diversity recruitment, had a strikingly different view. In their eyes, diversity fairs were largely impression management activities. Law firm hiring manager Kayla (white, female) explained, "I really do think it has to do with building brand name recognition and . . . I think it's just a great . . . tool just to be able to get your name out there." Diversity fairs, however, were not considered to be fruitful sources of new hires. Investment banking hiring manager Stephanie (white, female) confessed, "It gets our name out. We have a table; we answer questions. It's more than anything a PR effort—just get[ting] our name out there than actually getting anyone we met there to work for us."

When discussing why diversity fairs tended not to be successful sources of new hires, HR staff most frequently discussed how there was a disconnect between the "pedigree" or school prestige of fair attendees and the elite educational credentials desired by the revenue-generating professionals who interviewed candidates and made actual hiring decisions. As a result, employers reported meeting with candidates at diversity fairs and collecting resumes, but HR staff passed very few of them on to recruiting committees because most candidates did not meet firms' strict criterion of "school." Legal hiring manager Brent (white, male), who helped run diversity events for his firm, discussed how his firm typically does not consider applicants from diversity fairs unless they are attending a "core" or "target" school and, thus, already in the pipeline:

Brent: I think it's important for us to go, just to show those communities that we are interested in and finding diverse candidates, which we are. Those specific efforts aren't the most effective in getting candidates. If we see someone at one of those events who we also see on campus for interviews, then we're seeing them anyway. . . . But to be honest, I can't think of anyone we had seen just at one of those job fairs that we then hired.

Interviewer: Why do you think?

Brent: We don't see a lot of students from top-tier schools at those job fairs; we're seeing mostly students from middle- to what we would consider lower-tier schools. . . . We have plenty of really good students from top schools that we don't have to. . . .

Interviewer: Why do you think prestige is important?

Brent: Because that's the base the firm wants. Because the partners are from those schools.

Such pressures could result in a glass ceiling for diversity students outside top-ranked schools. In theory, these students are being given opportunities to enter the pipeline, but in practice they are typically excluded from consideration because they are not at a top-tier school. Of course, there are exceptions. Such exceptions include, for example, students who had sufficiently high-status connections to a firm, had been selected by third-party organizations to participate in special early diversity internships (e.g., Sponsors for Educational Opportunity), or, in the case of law firms, had clerked for a reputable judge. However, as these types of inroads also tended to be differentially distributed by school prestige (as well as socioeconomic status), diverse students outside of elite schools faced a catch-22. This predicament was perhaps most evident at an interviewing panel I observed during a law firm diversity fair. On the panel, partners gave job-seekers practical tips for interview success. In the question-and-answer period, an African American female, who appeared to be in her midtwenties, stood up and asked hopefully, "I'm a [third year] at Pace. I wanted a firm job, but they told me I needed to clerk first. But they told me I can't get a clerkship without firm experience. It's like the chicken and the egg. What should I do?" A partner responded, "You need to just go clerk," and turned to the next question. Consequently, as HR managers openly acknowledged, diversity job fairs tended to serve as important public relations tools but did little to increase the diversity of new hires.

In-reach. In addition to diversity job fairs, firms also participated in targeted recruitment events at "core" and "target" schools, which were aimed at increasing the proportion of minority candidates who actually applied from these campuses. Whereas outreach activities were viewed primarily as impression management activities, on-campus—or what I term in-reach—activities were viewed as legitimate opportunities to increase the diversity of incoming classes.

In-reach events took various forms. Some firms sponsored events (e.g., confer-ences, speakers) hosted by student affinity groups to demonstrate their commit-ment to diversity not only in words but in dollars. Firms also frequently sent employees from underrepresented groups to speak on career panels hosted by university career services to "show a diverse face for the firm" (Ella, consultant, white, female). Finally, many firms held social events at local bars or restaurants where diverse students could mingle directly with firm employees over cocktails and canapés. Firms varied in whether they chose to target a single diversity cate-gory at a time (e.g., racial minorities, women, LGBT students) or all diversity groups together. In general, the more prestigious the campus or the firm, the more in-reach networking events took place.

The purpose of networking events was threefold. The first was, again, to "show a diverse face" and signal commitment to diversity. The second was to collect contact information from diversity candidates so that HR representatives could follow up with them, encourage them to apply, and remind them to submit appli-cations as deadlines approached. Third, these events gave diversity candidates opportunities to learn more tacit knowledge about a firm and industry—informa-tion that respondents reported that diversity candidates may lack if they do not have friends or family "in the business"—solicit interview tips, and meet indi-viduals who could perhaps serve as advocates for them in the actual interview process. Consultant Emma (white, female) summarized the purpose of network-ing events:

> It's to dispel some of the myths that typically come with consulting. . . . We have like a women's group, we have an African American affinity group, and a gay and transgen-der group. We have got groups that support people from those groups here and it's terrific. So . . . the events are hooking candidates up with the types of groups and types of people they could ask the tough questions to . . . and then we can reach out to [employees from] those groups to help us identify candidates who would be good for us to interview.

Although in-reach events could provide significant opportunities for diversity candidates to apply to firms and prepare for interviews, the degree to which such events actually increased the representation of these candidates in new hires is unclear. When I asked whether she thought on-campus events aimed at increas-ing the diversity of the applicant pool are successful in increasing diversity in her investment bank, Laura (white, female) sighed: "Trying to be realistic. Maybe not, except you do just have a more diverse candidate pool when you get to that final round. So it does increase the odds, the more you have, the more of a chance they could get hired, but I don't think it ultimately drives decisions." As such, targeted recruitment events were seen as crucial ways to solicit interest and applications from minority candidates, but professionals expressed skepticism about their actual effectiveness in diversifying new hires. Perhaps tellingly, out-reach and in-reach diversity events were referred to as "marketing events" and even "community service" by HR staff and evaluators.

The great divide

A second barrier firms faced in converting diversity candidates into hires was the design of the hiring process itself. Recruitment activities were intentionally separated from hiring decisions. In addition, these two types of activities were generally overseen by different individuals. HR staff, including diversity managers, were responsible for overseeing diversity recruitment and handling the logistical and administrative aspects of hiring. However, it was revenue-generating professionals (i.e., bankers, consultants, and lawyers) who were responsible for actually evaluating candidates in interviews and making hiring decisions. These two groups tended to have different priorities and power in hiring.

Last stop: resume screening. After identifying diversity candidates at in-reach events, HR representatives typically were successful in increasing the representation of these candidates in first-round, on-campus interview pools at elite schools. They were able to do so because they had some authority in resume screening—firms often charged HR staff with making a "first cut" of resumes due to the large number of applications received, even from a single school—and because doing so was consistent with firms' philosophy of diversifying the applicant pool. In addition, although less than 10 percent of individuals who screened resumes reported that diversity was a criterion that they actively used in evaluating resumes (Rivera 2011b), many described how diversity could serve as a tiebreaker in the case of two equally qualified candidates. Attorney Nicole (white, female) explained, "It plays a role if you have two, you know, very qualified candidates on the same level."

"The same as everyone else." However, diversity recruitment programs typically ended at the point of the first-round interview. This primarily occurred for two reasons. First, HR and diversity staff—who both oversaw diversity recruitment programs and had vested interests in promoting diversity because it was part of their job description—were typically not involved in interviewing candidates or making hiring decisions. The delineated authority of HR was due partially to a strong belief within firms that only revenue-generating professionals are equipped to evaluate merit. Banker Oliver (white, male) expressed a common opinion about HR:

> From a scheduling perspective and sort of management perspective they're very good because they understand how hard people work and that by doing a lot of sort of setting up events they take a lot of pressure off the school team [the professionals]. . . . But they're out of touch with what we actually do; they can't really relate to it.

So, as banker Heather (white, female) said bluntly of decision-making, "HR stays out of it, which is good."

Compounding the perception that HR does not know "what it takes" to be a good banker, consultant, or lawyer, there are salient status divides between HR and professionals who serve as evaluators. First, HR was not perceived as contributing to companies' bottom line. Kelly (white, female), who ran recruitment and diversity recruitment for her investment bank, felt that she, like HR as a whole, was stigmatized:

> I've learned through this business that if you work for a department that does not make money, you're less rewarded. You're not earning your keep every day. You're draining what other people are producing, quote unquote. Even though you're really bring[ing] them new talent. But they don't see it that way. You're dead weight.

Second, there tended to be differences in educational prestige between HR staff and revenue-generating professionals. As discussed previously, professionals tended to interpret educational prestige as a critical signal of intellectual, social, and moral worth. Whereas revenue-generating professionals frequently were graduates of elite and superelite schools, HR staff typically had more modest "pedigrees." Banking managing director Tim (white, male) described why he personally did not trust HR staff to evaluate merit: "Maybe if they're lucky, [they] have a degree from SUNY Stonybrook. Not to knock the school or anything, but they don't have a degree from Harvard." Consequently, HR and diversity staff faced significant obstacles in increasing diversity beyond the point of composing the first-round interview pool because they lacked the power and status within their firms to do so.

The fundamental divide between diversity recruitment and hiring was perhaps most evident at Holt. Two professionals interviewed each candidate in first-round interviews. At the end of the day, these interviewers had to debrief with one another and submit their final rankings (out of ten to twelve candidates) to HR to pass on to the second round. Several HR representatives, including myself, sat in on these conversations as official "debriefers." In addition to recording data about interviewers' decisions, more than what they had written on their evaluation forms, we were given a list of the names of diversity candidates in the interview pool. The diversity manager instructed us that when there was a "borderline" candidate, we were to scan the list to see if this candidate was also a diversity candidate. If they were, we were to communicate this to the interviewers. However, there was no formal policy about how such situations should be handled; it was up to the discretion of the interviewers to interpret this information and make decisions as they wished. In the debriefings that I conducted, I received various reactions to the announcement that someone was a diversity candidate, ranging from thank-yous to eye-rolls to one case where an evaluator asked me to refrain from speaking for the rest of the debriefing. In one of my debriefings, an evaluator (white, male) said of a borderline candidate (black, male), "List him as a no, unless we *really* need diversity"; but he did not change his written evaluation or ranking of the candidate. The most common response, however, was a lack of response.

Moreover, when it came to final group deliberations about who would ultimately would be brought back for second-round interviews or be hired, the diversity recruitment manager was asked to leave the room. The contrast between how the diversity manager was treated versus professionals with the right "pedigree" was stark. For example, the diversity manager was actively excluded from hiring committee deliberations, but a former employee who was a current student at the school from which we were recruiting was, so that she could include her personal impressions derived from the classroom or school social events to help determine close calls.

Of course, the degree to which particular HR and diversity staff were included or excluded from decision-making did vary among firms. One factor that seemed to make an important difference was whether specific HR staff members had experience as a revenue-generating professional in their industry, preferably in their firm. In these cases, which were most frequently women who had left part-ner tracks for HR roles, they were still typically not allowed to interview candi-dates but often were included in candidate deliberations. Moreover, when they did speak up, participants reported listening to them. Manager Logan (white, male) described why he took seriously the opinions of his office's HR manager, who had worked as a consultant in his firm before entering her HR role: "She knows both sides. It is not just your, you know, administrator who doesn't under-stand the consulting business."

But such cases were uncommon. When diversity staff were not included in conversations or when their voices were not considered to be legitimate, conversa-tions with evaluators and my observations at Holt revealed how diversity, particu-larly racial diversity, was typically tabled as a criterion of evaluation for individual candidates because, for many, the sheer act of considering diversity meant "lower-ing the bar." As asserted by investment banking managing director Max (white, male), "We only go so far for diversity candidates." As such, once diversity candi-dates entered the interview stage, they were, in the words of consultant Lucy (white, female), "treated the same as everyone else." Evaluators emphasized how diversity candidates needed to perform at an equal level as traditional candidates on all dimensions in interviews to be passed on to second-round interviews or receive an offer to join the firm. Consulting manager Kai (white, male) explained, "It's just taken off the table and that means over time that if we pick the best can-didate that they're going to be a representative sample of the global population overall . . . the firm isn't yet, but hopefully we'll get there."

However, not all groups were perceived as being equally good interviewees. Evaluators described how they felt many black and Latino candidates fell short on the dimension of "polish," or communication skills required in these client-facing jobs—a sentiment that was supported by significantly lower ratings on average of black and Latino candidates on this dimension in written interview reports at Holt. Firms typically provided no guidance as to how to assess polish in interviews. Rather, they relied on evaluators' gut reactions and feelings of comfort while interacting with candidates. Evaluators' perceptions of decreased polish among blacks and Latinos could be due to stereotypes, unconscious negative emotional responses toward racial minorities, or actual behavior (see Dovidio, Glick, and Rudman [2005] for a review). In addition, as banker Ryan (black, male) highlighted, there could be a potential socioeconomic basis or bias inherent in such perceptions:

> It doesn't matter how smart you are; it's hard to compete, even if you're middle or upper middle class, with someone whose dad was a partner at Goldman or was a manager at a hedge fund and who grew up talking about investing all his life. Of course, when that person comes into interview, he'll be more polished, know more about the business and answer questions more in a more informed and articulate way. . . . [I]f you have very few executives who are minorities, you'll have very few children of executives who are minorities, and those children are simply way ahead from day one.

Still, Ryan saw the solution to this dilemma as providing soft skills training to underrepresented minorities either in college or high school to increase their polish rather than developing more standardized or inclusive measures of communication or client-facing abilities.

Deliberations. Although diversity was typically tabled in evaluations of individual performance, it could resurface in final deliberations, where recruiting committees meet to review evaluators' interview rankings and make offer decisions. Diversity was not a formal aspect of these discussions, and again the diversity manager was not included in them. However, according to my own observation at Holt and reports of evaluators in other firms, evaluators occasionally raised the issue of what the "portfolio" of potential hires looked like in terms of "diversity numbers." Perhaps interestingly, these discussions at Holt were often initiated by male partners and were raised almost exclusively about gender. This could be the case either because (1) gender was easier than race to benchmark to the composition of newly minted elite graduates or (2) gender was considered to be a more valid diversity statistic or criterion for hire than race. There was support for both processes in my ethnographic and interview data.

The divergent treatment of gender and race in final decisions was most evident in a deliberation I sat in on at Holt. Shortly before recruiting season, Holt received a notice from a compliance organization notifying them that they were under investigation for underhiring candidates from a particular racial group.[9] Taking this charge seriously, they reviewed the resumes of the candidates they had interviewed for the period under question and found that there was nothing on resumes or interviewers' scoring sheets that could explain why members of this group were not hired while members of other groups with similar qualifications and interview scores were. In the next recruiting season, the issue of bias against this group was brought up not only by HR managers but also by partners in informal discussions of recruitment goals and formal presentations by the firm's legal counsel about issues of compliance. Yet after interviews, in final deliberations for the region where discrimination was possibly an issue, there were again no candidates from this ethnic group on the list of first pick new hires. A partner (white, male) chuckled nervously as he looked at the list and shook his head: "We've done it again." However, instead of questioning whether the interviewer reports or their own readings of these documents might be biased against members of this ethnic group, I watched as he and another partner (Indian, male) erased interview scores of candidates from this group and replaced them with artificially lower ones so that the firm "won't have trouble" from the monitoring compliance organization. Less than 20 minutes before, these same two partners had decided to add an additional female versus male borderline candidate to balance out the gender "portfolio" of the class.

Conclusion

To summarize, this article has sought to provide an inside look into diversity recruitment programs in elite professional service firms. Although these firms have made great progress in diversifying over the past 30 years, particularly in the domain of gender, I have highlighted how there is a fundamental disconnect between diversity recruitment programs and actual decision-making that may stymie these programs' effectiveness in increasing the racial diversity of new hires. The employers in my sample believed that the problem of diversity was one of the pipeline rather than one of the hiring process. As such, they focused recruitment programs on the point of application rather than the point of hire. Although increasing the diversity of the applicant pool may indeed increase the odds of hiring candidates from underrepresented backgrounds, (1) structural and status divides between those responsible for overseeing diversity recruitment versus those who have the power and authority to make hiring decisions and (2) widespread cultural beliefs among decision-makers that university prestige is an essential signal of merit but that diversity is an invalid one may thwart firms' ability not only to receive applications from but actually hire diversity candidates.

Implications for policy and practice

My findings have several important implications for scholars and practitioners interested in increasing the demographic diversity of elite professional service firms. Although analyzing diversity programs after the point of entry is out of the scope of this analysis, my results suggest several means through which elite professional service employers can potentially increase the diversity of new hire classes, which constitute the bulk of their future managers. First, restricting competition for jobs to students at elite and superelite schools may artificially lower the racial and socioeconomic diversity of new hires, given the demographic composition of these schools (Bowen and Bok 1998; Karabel 2005). Firms that want to increase their diversity in either respect could adopt a more expansive definition of educational quality to include universities not only within the golden pipeline but also those that exhibit both high levels of academic achievement (including job-relevant coursework) and diversity. To help them to cope with a wider pipeline, firms could perform more intensive screens on grades, which can be a fairly reliable measure of job success (Rosenbaum and Binder 1997) but are currently used by firms only as a basic floor in candidate evaluation, if they are used at all (see Rivera 2011b).

Second, my results suggest that to be successful in translating diversity recruitment programs into hiring results, those charged with overseeing diversity programs need not only formal organizational authority but also sufficient power and status to be influential in decision-making. Firms could accomplish this by vesting HR staff, including diversity managers, with decision-making power, thereby eliminating the divide between diversity recruitment and actual hiring. Doing so could potentially not only increase the diversity of new hires by having individuals who are responsible for managing diversity select candidates but also improve efficiency by having highly paid professionals concentrate on revenue-generating client work rather than traveling from school to school over several months every year, interrupting team and client work, and costing each firm between tens and hundreds of thousands of dollars per year in recruiting travel expenses alone. However, due to the strong cultural belief prevalent among evaluators that only revenue-generating professionals are equipped to judge merit, this strategy is likely to encounter fierce resistance.

A more realistic but still promising strategy would be to erode the status divide between those charged with diversity recruitment and those charged with decision-making. Among the firms represented in my interview sample, the few cases where HR and diversity staff had strong voices not only in recruitment but also in hiring occurred when they had previous revenue-generating professional experience in their firms. As such, from a policy perspective, firms seeking to increase the effectiveness of diversity recruitment programs could assign revenue-generating professionals to diversity roles rather than relying on HR departments. Or, they may want to charge HR professionals who have previous experience on the revenue-generating side of the business and similar "pedigrees" as evaluators with diversity recruitment. Doing so could help to legitimize and raise the status of diversity recruitment activities and professionals and increase the likelihood of their success.

Third, in line with prior research demonstrating that diversity practices do not benefit all demographic groups equally (e.g., Kalev, Dobbin, and Kelly 2006), my findings suggest that gender and race may operate in different ways in hiring; it is very likely that in the case of diversity recruitment, one program design does not fit all. Future research should parse out which on-the-ground practices tend to be most beneficial for women, men, and specific ethnic/racial groups.

Finally, given that racial minorities were most commonly "dinged" in interviews on the evaluative criterion of polish, it is possible that it is necessary to change not only the composition of the pipeline and the status of those charged with diversity recruiting but also the very manner in which merit is assessed in interviews. As discussed earlier in this article, firms typically provided no guidance as to how to assess polish in interviews, relying instead on evaluators' gut reactions and feelings of comfort while interacting with candidates. Instead of such highly idiosyncratic measures, which open the door to judgments made on the basis of stereotypes as well as explicit and implicit biases (see Jolls and Sunstein 2006), firms could provide evaluators with more systematic methods to assess polish in interviews. For example, one consulting firm represented in this sample assessed candidates' polish through a client role-play exercise. Given that more standardized interview protocols are often associated with reduced subjectivity in evaluation (Reskin and McBrier 2000), it is possible that such changes could benefit minority candidates by providing more concrete information about communicative competence than what is available via gut reactions and stereotypes. Together, such structural, status, and evaluative changes could begin to narrow the current divide between diversity recruitment and hiring decisions and help to increase the racial diversity of new hires in elite firms.

Notes

1. These firms frequently appear in national rankings of "best companies" for women and working mothers by third-party organizations (e.g., *Fortune Magazine, Working Mother Magazine*, etc.).

2. For a discussion of differences and their effects on evaluation, see Rivera (2011a).

3. The most elite law schools are exceptions; career offices force firms to interview anyone who signs up.

4. I identified firms on the basis of national and major-market prestige rankings.

5. The title of this section and of the article as a whole are plays both on firms' diversity in-reach programs and on the name of the home furnishings company Design within Reach. The mission of the latter is to sell modern designer furniture to individuals who would not ordinarily have access to this market due to a lack of connections to designers, sky-high prices, or endless waits. In theory, they are attempting to democratize access to this market. However, in practice, their products are priced in such a manner that they are still out of reach for the vast majority of middle- and upper-middle-class consumers; as a result, they end up providing easier access and lower prices but typically to those who already had the financial and social resources to participate in this market. In the same manner, elite professional service firms in theory try to expand access to careers to diversity candidates at large through outreach efforts, such as job fairs. But in practice, competition is limited to those diversity candidates who already would have had access to firms through on-campus recruitment in the golden pipeline, high-status connections, and so on.

6. Women and minorities remain significantly underrepresented at the partner levels.

7. In law firms, diversity statistics are made public on an annual basis.

8. For example, see http://grad-schools.usnews.rankingsandreviews.com/grad/law/law_diversity.

9. Details are intentionally minimal to protect the identity of the firm.

References

Bowen, William, and Derek Bok. 1998. *The shape of the river*. Princeton, NJ: Princeton University Press.

Charmaz, Kathy. 2001. Grounded theory. In *Contemporary field research: Perspectives and formulations*, 2nd edition, ed. Robert M. Emerson, 335–52. Prospect Heights, IL: Waveland.

Cohen, Phillip, and Matt Huffman. 2007. Black underrepresentation in management across U.S. labor markets. *The Annals of the American Academy of Political and Social Science* 609:181–99.

Dobbin, Frank. 2009. *Inventing equal opportunity*. Princeton, NJ: Princeton University Press.

Dovidio, John, Peter Glick, and Laurie Rudman. 2005. *On the nature of prejudice: Fifty years after Allport*. Malden, MA: Blackwell.

Edelman, Lauren. 1992. Legal ambiguity and symbolic structures: Organizational mediation of civil rights law. *American Journal of Sociology* 97:1531–76.

Edelman, Lauren, and Stephen Petterson. 1999. Symbols and substance in organizational response to civil rights law. *Research in Social Stratification and Mobility* 17:107–35.

Guren, Adam, and Natalie Sherman. 22 June 2008. Harvard graduates head to investment banking, consulting. *Harvard Crimson*.

Heinz, John P., Robert L. Nelson, Rebecca L. Sandefur, and Edward O. Laumann. 2005. *Urban lawyers: The new social structure of the bar*. Chicago, IL: University of Chicago Press.

Huffman, Matt, and Philip Cohen. 2004. Occupational segregation and the gender gap in workplace authority: National versus local labor markets. *Sociological Forum* 19:121–47.

Jolls, Christine, and Cass Sunstein. 2006. The law of implicit bias. *California Law Review* 94:969–96.

Kalev, Alexandra, Frank Dobbin, and Erin Kelly. 2006. Best practices or best guesses? Diversity management and the remediation of inequality. *American Sociological Review* 71:589–617.

Kalfayan, Michael. 2009. Choosing financial careers at Harvard. AB Honors Thesis, Harvard University, Cambridge, MA.

Karabel, Jerome. 2005. *The chosen: The hidden history of admission and exclusion at Harvard, Yale, and Princeton*. New York, NY: Houghton Mifflin.

Kidder, Deborah, Melenie Lankau, Donna Chrobot-Mason, Kelly Mollica, and Raymond Friedman. 2004. Backlash toward diversity initiatives: Examining the impact of diversity program justification, personal and group outcomes. *International Journal of Conflict Management* 15:77–104.

Lamont, Michèle. 2009. *How professors think*. Cambridge, MA: Harvard University Press.

Pager, Devah, and Lincoln Quillian. 2005. Walking the talk? What employers say versus what they do. *American Sociological Review* 70:355–80.

Paluck, Elizabeth Levy, and Donald Green. 2009. Prejudice reduction: What works? *Annual Review of Psychology* 60:339–67.

Reskin, Barbara. 1998. *The realities of affirmative action in employment*. Washington, DC: American Sociological Association.

Reskin, Barbara, and Debra McBrier. 2000. Why not ascription? Organizations' employment of male and female managers. *American Sociological Review* 65:210–33.

Rivera, Lauren. 2011a. Hiring as cultural matching: Homophily in job interviews. Northwestern University Working Paper, Evanston, IL.

Rivera, Lauren. 2011b. Ivies, extracurriculars, and exclusion: Elite employers' use of educational credentials. *Research in Social Stratification and Mobility* 29:71–90.

Rosenbaum, James, and Amy Binder. 1997. Do employers really need more educated youth? *Sociology of Education* 70:68–85.

Roth, Louise M. 2006. *Selling women short*. Princeton, NJ: Princeton University Press.

Saez, Emmanuel. Winter 2008. Striking it richer: The evolution of top incomes in the United States. *Pathways Magazine*, 6–7.

Zimmerman, Eilene. 24 January 2009. Chill of salary freezes reaches top law firms. *New York Times*.

Zweigenhaft, Richard, and G. William Domhoff. 1998. *Diversity in the power elite: Have women and minorities reached the top?* New Haven, CT: Yale University Press.

Developmental Practices, Organizational Culture, and Minority Representation in Organizational Leadership: The Case of Partners in Large U.S. Law Firms

By
FIONA M. KAY
and
ELIZABETH H. GORMAN

Explanations of minority underrepresentation among organizational managers have focused primarily on either employee deficits in human and social capital or employer discrimination. To date, research has paid little attention to the role of developmental practices and related cultural values within organizations. Using data on large U.S. law firms, the authors investigate the role of formal developmental practices and cultural values in the representation of three minority groups among firm partners: African Americans, Latinos, and Asian Americans. The authors find that formal practices and cultural values intended to aid employee growth and development do not "level the playing field" for minorities. Formal training and mentoring programs do not increase minority presence, while a longer time period to promotion, a cultural commitment to professional development, and a cultural norm of early responsibility are all negatively associated with minority representation. Although the pattern is broadly similar across all three groups, some effects vary in interesting ways.

Keywords: lawyers; promotion; race; organizational culture; law firms

Fiona M. Kay is a professor in the Department of Sociology at Queen's University. Her research interests include gender and race inequality, stratification and mobility, and professions. Her research on mentorship and women's career paths has been published in the American Sociological Review, Law Society Review, *and* Law and Policy.

Elizabeth H. Gorman is an associate professor in the Department of Sociology at the University of Virginia. Her research interests include gender and race inequality, organizations, and professional and knowledge-based work. Her research on organizational characteristics influencing women's hiring and promotion has been published in the American Sociological Review, *the* American Journal of Sociology, *and* Social Forces.

NOTE: The authors acknowledge that the data analyzed in this study were licensed to them by the National Association for Law Placement (NALP). The views and conclusions stated herein are those of the authors and do not necessarily reflect the views of NALP or of any individuals associated with NALP. This research was supported by a grant from the Law School Admissions Council.

DOI: 10.1177/0002716211420232

Racial and ethnic minorities are scarce among managers and executives within organizations in the United States. Studies reveal that racial and ethnic minorities face lower chances of promotion (Miller, Kerr, and Reid 2010) and attain lower organizational rank or authority (Elliott and Smith 2004) than do their white counterparts. As a result, minorities are underrepresented among managers relative to their presence at lower organizational levels (Cohen and Huffman 2007).

Previous investigations of this underrepresentation have pointed to processes at the individual, organizational, and environmental levels. At the individual level, professionals' preferences and skills (S. Smith 2005) and organizational decision-makers' cognitive biases (DiTomaso et al. 2007) shape career outcomes for professionals. At the organizational level, the characteristics of jobs and workplace settings constrain or enable the operation of individual-level processes (Reskin 2003). At the level of the industry or organizational field, legal regulations, institutionalized practices, and market competition shape organizational actions and employees' career prospects (Skaggs 2009).

However, to date, scholars examining the determinants of racial and ethnic minority access to managerial positions have paid relatively little attention to the role of developmental practices and related cultural values within organizations. Yet such practices and values might counteract or diminish informal processes that place minorities at a disadvantage in obtaining the training, mentoring, and other opportunities that are vital for promotion into management (Thomas and Gabarro 1999). Of course, minority representation in management reflects not only the rate of minority promotion but also the inflow of minority managers through external hiring and their outflow through retirement and other forms of termination. Nevertheless, organizational practices that benefit nonmanagement minority employees can have a discernible impact on the presence of minorities among an organization's managers (Kalev 2009).

In this study, we ask whether organizations' practices and cultural values relating to employee development influence the representation of racial minorities among partners in large law firms. We also contribute to the literature on racial workplace inequality by examining multiple minority groups. Most studies that have examined racial inequality in workplace outcomes have focused on a comparison of whites and African Americans (e.g., Kalev, Dobbin, and Kelly 2006; Stainback and Tomaskovic-Devey 2009). In our study, using data on large law firms across the United States, we investigate the representation of three minority groups: African Americans, Latinos, and Asian Americans.

Individual and Interactional Sources of Minority Underrepresentation in Management

Previous research points to three processes that might lead organizational decision-makers to choose whites over minorities when selecting candidates for promotion into management. First, minorities may enter organizations with lower levels of the abilities and skills valued by employers, and these deficits may remain relatively constant as both white and minority employees progress toward promotion. Usually thought of as the "human capital" view, this argument also extends to resources beyond cognitive and technical skill, such as cultural competence and social ties (Nee and Sanders 2001). Importantly, this explanation does not necessarily blame minorities themselves for these deficits, which may be the result of earlier educational, cultural, and social disadvantages. Consistent with this view, empirical evidence indicates that at least a portion of the racial gaps in promotion and managerial representation is explained by differences in education and technical skill across racial groups (R. Smith 2005). Some qualitative studies find that minorities feel less culturally at ease than whites in corporate work environments (Bell and Nkomo 2001). Minorities often have fewer effective social networks (McGuire 2000) as well, and racial differences in social network composition play a role in explaining the racial gap in organizational mobility (Thomas and Gabarro 1999).

A second explanation of race disparities in promotions holds that, even though whites and minorities may possess the same levels of technical, cultural, and social resources, conscious or unconscious cognitive biases lead employers to assess minorities less favorably than whites. These biases, which are based on racial stereotypes or (for white decision-makers) explicit or implicit in-group favoritism, may lead organizational leaders to perceive minority employees as less competent than whites (Reskin 2001). Empirical evidence suggests that employers tend to hold minorities to stricter standards for demonstrating ability (Foschi 2009).

A third possibility is that minority and white employees enter organizations with relatively similar levels of technical, cultural, and social resources, but whites pull ahead during the course of employment as a result of better developmental opportunities. Senior employees typically have considerable discretion in deciding whether they will mentor or sponsor someone for developmental experiences. Due to cognitive biases, organizational decision-makers often perceive white employees as having greater potential. As a result, through a series of small, informal, and largely unplanned decisions, whites are likely to receive more on-the-job training, more mentoring, and more opportunities to perform challenging tasks that build skills. Although there may be no deliberate intention to exclude minorities, they may experience "benign neglect" (Sander 2006) or an "absence of advantage" (DiTomaso et al. 2007) while colleagues and superiors invest heavily in the career development of white employees. Research evidence suggests that, compared to whites, minorities are less likely to form informal developmental relationships and/or to receive developmental experiences (Sander 2006; Wilkins and Gulati 1996). In particular, minorities are less likely than whites to form a developmental relationship with a white mentor (García-López 2008), and relationships with white mentors provide improved opportunities for advancement (Elliott and Smith 2004). When minorities do forge cross-race developmental relationships with white mentors, they receive less guidance and support than those in same-race relationships (Cox and Nkomo 1991).

Developmental relationships and experiences are vitally important for the cultivation of needed capabilities and resources (Thomas and Gabarro 1999). Whereas formal education imparts abstract principles and general analytical skills, the more practical forms of knowledge and skills that are essential for effective functioning are typically acquired in the workplace itself (Schleef 2006). Pivotal to the idea of mentoring is the claim that mentors provide channels for upward mobility and support to their protégés' careers (Ragins 1997). Mentors serve as advisors, teachers, exemplars, and career advocates (McManus 2005). Thus, over time, differential access to developmental opportunities is likely to produce an observable gap in technical, cultural, and cognitive resources between whites and minorities, even if they entered employment with similar levels of these resources. Indeed, there is evidence that less extensive and effective developmental experiences explain a portion of the racial gap in upward organizational mobility (R. Smith 2005).

The Role of Organizations' Developmental Practices and Cultural Values

Characteristics of jobs, workplaces, firms, and organizational environments moderate the impact of individual and interactional processes by constraining or enabling their operation (Reskin 2003). Here, we focus on organizational employment practices and cultural values relating to the professional development of employees prior to promotion into management. Formal development practices can narrow differences in developmental experiences and the gaps that result in technical, cultural, and social resources by compensating for minorities' reduced access to more informal developmental relationships. Cultural values that encourage supportive and nurturing behavior toward junior employees may lead organizational leaders to offer informal training, mentoring, and developmental assignments more widely and not only to those junior employees who are perceived as future stars.

Formal developmental practices. Many organizations offer formal training programs to their junior professionals and aspiring managers.[1] Formal training programs are intended to ensure that all employees obtain the same baseline level of knowledge and skill, including firm-specific skills such as knowledge of organizational procedures and routines. Formal training programs can have substantial positive effects on employee performance as well as on job satisfaction and commitment (Saks 1996). We suspect that formal training programs are likely most successful at building technical and cognitive skills and are less effective at conveying culturally valued styles of communication or fostering social network ties to colleagues and clients. Still, to the extent that formal programs make training accessible to all junior employees, they should serve to reduce any skill and productivity gap that might otherwise exist between minorities and whites and improve minorities' chances for promotion into management.

Organizations may also offer formal mentoring programs that match new employees to more senior colleagues (Blake-Beard 2001). A formal mentoring program ensures that each junior employee is assigned a contact for guidance. Of course, the benefits of formal mentoring are likely to be weaker than those of informal mentoring relationships, which develop spontaneously and typically last longer than formal relationships. Indeed, in a quantitative meta-analytic review, Underhill (2006) reveals that informal mentoring produces larger and more significant effects on career outcomes than formal mentoring. Nonetheless, formal mentoring programs have generally been found to be satisfying to employees and offer such benefits as learning, coaching, psychosocial support (Eby and Lockwood 2004), development of self-confidence and professional direction (Wanberg, Kammeyer-Mueller, and Marchese 2006), and opportunities for career progress (Kay, Hagan, and Parker 2009). Formal mentoring programs may be particularly beneficial to racial and ethnic minorities, who might otherwise have difficulty gaining access to mentoring (McManus 2005). Indeed, research suggests extensive benefits of formal mentoring programs for racial minorities (Ortiz-Walters and Gilson 2005), and at least one study has found that formal mentoring programs are positively associated with the representation of African Americans among managers (Kalev, Dobbin, and Kelly 2006).

Another important organizational employment practice is the length of the expected or typical probationary period leading up to promotion. The duration of time until promotion decisions could have either positive or negative consequences for minorities. On one hand, a longer track until promotion could aid minorities by affording them the time to overcome conscious or unconscious employer bias through repeated strong performances. Research suggests that minority corporate managers who attain the executive level often take longer to achieve promotion than their white colleagues (Thomas and Gabarro 1999). On the other hand, a longer time until promotion could increase the impact of processes of cumulative advantage and disadvantage. If organizational decision-makers disproportionately select whites for informal training, mentoring, and developmental assignments, whites are likely to gain greater skills, further solidifying the impression that they are more competent and better suited for positions of responsibility and increasing their advantage in the next round of selection. A longer expected period until promotion could worsen minorities' disadvantage by allowing this cycle to repeat.

Cultural values. In addition to formal structures and practices, organizational culture has an important influence on employee behavior (Wallace and Leicht 2004). We understand "organizational culture" to encompass the beliefs, values, and norms that are widely shared or acknowledged within an organization (Trice and Beyer 1993). Here we consider three aspects of organizational culture: a commitment to the professional development of junior employees, a norm of giving substantial responsibility to employees at early stages in their careers, and an emphasis on collegiality.

Some organizations are characterized by the value they place on the internal development of junior employees. In these organizations, training, mentoring, and sponsorship are understood as professional obligations of the firm (McManus 2005). Senior employees are expected to take on responsibility for the formation of less experienced employees through mentoring and sponsorship, as a service to the firm rather than for the purpose of enhancing their own status or political clout. Like a longer partnership track, a cultural commitment to professional development could be either beneficial or detrimental to the advancement of minorities. Such an atmosphere could be beneficial if it leads senior employees and decision-makers to offer informal mentoring and developmental experiences more inclusively and consistently to junior employees of all races and ethnicities. If so, a cultural emphasis on professional development would increase the probability that whites and minorities receive similar developmental experiences, which should in turn reduce the disparity in their prospects for promotions into management. Consistent with this reasoning, at least one study has found that an organizational emphasis on the internal development of employees is positively associated with the presence of African Americans among managers (Fields, Goodman, and Blum 2005). In contrast, a cultural commitment to professional development could be detrimental to minorities if senior employees respond by focusing their developmental efforts along the lines of homophily toward junior employees who are socially similar to themselves. In that case, since most senior employees in major organizations are white, this cultural value would only aggravate the disadvantage that minorities face in gaining access to developmental experiences.

The nature and direction of the effect may depend on organizational size. A commitment to professional development of junior employees in general may more easily translate into particularistic ties based on homophily in smaller organizations. In smaller organizations, where there are relatively few junior employees, it is easier for potential mentors to justify their choice of socially similar protégés by pointing to their individual strengths and apparently greater promise. In larger organizations, which are usually both more bureaucratic and more visible within their organizational fields than smaller organizations, a cultural commitment to professional development may more readily take on an inclusive tone and be viewed as a policy that applies to all. Some research suggests that in the case of gender, larger bureaucratic organizations may be more inclusive when it comes to career development and promotion of women (Hagan et al. 1991).

The effect of a cultural value on fostering professional development could also depend on the representation of minorities among junior employees. It may be easier for potential mentors, who are predominantly white in most organizations, to maintain an inclusive, even-handed commitment to the professional growth of all junior employees when there are relatively few minorities among them. As the minority presence among junior employees grows, white senior employees and organizational leaders may feel increasingly uncomfortable and may gravitate—consciously or unconsciously—more strongly toward white protégés.

A second important aspect of organizational culture is the extent to which an organization has established norms for providing employees with a significant amount of responsibility early in their careers, as opposed to keeping them under close supervision during a lengthy period of gradual experimentation and skill-building. Once again, it is possible to foresee both advantages and disadvantages for minorities. On one hand, early responsibility for strategy formulation and relationships with major clients or customers is highly desirable to the career advancement of junior employees who are aiming for management. Because minority employees may be more likely to find themselves confined to support roles and "back office" tasks than their white counterparts (Sander 2006), a norm of giving early responsibility may be especially valuable for them. On the other hand, early responsibility could operate as a screening device for those who already have the necessary skills (or are quickly able to acquire them on their own) and "weed out" the rest. Early responsibility would then signal a "sink or swim" philosophy that places the burden of responsibility for skill development on junior employees, rather than on the firm. In that case, a norm of early responsibility could intensify the disadvantage of minorities, whose early missteps are likely to be perceived as evidence confirming weaker abilities.

A third significant dimension of organizational culture is the value placed on collegiality. By "collegiality," we understand both a positive social atmosphere of trust and a relatively nonhierarchical, team-based, decentralized way of organizing work and managing the firm (Greenwood and Empson 2003). Under the conditions of uncertainty that typically surround managerial work, people feel more comfortable trusting and relying on others who are socially similar to themselves; this in turn leads to the "homosocial reproduction" of management (Kanter 1977). A sustained cultural emphasis on collegiality—rather than on competition or hierarchy—may help to overcome these tendencies on the part of organizational decision-makers. Rather than reinforcing group boundaries along racial lines, a culture of collegiality could help employees of all races to redefine the "in-group" as inclusive of all members of the organization. Thus, even in the absence of a cultural commitment to professional development, an atmosphere of collegiality could ensure that developmental opportunities are more accessible to minorities.

Research Setting and Data

We apply the ideas discussed above to the case of large law firms that serve corporate clients. Most large firms now have multiple offices in major cities throughout the United States and abroad. Although major strategic directions are determined centrally, individual offices often maintain somewhat different policies, practices, and cultures. Law firms are typically organized as partnerships. The partners are both the owners and the managers of the firm. Partners typically supervise small teams of lawyers that are assembled for a given case or transaction. Executive groups or committees oversee the day-to-day management of the office and the firm as a whole, but the entire partnership usually must approve major changes in firm strategy or structure.

Large firms also employ junior lawyers as "associates" during a "partnership track" period that typically lasts between 6 and 10 years. At the end of this period, the firm's partners consider the members of an associate class for promotion to partnership (Galanter and Palay 1991). Firms traditionally maintained an "up-or-out" policy, so that associates who were "passed over" for partnership were expected to leave the firm; but in recent years many firms have begun to employ some experienced lawyers in non-partnership-track positions on a permanent basis (Gorman 1999). As of 2005, minorities represented 8.9 percent of lawyers and 4.9 percent of partners in the average major law firm office (Gorman and Kay 2010). The corresponding figures for specific groups were as follows: African Americans, 2.5 percent of lawyers and 1.6 percent of partners; Latinos, 2.3 percent of lawyers and 1.6 percent of partners; Asian Americans, 4.1 percent of lawyers and 1.7 percent of partners.

In this study, we analyze data on more than 1,300 law firm offices across the United States from the 2005–2006 edition of the *National Directory of Legal Employers* (National Association for Law Placement 2005) compiled by the National Association for Law Placement (NALP), a nonprofit organization established to provide information about employment to law schools and their students. The NALP conducts an annual survey of all law firms that carry out on-campus recruiting at law schools, asking for both quantitative and qualitative information, and compiles the results in annual editions of the *NALP Directory*. Firms report information as of February 1 of the publication year. Our unit of analysis is the office, not the entire firm. In most cases, law firms with multiple offices provide information pertaining to each office separately; the few firms that did not provide office-specific information were eliminated from our sample. We also removed from the sample any nonfirm employers (e.g., government agencies or public-interest law offices), offices located outside the United States, and offices with fewer than five lawyers. The final sample includes 1,394 offices.

Measures

Dependent variables. In the analyses that follow, we model the proportion of partners who belong to any of three racial or ethnic minority groups: African American, Latino, and Asian American. We also examine the proportions of partners who are members of each group separately. We follow previous research (Gorman 2005; Kalev 2009; Reskin and McBrier 2000) in transforming these proportions into their log odds to avoid predicted proportions below zero and above one, and because the functional form is likely to provide a better fit to the data.

Independent variables. The first set of independent variables captures formal professional development practices. Binary variables (coded 0–1) indicate whether an office offers a *formal training program* or a *formal mentoring program*. The typical period of time from entry to promotion, or *partnership track length*, is measured in years (ranging from four to nine and one-half years).

Measures of organizational culture were obtained from the narrative statements that firm offices provide in conjunction with their NALP survey responses.[2] These narrative statements were coded by three student research assistants. An initial subsample of fifty cases was coded by all three research assistants, resulting in high intercoder reliabilities. Before the assistants proceeded with additional coding, discrepancies in this subsample were discussed and resolved. Three binary variables (coded 0–1) measure whether the office's culture includes *a commitment to professional development, a norm of early and substantial responsibility*, and *an emphasis on collegiality*.

Control variables. The rate at which minorities are promoted to partnership depends on their presence among associates. *Minority group presence among associates* is measured by the proportion of associates who belong to the relevant group.

Various aspects of jobs and workplaces are also likely to influence the representation of minorities in managerial positions. Organizational size is a perennial subject of interest because it is closely associated with so many organizational processes. Larger, more visible organizations are also more susceptible to institutional pressures (Edelman 1990) that should operate to promote diversity. Size may also affect minority representation because it is closely associated with bureaucratization, which may help disadvantaged groups by establishing objective standards and procedures for employee evaluation (Baron et al. 2007). Organizational size is tapped by two measures: *office size* (the number of lawyers in the establishment as reported in the 2005–2006 *NALP Directory*) and whether the establishment's firm was included the 2005 *AmLaw 200* rankings published by *American Lawyer* magazine. Similar to the *Fortune 500* for corporations, this data source ranks the top 200 U.S. law firms by their gross revenues; because revenues are generated by lawyers' billable hours, revenues are highly correlated with firm size. To capture bureaucratization more directly, we also include a measure of whether an office is divided by *departments* (0 if no, 1 if yes).

If employers tend to place whites ahead of minorities in their "labor queues" for hiring and promotion (Alon 2004; Reskin and Roos 1990), then minorities' prospects depend on the number of available positions relative to the number of white candidates interested in filling those positions. Thus, characteristics that make jobs more attractive are likely to be negatively associated with the representation of minorities, presumably because they then face greater competition from whites (and, conversely, characteristics that make jobs less attractive are likely to be positively linked to minority presence). At least one study has found a negative relationship between salary level and minority presence among managers (Fields, Goodman, and Blum 2005). Although we do not have data for all cases on partner compensation, we do have a measure of the starting salary paid to associates. Associate and partner compensation are likely to be at least loosely linked. Because starting salaries vary across cities, we use the difference between an office's starting salary and the city mean.

We also include three structural characteristics that are likely to limit lawyers' opportunities for advancement, recognition, and self-actualization, thus making jobs less appealing to white competitors: leverage, a two-tier partnership, and branch office status (see Gorman and Kay 2010). *Leverage* is measured as the ratio of nonpartner lawyers to partners within the office. Higher leverage is associated with lower chances of making partner and, for those who do become partner, greater pressure to generate business to keep associates employed (but also greater profits in the event of success).[3] A dichotomous variable (coded 0–1) indicates the presence of a *two-tier partnership* including both traditional, equity-holding partners and salaried lawyers who bear the title of "partner" without its traditional ownership rights. Another dichotomous variable indicates whether the office is a *branch office* (0 if headquarters, 1 if branch office); lawyers in a firm's principal office are likely to have better prospects and perform more interesting work.

Finally, three dichotomous variables indicating *region of the United States* (Midwest, South, and West, with Northeast as the reference category) were included to tap geographical variation in racial and ethnic presence.

Results

Table 1 reports means, standard deviations, and ranges for the variables used in the analysis. In the average establishment, minorities represented 14 percent of associates and just 5 percent of partners. When we consider minority groups separately, we find African Americans made up 4 percent of associates and 1.6 percent of partners; Latinos, 3 percent of associates and 1.6 percent of partners; and Asian Americans, 7 percent of associates and 1.7 percent of partners. Thus, all three minority groups start out at different levels of representation in the lower ranks of firms but end up with a similar presence (1.6 to 1.7 percent) among partners. Formal training programs were more common (present in 39 percent of offices) than formal mentoring programs (less than 21 percent of offices offered these). A sizable share of establishments (41 percent) encouraged junior employees to take on significant responsibilities early, and the same percentage maintained a cultural value of fostering the professional development of junior employees. An emphasis on collegiality was present in only 22 percent of establishments.

The results of the multivariate regression analyses are presented in Tables 2 through 5. Huber-White standard errors are used because of likely violations of the assumptions that errors are independent and identically distributed.

TABLE 1
Descriptive Statistics for Variables Used in the Analysis

Variable	Mean	SD	Min.	Max.
Group presence among partners				
Proportion minority	.049	.089	0	1
Proportion African American	.016	.055	0	1
Proportion Latino	.016	.045	0	.455
Proportion Asian American	.017	.049	0	.583
Formal training program	.391	.488	0	1
Formal mentoring program	.205	.404	0	1
Partnership track length	7.66	.821	4	9.5
Cultural value on professional development	.406	.491	0	1
Cultural norm of early responsibility	.406	.491	0	1
Cultural value on collegiality	.450	.498	0	1
Group presence among associates				
Proportion minority	.138	.129	0	1
Proportion African American	.040	.062	0	1
Proportion Latino	.032	.064	0	.833
Proportion Asian American	.067	.093	0	1
Establishment size	81.604	86.042	5	809
AmLaw 200	.600	.490	0	1
Departments	.713	.453	0	1
Starting salary (difference from city mean)	−14.99	8,704.761	0	1
Two-tier partnership	.500	.500	0	1
Leverage	1.427	1.055	.133	12.333
Branch	.559	.497	0	1
Region Midwest	.149	.356	0	1
Region Northeast	.306	.461	0	1
Region South	.271	.445	0	1
Region West	.274	.446	0	1

All minorities. Table 2 presents the equations modeling the proportion of partners who belong to any of the three minority groups. Model 1 is a baseline model including only control variables. As expected, the proportion of minorities among associates has a strong positive effect on minority presence among partners. Surprisingly, establishment size has a negative effect. The coefficient on a firm's membership in the *AmLaw 200* is also negative, but the effect does not reach statistical significance. Also unexpected is the negative impact of departmentalization. As we anticipated, minority presence among partners is positively associated with leverage (the ratio of nonpartners to partners) and with status as a branch office, but a two-tier partnership has no significant effect. Geographically,

TABLE 2
Regressions of Log Odds of Proportion of Minorities among Partners on Selected
Organizational Characteristics

Variable	Model 1	Model 2	Model 3	Model 4
Professional development practices				
Formal training program		.008 (.058)	.012 (.058)	-.001 (.055)
Formal mentoring program		-.079 (.057)	-.081* (.056)	-.066 (.056)
Partnership track length		-.076*** (.033)	-.076*** (.033)	-.074*** (.032)
Cultural values and norms				
Cultural value on professional development		-.089** (.049)	-.092** (.049)	-.079** (.047)
Cultural value on professional development × office size			.001** (.001)	
Cultural value on professional development × group presence among associates				-1.059** (.508)
Cultural norm of early responsibility		-.089** (.046)	-.091** (.046)	-.092** (.045)
Cultural value on collegiality		.050 (.046)	.051 (.046)	.050 (.046)
Control variables				
Group presence among associates				
Proportion minority	2.632**** (.456)	2.703**** (.453)	2.716**** (.452)	2.639**** (.408)
Establishment size	-.002**** (.000)	-.002**** (.000)	-.002**** (.000)	-.002**** (.000)
AmLaw 200	-.059 (.063)	-.032 (.061)	-.032* (.061)	-.023* (.060)
Departments	-.167*** (.058)	-.141*** (.055)	-.136*** (.055)	-.151*** (.055)
Starting salary (difference from city mean)	.000 (.000)	.000 (.000)	.000 (.000)	.000 (.000)
Two-tier partnership	-.010 (.049)	-.005 (.053)	-.001 (.053)	-.002 (.053)
Leverage	.266**** (.028)	.278**** (.030)	.279**** (.030)	.276**** (.029)
Branch	.250**** (.071)	.290**** (.072)	.287**** (.073)	.295**** (.071)
Region Midwest[a]	.215*** (.068)	.195*** (.069)	.194*** (.069)	.196*** (.068)
Region South	.391**** (.059)	.337**** (.056)	.339**** (.056)	.339**** (.056)
Region West	.380**** (.060)	.344**** (.060)	.346**** (.060)	.351**** (.060)
Constant	-3.681**** (.100)	-3.113**** (.268)	-3.307**** (.267)	-2.784**** (.261)
R^2	.328	.358	.360	.362
N	1,384	1,353	1,353	1,353

NOTE: Standard errors appear in parentheses.
a. Comparison category is the Northeast region.
*p < .10. **p < .05. ***p < .01. ****p < .001.

minority representation is especially high in the West and South and lowest in the Northeast. These control variable effects do not change substantially across models, except that the coefficient on membership in the *AmLaw 200* becomes

TABLE 3
Regressions of Log Odds of Proportion of African Americans among Partners on Selected Organizational Characteristics

Variable	Model 1	Model 2	Model 3	Model 4
Professional development practices				
Formal training program		-.005 (.046)	.001 (.046)	-.024 (.044)
Formal mentoring program		.015 (.046)	.013 (.045)	.021 (.045)
Partnership track length		-.010 (.028)	-.010 (.028)	-.010 (.027)
Cultural values and norms				
Cultural value on professional development		-.123*** (.042)	-.129*** (.043)	-.119*** (.042)
Cultural value on professional development × office size			.001** (.001)	
Cultural value on professional development × group presence among associates				-2.983** (1.281)
Cultural norm of early responsibility		-.057* (.038)	-.060* (.038)	-.051* (.038)
Cultural value on collegiality		.029 (.040)	.031 (.041)	.020 (.040)
Control variables				
Group presence among associates				
Proportion African American	2.717*** (1.053)	2.875*** (1.037)	2.882*** (1.032)	2.425*** (.786)
Establishment size	-.005**** (.001)	-.005**** (.001)	-.005**** (.001)	-.005**** (.001)
AmLaw 200	.012 (.053)	.024 (.052)	.024 (.053)	.041 (.050)
Departments	-.182*** (.054)	-.158**** (.049)	-.149**** (.050)	-.163**** (.048)
Starting salary (difference from city mean)	.000 (.000)	.000 (.000)	.000 (.000)	.000 (.000)
Two-tier partnership	-.016 (.043)	.011 (.046)	.018 (.046)	.019 (.046)
Leverage	.332**** (.029)	.338**** (.030)	.338**** (.030)	.340**** (.028)
Branch	.242**** (.064)	.286**** (.068)	.282**** (.068)	.273**** (.068)
Region Midwest[a]	.179*** (.062)	.172*** (.063)	.170*** (.064)	.175*** (.063)
Region South	.226**** (.056)	.183**** (.051)	.187**** (.051)	.188**** (.051)
Region West	.103* (.053)	.097* (.056)	.102* (.056)	.094* (.056)
Constant	-3.698**** (.106)	-3.646**** (.244)	-4.126**** (.244)	-3.585**** (.234)
R^2	.428	.468	.473	.475
N	1,384	1,353	1,353	1,353

NOTE: Standard errors appear in parentheses.

a. Comparison category is the Northeast region.

*$p < .10$. **$p < .05$. ***$p < .01$. ****$p < .001$.

TABLE 4
Regressions of Log Odds of Proportion of Latinos among Partners on Selected Organizational Characteristics

Variable	Model 1	Model 2	Model 3	Model 4
Professional development practices				
Formal training program		-.047 (.048)	-.041 (.048)	-.048 (.048)
Formal mentoring program		-.099** (.051)	-.101** (.050)	-.101** (.050)
Partnership track length		-.066*** (.027)	-.065*** (.027)	-.066*** (.027)
Cultural values and norms				
Cultural value on professional development		-.058* (.041)	-.064* (.043)	-.059* (.041)
Cultural value on professional development × office size			.001** (.001)	
Cultural value on professional development × group presence among associates				.444 (.826)
Cultural norm of early responsibility		-.001 (.042)	-.002 (.042)	-.003 (.042)
Cultural value on collegiality		.012 (.040)	.014 (.041)	.011 (.041)
Control variables				
Group presence among associates				
Proportion Latino	3.251**** (.489)	3.360**** (.486)	3.393**** (.482)	3.320**** (.501)
Establishment size	-.006**** (.001)	-.006**** (.001)	-.006**** (.001)	-.006**** (.001)
AmLaw 200	-.064 (.058)	-.039 (.058)	.039 (.057)	-.038 (.058)
Departments	-.162*** (.043)	-.163*** (.043)	-.154*** (.044)	-.164*** (.044)
Starting salary (difference from city mean)	.000 (.000)	.000 (.000)	.000 (.000)	.000 (.000)
Two-tier partnership	-.047 (.041)	-.051 (.044)	-.045 (.044)	-.052 (.044)
Leverage	.384**** (.030)	.386**** (.031)	.387**** (.032)	.386**** (.032)
Branch	.323**** (.067)	.363**** (.069)	.360**** (.068)	.363**** (.069)
Region Midwest[a]	.111** (.058)	.095 (.059)	.093 (.059)	.095 (.059)
Region South	.279**** (.048)	.261**** (.050)	.264**** (.050)	.261**** (.050)
Region West	.245**** (.048)	.222**** (.050)	.225**** (.050)	.222**** (.050)
Constant	-3.807**** (.094)	-3.301**** (.217)	-3.809**** (.217)	-3.215**** (.218)
R^2	.565	.571	.575	.572
N	1,384	1,353	1,353	1,353

NOTE: Standard errors appear in parentheses.
a. Comparison category is the Northeast region.
°$p < .10.$ °°$p < .05.$ °°°$p < .01.$ °°°°$p < .001.$

TABLE 5

Regressions of Log Odds of Proportion of Asian Americans among Partners on Selected Organizational Characteristics

Variable	Model 1	Model 2	Model 3	Model 4
Professional development practices				
Formal training program		-.077** (.043)	-.073** (.043)	-.080** (.043)
Formal mentoring program		-.043 (.046)	-.044 (.046)	-.034 (.047)
Partnership track length		-.074*** (.026)	-.074*** (.026)	-.075*** (.026)
Cultural values and norms				
Cultural value on professional development		-.006 (.045)	-.010 (.045)	-.002 (.045)
Cultural value on professional development × office size			.001* (.001)	
Cultural value on professional development × group presence among associates				-1.181** (.513)
Cultural norm of early responsibility		-.094** (.037)	-.096*** (.037)	-.092*** (.037)
Cultural value on collegiality		.040 (.037)	.041 (.037)	.039 (.037)
Control variables				
Group presence among associates				
Proportion Asian American	1.625**** (.400)	1.582**** (.409)	1.597**** (.407)	1.570**** (.363)
Establishment size	-.006**** (.001)	-.006**** (.001)	-.005**** (.001)	-.005**** (.001)
AmLaw 200	-.094* (.054)	-.072 (.055)	.072 (.054)	-.068 (.054)
Departments	-.177**** (.048)	-.179**** (.047)	-.173**** (.048)	-.192**** (.048)
Starting salary (difference from city mean)	.000 (.000)	.000 (.000)	.000 (.000)	.000 (.000)
Two-tier partnership	-.081** (.041)	-.092* (.046)	-.088* (.046)	-.094** (.046)
Leverage	.337**** (.028)	.341**** (.029)	.341**** (.029)	.337**** (.029)
Branch	.345**** (.068)	.388**** (.068)	.386**** (.068)	.397**** (.068)
Region Midwest[a]	.055** (.058)	.034 (.059)	.034 (.059)	.036 (.058)
Region South	.027 (.047)	-.009 (.047)	-.005 (.047)	-.009 (.046)
Region West	.330**** (.052)	.297**** (.053)	.299**** (.052)	.300**** (.052)
Constant	-3.643**** (.093)	-3.047**** (.216)	-3.499**** (.212)	-2.927**** (.209)
R^2	.532	.538	.539	.541
N	1,384	1,353	1,353	1,353

NOTE: Standard errors appear in parentheses.
a.Comparison category is the Northeast region.
*$p < .10$. **$p < .05$. ***$p < .01$. ****$p < .001$.

marginally significant ($p < .10$) when interaction terms are included in models 3 and 4.

Model 2 introduces the professional development variables. Neither formal training programs nor formal mentoring programs are significantly associated with overall minority presence among partners. Longer partnership tracks reduce minority representation. Interestingly, a cultural value of fostering the professional development of junior employees has a significant negative effect, consistent with our second alternative conjecture about the role of this variable. A cultural norm of encouraging early responsibility is also negatively linked to minority presence among partners, in line with our second alternative argument. A cultural emphasis on collegiality is not significantly associated with the proportion of minority partners.

In model 3, we add an interaction between a cultural commitment to professional development and office size. Model 4 substitutes an interaction between a cultural emphasis on professional development and minority presence among associates. Because both continuous variables were centered before the multiplicative interaction terms were created, the coefficients on the cultural value variable reflect its effect when office size (in model 3) and proportion of minorities among associates (in model 4) are at their means. In model 3, as we anticipated, the coefficient on the interaction with office size is positive and significant, indicating that the negative effect of a cultural value on fostering professional development is weaker in larger offices.[4] Conversely, the negative effect of organizational size is only half as strong in offices with a stronger cultural commitment to professional development. The coefficient on the formal mentoring program indicator also becomes marginally significant ($p < .10$) and negative in this model.

In model 4, also as expected, the coefficient on the interaction with minority group presence among associates is negative, indicating that the negative impact of a cultural value on fostering professional development is especially strong when minorities hold a greater share of associate positions. At the same time, the positive effect of high representation of minorities among the associate ranks is diminished when an organizational culture places greater emphasis on professional development.

Specific minority groups. Table 3 presents results for African American partners. While the pattern of results is similar to those for all minorities jointly, a few differences are worth noting. Partnership track length is not significantly associated with African American presence among partners, whereas it was for minorities overall. The coefficient on a cultural emphasis on professional development is more negative for African Americans than it is for all minorities together, and the coefficient on the interaction between this cultural value and group presence among associates is nearly three times as large in absolute value for African Americans as it is for minorities overall. Finally, the negative impact of a norm of early responsibility is only marginally significant for African Americans.

Results for Latinos are reported in Table 4. In contrast to the results for all minorities together, formal mentoring programs are significantly negatively associated with Latino representation among partners. Interestingly, the negative impact of a cultural value on professional development is only marginally significant for Latinos ($p < .10$), and the interaction between this cultural value and group presence among associates is not statistically significant here. A norm of early responsibility also has no significant effect.

Finally, Table 5 presents results for Asian Americans. Relative to the results for all minorities together, Asian Americans are distinctive in that the presence of a formal training program is negatively associated with their representation among partners. Intriguingly, a cultural emphasis on professional development has no significant impact for Asian Americans. However, similar to African Americans but unlike Latinos, the interaction between this cultural value and group presence among associates is negative, indicating that the effect of this cultural value becomes more negative as the Asian American share of associate positions increases. Finally, it is clear that Asian Americans are primarily responsible for the negative impact of norms of early responsibility that we saw for all minorities together in Table 2.

There is notable consistency across the different racial groups when we examine the control variables. The proportions of all three groups among partners increase with their group's current representation among associates. Larger offices and establishments with departments have negative effects on the proportions of all three racial groups among firm partners. Both leverage and status as a branch office are positively associated with presence among partners for all three racial groups. Only the role of a two-tier partnership varies: it is negatively linked to representation among partners for Asian Americans but not for the other two groups.

Discussion and Conclusion

Organizations that hope to fill a substantial number of their management positions through internal promotion have an interest in the growth and development of their nonmanagement employees. Such organizations often maintain both formal practices and cultural values intended to bolster nonmanagement employees' technical skills, interpersonal competencies, and social connections. Although these practices and values are not specifically aimed at fostering diversity, it is intuitively appealing to think that minority employees might derive particular benefit from them. Whites are likely to have better access to informal developmental opportunities (Kay, Hagan, and Parker 2009), so organizational efforts to make developmental experiences uniformly available should help to "level the playing field."

Our findings suggest that this intuitive expectation is misguided. Strikingly, none of the practices or cultural characteristics considered was positively associated with the presence of minorities among partners—the management tier of large law firms. All of them had either negative effects or no effects.

Perhaps the most notable finding is that an organizational culture of fostering and taking responsibility for employees' professional development works to *decrease* the proportions of minorities in management. Yet as institutional theorists have reminded us (Meyer and Rowan 1977), there is often a "loose coupling" between organizations' formal pronouncements and their implementation. A firm may articulate and celebrate a cultural commitment to the growth and development of employees, but in practice that culture may not be fully inclusive. Indeed, senior managers who receive cultural encouragement to nurture the progress of nonmanagement juniors may simply direct their attention even more vigorously to protégés who are socially similar to themselves. If this interpretation is correct, it may help to explain the unanticipated finding that the negative effect of a cultural emphasis on professional development is strongest for African Americans, marginal for Latinos, and nonsignificant for Asian Americans. It is possible that white senior managers feel the least social dissimilarity and discomfort with Asian American protégés, somewhat more with Latinos, and considerably more with African Americans.

Loosening long-standing patterns of occupational segregation will require that organizations move beyond well-intended cultures of professional development and collegiality to implement programs that are fully inclusive of racial minorities in their day-to-day reality. An important policy implication of our findings is that mentoring and training programs within organizations need to be purposely designed with minorities in mind and monitored on an ongoing basis to ensure inclusivity as well as assessed in terms of outcomes for all employees. Interestingly, we found that both organizational size and the representation of minorities among nonmanagement employees moderate the impact of a cultural emphasis on professional development. In the case of organizational size, the interaction is positive, so that the negative effect of a cultural emphasis on professional development becomes weaker as organizational size increases. Although additional research is needed, it is possible that larger organizations are better able to translate their cultural values into actual behavior on the part of senior managers. Furthermore, in larger organizations, mentors and sponsors may be more aware of the organizational context surrounding them and more likely to understand themselves as enacting organizational roles, rather than merely forming personal bonds with protégés. It is also worth noting that, conversely, a cultural value on professional development lessens the negative effect of organizational size. The decline in the proportion of minority partners as office size increases hints that once a firm has demonstrated its political and institutional legitimacy by including a certain number of minorities in its management ranks, further increases in minority presence are seen as unnecessary, regardless of size. A cultural emphasis on professional development may exert pressure to lessen this sort of tokenism.

The interaction between a cultural commitment to professional development and group presence at lower levels is negative, so that the negative effect becomes stronger as a greater share of nonmanagement positions are filled by minorities. More research is needed, but it seems that as minority group presence among nonmanagement employees increases, organizations have increasing difficulty in implementing this cultural commitment in an even-handed way. Sociologists have long argued that racial and ethnic prejudice and discrimination increase as a minority group increases in size and is perceived to pose a greater threat to the dominant group (Blalock 1967). Consistent with this idea, it may be that, as minority presence among nonmanagement employees grows, white senior managers increasingly respond to their firm's cultural mandate by concentrating their mentoring and sponsorship efforts toward white protégés.

Some research suggests that racial minorities are disadvantaged by a lack of opportunity to take on significant responsibility early in their careers (Sander 2006). Because they are asked to prove their competence repeatedly before being trusted with challenging tasks, they have fewer opportunities to gain visibility and take longer to advance than their white counterparts (Thomas and Gabarro 1999). However, early responsibility can be a double-edged sword for minority employees: if they are assigned responsibility and make mistakes, those mistakes are likely to be viewed much more negatively—and more conclusively attributed to weak ability—than the comparable missteps of whites. Our finding that a norm of early responsibility is negatively associated with minority representation at the partner level suggests that the second process outweighs the first.

Formal practices intended to aid nonmanagement employees in building and demonstrating skills and resources also fail to benefit minorities. One might expect that formal training and mentoring programs would help by offsetting minorities' likely disadvantage in access to informal developmental opportunities. Yet neither type of program has a positive effect on minority representation among partners. Although formal training programs may provide certain important information and limited opportunities to practice new skills, they likely fall far short of imparting the full range of technical and interpersonal skills that are vital to being perceived as having managerial potential—let alone the social connections and alliances that are essential for success. Formal mentoring programs, as well, are likely too limited in their effects to make a real difference. Research suggests that formal mentoring arrangements tend to be shorter in duration and less close than informal mentoring and focused primarily on technical skills and procedures rather than on career planning, advice on office politics, emotional support, and reputation building (Kay, Hagan and Parker 2009; Ragins and Cotton 1999). In formal mentoring programs, where matches are assigned rather than arising from interpersonal compatibility, mentors may lack motivation to act on behalf of their associates. Studies have documented the challenges of formal mentoring programs, including unmet expectations (on the part of associates), lack of attraction for identification, failure to forge a postprogram relationship, scheduling difficulties, mentor neglect, and feelings of personal inadequacy (by mentors) (Blake-Beard 2001; Eby and Lockwood 2004). Thus, while formal training and mentoring programs may be better than nothing, they typically yield more modest career outcomes than informal arrangements (Underhill 2006). More difficult to understand are the unanticipated negative effects of formal training programs for Asian Americans and of formal mentoring programs for Latinos.

The length of the typical or expected time until promotion into management—in law firms, the partnership track—also plays a role in shaping racial minorities' representation among managers. Longer "probationary" periods of this sort are sometimes thought to be beneficial to employees who face a disadvantage of some kind. For example, "mommy tracks" in corporations and paused tenure clocks in universities are meant to allow parents additional time to establish a strong record of performance. Moreover, there is evidence that minorities often require more time than whites to attain promotion (Thomas and Gabarro 1999). However, if the same lengthened period is made available to employees who are *not* disadvantaged—in this case, whites—the extended period may worsen minorities' promotion prospects by enabling repeated cycles of cumulative advantage for whites and cumulative disadvantage for minorities. As a result, by the time the normative period to promotion expires, minority employees may, on average, have acquired fewer important skills than their white counterparts, thus limiting their prospects even if the promotion process is entirely fair. Moreover, minority employees, recognizing the compounding effects of being repeatedly passed over for career development experiences, are less likely than whites to feel committed to a future with the firm and more likely to leave in search of better opportunities elsewhere.

These interpretations of our results are necessarily tentative, because our data are subject to several important limitations. First, we lack information on processes at the individual and interactional levels, such as characteristics of and ties between minority partners, their white peers, and the decision-makers who originally chose to admit them to the partnership. Second, our data are cross-sectional, so we are unable to determine causal order with certainty. However, the reverse causal order does not seem plausible; it is hard to see why a greater minority presence among partners would make firms less likely to establish practices or uphold values aimed at the internal growth and development of nonmanagement employees. Finally, we have information only on "stocks" and not on "flows." In other words, we have data on the proportions of partners who were members of various minority groups at a given point in time, but we lack information on the number of minorities and whites entering the partnership through promotion or external hiring and the number leaving the partnership through retirement or departure.

However, processes of internal upward mobility remain important for increasing racial and ethnic diversity and equality among managers. Broadly speaking, our findings align with the view that the formalization of human resources policies furthers these ends by checking bias and introducing procedural fairness (Reskin 2000). Although formal developmental practices do little to help minorities, our findings suggest that informal, cultural approaches to professional development actively hurt them. No matter how well intentioned such approaches may be, day-to-day behavior in organizations is only loosely coupled with organizational ideals, and policies that are intended to be even-handed may not be implemented in that fashion. Hearing organizational encouragement to provide mentoring and support, senior managers may simply direct their efforts more energetically to aiding protégés who are socially similar to themselves.

Notes

1. By the term "formal training program," we intend to refer to relatively intensive and sustained classroom-style sessions—not brief orientation sessions or occasional workshops—in which managers and senior colleagues present information and attempt to impart skills.

2. In most cases, offices provide statements independently, but a few firms supply the same statement for all offices.

3. Leverage could also have a negative influence on minority presence among managers, because it is associated with a steeper hierarchical structure and fewer managerial positions to fill. Thus, leverage could mean that employers find it easier to meet their staffing needs with whites and are not pushed to go deeper into their "labor queues."

4. The effect does not actually become positive until office size reaches 174, nearly the 90th percentile of the office size distribution in our sample.

References

Alon, Sigal. 2004. The gender stratification of employment hardship: Queuing, opportunity structure and economic cycles. *Research in Social Stratification and Mobility* 20:115–43.

Baron, James N., Michael T. Hannan, Greta Hsu, and Özgecan Koçak. 2007. In the company of women: Gender inequality and the logic of bureaucracy in start-up firms. *Work and Occupations* 34:35–66.

Bell, Ella, and Stella Nkomo. 2001. *Our separate ways: Black and white women and the struggle for professional identity.* Boston, MA: Harvard Business School Press.

Blake-Beard, Stacy D. 2001. Taking a hard look at formal mentoring programs: A consideration of potential challenges facing women. *Journal of Management Development* 20 (4): 331–45.

Blalock, Hubert M. 1967. *Toward a theory of minority-group relations.* New York, NY: John Wiley.

Cohen, Philip N., and Matt L. Huffman. 2007. Black under-representation in management across U.S. labor markets. *The Annals of the American Academy of Political and Social Science* 609:181–99.

Cox, Taylor H., and Stella M. Nkomo. 1991. A race and gender-group analysis of the early career experience of MBAs. *Work and Occupations* 18:431–46.

DiTomaso, Nancy, Corinne Post, D. Randall Smith, George Farris, and Rene Cordero. 2007. Effects of structural position on allocation and evaluation decisions for scientists and engineers in industrial R&D. *Administrative Science Quarterly* 52:175–207.

Eby, Lillian T., and Angie Lockwood. 2004. Protégés' and mentors' reactions to participating in formal mentoring programs: A qualitative investigation. *Journal of Vocational Behavior* 67:619–36.

Edelman, Lauren B. 1990. Legal environments and organizational governance: The expansion of due process in the workplace. *American Journal of Sociology* 97:1531–76.

Elliott, James, and Ryan Smith. 2004. Race, gender, and workplace power. *American Sociological Review* 69:365–86.

Fields, Dail L., Jodi S. Goodman, and Terry C. Blum. 2005. Human resource dependence and organizational demography: A study of minority employment in private sector companies. *Journal of Management* 31:167–85.

Foschi, Martha. 2009. Gender, performance level, and competence standards in task groups. *Social Science Research* 33:447–57.

Galanter, Marc, and Thomas Palay. 1991. *Tournament of lawyers: The transformation of the big law firms.* Chicago, IL: University of Chicago Press.

García-López, Gladys. 2008. "Nunca te toman en cuenta [They never take you into account]": The challenges of inclusion and strategies for success of Chicana attorneys. *Gender & Society* 22 (5): 590–612.

Gorman, Elizabeth H. 1999. Moving away from "up or out": Determinants of permanent employment in law firms. *Law & Society Review* 33 (3): 637–66.

Gorman, Elizabeth H. 2005. Gender stereotypes, same-gender preferences, and organizational variation in the hiring of women: Evidence from law firms. *American Sociological Review* 70:702–28.

Gorman, Elizabeth H., and Fiona M. Kay. 2010. Racial and ethnic minority representation in large U.S. law firms. *Studies in Law, Politics, and Society* 52:211–38.

Greenwood, Royston, and Laura Empson. 2003. The professional partnership: Relic or exemplary form of governance? *Organizational Studies* 24 (6): 909–34.

Hagan, John, Marjorie Zatz, Bruce Arnold, and Fiona Kay. 1991. Cultural capital, gender and the structural transformation of legal practice. *Law & Society Review* 25 (2): 239–62.

Kalev, Alexandra. 2009. Cracking the glass cages? Restructuring and ascriptive inequality at work. *American Journal of Sociology* 114:1591–1643.

Kalev, Alexandra, Frank Dobbin, and Erin Kelly. 2006. Best practices or best guesses? Assessing the efficacy of corporate affirmative action and diversity policies. *American Sociological Review* 71:589–617.

Kanter, Rosabeth Moss. 1977. *Men and women of the corporation.* New York, NY: Basic Books.

Kay, Fiona M., John Hagan, and Patricia Parker. 2009. Principals in practice: The importance of mentorship in the early stages of career development. *Law & Policy* 31 (1): 69–110.

McGuire, Gail M. 2000. Gender, race, ethnicity, and networks: The factors affecting the status of employees' network members. *Work and Occupations* 27:501–23.

McManus, Elizabeth K. 2005. Intimidation and the culture of avoidance: Gender issues and mentoring in law firm practice. *Fordham Urban Law Review* 33:217–31.

Meyer, John, and Brian Rowan. 1977. Institutionalized organizations: Formal structure as myth and ceremony. *American Journal of Sociology* 83:340–63.

Miller, Will, Brinck Kerr, and Margaret Reid. 2010. Descriptive representation by gender and race/ethnicity in municipal bureaucracies: Change in U.S. multiethnic cities, 1987–2001. *Journal of Women, Politics & Policy* 31:217–42.

National Association for Law Placement. 2005. *Directory of Legal Employers - 2005-2006.* Washington, DC: National Association for Law Placement.

Nee, Victor, and Jimy Sanders. 2001. Understanding the diversity of immigrant incorporation: A forms-of-capital model. *Ethnic and Racial Studies* 24 (3): 386–411.

Ortiz-Walters, Rowena, and Lucy L. Gilson. 2005. Mentoring in academia: An examination of the experiences of protégés of color. *Journal of Vocational Behavior* 67:459–75.

Ragins, Belle Rose. 1997. Antecedents of diversified mentoring relationships. *Journal of Vocational Behavior* 51:90–109.

Ragins, Belle Rose, and John L. Cotton. 1999. Mentor functions and outcomes: A comparison of men and women in formal and informal mentoring relationships. *Journal of Applied Psychology* 84:529–50.

Reskin, Barbara F. 2000. The proximate causes of employment discrimination. *Contemporary Sociology* 29:319–28.

Reskin, Barbara F. 2001. Employment discrimination and its remedies. In *Sourcebook of labor markets: Evolving structures and processes,* eds. Ivar Berg and Arne Kalleberg, 567–99. New York, NY: Kluwer Academic/Plenum.

Reskin, Barbara F. 2003. Including mechanisms in our models of ascriptive inequality. *American Sociological Review* 68:1–21.

Reskin, Barbara F., and Debra B. McBrier. 2000. Why not ascription? Organizations' employment of male and female managers. *American Sociological Review* 65:210–33.

Reskin, Barbara F., and Patricia Roos. 1990. *Job queues, gender queues: Explaining women's inroads into male occupations.* Philadelphia, PA: Temple University Press.

Saks, Alan M. 1996. The relationship between the amount and helpfulness of entry training and work outcomes. *Human Relations* 49 (4): 429–51.

Sander, Richard. 2006. The racial paradox of the corporate law firm. *North Carolina Law Review* 84:1755–822.

Schleef, Debra. 2006. *Managing elites: Professional socialization in law and business schools.* Lanham, MD: Rowman & Littlefield.

Skaggs, Sheryl. 2009. Legal-political pressures and African American access to managerial jobs. *American Sociological Review* 74:225–44.

Smith, Ryan A. 2005. Do the determinants of promotion differ for white men versus women and minorities? An exploration of intersectionalism through sponsored and contest mobility processes. *American Behavioral Scientist* 48:1157–81.

Smith, Sandra. 2005. "Don't put my name on it": Social capital activation and job-finding assistance among the black urban poor. *American Journal of Sociology* 111:1–57.

Stainback, Kevin, and David Tomaskovic-Devey. 2009. Intersections of power and privilege: Long-term trends in managerial representation. *American Sociological Review* 74:800–20.

Thomas, David A., and John J. Gabarro. 1999. *Breaking through: The making of minority executives in corporate America.* Boston, MA: Harvard Business School Press.

Trice, Harrison M., and Janice M. Beyer. 1993. *The cultures of work organizations.* Upper Saddle River, NJ: Prentice Hall.

Underhill, Christina M. 2006. The effectiveness of mentoring programs in corporate settings: A meta-analytical review of the literature. *Journal of Vocational Behavior* 68:292–307.

Wallace, Michael, and Kevin Leicht. 2004. Culture wars in the workplace? Cultural antecedents of workers' job entitlement. *Work and Occupations* 31 (1): 3–37.

Wanberg, Connie R., John Kammeyer-Mueller, and Marc Marchese. 2006. Mentor and protégé predictors and outcomes of mentoring in a formal mentoring program. *Journal of Vocational Behavior* 69:410–23.

Wilkins, David, and Mitu Gulati. 1996. Why are there so few black lawyers in corporate law firms? An institutional analysis. *California Law Review* 84:493–625.

If You're So Smart, Why Aren't You the Boss? Explaining the Persistent Vertical Gender Gap in Management

By
HEATHER A. HAVEMAN
and
LAUREN S. BERESFORD

Since 1970, women have made substantial inroads into management jobs. But most women are in lower- and middle-management jobs; few are in top-management jobs. Human capital theory uses three individual-level variables to explain this vertical gender gap: women acquire fewer of the necessary educational credentials than men, women prefer different kinds of jobs than men, and women accumulate less of the required work experience than men. The authors argue that cultural schemas, specifically gender roles and gender norms, explain most individual-level differences between men and women and that when cultural factors are ignored, any observed effects of these factors can be dismissed as spurious. This analysis is based on data on nationally representative samples and the results of published research.

Keywords: gender gap; management; culture

Over the past four decades, women have made substantial inroads into management jobs. But most women are in lower- and middle-management jobs; few are in top-management

Heather A. Haveman is a professor of sociology and business at the University of California, Berkeley. She studies how organizations, industries, and employees' careers evolve. Her work has appeared in Administrative Science Quarterly, American Sociological Review, American Journal of Sociology, Poetics, Organization Science, Journal of Business Venturing, and Academy of Management Journal. Her current research involves the evolution of antebellum American magazines and corporate governance in twenty-first-century Chinese corporations.

Lauren S. Beresford is a PhD candidate in sociology at the University of California, Berkeley. She studies labor-market stratification, inequality in educational outcomes, and the role organizations play in producing and reproducing these inequalities. Her dissertation explores how gender inequality among managers is affected by employing organizations, the industries these organizations operate in, and general economic conditions.

NOTE: We thank the Institute for Research on Labor and Employment at the University of California, Berkeley, for financial support.

DOI: 10.1177/0002716211418443

jobs (Reskin and Ross 1992; L. Cohen, Broschak, and Haveman 1998; Carter and Silva 2010). This vertical gender gap occurs even among those with elite educational credentials. Female graduates of highly ranked MBA programs take lower-status jobs than do their male counterparts, even after controlling for years of work experience, children living at home, industry, region, and aspirations to be senior executives (Carter and Silva 2010). Moreover, these female MBA graduates lag behind their male counterparts at all stages. This vertical gender gap in management has important implications. Because women are less likely than men to be in top management jobs, they tend to earn less than men and to have less formal authority than men.

Human capital theory (Mincer 1970; Becker 1975) predicts that women are less likely than men to be promoted to top management for three related reasons: women acquire fewer of the necessary educational credentials than men, women prefer different kinds of jobs than men, and women accumulate less of the required work experience than men. After discussing the impact of these individual differences on men's and women's advancement into the upper ranks of management, we argue that cultural schemas, specifically gender roles and gender norms, explain most of these gender differences.

Our analysis focuses on managers in the private sector because over four-fifths of the labor force works in the private sector (U.S. Census Bureau 2010) and the most powerful and most highly compensated management jobs are in that sector. We analyze data on nationally representative samples, along with the results of published research, to reveal trends over the past four decades—when women began to enter the managerial workforce in large numbers.

The Vertical Gender Gap in Management

American women have entered management in increasing numbers. As Figure 1 shows, in 1970, only 13 percent of managers in the private sector were women; in 1998, 45 percent were women, based on estimates from the Current Population Survey (U.S. Census Bureau 2010).[1] At that time, women's representation in management almost equaled women's share of the civilian labor force, which was 46 percent (U.S. Census Bureau 2000, Table 646). In recent years, the percentage of female managers in the private sector declined, reaching 41 percent in 2010, even though women's share of the civilian labor force rose to 47 percent (U.S. Census Bureau 2011, Table 604).

This long-term trend toward gender equality in management, tempered as it is by a recent countertrend, is not seen at all ranks of management. Instead, women remain disproportionately segregated in lower levels of management and are scarcely represented at the top. As Figure 1 shows, 12 percent of executives in the private sector were women in 1970; that figure rose to 39 percent in 1991 and then dropped to 28 percent in 2010.[2] The upward trend in women's representation was less strong for executives (12 to 39 percent women, an increase of 225 percent) than for managers as a whole (12 to 45 percent women, an increase of 275

FIGURE 1

Percentage of Managers in the Private Sector Who Are Female, 1970–2010

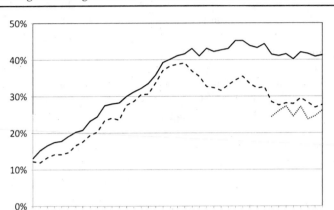

—% Female Managers   – – % Female Executives   ······ % Female CEOs

SOURCE: U.S. Census Bureau (2010).

percent), and the recent downward trend was more pronounced for executives (39 to 28 percent women, a decline of 28 percent) than for managers as a whole (45 to 41 percent women, a decline of 9 percent). We wanted to conduct this trend analysis for chief executive officers (CEOs), but valid data for CEOs do not start until 2003. From 2003 to 2010, the percentage of female CEOs was stagnant, ranging between 24 and 27 percent.

The vertical gender gap is most pronounced in the largest firms. From 1992 to 2004, women constituted, on average, 1.3 percent of CEOs in Standard & Poor's 1,500 firms (Wolfers 2006). In 1995, the first year *Fortune* published a combined list for industrial and service firms, there were no female CEOs in the Fortune 500 and just two in the Fortune 501–1,000; in 2010, eleven Fortune 500 companies had female CEOs, while fourteen Fortune 501–1,000 companies did (Catalyst 2010). Thus, even today, women constitute a mere 2.5 percent of the top at the largest and most powerful private sector firms.

The Impact of Individual Differences between Men and Women

Human capital theory proposes that three differences between men and women explain their differing representation in management, especially in the top ranks: educational attainment, job preferences, and accumulated work experience. We review each in turn.

FIGURE 2
Percentage of College Degrees Awarded to Women, 1970–1971 and 2008–2009

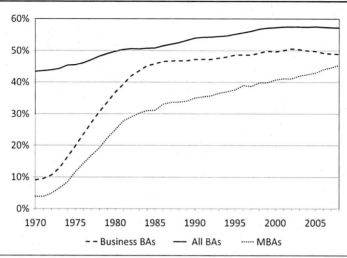

SOURCE: National Center for Education Statistics (2011).

Education. Higher education is an increasingly critical pathway into top management. An increasing fraction of managers have bachelor's degrees; more and more also have advanced degrees. In 1970, 21 percent of managers in the private sector had bachelor's degrees while 4 percent also had advanced degrees; in 2010, 35 percent had bachelor's degrees while 19 percent also had advanced degrees (U.S. Census Bureau 2010). These higher-education credentials have always been far more common among managers than in the population at large. In 1970, 9 percent of Americans had bachelor's degrees while 3 percent had advanced degrees. In 2010, 21 percent had bachelor's degrees while 11 percent had advanced degrees (U.S. Census Bureau 2010).

Higher education credentials are especially important for top managers in the largest and most powerful firms. Analysis of 2,727 senior managers in 208 large manufacturing and finance firms taken from the 1977 *Fortune* lists (Useem and Karabel 1986) revealed that 83 percent of senior managers had bachelor's degrees while 44 percent also had advanced degrees. In that same year, among private sector firms of all sizes, only 26 percent of managers had bachelor's degrees while 6 percent also had advanced degrees (U.S. Census Bureau 2010).

Over the past 40 years, American women's educational attainment has outpaced men's. As Figure 2 shows, women earned 43 percent of bachelor's degrees in 1970–1971 (National Center for Education Statistics 2011). In 2008–2009, women earned 57 percent of bachelor's degrees. This trend was evident at all levels: women earned 40 percent of master's degrees and 14 percent of doctorates in 1970–1971, compared to 60 percent of master's degrees and 52 percent of doctorates in 2008–2009. In 2010, women made up just over 50 percent of the civilian workforce with college degrees (U.S. Census Bureau 2010).

The change in women's educational attainment has been especially rapid in the field of business, the training ground for many managers. As Figure 2 shows, women earned 9 percent of business BAs and 4 percent of MBAs in 1970–1971, compared with 49 percent of business BAs and 45 percent of MBAs in 2008–2009. Thus, women are almost as likely as men to earn MBAs, given that they constitute 47 percent of the labor force (U.S. Census Bureau 2011, Table 604). The remarkable correspondence between Figures 1 and 2 suggests that American women's increased educational attainment in the field of business has given them easier entrée into management. Through the mid-1990s, the increase in women earning business BAs and MBAs paralleled the increase in women in management. But in recent years, trends for women's educational attainment and representation in management diverged, as the percentage of female managers declined slightly, while the percentage of women earning business BAs and MBAs continued to rise.

Although overall, women's educational attainment has exceeded men's, educational attainment can still help to explain the vertical gender gap in management. Educational fields continue to be gender-segregated, with women less likely to be in fields that require mathematical skills. In 1970, women earned just 18 percent of bachelor's degrees in the fields of science, technology, engineering, and mathematics (STEM); in 2004, women earned 38 percent of bachelor's degrees in STEM fields (National Science Foundation 2007). Although women's representation among graduates of STEM fields doubled, in 2004 women constituted only 25 percent of the STEM workforce (Carrell, Page, and West 2009). Among MBAs, women are less likely to acquire expertise in the mathematics-heavy field of finance (Bertrand, Goldin, and Katz 2010). Women's underrepresentation in STEM fields and finance has kept them out of pipelines to upper management. Starting in the 1970s, the top ranks of large American corporations have been increasingly filled by people with backgrounds in finance (Fligstein 1987; Zorn 2004). And beginning in the 1980s, the top ranks of large corporations have been increasingly filled by people with backgrounds in production and technology (Ocasio and Kim 1999), which usually require education in STEM fields.

Women's access to business education is stratified by institutional prestige, which can also help to explain why female managers are generally at lower levels than male managers. Women constitute a smaller fraction of students in the highest-ranked MBA programs than in lower-ranked programs. Only 31 percent of MBA students in the top U.S. business schools are female (*Financial Times* 2010), compared with 45 percent across all MBA programs.[3] Students from top MBA programs have easier access to the best management jobs, due to their schools' reputations and their ability to foster ties to other elite students, so the scarcity of women in top MBA programs means that women have less easy access to the highest-status positions. Thus educational stratification—fewer women in top-ranked MBA programs and more in lower-ranked programs—helps to maintain gender inequality in management (S. Lucas 2001).

Job preferences. There is some evidence of gender differences in job preferences. Longitudinal analysis of high school seniors' value orientations along three dimensions (concern and responsibility for the well-being of others, emphasis on material benefit and competition, and concern with finding purpose and meaning in life) revealed substantial and persistent gender differences on all three measures (Beutel and Marini 1995). From the mid-1970s through the early 1990s, young women were consistently more likely than young men to express concern and responsibility for the well-being of others, less likely than young men to accept materialism and competition (the values that are strongly held in corporate America), and more likely than young men to indicate that finding purpose and meaning in life is extremely important. There was no evidence that young men's and women's values converged over time.

Perhaps more relevant to the question of male versus female managers' job preferences is a pair of studies analyzing data on adult workers from the General Social Survey (GSS). The first analyzed all workers from 1973 to 1993 (Rowe and Snizek 1995); the second, married workers only from 1973 to 1994 (Tolbert and Moen 1998). Both examined preferences for five job characteristics: high income, job security, opportunities for advancement, a sense of accomplishment, and short hours. Human capital theory would predict that men would prefer the first three job characteristics more than women, while women would prefer the last two job characteristics more than men. The first study offered little support for human capital theory. Men and women had the same rank-order preferences among job characteristics. Moreover, gender differences in the ranks assigned to job characteristics were very small. After controlling for age, education, marital status, occupational prestige, job satisfaction, spouse's work status, and year, there were few differences between men's and women's work values. Men were slightly less likely than women to value job security and short hours. Regardless of gender, preferences for particular job characteristics depended mostly on age, education, and occupational prestige.

The second study offered partial support for human capital theory. After controlling for age, education, race, occupation, number of children, and time period, married men valued promotion opportunities and job security more than married women, while married women valued a sense of accomplishment more than did married men. Counter to human capital theory, there were no significant differences between married men's and women's preferences for high incomes or short hours. As in the first study, most statistically significant gender gaps in job preferences were small in magnitude. Gender gaps were widest among young married workers, and there was no evidence that they declined over time; both findings are consistent with previous research on high school students (Beutel and Marini 1995).

The situation is complicated by the fact that any differences we observe between men's and women's job preferences may not be exogenous; they may instead be due to the jobs men and women currently hold and those they held in the past (Kanter 1977; Brief, Rose, and Aldag 1977; Rowe and Snizek 1995). Since women, including female managers, tend to work in lower-status positions than men, women may react by placing less value on their careers (Kanter 1977); if so, women may prefer short hours and a sense of accomplishment more than men. Much evidence supports the hypothesis of endogenous job preferences: after taking into consideration differences between men's and women's jobs, there are no gender differences in attitudes toward work (Brief, Rose, and Aldag 1977; Bielby and Bielby 1989; Rowe and Snizek 1995). Men and women engaged in similar work have almost equal commitment to work, and men and women engaged in similar family roles have almost equal commitment to family (Bielby and Bielby 1989). A study of female finance executives found that the most successful of these women had the strongest devotion to work; indeed, female executives' attitudes toward work were virtually identical to those of their male counterparts (Blair-Loy 2003).

Work experience. Four decades ago only 41 percent of American women were in the labor force, compared to 76 percent of American men; by 2009, the figures for men and women had converged slightly: 54 percent of American women and 65 percent of American men were in the labor force (U.S. Census Bureau 2011, Table 586). Married women entered the labor force alongside single women: for single women, labor force participation rates rose from 57 percent in 1970 to 64 percent in 2009; for married women, these rates rose from 41 percent in 1970 to 61 percent in 2009 (U.S. Census Bureau 2011, Table 596). As a result of married women's entry into the labor force, the percentage of two-income couples rose from 50 percent in 1986 (the earliest year such data are available) to 55 percent in 2009 (U.S. Census Bureau 2011, Table 600). Not only have women entered the labor force in greater numbers, they have increasingly worked full time: among female workers, the ratio of full-time to part-time workers rose from 2.5 in 1972 to 3.3 in 2008 (GSS 2010). Moreover, in more and more households with young children, both men and women work: the percentage of working married mothers with husbands present and children under six rose from 30 percent in 1970 to 59 percent in 1990 and 62 percent in 2009 (U.S. Census Bureau 2011, Table 598). Taken together, these trends indicate that women's lives have come to resemble those of men's: women are increasingly likely to work for pay, full time, even when they have young children and husbands present.

Notwithstanding these trends toward gender equality, women tend to accumulate less of the work experience that is needed to get into management than men do. We do not have good data on work experience, but we do have data on one component of work experience—tenure with one's current employer. In 2008, median firm tenure for male workers 20 years and older was 4.5 years; median firm tenure for female workers was 4.2 years (U.S Census Bureau 2011, Table 611). To the extent that women take more time out from work than men to tend to children, gaps between men's and women's work experience will increase with age. We see such a pattern across most age ranges. Median tenure for men ages 25–34 was 2.8 years; for men ages 35–44, 5.2; for men ages 45–54, 8.2; and for men ages 55–64, 10.1. For women, median tenure was lower for all age groups, and the gap between men's and women's tenure generally widened with age: median tenure for women ages 25–34 was 2.6 years (0.2 years less than men); for women ages 35–44, 4.7 years (0.5 years less than men); for women ages 45–54, 7.0 years (1.2 years less than men); and for women ages 55–64, 9.8 years (0.3 years less than men). Such increasing gaps in accumulated experience can help to explain the vertical gender gap in management (Bertrand, Goldin, and Katz 2010).

Since many managers have college degrees, it is worthwhile to assess differences in work experience for male and female college graduates. In the first decade after leaving college, women tend to have about the same amount of work experience as men; after that point, female college graduates tend to work fewer hours than males, and female college graduates are more likely than males to interrupt their careers to raise children (Black et al. 2008). Thus, over their careers, female college graduates accumulate less work experience than males. But this accumulated experience gap has declined over time, at least for those with elite educational credentials. Among Harvard graduates, spells of women's nonemployment, explained by the presence of young children, were longest for 1970 graduates, intermediate for 1980 graduates, and shortest for 1990 graduates (Goldin and Katz 2008).

Cultural Factors Are the Cause of Individual Differences: Gender Roles and Gender Norms

Widely held cultural schemas about what is appropriate for men and women to do (gender norms) and what it is that men and women do well (gender roles) may be the root cause of differences between men's and women's educational attainment, job preferences, and work experience. If so, cultural schemas would explain gender differences in managers' career trajectories. We focus on three cultural schemas that are especially relevant to the vertical gender gap in management: (1) men are better than women at math and science, (2) men belong at work and women belong at home, and (3) men are more natural managers and leaders than women.

Gender and mathematics/science. Culture can explain women's reluctance to study fields that require mathematical skills and that are gateways to top management jobs. There is only weak evidence of actual gender differences in mathematics skills (Hyde, Fennema, and Lamon 1990; Baker and Jones 1993). Moreover, any gender differences that do exist in actual mathematics skills have been attributed to cultural factors, such as women's social status (Penner 2008). But even today, most college students believe men are better at mathematics than women (Nosek, Banaji, and Greenwald 2002).

Widely held beliefs about competence bias individuals' perceptions of their own competence at career-relevant tasks and so shape their decisions about field of study. In particular, gender stereotypes about mathematics skills affect students' attitudes toward, participation in, and performance in mathematics and science courses (Eccles 1987; Hyde et al. 1990; Spencer, Steele, and Quinn 1999). Even those female students who believe they are good at mathematics are susceptible to this stereotype (Nguyen and Ryan 2008). Thinking more broadly, if most people—parents, teachers, and students—perceive female students' mathematics skills to be inferior to male students', female students will be influenced by these widely held stereotypes and will be less likely than male students to study fields that require mathematical skills (Correll 2001, 2004).

Finally, powerful stereotypes associate careers in science and engineering, which have increasingly led to upper-management jobs, with men and not with women. These stereotypes are held by men and women equally (Smyth, Greenwald, and Nosek 2010) and are reinforced by experience—by men's domination of science and engineering jobs, which shapes men's and women's career choices (Xie and Shauman 2003).

Gender and work/family. As married women have entered the workforce in ever greater numbers, Americans have increasingly accepted the idea of married women working. In Gallup polls, acceptance of married women working was 55 percent in 1969 (Erskine 1971); in the GSS, acceptance of married women working rose to 68 percent in 1972 before dropping to 65 percent in 1977 (Spitze and Huber 1980).[4] Analysis of related GSS questions between 1977 and 1996 revealed that both cohort succession and within-cohort attitude shifts led to increasingly positive attitudes about women, including mothers, working (Mason and Lu 1988; Brewster and Padavic 2000). Still, most Americans continue to believe that married women with young children belong at home, not at work. The most recent data we have on this specific gender schema come from 1994, when 84 percent of Americans approved of married women without children working full time, but only 11 percent approved of married women with pre-school-age children working full time; a further 34 percent approved of married women with pre-school-age children working part time, and 55 percent preferred they not work at all (Treas and Widmer 2000).

Cultural schemas create behavioral traces that allow us to pinpoint temporal shifts. One behavioral trace of the gender and work-family schema involves use of time for paid work, housework, or leisure. Because traditional gender roles involve women doing more housework and childcare than men, working women who fulfill their expected gender role are forced to take on a "second shift" of housework and childcare after working hours, while working men who fulfill their expected gender role can concentrate more on work or spend more time on leisure (Hochschild 1989). These behavioral traces of traditional gender roles have persisted, even though more married women work and more work full time. Time-diary studies covering the years 1965, 1975, and 1998 reveal that women continue to do more housework than men, although men increasingly help with core household duties such as cooking, cleaning, and childcare (Bianchi et al. 2000; Sayer 2005; Bianchi 2011). Male-female differences in time use are especially pronounced for parents. Compounding the effect of stable gender roles for time use, especially for parents, is the fact that managers work ever longer hours (Jacobs and Gerson 2004; Collinson and Collinson 2004). A recent survey showed medians of 56 hours per week for male managers and 52 hours per week for female managers; moreover, 29 percent of male managers and 11 percent of female managers worked over 60 hours per week (Brett and Stroh 2003). This suggests that female managers experience especially strong work-family conflicts (Jacobs and Gerson 2004).

In the middle and upper-middle classes, from whose ranks most managers are drawn, there is increasing cultural pressure for mothers to tend to their children themselves, rather than working full time and delegating childcare to nannies, preschools, boarding schools, or babysitters (Epstein 2004; Stone 2007). These mothers are expected to make the switch from managing bureaucracies to managing their children's increasingly bureaucratized lives: to tutor children after school, help schools raise funds, coach children's sports teams, and chauffeur children around (Lareau 2003; Lareau and Weininger 2008). There are many journalistic accounts of highly educated and high-achieving women leaving managerial jobs to stay home with their children (e.g., Belkin 2003; Story 2005). But the news media have not just reported on this trend; they have also accentuated it, by excoriating women who hire others to care for their children (e.g., Flanagan 2004). This recent cultural backlash against middle- and upper-middle-class mothers delegating childcare intensifies the already-strong work-family conflicts that female managers experience.

Because cultural schemas affect the amount of time men and women spend at work rather than home, they affect the type and amount of work experience men and women accumulate. The persistence of the gender gap in housework and childcare creates role conflicts for working women, especially those with children. Women may try to "balance" work and family by choosing jobs with lower time commitments and greater flexibility, by working fewer hours, and by staying at home when their children are very young. Thus, traditional expectations about gender roles at work versus at home, especially for married women with young children, may explain why female managers accumulate less work experience than their male counterparts and so may help to explain the vertical gender gap in management. This conclusion is supported by research showing that women in management often got there by forgoing marriage and children altogether: female managers are less likely to be married than their male counterparts (Davidson and Burke 2000). And a study of female executives in finance showed that after women have children, their choices of career trajectories—to pursue senior-management positions, stay at home, or work part time—are influenced by two conflicting cultural schemas: family devotion and work devotion (Blair-Loy 2003). The work devotion schema characterizes the culture of the finance industry; it demands that executives put the firm and clients first by working long hours. The family devotion schema characterizes children as vulnerable and in need of attention, particularly from their mothers. Women who try to have it both ways and go part time are marginalized for their lack of devotion to the firm and cut off from promotion to upper management.

Gender and management. Cultural schemas about men and women at work also shape perceptions of who should be in positions of corporate leadership and so may explain the dearth of female managers in the top managerial ranks. People who score high on three of the "big five" personality traits—conscientiousness, extraversion, and openness to experience—are more likely to become leaders and to be effective leaders (Judge et al. 2002).[5] Men and women exhibit similar levels of extraversion, openness to experience, and conscientiousness, although there are differences between men and women on subcomponents of extraversion and openness to experience (Costa, Terracciano, and McCrae 2001). Therefore, personality differences cannot explain women's underrepresentation among corporate leaders. Perhaps differences in interpersonal skills can. People who have greater emotional intelligence, meaning greater ability to perceive emotions, understand emotions, use emotions to facilitate thought, and regulate emotions (Mayer et al. 2001), may be more likely to be leaders. Women tend to score higher than men on emotional intelligence (Brackett et al. 2006), so if this skill helps people to get into formal leadership positions, we would expect women to outnumber men among managers. This is especially likely in the top ranks because senior management jobs have a large symbolic component (Selznick 1957; Pfeffer 1981). In sum, little evidence suggests that differences between men and women in personality traits and interpersonal skills can explain women's underrepresentation in top management; instead, such differences are due to cultural factors.

Powerful stereotypes associate managerial roles with men and not with women. Put simply, when people "think manager," they "think male" (Schein 2001). Such stereotypes are reinforced by experience; the fact that men dominate the ranks of management, especially at the top, contributes to this stereotype (Marini and Brinton 1984). Because of this stereotype, people expect managers to do things that are typically associated with masculinity, such as competing with peers, imposing their wishes on subordinates, behaving assertively, and standing out from the group (Miner 1993; Atwater et al. 2004). That is why people who assess "men," "women," and "successful managers" rate managers and men as similar on many individualistic and agentic characteristics, such as being competitive, self-confident, aggressive, and ambitious (Schein 2001; Sczesny 2003). In contrast, ratings of women and managers are similar on only a few communal characteristics, such as being intuitive and helpful.

Because cultural schemas constrain behavior, men and women exhibit different leadership styles, despite having similar personality traits. Women are "outsiders" to management and must negotiate two roles—woman and manager—and reconcile the communal qualities people prefer in women with the agentic qualities that people expect in managers. As a result, female managers are more likely than male managers to have democratic, participative, and collaborative styles (Eagly and Johnson 1990). But the gender gap in managerial style is narrower among more senior managers. Moreover, between-gender differences are small compared to within-gender variation.

Women who embrace the "think manager–think male" stereotype are less likely to aspire to managerial positions (van Vianen and Keizer 1996; Davies, Spencer, and Steele 2005). Even women who reject this stereotype and aspire to management may perform more poorly compared to men, due to stereotype threat (for a review of research on stereotype threat, see Steele, Spencer, and Aronson 2002). If women are not expected to be managers, especially not top managers, and if women are aware that others believe this stereotype, then women are at risk of confirming this stereotype. Simply being aware of this stereotype may create concerns about fulfilling it, which may hinder task performance. Stereotype threat has been shown to diminish female MBA students' performance in many managerial tasks, such as negotiating (Kray, Thompson, and Galinsky 2001).

When those who evaluate potential managers for promotion embrace the stereotype of managers as male, they are less likely to perceive female candidates for managerial jobs—especially at the top, where women are rare—as positively as their male rivals (Eagly and Karau 2002). To be promoted to upper management, one must demonstrate competence. But surveys and laboratory experiments alike reveal that people perceive men as more competent than women (e.g., Heilman et al. 1989; J. Lucas 2003). Even when women enter management positions, they are in a double bind: as women, they are expected to be communal, collaborative, and democratic; but as managers, they are expected to be agentic and authoritative. The situation is complicated by the fact that higher-ranking managerial jobs tend to involve greater uncertainty—they focus more on strategy and less on tactics to achieve a strategic goal. Such uncertainty should accentuate decision-makers' reliance on gender as an indicator of competence (Gorman and Kmec 2009).

Conclusion

Widely held cultural expectations about what men and women can and should do—gender stereotypes about who can do mathematics, who should work and who should care for children and the home, and who should lead—are the basic cause of observed gender differences in educational attainment, job preferences, and work experience. Figure 3 shows our causal model. It makes clear that research on the vertical gender gap in management that seeks to show effects of education, job preferences, or work experience must account for these cultural factors. If cultural factors are ignored, any observed effects of these factors can be dismissed as spurious. And as Figure 3 indicates, the individual differences that human capital theory focuses on have common cultural origins; therefore, their effects cannot be entirely separated. In addition, the cultural schemas we highlight feed stereotypes about men as managers that prevent women from aspiring to or getting into management positions, especially at the top.

Our basic conclusion is that, contrary to human capital theory, it is not all about choices. Instead, choices—including what field to study, how much education to get, whether to work outside the home, how much to work, and what kind of job is most desirable—are constrained by culture. We risk sounding unoriginal

FIGURE 3

The Impact of Cultural Schemas on Human Capital and the Vertical Gender Gap in Management

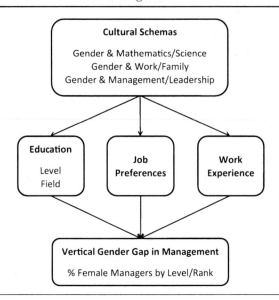

by echoing Duesenberry's (1960, 233) quip that "Economics is all about how people make choices. Sociology is all about why they don't have any choices to make." But we take this risk because our point is one that many scholars seem to have forgotten. We read a plethora of studies that take behavioral indicators of "managerial" talent (e.g., mathematics test scores, years of experience) at face value and ignore the power of culture to drive men and women to display different amounts of such talent.

Policy implications. If the root cause of the vertical gender gap in management is culture, then corporate or public policies that seek to reduce this gap must focus on culture. In general, to change culture, you have to change people's hearts and minds. Therefore, culture is arguably the hardest thing to change through policy. In the United States, policies that target a single group, such as women, have been subject to backlash and retrenchment (Skocpol 1991; Alesina and Glaeser 2006). Americans simply refuse to pay for something that does not benefit them (Korpi and Palme 1998). One way around this is to nest policies that benefit women within policies that benefit both men and women. For instance, family-friendly policies could place a ceiling on working hours for all salaried workers (e.g., 50 hours per week) or mandate on-site employer-sponsored childcare for workplaces over a certain size, while education policies could create programs, available to both sexes, to foster student participation in science and mathematics programs in secondary schools as well as in colleges.

Notes

1. This figure includes all Census Bureau occupation codes that are relevant to the private sector: occ1990 = 4, 7, 8, 13, 14, 15, 16, 17, 18, 19, 21, and 22. Similar trends are seen when using data from the decennial census and the Equal Employment Opportunity Commission (P. Cohen, Huffman, and Knauer 2009).

2. Before 2003, the Current Population Survey had a valid count for executives, but not for CEOs (Mary Bowler, U.S. Census Bureau, personal communication, December 2010). Occupation codes were revised between 2002 and 2003, when a valid code for CEO was created (occ = 1, which improved on occ1990 = 4). Before 2003, figures for executives are based on the occupation code "managers n.e.c." ("not elsewhere classified," occ1990 = 22); most executive-rank employees are in this category, and most employees in this category are executives (Mary Bowler, U.S. Census Bureau, personal communication, December 2010). After 2003, figures for executives include both managers n.e.c. (occ1990 = 22) and the new CEO code (occ = 1/occ1990 = 4).

3. Fifty-six of the top U.S. schools were in this global top one hundred list; almost all were in the *Business Week* or *U.S. News and World Report* top fifty.

4. The Gallup Poll question was "Do you approve of a married woman earning money in business or industry if she has a husband capable of supporting her?" The GSS added "or disapprove" to this question, so the two surveys are quite comparable.

5. Conscientiousness involves achievement orientation and dependability. Extraversion involves sociability, assertiveness, activity, and positive emotions. Openness to experience involves creativity, nonconformity, autonomy, and unconventional qualities. The personality traits that have not been empirically linked to leadership are neuroticism and agreeableness. Neuroticism involves poor emotional adjustment and negative emotions, while agreeableness involves caring, trusting, compliant, and gentle qualities.

References

Alesina, Alberto, and Edward L. Glaeser. 2006. *Fighting poverty in the U.S. and Europe: A world of difference*. New York, NY: Oxford University Press.

Atwater, Leanne E., Joan F. Brett, David Waldman, Lesley DiMare, and Mary Virginia Hayden. 2004. Men's and women's perceptions of the gender typing of management subroles. *Sex Roles* 50:191–99.

Baker, David P., and Deborah P. Jones. 1993. Creating gender equality: Cross-national gender stratification and mathematical performance. *Sociology of Education* 66:91–103.

Becker, Gary S. 1975. *Human capital*. 2nd ed. Chicago, IL: University of Chicago Press.

Belkin, Lisa. 26 October 2003. The opt-out revolution. *New York Times Magazine*.

Bertrand, Marianne, Claudia Goldin, and Lawrence F. Katz. 2010. Dynamics of the gender gap for young professionals in the financial and corporate sectors. *American Economic Journal: Applied Economics* 2:228–55.

Beutel, Ann M., and Margaret Mooney Marini. 1995. Gender and values. *American Sociological Review* 60:436–48.

Bianchi, Suzanne M. 2011. Family change and time allocation in American families. *Annals of the American Academy of Political and Social Science* 638.

Bianchi, Suzanne M., Melissa A. Milkie, Liana C. Sayer, and John P. Robinson. 2000. Is anyone doing the housework? Trends in the gender division of household labor. *Social Forces* 79:191–228.

Bielby, William T., and Denise D. Bielby. 1989. Family ties: Balancing commitments to work and family in dual earner households. *American Sociological Review* 54:776–89.

Black, Dan A., Amelia M. Haviland, Seth G. Sanders, and Lowell J. Taylor. 2008. Gender wage disparities among the highly educated. *Journal of Human Resources* 43:630–59.

Blair-Loy, Mary. 2003. *Competing devotions*. Cambridge, MA: Harvard University Press.

Brackett, Marc A., Susan E. Rivers, Sara Shiffman, Nicole Lerner, and Peter Salovey. 2006. Relating emotional abilities to social functioning. *Journal of Personality and Social Psychology* 91:780–95.

Brett, Jeanne F., and Linda K. Stroh. 2003. Working 61 plus hours a week: Why do managers do it? *Journal of Applied Psychology* 88:67–78.

Brewster, Karin L., and Irene Padavic. 2000. Change in gender ideology 1977–1996. *Journal of Marriage and the Family* 62:477–87.

Brief, Arthur P., Gerald L. Rose, and Ramon J. Aldag. 1977. Sex differences in preferences for job attributes revisited. *Journal of Applied Psychology* 62:645–46.

Carrell, Scott E., Marianne E. Page, and James E. West. 2009. Sex and science: How professor gender perpetuates the gender gap. National Bureau of Economic Research Working Paper 14959, Philadelphia, PA.

Carter, Nancy, and Christine Silva. 2010. *The pipeline's broken promise*. New York, NY: Catalyst.

Catalyst. 2010. *Women CEOs in the Fortune lists: 1972–2010*. New York, NY: Catalyst.

Cohen, Lisa E., Joseph P. Broschak, and Heather A. Haveman. 1998. And then there were more? The effect of organizational sex composition on the hiring and promotion of managers. *American Sociological Review* 63:711–27.

Cohen, Philip N., Matt L. Huffman, and Stephanie Knauer. 2009. Stalled progress? Gender segregation and wage inequality among managers, 1980–2000. *Work and Occupations* 36:318–42.

Collinson, David L., and Margaret Collinson. 2004. The power of time: Leadership, management, and gender. In *Fighting for time: Shifting boundaries of work and social life*, eds. Cynthia Fuchs Epstein and Arne L. Kalleberg, 219–46. New York, NY: Russell Sage Foundation.

Correll, Shelley J. 2001. Gender and the career choice process. *American Journal of Sociology* 106: 691–730.

Correll, Shelley J. 2004. Constraints into preferences: Gender, status, and emerging career aspirations. *American Sociological Review* 69:93–113.

Costa, Paul T., Jr., Antonio Terracciano, and Robert R. McCrae. 2001. Gender differences in personality traits across cultures. *Journal of Personality and Social Psychology* 81:322–31.

Davidson, Marilyn, and Ronald Burke. 2000. *Women in management: Current research issues*. Vol. II. London: Sage.

Davies, Paul G., Steven J. Spencer, and Claude M. Steele. 2005. Clearing the air: Identity safety moderates the effects of stereotype threat on women's leadership aspirations. *Journal of Personality and Social Psychology* 88:276–87.

Duesenberry, James S. 1960. Comment on Becker: An economic analysis of fertility. In *Demographic and economic change in developed countries*, 231–34. Princeton, NJ: Princeton University Press.

Eagly, Alice H., and Blair T. Johnson. 1990. Gender and leadership style. *Psychological Bulletin* 108:233–56.

Eagly, Alice H., and Steven J. Karau. 2002. Role congruity theory of prejudice toward female leaders. *Psychological Review* 109:573–98.

Eccles, Jacquelynne S. 1987. Gender roles and women's achievement-related decisions. *Psychology of Women Quarterly* 11:135–72.

Epstein, Cynthia Fuchs. 2004. Border crossings: The constraints of time norms in transgressions of gender and professional roles. In *Fighting for time: Shifting boundaries of work and social life*, eds. Cynthia Fuchs Epstein and Arne L. Kalleberg, 317–40. New York, NY: Russell Sage Foundation.

Erskine, Hazel. 1971. The polls: Women's role. *Public Opinion Quarterly* 35:275–90.

Financial Times. 2010. Global MBA rankings 2010. Available from http://rankings.ft.com/businessschool-rankings/global-mba-rankings.

Flanagan, Caitlin. 2004. How serfdom saved the women's movement. *The Atlantic* 293(2): 109–228.

Fligstein, Neil. 1987. The intraorganizational power struggle: Rise of finance personnel to top leadership in large corporations, 1919–1979. *American Sociological Review* 52:44–58.

General Social Survey (GSS). 2010. *1972–2008 Cumulative Data Release 3*. Chicago, IL: National Opinion Research Center.

Goldin, Claudia, and Lawrence Katz. 2008. Transitions: Careers and family life cycles of the educational elite. *American Economic Review* 98:363–69.

Gorman, Elizabeth H., and Julie A. Kmec. 2009. Hierarchical rank and women's occupational mobility: Glass ceilings in corporate law firms. *American Journal of Sociology* 114:1428–74.

Heilman, Madeline E., Caryn J. Block, Richard F. Martell, and Michael C. Simon. 1989. Has anything changed? Current characterizations of men, women, and managers. *Journal of Applied Psychology* 74:935–42.

Hochschild, Arlie Russell. 1989. *The second shift*. New York, NY: Avon Books.

Hyde, Jane Shibley, Elizabeth Fennema, and Susan J. Lamon. 1990. Gender differences in mathematics performance. *Psychological Bulletin* 107:139–55.

Hyde, Jane Shibley, Elizabeth Fennema, Marilyn Ryan, Laurie A. Frost, and Carolyn Hopp. 1990. Gender comparisons of mathematics attitudes and affect. *Psychology of Women Quarterly* 14:299–324.

Jacobs, Jerry A., and Kathleen Gerson. 2004. *The time divide*. Cambridge, MA: Harvard University Press.

Judge, Timothy E., Joyce E. Bono, Remus Ilies, and Megan W. Gerhardt. 2002. Personality and leadership. *Journal of Applied Psychology* 87:765–80.

Kanter, Rosabeth Moss. 1977. *Men and women of the corporation*. New York, NY: Basic Books.

Korpi, Walter, and Joakim Palme. 1998. The paradox of redistribution and strategies of equality: Welfare state institutions, inequality, and poverty in the Western countries. *American Sociological Review* 63:661–87.

Kray, Laura J., Leigh Thompson, and Adam D. Galinsky. 2001. Battle of the sexes: Gender stereotype activation in negotiations. *Journal of Personality and Social Psychology* 80:942–58.

Lareau, Annette. 2003. *Unequal childhoods*. Berkeley: University of California Press.

Lareau, Annette, and Elliot B. Weininger. 2008. Time, work, and family life. *Sociological Forum* 23:419–54.

Lucas, Jeffrey W. 2003. Status processes and the institutionalization of women as leaders. *American Sociological Review* 68:464–80.

Lucas, Samuel R. 2001. Effectively maintained inequality: Education transitions, track mobility, and social background effects. *American Journal of Sociology* 106:1642–90.

Marini, Margaret Mooney, and Mary C. Brinton. 1984. Sex stereotyping in occupational segregation. In *Sex segregation in the workplace*, ed. Barbara Reskin, 192–232. Washington, DC: National Academy Press.

Mason, Karen Oppenheim, and Yu-Hsia Lu. 1988. Attitudes toward U.S. women's familial roles, 1977–1985. *Gender and Society* 2:39–57.

Mayer, John D., Peter Salovey, David R. Caruso, and Gill Sitarenios. 2001. Emotional intelligence as a standard intelligence. *Emotion* 1:232–42.

Mincer, Jacob. 1970. The distribution of labor income. *Journal of Economic Literature* 8:1–26.

Miner, John B. 1993. *Role motivation theories*. New York, NY: Routledge.

National Center for Educational Statistics. 2011. *Digest of education statistics*. Available from http://nces .ed.gov/quicktables/.

National Science Foundation. 2007. *Science and engineering degrees: 1966–2004*. NSF 07-307. Available from www.nsf.gov/statistics/nsf07307/.

Nguyen, Hannah-Hanh D., and Ann Marie Ryan. 2008. Does stereotype threat affect test performance of minorities and women? *Journal of Applied Psychology* 93:1314–34.

Nosek, Bryan A., Mahzarin R. Banaji, and Anthony G. Greenwald. 2002. Math = male, me = female, therefore math ≠ me. *Journal of Personality and Social Psychology* 83:44–59.

Ocasio, William E., and Hyosun Kim. 1999. The circulation of corporate control: Selection of functional backgrounds of new CEOs in large U.S. manufacturing firms, 1981–1992. *Administrative Science Quarterly* 44:532–62.

Penner, Andrew M. 2008. Gender differences in extreme mathematical achievement. *American Journal of Sociology* 114:S138–S170.

Pfeffer, Jeffrey. 1981. Management as symbolic action. *Research in Organizational Behavior* 3:1–52.

Reskin, Barbara F., and Catherine E. Ross. 1992. Authority and earnings among managers: The continuing significance of sex. *Work and Occupations* 19:342–65.

Rowe, Reba, and William E. Snizek. 1995. Gender differences in work values. *Work and Occupations* 22:215–29.

Sayer, Liana C. 2005. Gender, time, and inequality. *Social Forces* 84:285–303.

Schein, Virginia. 2001. A global look at psychological barriers to women's progress in management. *Journal of Social Issues* 57:675–88.

Sczesny, Sabine. 2003. A closer look beneath the surface: Various facets of the think-manager–think-male stereotype. *Sex Roles* 49:353–63.

Selznick, Philip. 1957. *Leadership in administration*. Berkeley: University of California Press.

Skocpol, Theda. 1991. Targeting within universalism. In *The urban underclass*, eds. Christopher Jencks and Paul E. Peterson, 411–36. Washington, DC: Brookings Institution.

Smyth, Frederick L., Anthony G. Greenwald, and Brian A. Nosek. 2010. Implicit gender-science stereo-type outperforms math scholastic aptitude in identifying science majors. Working Paper, University of Virginia.

Spencer, Steven J., Claude M. Steele, and Diane M. Quinn. 1999. Stereotype threat and women's math performance. *Journal of Experimental Social Psychology* 35:4–28.

Spitze, Glenna, and Joan Huber. 1980. Changing attitudes toward women's roles: 1938–1978. *Sociology of Work and Occupations* 7:317–35.

Steele, Claude M., Steven J. Spencer, and Joshua Aronson. 2002. Contending with group image: The psychology of stereotype and social identity threat. *Advances in Experimental Social Psychology* 34:379–440.

Stone, Pamela. 2007. *Opting out? Why women really quit careers and head home.* Berkeley: University of California Press.

Story, Louise. 20 September 2005. Many women at elite colleges set career path to motherhood. *New York Times*, A18.

Tolbert, Pamela S., and Phyllis Moen. 1998. Men's and women's definitions of "good" jobs: Similarities and differences by age and across time. *Work and Occupations* 25:168–94.

Treas, Judith, and Eric D. Widmer. 2000. Married women's employment over the life course. *Social Forces* 78:1409–36.

U.S. Census Bureau. 2000. *Statistical abstract of the United States: 2000.* Washington, DC: Government Printing Office.

U.S. Census Bureau. 2010. *Current Population Survey, March supplement.* Available from www.census .gov/cps/.

U.S. Census Bureau. 2011. *Statistical abstract of the United States: 2011.* Washington, DC: Government Printing Office.

Useem, Michael, and Jerome Karabel. 1986. Pathways to top corporate management. *American Sociological Review* 51:184–200.

van Vianen, Annelies E. M., and Wim A. J. Keizer. 1996. Gender differences in managerial intention. *Gender, Work, and Organization* 3:103–14.

Wolfers, Justin. 2006. Diagnosing discrimination: Stock returns and CEO gender. *Journal of the European Economic Association* 4:531–41.

Xie, Yu, and Kimberlee Shauman. 2003. *Women in science.* New York, NY: Cambridge University Press.

Zorn, Dirk M. 2004. Here a chief, there a chief: The rise of the CFO in the American firm. *American Sociological Review* 69:345–64.

Women's Mobility into Upper-Tier Occupations: Do Determinants and Timing Differ by Race?

By
GEORGE WILSON

Data from the 1998 to 2005 waves of the Panel Study of Income Dynamics are used to assess the particularistic mobility thesis, which maintains that among women there is a racialized continuum in the determinants of and timing to mobility into two "upper-tier" occupational categories. Findings support this theory, though racial gaps along the continuum are greater for professional/technical than for managerial/administrative positions. Specifically, the route to mobility for African Americans is relatively narrow and structured by traditional stratification causal factors, including human capital, background status, and job/labor market characteristics. In contrast, the route to mobility for whites is relatively broad and unstructured by the stratification-based causal factors, and they experience mobility the quickest. Along both dimensions, Latinas occupy an intermediate position between African Americans and whites. Implications of the findings for understanding racial inequality among managers, executives, and professionals are discussed.

Keywords: workplace inequality; mobility; race; women

Pursuant to women's increasing representation in the U.S. labor market, an enormous literature has examined their stratification-based experiences. Along these lines, the overwhelming majority of this work has explicated the dynamics of gender stratification by comparing men and women and uncovering a primary and deep-rooted form of inequality (for reviews, see Jacobs 1989; Reskin and Bielby 2005). Overall, encompassing hundreds of research pieces—journal articles, books, and essays—this literature documents that both structural

George Wilson is a professor of sociology at the University of Miami. His research interests focus on the institutional production of racial/ethnic inequality in the American workplace as well as the sources and consequences of race/ethnic-specific beliefs about the American stratification system.

DOI: 10.1177/0002716211422339

(e.g., occupational segregation/crowding of women into devalued "sex typical" occupations [see Tomaskovic-Devey 1993; Jacobs 1989]) and ideologically based (e.g., patriarchal dominant ideologies of workplace governance [see Risman 2004; Ridgeway and Smith-Lovin 1999]) factors explain gender inequality across the wide range of workplace-based rewards.

As several sociologists have pointed out, however, the sheer magnitude of gender differences has deflected attention away from examining intragender group stratification among women on potentially critical bases such as race (Higginbotham and Weber 1992; England, Christopher, and Reid 1999). Indeed, assessing race within a disadvantaged status, that is, among women, broadens our understanding of racial stratification in the American workplace: our knowledge of racial stratification among women—relative to our knowledge among men—is limited in terms of the range of socioeconomic outcomes considered, and the sources of documented racial differences have been characterized as "virtually non-existent" (Reskin 2000, 322). Overall, among women, we know that African Americans and Latinas, relative to whites, receive lower earnings and socioeconomic status "returns" from human capital investments, such as educational attainment and workforce experience (Farley 2004; Jaynes and Williams 1989). In addition, they have limited access to reward-generating structural characteristics of jobs, including, most conspicuously, supervisory responsibility (R. Smith 2002), and are disadvantaged in occupational mobility rates—both upward and downward (Spalter-Roth and Deitch 1999; Wilson and McBrier 2005).

Among these socioeconomic outcomes, the sources of racial gaps among women moving upward into well-rewarded and prestigious occupational destinations, such as "upper-tier" (Wilson, Sakura-Lemessy, and West 1999) managerial, professional, and executive positions, emerge as particularly worthy of in-depth investigation. Upper-tier slots offer material (e.g., income, benefits, and retirement packages) and symbolic rewards (e.g., prestige, honor) that enhance life-chance opportunities on an intragenerational basis and secure resources to assist in the intergenerational transmission of status (Wilson, Sakura-Lemessy, and West 1999; Leicht and Fennell 2001). These slots are also associated, for example, with salutary job and generalized social psychological orientations (e.g., esteem, job and life satisfaction and intellective functioning), many of which are also transmitted to one's children, thereby enhancing their quality of life and that of future generations (Kohn 1969).

Among men, the old adage that minorities "have to work twice as hard to get ahead" has been demonstrated in the context of the particularistic mobility thesis (Wilson, Sakura-Lemessy, and West 1999; Wilson 1997; Stainback, Robinson, and Tomaskovic-Devey 2005): employers' decisions regarding promotion are based on employees' demonstrating the range of informal, requisite criteria (e.g., perceived loyalty, sound judgment, and trust). Minorities, lacking opportunities to demonstrate them, are restricted to attaining mobility along a relatively formal and circumscribed route. Accordingly, the low mobility rates of African Americans and Latinos into managerial/administrative and professional/technical census categories (Wilson 2005) as well as mobility into unspecified occupational destinations (Baldi and McBrier 1997; R. Smith 2005) are captured by traditional stratification criteria, such as attaining substantial human capital (e.g., educational attainment, substantial workplace experience, and tenure with current employer), coming from a privileged background, and having favorable job/labor market characteristics (e.g., union status, sector [Wilson, Sakura-Lemessy, and West 1999; R. Smith 2001]). Conversely, whites—in addition to relying on this formal path—can utilize a more informal networking route based on demonstrating informal criteria, which, overall, translates into discrete mobility paths.

To date, no work has examined whether a similar association exists between mobility rates and the process of attaining upper-tier occupations on the basis of race within a disadvantaged status, namely, being a woman. Furthermore, no work has examined an auxiliary mobility issue—also absent in analyses of men— namely, the temporal sequencing of upward mobility. What is significant is that the earlier that mobility takes place in one's career, the greater the time spent enjoying the material and symbolic rewards of incumbency in an upper-tier slot. In fact, the earlier that mobility is attained, the more resources can be accumulated and the more time can be spent cultivating the important networks that help to ensure the intergenerational transmission of an occupational position (Maume 1999; Wilson and Roscigno 2010).

This study fills this void by using data from a nationally representative sample to assess whether the particularistic mobility thesis can (1) explain the process of mobility into upper-tier occupations among white, African American, and Latina women; and (2) explain race-specific timing to mobility into upper-tier occupations among white, African American, and Latina women.

Theory

Extending the particularistic mobility thesis to explain the process and timing of race-based disadvantage among women derives from a synthesis of the approximately twenty existing survey-based studies, case studies, and review/theoretical essays that address race-based promotion practices among women who work in predominantly white-owned and -managed firms/businesses (Kennelly 1999; Browne and Misra 2003; Feagin and Sikes 1994; Tomaskovic-Devey 1993; Bell and Nkomo 2001; Fernandez 1981; Fosu 1992; Tomkiewitz and Brenner 1996; Reskin and Padavic 1994; Mundra, Moellner, and Loez-Aqueres 1995; James 2000; King 1995; Higginbotham and Weber 1992). These studies tend to be rooted in "intersectionality" theory (P. Collins 2008; Browne and Misra 2003) and establish that the statuses of race and gender constitute interrelated but distinct stratification systems. Accordingly, dynamics associated with the racialized system, for example, occupational segregation and unequal access to educational and training opportunities (Browne and Misra 2003), may compound disadvantage, operating within the gendered system, for example, occupational segregation and the devaluation of female jobs (Reskin and McBrier 2000).

In terms of causal mechanisms, this body of work maintains that the tendency of minority women to receive unfavorable performance evaluations, relative to white women, constitutes a form of disadvantage in the mobility process. Specifically, it identifies the employment practices that reinforce negative race-based stereotypes unique to minority women that, ultimately, render promotion difficult relative to white women. Accordingly, this literature documents that an element of "modern racism" (Pettigrew 1985) permeates the mobility process within a disadvantaged gender status. This form of racism—consistent with broad formulations that have no specific gender referent, such as "laissez-faire racism" (Bobo, Kluegel, and Smith 1997) and "color-blind racism" (Bonilla-Silva 2004)— is subtle, institutional, and even ostensibly nonracial in nature, and it tends to produce disparate outcomes by race without reference to the traditional ill will associated with classic "Jim Crow" discrimination (Pettigrew and Martin 1987; Bobo, Kluegel, and Smith 1997). Overall, dynamics that drive this subtle form of racism range from the perceived "business necessity" of maintaining a stable workforce and customer/client base (Wilson 1997; Pettigrew 1985) to cognitive distortions inherent to such social psychological constructs as "statistical discrimination" (Tomaskovic-Devey and Skaggs 1999) to "self-serving attributional bias" (Pettigrew and Martin 1987) that is associated with stereotypes about the fitness and suitability to be a productive worker.

A first line of studies highlights the dynamics of allocation of African American women and Latinas into internship/mentoring and training programs. These women, specifically, are allocated into programs that are segregated along race/gender lines (e.g., Latinas work alongside Latinas) and that are supervised by coracial women (e.g., Latinas workers are supervised by Latinas) so that minority women are restricted to "hyper-segregated" (Bell and Nkomo 2001) job networks (Tomkiewitz and Brenner 1996; Bell and Nkomo 2001; Kennelly 1999; Higginbotham and Weber 1992). Restriction to these networks, in turn, limits cross-racial interactions, thus reaffirming negative race-based stereotypes that have an "intersecting race/gender content" (Browne and Misra 2003). These stereotypes range from being tardy or unreliable (Kennelly 1999) and having a penchant for complaining about work assignments and perceived discrimination (Kennelly 1999; McGuire 2002) to being prone to hostile outbursts toward coworkers and customers and impatience and lack of loyalty toward supervisors (Feagin and Sikes 1994).

A second set of studies emphasizes inequities in race-based allocation to job tasks among minority women. Specifically, African American women and Latinas are channeled into "racialized" job functions that revolve around producing services used or concerned with minority populations and those that assign minority women, relative to white women, to less substantively complex tasks that involve less reading, less writing, and less complex computer skills (James 2000; Feagin and Sikes 1994) Allocation into these positions serves to stigmatize minority women, reaffirming invidious stereotypes, and places them in positions that are unconnected to mobility ladders.

Predictions

Determinants

The line of research that extends the particularistic mobility thesis to women posits that dynamics associated with allocation on the basis of race among women disadvantage Latinas and African American women in mobility prospects, relative to white women. Specifically, the "double disadvantage" experienced by minority women—that is, discrimination within a disadvantaged gender status—that is fueled by unique intersecting negative stereotypes renders minority group women, relative to white women, disadvantaged in a manner analogous to men: that is, on a particularistic basis. Accordingly, relative to white women, minority women are favorably assessed for promotion on a relatively narrow basis. They must compensate, being forced to rely on a relatively formalistic and narrow route to promotion that is captured, relative to whites, by traditional stratification-based causal factors that encompass human capital, background status, and job/labor market characteristics.

Timing

It is further hypothesized that—in accordance with dynamics associated with the particularistic mobility thesis—minority women, on average, should take longer to achieve mobility than white women. Along these lines, having to rely on relatively formal means—including, most notably, the acquisition of significant human capital—as a prerequisite to promotion is a slow and deliberate process. Thus, for minority women, the time required to overcome negative stereotypes, it is assumed, is longer than that required to utilize networking and other informal strategies more often employed by white women to attain mobility.

Refinement to Theory

Studies comprising the particularistic mobility thesis provide a basis for further differentiating how causal dynamics posited by this perspective should impact the determinants of and timing to mobility into upper-tier occupations among minority women. Latinas, specifically, should be less prone to particularistic bias than are African American women. First, anecdotal evidence from several case studies of race-based experiences at work suggest that Latinas are allocated to less segregated task groups and internship programs than African American women, leaving them better able to communicate relevant job-related personal characteristics (Fernandez 1981; Yaffee 1995). Second, survey research has demonstrated that whites hold less invidious stereotypes toward Latinas than they do toward African American women (see Kluegel and Bobo 2001; Bobo and Massagli 2001). As such, relatively benign perceptions of Latinas regarding job-related personal characteristics, such as work ethic, intelligence, and penchant for criminality, translate into, relative to African Americans, a more favorable set of baseline personal characteristics. Accordingly, these relatively benign perceptions may be the basis of less severe forms of cognitive distortion, such as self-serving attribution bias and statistical discrimination in the promotion process.

Overall, based on these studies, racial differences in the determinants of and timing to occupational mobility into upper-tier occupations along lines enunciated by the particularistic mobility thesis should operate along a racialized continuum. Specifically, the path to mobility for African American women should be most narrow and circumscribed; that is, it is most dependent on traditional stratification-based causal factors, including, most notably, human capital. Conversely, the route to upper-tier slots for white women should be broadest, meaning it is most generalizable and least dependent on traditional stratification-based causal factors. Finally, Latinas should occupy an intermediate ground between African Americans and whites. In addition, as the timing of mobility into upper-tier occupations is a function of opportunities to reach them, race-based patterns in timing should proceed along a parallel track to the determinants of mobility. Accordingly, African Americans should experience the slowest movement into upper-tier occupations, while whites should move into these occupations most rapidly. Furthermore, Latinas should ascend into them in a temporally intermediate fashion between African American and white women.

Data and Methods

Data from the 1998 through 2005 waves of the Panel Study of Income Dynamics (PSID) were pooled to examine racial differences among women in the determinants of and timing to mobility into upper-tier occupations (see Hill [1992] for a detailed description of the PSID data set). The PSID originated in 1968 and is an ongoing longitudinal survey of all members of 5,000 households to determine changes in their economic well-being. The sample for the current study consists of a cohort of 528 full-time non-self-employed African American women, 983 white women, and 266 Latinas who were between the ages of 18 and 55.[1] The variables used in the analyses are as follows.

Dependent variable

Upper-tier occupations consist of two of the eleven broad-based 1970 census-based occupational categories—managers/administrators and professional/technical workers. The managers/administrators category includes jobs that are high on a "supervisory dimension" (Hout 1988), that is, having decision-making responsibility over the size, personnel, and direction of firms (Parcel and Mueller 1983; Bridges and Villemez 1994). The professional/technical category includes positions that put a premium on the attainment of formalized training in specialty areas and typically involve relatively high levels of formalized credentialing as a prerequisite for entry (Leicht and Fennell 2001).

Predictor variables

The influence of several categories of factors in structuring the determinants of and timing to occupational mobility among African American and white women as well as Latinas are included.

Race and socioeconomic background. Race is coded as 1 for African Americans and Latinas, with white women serving as the reference category. Background status is measured with two variables. The first is years of mother's education (years).[2] The second is whether the respondent came from an "intact family" when growing up. This variable is coded 1 if the worker had both parents in the household until age 16 and 0 if the worker did not have both parents in the household until age 16.[3]

Human capital credentials. The influence of several human capital credentials is assessed. First, level of educational attainment is coded as a series of dummy variables, specifically, "postcollege" and "college," with "less than college" serving as the reference category. Second, consistent with prior research, attendance at work is used as an indicator of job commitment (Mueller and Price 1992; Wilson and McBrier 2005). Specifically, job commitment is operationalized as the mean number of job absences among respondents in a year. Job absences are reverse-coded so that higher scores reflect greater commitment (i.e., fewer absences) and lower scores reflect lesser commitment (i.e., more absences). Third, time spent at present employer is included, which is measured by the number of months the respondent has worked for her present employer. The fourth human capital characteristic included is prior work experience, which is measured by the number of years the respondent has worked full time in the labor force since age 18. Finally, the number of hours worked per week is included as a control variable.

Job/labor market characteristics. The influence of several job/labor market characteristics is assessed. First, union status of job is coded as 1 = yes, 0 = no. Second, sector of employment is coded as 1 = public, 0 = private.

Finally, this study uses an interaction-based strategy to assess the determinants of mobility into upper-tier occupations for African American and white women as well as Latinas. Accordingly, interaction terms are created for race and all independent variables in the model, with whites serving as the reference category (coded 0) so that the paths to promotion for the two groups of minority women is compared to that of whites. Overall, this strategy is appropriate for our purposes: it controls on all independent variables, thereby assessing whether the vector of predictors operates in a significantly different fashion for minorities vis-à-vis white women.

Statistical model

Multinomial logistic regression is used to assess the determinants of the two occupational categories. This multivariate technique is used for evaluating categorical dependent variables that are treated as distinct and unordered, and the issue of interest is to identify factors that contribute to being in a particular upper-tier occupational category rather than not being employed in either of them. The output from the multinomial logit analysis includes one fewer vector of coefficients than there are choices in the model. The B estimates represent the log odds of being in a particular category relative to a base category resulting from a one-unit change in the independent variable of interest. Thus, for the analysis of the three-category dependent variables, occupational categories, two vectors of coefficients are produced. Because the base category for these analyses is occupational categories other than the managers/administrators or professional/ technical ones, the coefficients represent the net effect of the independent variables on the probability of being employed in the two white-collar occupational categories rather than being employed in either of them. In addition, for multinomial logistic regression analyses, odds ratios are constructed by computing the antilog of each coefficient.

Last, mobility into upper-tier positions is identified by tracking occupations of respondents across survey years. In particular, a discrete-time hazard rate model—a form of event-history analysis—is used to track career experiences (Allison 1984). The dependent variable in event-history analysis is the hazard rate, an unobserved variable that indicates the probability that a person will experience an event at a particular time given that the person has not yet experienced the event. Event-history analysis estimates the probability of becoming upwardly mobile for each person-year of exposure to the risk of experiencing the event; this entails treating each person-year of exposure to the risk of moving upward from a non-upper-tier occupation during the eight waves as if it were a separate observation and pooling these observations.

Workers were defined as "being at risk" for becoming mobile if they worked in a non-upper-tier occupation and were paid by an employer. Beginning in 1998, workers were followed until they experienced a career transition, specifically, moving to an upper-tier occupation, or a move to unemployment or self-employment. When experiencing a transition to an upper-tier slot, the worker is no longer in the risk set and is dropped from the analysis. Thus, the number of cases contributing to the pooled set decreases each year. Respondents excluded from the initial sample in 1998 could enter the risk set in later years if they met the selection criteria. Similar to those selected in 1998, these workers remained in the risk set until they experienced a career transition. The total number of person-years in the 1998 to 2005 pooled data set was 2,911 white, 1,556 African American, and 721 Latina.

Overall, after pooling the eight years of observations, a multinomial logistic regression equation is specified, which models the odds of being mobile between year and year $t = 1$. As tenure is controlled, the model estimates the likelihood of

TABLE 1
Rates of Mobility into Upper-Tier Occupations (in Percentages)

Professional/Technical			Managerial/Administrative		
African American	White	Latina	African American	White	Latina
18.9[a]	35.6	24.1[b]	18.1	22.8	19.5

a. African American–white $p < .001$.
b. Latina–white $p < .01$.

becoming mobile given the failure to have been mobile at an earlier duration. Results from this model approximate a discrete-time hazard rate, which accommodates time-varying covariates (Allison 1984; Teachman 1983).

Results

The first stage of analysis used descriptive statistics to address the race-specific incidence of mobility for the white, African American, and Latina sample of women into both census-based upper-tier occupational categories during the 1998 to 2005 period. Table 1 reports these results from an analysis of variance (ANOVA) procedure).

The findings indicate that there is variation in the distribution of race-based representation across the two upper-tier categories among the sample of women. The racial gap between whites and the two minority groups of women is pronounced in the professional/technical category. Specifically, 35.6 percent of whites, 18.9 percent of African Americans, and 24.9 percent of Latinas experience mobility into the professional/technical category.[4] Furthermore, access is significantly different between whites and the two groups of minority women. The racial gap, however, between whites and the two groups of minority women in access to the managers/administrators category is less, and there are no significant differences between whites and either minority group. Specifically, 22.8 percent of white women, 18.1 percent of African American women, and 19.5 percent of Latinas experience mobility into the managers/administrators category.

Determinants of mobility

Table 2 reports results from multinomial logistic regression models for the determinants of mobility into the professional/technical and managers/administrators occupational categories among white and African American women as well as Latinas.

TABLE 2
Multinomial Logistic Regressions for Determinants of Mobility into Upper-Tier
Occupations

	Professional/Technical		Managerial/ Administrative	
Variable	Coefficient	Odds Ratio	Coefficient	Odds Ratio
Main effects				
Sociodemographic				
African American	−.38°°°	.69	−.23°°	.75
Latina	−.22°°	.76	−.17°	.82
Background				
Mother's education	.03°°	1.03	.01	1.01
Intact family	.17°°	1.18	.05	1.05
Human capital				
Postcollege	.16°°	1.16	.17°	1.17
College	.18°°	1.19	.07	1.07
High school	.03	1.03	−.04	.96
Commitment	.06°°°	1.06	.02°	1.02
Time with employer	.05°°°	1.05	−.01	.99
Work experience	.04°°°	1.05	.01	1.01
Job/labor market				
Union	.28°°°	1.30	.14°	1.14
Public	.05	1.05	.08	1.08
Interactions with race				
Background				
Mother's education—African American	.01	1.01	.02°	1.02
Mother's education—Latina	.01	1.01	.01	1.01
Intact family—African American	.17°°	1.17	.05	1.05
Intact family—Latina	.13°	1.13	.01	1.01
Human capital				
Postcollege—African American	.13°	1.13	.17°	1.17
Postcollege—Latina	.20°°	1.22	−.01	.99
College—African American	.18°°	1.19	.07	1.07
College—Latina	−.01	.99	.01	1.01
High school—African American	.03	1.03	−.04	.96
High school—Latina	.01	1.01	.01	1.01
Commitment—African American	.06°°°	1.06	.02°	1.02
Commitment—Latina	.03°°	1.03	.02°	1.02
Time with employer—African American	.05°°°	1.05	.02°	1.02
Time with employer—Latina	.01	1.01	−.01	.99
Work experience—African American	.04°°°	1.05	.01	1.01
Work experience—Latina	.03°°	1.03	.01	1.01

(continued)

TABLE 2 (CONTINUED)

Variable	Professional/Technical		Managerial/ Administrative	
	Coefficient	Odds Ratio	Coefficient	Odds Ratio
Job/labor market				
Union—African American	.28°°°	1.30	.14°	1.14
Union—Latina	.20°°	1.22	.06	1.06
Public—African American	.05	1.05	.08	1.08
Public—Latina	.05	1.05	.07	1.07
Constant	−2.67		−2.64	
Log-likelihood	−311.57		−308.58	

°$p < .05.$ °°$p < .01.$ °°°$p < .001.$

Professional/technical. Findings indicate there is greater support for prediction from theory in the context of the determinants of mobility into professional/technical occupations. First, at least half the interaction terms—specifically, seven out of nine for African Americans vis-à-vis whites and five out of nine for Latinas vis-à-vis whites—exert significant differences. Second, the effects of these variables are along lines predicted by theory; that is, they produce a more narrow and more scrutinized path to mobility for minority women, relative to white women. Furthermore, the effect of these variables is pronounced: of the seven significant among African Americans, six—the overwhelming majority—exert either robust ($p < .001$) or moderate ($p < .01$) effects; of the five significant variables for Latinas, four exert moderate effects and one exerts a modest effect ($p < .05$). In particular, African Americans' attainment of professional/technical jobs, relative to whites, increases, respectively, by 1.06, 1.04, 1.06, and 1.05 times the marginal odds of not reaching this occupational category with unit increases in job commitment, time with present employer, and work experience. Furthermore, African Americans' attainment of the professional/technical jobs, relative to whites, increases, respectively, by 1.17, 1.13, and 1.19 times the marginal odds of not reaching this occupational category if they come from an intact family and have either a postcollege or college education. Finally, among variables measuring job/labor market characteristics, findings indicate that African Americans' attainment of the professional/technical jobs, relative to whites, increases by 1.30 times the marginal odds if they work in a unionized position.

Similar results—though not as pronounced—are found among Latinas, relative to white women. Specifically, Latinas' attainment of jobs in the professional/technical category, relative to white women, increases by 1.03 times the marginal odds of not reaching this occupational category with unit increases in job commitment and work experience. Furthermore, Latinas' attainment of jobs in the professional/technical category, relative to whites, increases respectively by 1.13,

TABLE 3
Timing to Mobility into Upper-Tier Occupations (in Months)

	Professional/Technical			Managers/Administrators		
Tenure Year	White	African American	Latina	White	African American	Latina
1	67	89	75	71	83	78
4	55	80	68	63	71	69
8	45	74	61	56	67	62

1.22, and 1.22 times the marginal odds of not reaching this occupational category if they come from an intact family, have a postcollege education, or work in a unionized slot.

Managerial/administrative. Findings from Table 2 also support predictions from theory in the context of the determinants of mobility into managerial/administrative occupations. However, while whites are favored along lines predicted by theory, gaps are minor relative to findings regarding entry into professional/technical slots. First, four out of nine interaction terms exert significant effects for African Americans, vis-à-vis whites, and two out of nine exert significant effects for Latinas, vis-à-vis whites. Furthermore, the magnitude of all significant variables for both groups, vis-à-vis whites, is modest. In particular, African Americans' attainment of occupations in the managerial/administrative category, relative to whites, increases respectively by 1.02 times the marginal odds of not reaching this occupational category with unit increases in mother's education and job commitment. Furthermore, African Americans' attainment of positions in the managerial/administrative category, relative to whites, increases respectively by 1.17 and 1.14 times the marginal odds if they have a postcollege education or work in a unionized position. Finally, Latinas' attainment of jobs in the managerial/administrative category, relative to whites, increases by 1.02 times the marginal odds of not reaching this occupational category with unit increases in job commitment and time with employer.

Timing to mobility

Table 3 reports results from event-history analyses regarding the timing of experiencing upward mobility into each of the two upper-tier occupational categories among white women, African American women, and Latinas. The timing to mobility is determined by substituting the race-specific means on predictor variables from Table 1 into the models in Table 2. By allowing tenure to vary, the models predict the odds of experiencing movement at each year of tenure. After transforming the predicted odds to predicted probabilities, the cumulative product of one minus the duration-specific mobility probabilities yields a survival curve (highlighting findings for years one, four, and eight in tabular form). Plotting the survival curve against duration in the job will show how long the typical respondent in the PSID sample waits before becoming upwardly mobile.

The findings highlight a racialized continuum in the timing to mobility into both professional/technical and managerial/administrative categories along lines enunciated by the particularistic mobility thesis. Accordingly, in terms of timing to reach professional/technical slots, racial differences favoring white women over minority women should be relatively pronounced. Specifically, it is predicted that after eight years, 45 percent of white women will not have been upwardly mobile, meaning that 55 percent will have left the risk set and experienced mobility into upper-tier occupations. In contrast, in the eighth year, it is predicted that 74 percent of African Americans will not have been upwardly mobile, meaning that 26 percent of African American women will have experienced mobility into upper-tier slots. Finally, by the same logic, it is predicted that in the eighth year, 39 percent of Latinas will have experienced mobility into upper-tier slots.

The findings also indicate that racial gaps between white and minority women in timing to mobility into managerial/administrative occupation are not as great as gaps in timing into professional/technical occupations. Specifically, it is predicted that after eight years, 56 percent of white women will not have been upwardly mobile, meaning that 44 percent will have left the risk set and experienced mobility into upper-tier occupations. In contrast, in the eighth year, it is predicted that 70 percent of African Americans will not have been upwardly mobile, meaning that 30 percent of African American women will have experienced mobility into upper-tier slots. Finally, by the same logic, it is predicted that in the eighth year, 34 percent of Latinas will have experienced mobility into upper-tier slots.

Conclusion

The findings from analyses of the PSID sample of women support predictions from the particularistic mobility thesis, though gaps along the predicted racialized continuum are greater for the professional/technical category than they are for the managers/administrators upper-tier occupational category. Specifically, a racialized hierarchy, favoring whites and disadvantaging African Americans most, with Latinas occupying a middle ground, emerges in terms of both the determinants of and timing to mobility into both occupational categories. Specifically, the route to mobility for African Americans is most narrow and structured by traditional stratification causal factors, including background status and job/labor market characteristics, and they are slowest to experience mobility. The route to mobility for whites is the most broad and unstructured by the stratification-based causal factors, and they experience mobility the quickest. Along both issues, Latinas occupy an intermediate position between African Americans and whites.[5]

It is important to specify how findings constitute forms of disadvantage for Latinas and, especially, African American women. First, the narrower path to mobility appears deleterious: long-standing discriminatory barriers that impede the acquisition of, for example, human capital—such as access to postcollege education (Braddock and McPartland 1987) and high rates of job displacement (Wilson and McBrier 2005; Spalter-Roth and Deitch 1999)—serve to depress rates of mobility among minority women. Conversely, whites are not similarly handicapped. They attain upper-tier occupations in at least two ways: similar to African American women and Latinas, they advance through a relatively formal process, but they also do so through a variety of informal means unavailable to minority women. Overall, the greater range of options for white women would seem to translate into higher mobility rates. Second, the slower ascent to upper-tier occupations among minority women signals disadvantage. As mentioned earlier, the longer spell spent outside upper-tier occupations means minorities lose a greater amount of socioeconomic rewards—both material and symbolic—than whites, who have an advantage on an intragenerational and intergenerational basis. Furthermore, African American women and Latinas who climb the occupational ladder would seem to be handicapped in terms of an increasingly important dimension of stratification in the first decade of the new millennium, namely, the stability of jobs: in an era in which job displacement by way of layoffs, furloughs, and reductions to part-time status has accelerated, seniority status has become increasingly prized as a resource that insulates workers from job loss (B. Smith and Rubin 1997; Cappelli 2000).

What is significant, and not to be overlooked, is that the findings also indicate that among women, particularistic practices have varying effects across upper-tier occupational categories, with racial effects in the determinants of and timing to managerial/administrative slots being more pronounced than in professional/technical slots. In fact, several recent gender-based studies may help to explain variation in racial gaps in the determinants of and timing to professional/technical jobs vis-à-vis manager/administrator occupations. They suggest, in particular, that women—across racial categories—suffer from a pronounced form of "social closure" (Weber 1968) that includes institutional forms of exclusion from occupations that invoke supervisory responsibility (R. Smith 2002; Reskin 2000; Moller and Rubin 2008). Apparently, when firm control and direction is at stake, gender—across racial groups—acts to depress occupational attainment, thereby partially counteracting the race-specific impact of particularism. Conversely, in the context of professional/technical occupations, where incumbency translates into well-paid and prestigious positions but does not as directly offer opportunities to exercise control/power over firms (Leicht and Fennell 2001), particularism acts unencumbered to create greater variation by race in access to upper-tier slots among women.

Finally, there is reason to suspect these forms of minority group disadvantage produced by particularistic practices are not likely to recede any time soon. In particular, a hallmark of the "new restructured workplace" (Kalleberg 2009) is enhanced employer "flexibility," an outgrowth of increasing de-bureaucratization of workplace rules/regulations (Moller and Rubin 2008; Kalleberg 2009), the rise of short-term employment contracts (Cappelli 2008; Moller and Rubin 2008), and the loss of traditional employee-based equal employment opportunity protections (Skrentny 2001; Stainback, Robinson, and Tomaskovic-Devey 2005). Significantly, flexibility has increased discretion among employers when making promotion-relevant decisions, likely fueling particularistic practices (Kalleberg 2009; Cappelli 2008). Accordingly, vigorous policy is necessary if we are to "stem the tide" and reverse the impact of these recent developments in the workplace. In this regard, policies should be enacted that minimize employer discretion by establishing clear-cut guidelines for promotion that are based on objective criteria such as educational prerequisites and relevant work experience. In addition, policies should be enacted to ensure that African American women and Latinas are increasingly represented across the range of settings and contexts within firms that facilitate racially integrated informal and formal social networks. These measures—if enacted in a manner that makes firms "legally accountable and responsible" (Kalev, Dobbin, and Kelly 2007)—help to level the playing field with respect to providing opportunities to demonstrate the informal criteria that are important bases for promotion into upper-tier occupations.

In sum, the findings from this study provide additional evidence for the recent statement by Bonilla-Silva (2004) that in the contemporary American workplace—across both gender groups—a racialized continuum is coming to characterize stratification-based dynamics. Nevertheless, it must be emphasized that this study does not represent the "final word" regarding the race-based determinants of and timing to mobility of women into upper-tier occupations. Researchers, for example, should conduct more refined analyses. First, they should assess how particularism structures the determinants and timing of mobility across specific jobs, such as for lawyers, doctors, accountants, and so forth. In fact, occupational-level data may mask inequality generated by phenomena such as race-based job "ghettoization" (Vallas 2003) that have been documented to operate at the job level (Reskin 2000; S. Collins 1997). Second, researchers should more directly capture the influence of the causal mechanisms posited by the particularistic mobility thesis that produce racial inequities among women in mobility into upper-tier occupations. There is a limitation in a survey-based approach that bases its results on the explanatory power of a model with a particular focus on sets of variables that measure, for example, human capital credentials. Specifically, interpretations of occupational attainment processes that are based, in part, on the presence or absence of relationships between objective characteristics such as human capital and occupational attainment may be problematic because the lack of significance of it may be due to unmeasured factors. Accordingly, it is important for researchers to undertake case studies in specific organizations where the potential exists to observe firsthand the practices of employers that account for race-specific mobility dynamics. Overall, when these suggestions for research are implemented, we should further understand how, among women, racial stratification—in the context of occupational mobility—unfolds.

Notes

1. The PSID uses the 1970 census-based occupational classification scheme.

2. Large numbers of missing cases on father's education for African Americans necessitated the use of mother's education. Sociological research has found that there is a high positive correlation between measures of educational attainment for mothers and fathers' education (Parcel and Mueller 1983).

3. Missing values on all independent variables were coded to racial group means. No variable included in the final model had more than 8 percent missing values.

4. The Sheffe multigroup comparison procedure in the analysis of variance was used here.

5. No assertion is made here that minority women experience a "double disadvantage" based on a combined/interactive effect of race and gender; it is unclear from existing sociological research based on, for example, "queuing theory" (Lieberson 1980) whether African American women and Latinas are situated below minority male counterparts (Farley 2004; Reskin 2000).

References

Allison, Paul. 1984. *Event history analysis: Regression for longitudinal event data*. Newbury Park, CA: Sage.

Baldi, Stephane, and Debra McBrier. 1997. Do the determinants of promotion differ for blacks and whites? *Work and Occupations* 24:478–97.

Bell, Ella, and Stella Nkomo. 2001. *Our separate ways: Black and white women and the struggle for professional identity*. Cambridge, MA: Harvard Business School Press.

Bobo, Lawrence, James Kluegel, and Ryan Smith. 1997. Laissez-faire racism: The crystallization of a kinder, gentler, antiblack ideology. In *Racial attitudes in the 1990s*, eds. Steven Tuch and Jack Martin, 75–108. Westport, CT: Praeger.

Bobo, Lawrence, and Michael Massagli. 2001.Stereotyping and urban inequality. In *Urban inequality: Evidence from four cities*, eds. Alice O'Connor, Chris Tilly, and Lawrence Bobo, 89–162. New York, NY: Russell Sage Foundation.

Bonilla-Silva, Eduardo. 2004. From bi-racial to tri-racial: Towards a new system of racial stratification in the United States. *Ethnic and Racial Studies* 27:931–50.

Braddock, Jomills, and James McPartland. 1987. How minorities continue to be excluded from employment opportunities: Research on labor markets and institutional barriers. *Journal of Social Issues* 43:5–39.

Bridges, George, and Wayne Villemez. 1994. *The employment relationship*. New York, NY: Plenum.

Browne, Irene, and Joya Misra. 2003. The intersection of race and gender in the labor market. *Annual Review of Sociology* 290:487–513.

Cappelli, Peter. 2000. Examining the incidence of downsizing and its effects on establishment performance. In *On the job: Is long-term employment a thing of the past?* ed. David Neumark, 463–515. New York, NY: Russell Sage Foundation.

Cappelli, Peter. 2008. *Employment relationships: New models of white collar work*. Cambridge, MA: Harvard University Press.

Collins, Patricia Hill. 2008. *Black feminist thought: Knowledge, consciousness, and the politics of empowerment*. New York, NY: Routledge.

Collins, Sharon. 1997. *Black corporate executives: The making and breaking of a middle class*. Philadelphia, PA: Temple University Press.

England, Paula, Karen Christopher, and Lori Reid. 1999. The economic progress of Mexicana and Puerto Rican women. In *Latinas and African American women at work*, ed. Irene Browne, 139–82. New York, NY: Russell Sage Foundation.

Farley, Reynolds. 2004. *The American people*. New York, NY: Russell Sage Foundation.

Feagin, Joe, and Melvin Sikes. 1994. *Living with racism: The black middle-class experience*. Boston, MA: Beacon.

Fernandez, John. 1981. *Black managers in white corporations*. Lanham, MD: Lexington Books.

Fosu, Augustin. 1992. Occupational mobility of black women, 1958–1981: The impact of post-1964 antidiscrimination measures. *Industrial and Labor Relations Review* 45:281–94.

Higginbotham, Elizabeth, and Lynn Weber. 1992. Moving up with kin and community: Upward social mobility for black and white women. *Gender & Society* 6:416–40.

Hill, Martha. 1992. *The panel study of income dynamics: A user's guide*. Newbury Park, CA: Sage.

Hout, Michael. 1988. More universalism, less structural mobility: The American occupational structure in the 1980s. *American Journal of Sociology* 93:1358–1400.

Jacobs, Jerry. 1989. *Revolving doors: Sex segregation and women's careers*. Palo Alto, CA: Stanford University Press.

James, Erica. 2000. Race-related differences in promotions and support: Underlying effects of human and social capital. *Organization Science* 11:493–508.

Jaynes, Gerald, and Robin Williams. 1989. *A common destiny: Blacks and American society*. Washington, DC: National Academies Press.

Kalev, Alexandra, Frank Dobbin, and Erin Kelly. 2007. Best practices or best guesses? Assessing the efficacy of corporate affirmative action and diversity programs. *American Sociological Review* 72:353–97.

Kalleberg, Arne. 2009. Precarious work, insecure workers, and employment relations in transition. *American Sociological Review* 74:1–22.

Kennelly, Ivy. 1999. That single mother element: How white employers typify black women. *Gender & Society* 13:168–92.

King, Mark. 1995. Black women's labor market status: Occupational segregation in the United States and Britain. *Review of Black Political Economy* 24:23–43.

Kluegel, James, and Lawrence Bobo. 2001. Perceived group discrimination and policy attitudes: The sources and consequences for the race and gender gaps. In *Urban inequality: Evidence from four cities*, eds. Alice O'Connor, Chris Tilly, and Lawrence Bobo, 163–216. New York, NY: Russell Sage Foundation.

Kohn, Melvin. 1969. *Class and conformity: A study in values*. Chicago, IL: University of Chicago Press.

Leicht, Kevin, and Mary Fennell. 2001. *Professional work: A sociological approach*. Malden, MA: Blackwell.

Lieberson, Stanley. 1980. *A piece of the pie*. Berkeley: University of California Press.

Maume, David. 1999. Glass ceilings and glass escalators: Occupational segregation and race and sex differences in managerial promotions. *Work and Occupations* 26:483–509.

McGuire, Gail. 2002. Gender, race, and the shadow structure: A study of informal networks and inequality in a work organization. *Gender & Society* 16:303–22.

Moller, Stephanie, and Beth Rubin. 2008. The contours of stratification in service-oriented industries. *Social Science Research* 37:1039–60.

Mueller, Charles, and James Price. 1992. Employee commitment: Resolving some issues. *Work and Occupations* 19:211–36.

Mundra, Kenneth, Anthony Moellner, and William Loez-Aqueres. 1995. Investigating Hispanic underrepresentation in managerial and professional occupations. *Hispanic Journal of Behavioral Sciences* 25:513–29.

Parcel, Toby, and Charles Mueller. 1983. *Ascription and labor markets: Race and sex differences in earnings*. New York, NY: Academic Press.

Pettigrew, Thomas. 1985. New black-white patterns: How best to conceptualize them. *Annual Review of Sociology* 9:1–23.

Pettigrew, Thomas, and Joanne Martin. 1987. Shaping the organizational context of African American inclusion. *Journal of Social Issues* 43:41–78.

Reskin, Barbara. 2000. The proximate causes of discrimination. *Contemporary Sociology* 29:319–28.

Reskin, Barbara, and Denise Bielby. 2005. A sociological perspective on gender career outcomes. *Journal of Socioeconomic Perspectives* 19:71–86.

Reskin, Barbara, and Debra McBrier. 2000. Why not ascription? Organizations' employment of male and female managers. *American Sociological Review* 65:210–33.

Reskin, Barbara, and Irene Padavic. 1994. *Women and men at work*. Thousand Oaks, CA: Pine Forge Press.

Ridgeway, Cecilia, and Linda Smith-Lovin. 1999. The gender system and interaction. *Annual Review of Sociology* 25:191–216.

Risman, Barbara. 2004. Gender as a social structure. *Gender & Society* 18:429–50.

Skrentny, John. 2001. *Color lines: Affirmative action, immigration, and civil rights options for America.* Chicago, IL: University of Chicago Press.

Smith, Brian, and Beth Rubin. 1997. From displacement to reemployment: Job acquisition in the flexible economy. *Social Science Research* 26:282–308.

Smith, Ryan. 2001. Particularism in control over monetary resources at work. *Work and Occupations* 28:447–68.

Smith, Ryan. 2002. Race, gender, and authority in the workplace. *Annual Review of Sociology* 28:509–42.

Smith, Ryan. 2005. Do the determinants of promotion differ for white men versus women and minorities? An exploration of intersectionalism through sponsored and contest mobility processes. *American Behavioral Scientist* 48:1157–81.

Spalter-Roth, Roberta, and Cynthia Deitch. 1999. "I don't feel right sized, I feel out-of-work sized": Gender, race, ethnicity and the uneven costs of displacement. *Work and Occupations* 30:379–400.

Stainback, Kevin, Corre L. Robinson, and Donald Tomaskovic-Devey. 2005. Race and workplace integration: A politically mediated process? *American Behavioral Scientist* 48:1200–1228.

Teachman, Jay. 1983. Analyzing social processes: Life tables and proportional hazards models. *Social Science Research* 12:263–301.

Tomaskovic-Devey, Donald. 1993. *Gender and racial inequality at work.* Ithaca, NY: ILR.

Tomaskovic-Devey, Donald, and Sheryl Skaggs. 1999. An establishment-level test of the statistical discrimination hypothesis. *Work and Occupations* 26:422–45.

Tomkiewitz, James, and Orlando Brenner. 1996. The relationship between race (Hispanic) stereotypes and requisite management characteristics. *Journal of Social Behavior and Personality* 11:511–20.

Vallas, Steve. 2003. Rediscovering the color line within work organizations: The "knitting of racial groups" revisited. *Work and Occupations* 30:379–400.

Weber, Max. 1968. *Economy and society.* New York, NY: Vantage.

Wilson, George. 1997. Pathways to power: Racial differences in the determinants of job authority. *Social Problems* 48:148–64.

Wilson, George. 2005. Race and job dismissal: African American/white differences in their sources during the early work career. *American Behavioral Scientist* 48:1182–95.

Wilson, George, and Debra McBrier. 2005. Race and loss of privilege: African American/white differences in the determinants of job layoffs from upper-tier occupations. *Sociological Forum* 20:301–21.

Wilson, George, and Vincent Roscigno. 2010. Race and downward mobility from privileged occupations: African American/white dynamics across the early work-career. *Social Science Research* 39:67–77.

Wilson, George, Ian Sakura-Lemessy, and John West. 1999. Reaching the top: Racial differences in mobility paths to upper-tier occupations. *Work and Occupations* 26:165–86.

Yaffee, James. 1995. Latina managers in employment: Perceptions of organizational discrimination. *Hispanic Journal of Behavioral Sciences* 17:334–46.

Money, Benefits, and Power: A Test of the Glass Ceiling and Glass Escalator Hypotheses

By
RYAN A. SMITH

This article explores the manner in which race, ethnicity, and gender intersect to produce inequality in wages and employer benefits among "workers" (employees with no job authority), "supervisors" (employees with broad supervisory responsibilities), and "managers" (employees who can hire/fire and set the pay of others). Using data uniquely suited to examine these relationships, the author finds that, contrary to the glass ceiling hypothesis, the white male advantage over women and minorities in wages and retirement benefits generally does not increase with movement up the authority hierarchy net of controls. Instead, relative inequality remains constant at higher and lower levels of authority. However, in nontraditional work settings where white men report to minority and female supervisors, there is evidence that a glass ceiling stifles women and minorities while a glass escalator helps white men. Instead of representing mutually exclusive processes and outcomes, glass ceilings and glass escalators may actually overlap in certain employment contexts. The implications of these results for future analyses of workplace inequality are discussed.

Keywords: wages; employer benefits; glass ceiling; glass escalator; job authority; intersectionalism

In the past quarter-century, two dominant metaphors have come to symbolize the processes and outcomes associated with workplace inequality: *glass ceilings* and *glass escalators*. While originally conceived as blocked promotional

Ryan Alan Smith is an associate professor and Lillie and Nathan Ackerman Chair of Social Justice in the School of Public Affairs, Baruch College, City University of New York (CUNY). He has written extensively on race, ethnicity, and gender stratification at work. His publications have appeared in the American Sociological Review, *the* Annual Review of Sociology, Social Forces, *and* Work and Occupations. *He also serves as an organizational change consultant to public, private, and non-profit organizations.*

NOTE: This research is being supported, in part, by a PSC-CUNY research award. I thank Jim Elliott for original data and variable construction and for several conversations about key ideas presented in this article. Any errors remain those of the author.

DOI: 10.1177/0002716211422038

opportunities for women in the corporate hierarchy (Hymowitz and Schellhardt 1986), the concept of the glass ceiling has now been extended to include not only women but also racial minorities, and not employees only at the upper levels of corporations but throughout the lower and middle occupational ranks as well (Federal Glass Ceiling Commission 1995). Despite the glass ceiling metaphor's popularity and its influence on the way workplace inequality is understood, social scientific evidence as to whether it exists has produced two schools of thought. On one hand, opponents argue that general inequality may exist between women and men (Baxter and Wright 2000; Wright, Baxter, and Birkelund 1995; Morgan 1998) and between white men and women and racial minorities specifically (Zeng 2011), but they claim the disparities do not necessarily increase with movement up the authority hierarchy as the glass ceiling hypothesis implies. One researcher siding with this position has even gone as far as to call the glass ceiling idea a "myth" (Zeng 2011). On the other hand, a larger body of literature has documented the presence of a glass ceiling for women relative to men (Cotter et al. 2001; Huffman 2004; Jacobs 1992; Maume 1999, 2004; Morrison and Glinow 1990; Reskin and McBrier 2000; Reskin and Ross 1992), and for racial minorities and white women relative to white men (Elliott and Smith 2004; Maume 2004; Smith n.d.). These studies show increasing inequality between groups from lower levels of an outcome variable (e.g., authority, wages, managerial transitions) to higher levels.

Needless to say, the battle to prove or disprove the existence of glass ceiling inequality in the United States is a "winner take all" proposition. Understandably, the very idea that the glass ceiling is a myth would come as a major shock to students of workplace inequality, policy proponents, diversity advocates, practitioners, and scholars. After all, if there is no glass ceiling, the countless millions of dollars spent to dismantle it, the policy and legal prescriptions designed to combat it, and the research dollars set aside to study it may have all been for nought. The stakes are high indeed.

With less fanfare and far less empirical scrutiny, the concept of the glass escalator has influenced the way social scientists have come to understand the differential workplace rewards men and women receive when they work in predominantly female occupations (Budig 2002; Huffman 2004; Hultin 2003; Maume 1999; Williams 1992, 1995). Drawing on Rosabeth Moss Kanter's seminal work *Men and Women of the Corporation* (1977), Christine Williams (1992, 1995) argued, contrary to Kanter's theory of tokenism, that male tokens working in female-dominated jobs do not experience the same kind of discrimination women face when they are tokens working in male-dominated jobs. In fact, Williams argued that men working in female-dominated jobs (e.g., nurses, elementary school teachers, librarians, and social workers) experience a certain amount of favoritism at the point of hire and in promotions to higher-paying, more prestigious positions.

While less voluminous than glass ceiling inquiries, quantitative tests of the glass escalator hypothesis have also produced mixed results, with some studies providing evidence in support of the hypothesis (Huffman 2004; Hultin 2003; Maume 1999) while others show evidence to the contrary (Budig 2002; Snyder and Green 2008). One of the major limitations of past quantitative inquiries into this matter is the general impression that the glass escalator lifts all men (regardless of color) in female-dominated jobs to higher-paying positions with more authority. This assumption is contrary to a recent claim that glass escalators are both racialized and gendered such that white men are more likely than minority men to benefit from working in female-dominated jobs (Wingfield 2009). Thus, the second major goal of this article is to provide a formal test of this proposition. Specifically, I extend the glass escalator literature in four ways. First, I examine whether glass escalator inequality can be extended beyond female-dominated jobs to environments in which white men report to women and minority supervisors versus white male supervisors. Second, drawing a hypothesis from intersectional theory, I test the assumption that the glass escalator is both gendered and racialized—meaning that its exclusive benefits accrue only to white men and to not black men and Latinos. Third, I add employer-sponsored benefits to a traditional wage analysis of glass escalator effects, which enables an assessment of workplace inequality that takes into account the total compensation package. Finally, this study examines the possibility that glass ceilings and glass escalators are not necessarily mutually exclusive entities (Maume 1999; Williams 1992). If so, then *glass escalator* evidence should be marked by a clear advantage in wages and employer benefits for white men (relative to women and minorities) when they are employed in nontraditional work settings—such as when they report to women and minority supervisors. Under such circumstances, the advantage white men experience, relative to women and minorities, should increase with movement up the authority hierarchy as the *glass ceiling* hypothesis implies.

Background

Glass ceilings and glass escalators symbolize different kinds of blocked opportunities for women and racial minorities. The emerging subfield of organizational demography sheds light on the underlying social psychology that operates within these structures to limit the life chances of women and racial minorities, while the nascent area of "intersectional" scholarship offers an explanation as to *how* race, ethnicity, and gender may intersect to forge unique labor market advantages for white men and disadvantages for minority men and women. A brief review of each perspective is offered below.

Glass ceiling inequality

Baxter and Wright's (2000) provocative proposition denying the existence of gender-based glass ceiling inequality in the United States is rooted in a cross-national study of women and men in the United States, Australia, and Sweden. Using a six-level measure of authority, the authors find "weak" evidence of a glass ceiling for Australia and Sweden and no evidence of glass ceiling inequality in the United States. However, the authors did find significant gender differences at each stage of their authority measure, but the disparities did not increase with movement up the authority hierarchy—as the glass ceiling hypothesis implies. Much of the controversy resulting from their study stemmed from their definition of the glass ceiling, the lack of operational controls for glass ceiling inequality, and the cross-sectional nature of their data. Regarding definitional concerns, critics argued that the glass ceiling was not just about the hierarchical position of women relative to men. Instead, they noted that other dimensions of stratification should also be assessed, including income, prestige, and authority (Britton and Williams 2000). I heed this call in the present study as I employ wages and employer-sponsored benefits as chief outcome measures.

Another definitional objection quarreled with the proposition that glass ceiling inequality had to take place at higher rather than lower levels of an organization. Gender specialists Dana Britton and Christine Williams (2000) noted that the glass ceiling could also manifest itself at lower organizational levels in a manner akin to a "sticky floor." This study addresses this possibility, as it examines group differences in wages and employer-sponsored benefits among employees who are concentrated at lower to middle levels of job authority as defined by employees with no authority ("workers"), employees with broad supervisory responsibilities ("supervisors"), and employees with authority to hire/fire and set the pay of others ("managers"). Another complaint pointed to the lack of statistical controls for occupational gender segregation (Britton and Williams 2000)—an important point given that men and women are concentrated in different organizations with different hierarchical structures such that a manager in a female-dominated organization may be ranked much differently than a manager in a male-dominated organization. To this point, Britton and Williams lamented, "If the authors had controlled for the sex segregation of occupations in their analysis, they would have been able to compare similarly situated men and women in each hierarchical category" (2000, 806). One way the present study takes this issue into account is by controlling for percent female in an occupation. An additional criticism concerns the cross-sectional nature of Baxter and Wright's (2000) data. Ideally, assessments of glass ceiling inequality are better suited to longitudinal designs that allow researchers to track the career trajectories of the same incumbents over time (Cotter et al. 2001; Maume 1999, 2004; Zeng 2011). Baxter and Wright fully acknowledged the limitations of their cross-sectional data but concluded that when it comes to studying glass ceiling inequality, "cross-sectional evidence can be illuminating" (2000, 815). Additional investigations into the matter concur (Elliott and Smith 2004; Wright, Baxter, and Birkelund 1995).

The concerns about definitional clarity, statistical controls, and cross-sectionality notwithstanding, the weight of empirical evidence to date supports the presence of glass ceiling inequality in the United States. What is important is that the most convincing evidence in favor of glass ceiling inequality has proven to be quite responsive to Baxter and Wright's (2000) early critics. That is, scholars have extended tests of glass ceiling inequality by exploiting longitudinal designs, moving beyond a strict analysis of organizational hierarchy, predicting multiple dependent variables, and adding myriad statistical controls for workplace variables that might otherwise differentiate groups—including controls for occupation-based and job-based segregation. What has survived these innovations is Baxter and Wright's basic definition of glass ceiling inequality—the idea that inequality increases from lower to higher levels of an outcome measure, be it job authority, wages, or managerial positions. With this definition in mind, there is strong evidence to support the presence of a glass ceiling in the United States, whether conceived as a barrier women face relative to men (Cotter et al. 2001; Huffman 2004; Jacobs 1992; Morrison and Glinow 1990; Reskin and McBrier 2000) or as barrier minorities and women confront relative to white men (Maume 1999; Elliott and Smith 2004; Smith n.d.). In contrast, other scholars uncover group disparities throughout levels of authority structures but no evidence that the disparities increase with movement up the authority hierarchy (Baxter and Wright 2000; Wright, Baxter, and Birkelund 1995; Zeng 2011). A chief goal of this study is to provide data that will allow us to adjudicate between these two perspectives. If glass ceiling inequality exists, then it should be represented by a progressive increase in group differences (between white men versus women and minorities) in wages and employer benefits with movement up the authority hierarchy.

Glass escalator inequality

Christine Williams's (1992, 1995) in-depth interviews with seventy-six men and twenty-three women in female-dominated professions (e.g., nurse, elementary school teacher, librarian, and social worker) yielded a provocative conclusion. In contrast to the theory of tokenism, Williams argued that male tokens who work in female-dominated jobs did not experience the same kind of discrimination women tokens experienced when they worked in male-dominated jobs. In fact, she found that men were favored in the hiring process and encouraged to pursue the most masculine jobs in female-dominated professions—jobs that offered higher pay and more authority.

Compared with the voluminous body of literature on glass ceiling inequality (see Jackson and O'Callaghan's [2009] review), far fewer researchers have tested for glass escalator effects. There is substantial support for Williams's (1992, 1995) argument rooted in qualitative assessments of the matter (see Yoder [1991] for a review). However, as with the glass ceiling hypothesis, quantitative support for the glass escalator cuts across a variety of outcome measures, including wages (Huffman 2004), internal promotions (Hultin 2003), managerial promotions (Maume 1999), perceived job-related support, and advancement opportunities (Maume 2004). This research generally shows that men (specifically white men) do not suffer the same penalties as women (and racial minorities) for their token status. Recently, Wingfield (2009) has called on researchers to consider how race intersects with gender to stifle the benefits minority men receive from working in feminized occupations. Her study, based on seventeen semistructured interviews of black male nurses, concluded that unlike white men, black men do not get to ride the glass escalator to better-paying jobs and higher pay in the nursing profession. Maume's (1999, 2004) core findings, which may be regarded as quantitative tests of Wingfield's assumption, are largely supportive. An important contribution of Maume's work in this area is a shift in focus away from a concern for what happens in female-dominated jobs. That domain still remains salient, but it obscures the need to direct attention to other workplace conditions, such as when employees report to supervisors of a different race. On this point, Maume (2004) found that reporting to a female supervisor brought greater rewards for men than women in the form of more job-related support and career optimism—a pattern that is consistent with glass escalator effects. I extend this research to an examination of wages and employer-sponsored benefits. If glass escalator effects are present, inequity between white men and other groups should be most prevalent under anomalous work settings, such as when white men report to female and minority supervisors. If glass ceiling inequality is present, the wage and benefits disparities between white men and other groups should increase from lower to higher levels of authority.

Data

The data to test these expectations come from the Multi-City Study of Urban Inequality (MCSUI). The MCSUI is a multistage, stratified, clustered area-probability design with a sampling of whites and an oversampling of minority groups (blacks and Latinos) from Atlanta, Boston, and Los Angeles. The survey was conducted from 1992 to 1994.[1] The oversampling of minorities necessitated weighting all descriptive statistics but not the multivariate analyses (see Kmec 2003).[2]

The MCSUI data are good sources for testing for glass ceiling and glass escalator inequality. First, the MCSUI's multiethnic sample of men and women enables a study of Latino men and women in addition to whites and blacks, which makes it possible to test competing theories of *how* race/ethnicity and gender affect the relationship between wages and employer benefits and authority attainment. Second, the MCSUI provides detailed information on individual-level factors, family status indicators, and a full array of important structural determinants of wages and benefits (see the appendix for all variables).

Third, the MCSUI provides data on successive levels of workplace power and information on the race and gender of immediate superiors. These factors enable a test of whether inequality in wages and benefits stems from glass ceiling inequality (i.e., increasing inequality between white men and other groups at higher levels of power) and glass escalator inequality (i.e., white men's receipt of higher compensation via wages and retirement benefits when they work in settings that are supervised by minorities and women). Finally, the MCSUI offers data from local, urban labor markets and also job-level information that scholars now regard as strategic sites at which labor market opportunities are concentrated (Huffman 2004, 324; Kmec 2003). However, the data are cross-sectional, which eliminates the possibility of tracking the same employees throughout their career trajectory—a key criterion in some investigations of the glass ceiling (Cotter et al. 2001; Maume 2004).

Methods and Measures

Dependent variables: Wages and employer-sponsored benefits

The focus here is on two components of job-level rewards: wages and employer benefits. For employer-sponsored benefits, the MCSUI survey asked respondents, "Through your job, (are/were) any of the following available to you?" Choices included "paid sick leave; hospital or health insurance for yourself; hospital or health insurance for your family or dependents; and a retirement plan." Ordinary least squares (OLS) regression is used to predict hourly wages. For employment benefits, I use logit equations predicting the odds (yes/no) of each ethnoracial and gender group having employer-sponsored retirement plans, sick leave, individual health insurance, and family health insurance relative to white men net of control factors.

Hierarchical authority

The association between wages and job authority in studies of gender and race inequality at work has been well established (see Smith's [2002] review). This research shows that job authority is positively associated with wages; men earn a higher wage return to authority than do women (Reskin and Ross 1992; Wolf and Fligstein 1979), and whites receive a higher wage return than minorities for occupying similar positions of authority net of select controls (Kluegel 1978; McGuire and Reskin 1993; Smith 1997; Wilson 1997).

While much is known about the wage–job authority link, a search for research that examines the relationship between employer benefits and job authority yielded no results. This leaves open two important questions: Are employer benefits as unequally distributed among ethnoracial and gender groups as are wages? And are there group differences in the employment benefits returns employees receive for occupying similar levels of authority? As shown in Figure 1, the authority measure is based on a three-level index of workplace power that is derived from yes/no responses to questions that come from prior sociological research on workplace authority (Wolf and Fligstein 1979). Incumbents of *managerial control* positions have the power to hire, fire, and set the pay of others. Those with *supervisory authority* have generalized supervisory responsibilities. Remaining employees

FIGURE 1
Hierarchical Measure of Job Authority (Primary Dependent Variable)

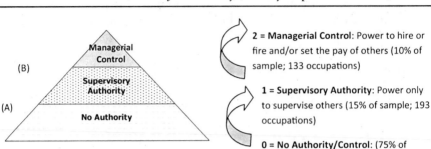

NOTE: Tests of increasing inequality compare odds of transition (A) to odds of transition (B), each relative to white men. If the relative gap grows larger from (A) to (B), there is evidence of increasing inequality with movement up the authority hierarchy, relative to white men.

have *no authority*. This measure has been shown to be a reliable and valid measure of workplace authority (Elliott and Smith 2004).[3]

Controls

To test for whether race/ethnicity intersects with gender to forge differential wage and employer-benefit opportunities for employees, dummy variables were constructed for each ethnoracial and gender group: white men, black men, Latinos, white women, black women, and Latinas. Standard controls include individual-level and family factors (i.e., age, education, total work experience, total work experience squared, prior job-specific experience, job tenure, English speaking ability, nativity, marital status, child status, and nonspousal adult living in the household).

Several job-relevant factors are also considered, including organizational size (natural log, which is often associated with formalized bureaucratic procedures [Dobbin et al. 1993]). To test for glass escalator effects and to offer a stricter test for glass ceiling effects, in some analyses the data are stratified by whether a respondent reports to a white male supervisor or a minority/female supervisor—the latter is combined to increase sample size. In addition, the multivariate models include controls for employment sector and occupational location,[4] socioeconomic status, unionized job, weekly job tasks (face-to-face, phone, read, write, computer), and city of residents, with the latter accounting for possible between-city differences in history, economy, and labor supply (Browne, Tigges, and Press 2001). Finally, since the likelihood of possessing authority declines for both men and women with increased representation of women in an occupation (Huffman and Cohen 2004), multivariate models take into account the percent female in an occupation. The next section begins with the analysis of wage inequality and is followed

FIGURE 2
Mean Hourly Wages (in Dollars), by Authority
Level (Data Are Weighted for Oversampling)

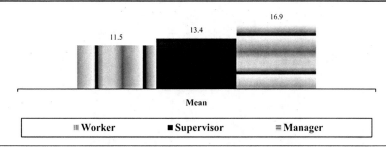

NOTE: Each category is significantly greater than the prior category at the .001 level.

by a separate analysis of employer-sponsored benefits.

Results

Do hourly wages vary by authority level?

Let us begin with a baseline analysis of whether hourly wages vary by authority level. There is ample reason to believe that managers will be paid more than supervisors who should, in turn, be paid more than workers who do not exercise any authority at all (Robinson and Kelley 1979, 43). To test this hypothesis, Figure 2 depicts mean hourly wages by authority level. The descriptive statistics indicate that wages increase steadily up the authority hierarchy from worker to supervisor to manager. Converted to full-time, year-round totals (40 hours per week for 52 weeks), workers in the sample would have mean earnings of roughly $36,239 (2011 dollars), compared with roughly $42,226 for supervisors and $53,255 for managers.[5] Each category is significantly greater than the prior category at the .001 level.[6]

Do hourly wages vary by group and authority level?

Figure 3 compares differences in mean hourly wages by group and by authority level, using white men as the comparison group. Generally speaking, hourly wages do, in fact, vary by ethnoracial and gender groups, and group differences in hourly wages are greater than wage differences by authority level. That is, without controls, group variation in wages exceeds authority wage differentials.

For example, based on full-time earnings, the average supervisor would earn $4,000 more per year than the average worker. By comparison, and assuming full-time status, the average black woman would earn $10,400 less than the

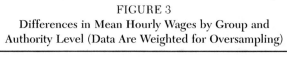

FIGURE 3
Differences in Mean Hourly Wages by Group and
Authority Level (Data Are Weighted for Oversampling)

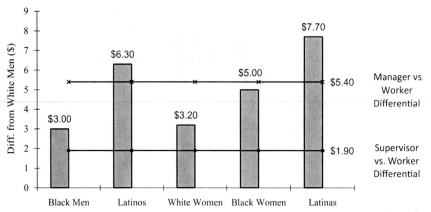

NOTE: All group differentials, relative to white men, are negative and statistically significant
at the .001 level; n = 3,480.

average white man. Put another way, the white male advantage over black women
is greater than the managerial wage advantage over nonsupervisory workers.
Also, as shown in Figure 3, black men average about $3 less per hour than white
men—without taking into account group differences in human capital. This difference is greater than the average difference between workers and supervisors
generally, which is only about $2 per hour. So although wage differences by
authority level are statistically significant (see Figure 2), they pale in comparison
to enduring ethnoracial and gender differences. For a more rigorous assessment
of these dynamics, a series of regression equations was estimated to examine how
wages and authority intersect and whether group differences in wage returns to
authority increase with movement up the authority hierarchy (controlling for
possible group disparities in a full set of control variables).

Wages and the glass ceiling

Are these general gaps in wages relative to white men generated, at least in
part, by increasing white male advantage with movement up the authority hierarchy, as glass ceiling proponents would predict? Based on a series of OLS estimates starting with controls for human capital and another model controlling for
human capital plus a full array of background factors, the answer is no. That is,
none of the interactions between ethnoracial/gender groups and authority level
are statistically significant in the OLS estimations (models not shown), which
implies, contrary to the glass ceiling hypothesis, that the observed wage gaps for
the respective groups, relative to white men, do not increase with movement

FIGURE 4
Hourly Wages Relative to White Men with Full Controls

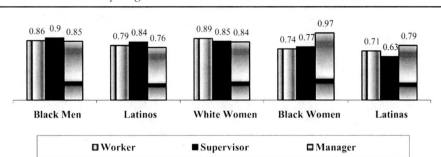

| Black Men | Latinos | White Women | Black Women | Latinas |

NOTE: The bars represent probabilities generated from ordinary least squares (OLS) regression models, with hourly wages regressed on an indicator for each ethnoracial/gender group, authority, and the product of the two controlling for known wage determinants and city of survey. OLS model: Hourly Wage = a + [Group] + [Authority Level] + [Group × Authority Level] + [years of school completed, total experience, total experience squared, previous work experience, job tenure, foreign-born, English speaking ability, age, marital status, child status, non-spousal adult in household, establishment size(logged), employment sector (public/private), socioeconomic index, occupational categories, percent female occupation, job complexity (face-to-face, phone, read, write, computer, math) + union status, city of survey (Atlanta, Los Angeles, Boston)]. The sample is restricted to employees who report to a white male supervisor, n = 1,325.

from worker to supervisory to managerial positions. Instead, the relative white male advantage remains the same at each level of authority for each ethnoracial and gender group.

White male supervisor versus female/minority supervisor wage effects

Do these patterns change in any way with the ethnoracial and gender identity of a respondent's superior? Since white men still occupy the largest share of decision-making positions, it stands to reason that glass ceiling inequalities, if present at all, should be greater for those who report to a white male superior than for those reporting to a woman or racial minority. A clear indication that such a pattern exists would mean that the wage gaps between white men and other groups working under white men should increase when moving up the authority hierarchy. If anything, the findings here suggest the very opposite. As shown in Figure 4, none of the observed wage gaps for the respective groups, relative to white men, increase with movement up the authority hierarchy, beyond what might occur by chance. Instead, consistent with Baxter and Wright (2000), the relative white male advantage remains the same at each level of authority for each group in question.[7]

However, the picture is quite different when employees report to non-white-male supervisors (Figure 5). In particular, relative to white men, Latinos,

FIGURE 5

Hourly Wages Relative to White Men, with Full Controls
among Those Not Supervised by White Men

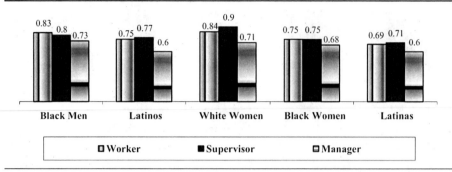

NOTE: The OLS model is the same as that depicted in Figure 4, except the sample is restricted to employees who do not report to a white male supervisor, n = 2,081. Controls for human capital are statistically significant at the .001 level.

Latinas, and, perhaps to a lesser extent, white women and black women experience increasing wage inequality from lower to higher levels of authority.[8] For black men, similar patterns are evident but not statistically significant. A comparison of Figures 4 and 5 suggests that, if anything, the white male advantage is more likely to increase with movement up the authority hierarchy outside settings supervised by white males—contrary to a strict interpretation of the glass ceiling hypothesis.

What emerges is a more nuanced pattern that is more consistent with a glass ceiling and glass escalator interpretation. This is because, even after extensive controls, white male supervisors and managers are paid better under dissimilar superiors than under white male superiors; the opposite is true for all other groups. To observe this pattern up close, consider the probabilities in Table 1. In support of both the glass ceiling and glass escalator hypotheses, the wage gaps between white men and other groups increase from supervisory to managerial authority, and the wage gaps are wider between white men and other groups in work settings where employees report to women and minorities. Among other things, this finding supports prior research showing that glass ceilings and glass escalators are not necessarily mutually exclusive phenomena (Maume 1999, 2011; Williams 1992).

While an important piece of the compensation puzzle, wages are not the only form of remuneration valued by workers. In fact, as argued at the outset, to paint a more complete picture of the consequences of authority for workplace compensation, it must be understood that, in lieu of wages, workers routinely receive employer-sponsored benefits, which include retirement plans, sick leave, individual health insurance, and family health insurance. With the cost of health care

TABLE 1
Average Hourly Wage for Respondents Reporting and Not Reporting to a White Male Supervisor Net of Controls

	White Men		Black Men		Latinos		White Women		Black Women		Latinas	
	White Male Supervisor	Non-White Male Supervisor	White Male Supervisor	Non-White Male Supervisor	White Male Supervisor	Non-White Male Supervisor	White Male Supervisor	Non-White Male Supervisor	White Male Supervisor	Non-White Male Supervisor	White Male Supervisor	Non-White Male Supervisor
Manager	15.9	18.4	13.7	13.5	12.2	11.0	13.4	13.1	15.5	12.5	12.8	11.0
Supervisor	13.7	14.0	12.1	11.1	11.6	10.6	11.6	12.5	10.8	10.4	8.6	9.8
Worker	13.1	12.6	11.3	10.4	10.5	9.4	11.6	10.6	9.7	9.4	9.4	8.7

NOTE: Identical OLS model as in Figure 4. If supervised by a male superior, n = 1,325. If not supervised by a male superior, n = 2,081.

FIGURE 6
Comparing Probability Differences in Benefits, by Group

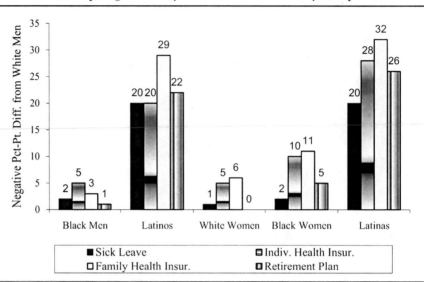

NOTE: All group differentials are relative to white men and negative. N = 3,291 to N = 3,456, due to missing cases.

at an all-time high, employers are increasingly transferring the burden of covering health care costs to workers. At the same time, the value of retirement benefits is constantly shrinking, causing older workers to stay on the job longer than they ordinarily would. What this means for the daily subsistence of workers is that employer benefits are a valued and increasingly scarce resource that, similar to wages, are likely to be unequally distributed by race, ethnicity, gender, and authority. The following section examines this likelihood.

Employer benefits

The absence of an extant literature that links employment benefits to job authority makes it difficult to formulate expectations about ethnoracial and gender differences in the employer benefits that workers receive for the authority positions they occupy. Notwithstanding this omission, the rising cost of health care and the fact that for-profit and public agencies are rapidly transferring health care costs to employees (Paulin and Dietz 1995) means that employer-sponsored benefits are an important, yet understudied, part of an employees' total compensation package. It comes as no surprise to learn that this shifting cost leaves low-income people and racial minorities in a particularly precarious state, as they are least able to absorb the cost associated with proper health care (Penner 2008). Similar constraints are associated with employer-provided retirement plans. According to reports, there are many ways to save for retirement (e.g., personal savings, equity in home ownership, pension plans, and personal retirement accounts), yet blacks and Hispanics are more likely than other groups to rely on Social Security benefits (Penner 2008). This suggests that, as with wages, employer-provided benefits are yet another source of compensation in which group disparities may flourish. Is there any evidence that employer-sponsored benefits vary by group and authority level? How might glass ceilings and glass escalators factor into the matter, if at all? These questions are addressed next.

Variation in employer benefits by group and authority level

Figure 6 presents the probability of each group having four types of employer benefits. The bars represent the percentage point differences between white men and each of the other groups in the likelihood of having employer benefits. All differentials are negative, which means that white men are more likely than any other group to have sick leave, individual health insurance, family health insurance, and retirement plans. For example, the 5 percentage point differential for black men's individual health insurance means that the probability of such a benefit is 5 percentage points lower than that of white men (72 versus 77 percent), but since the difference is not statistically significant at the .05 level, the gap may very well be due to chance.

Black women are significantly different from white men with respect to individual and family health insurance, as are white women. However, compared with the other groups, the difference between Latinos/Latinas and white men in the probability of having employer benefits is astounding. The probability of Latinos/Latinas having employer benefits is between 20 and 32 percentage points lower than that of white men, and the differences are statistically significant at the .05 level for all four types of benefits. In this case, the highest differential (modal category) occurs among those with family health insurance. For example, the probability of Latinos/Latinas having family health insurance is 29 and 32 percentage points, respectively, lower than white men's. In raw percentages, 67 percent of white men have family health insurance, compared with 38 percent of Latinos and 35 percent of Latinas.

Do group differences in employer benefits increase with movement up the authority hierarchy?

If glass ceiling inequality exists, it should be represented by a progressive increase in group differences in employer benefits with movement up the authority hierarchy. And if there is more than one glass ceiling, the increasing inequality between white men and other groups should vary from one group to another. To examine these possibilities, four logit models were generated predicting the odds (yes/no) of each ethnoracial and gender group having sick leave, individual health insurance, family health insurance, and retirement plans relative to white men. To assess what accounts for ethnoracial and gender gaps in employer benefits between white men and all other groups, a baseline model without controls was generated, followed by a model that controls for human capital differences and a final additive model that controls for human capital, additional individual-level factors, family and household characteristics, job/occupational variables, employment sector, union status, and city of residence.

The results of this exercise reveal the prominence of human capital attributes as a source of group differences in employer benefits. In particular, Latinos and white women experience increasing personal health insurance inequality, relative to white men, as they move from supervisory to managerial positions. The data show that a full 92 percent of white male managers have personal health insurance, compared with 60 and 79 percent of Latinos and white women, respectively. However, once differences in human capital are taken into account, evidence of increasing inequality disappears. With regard to family health insurance, there is evidence that Latinas experience increasing inequality, relative to white men, as they move from supervisory to managerial positions. Underlying percentages show that 86 percent of white men have family health insurance compared with only 40 percent of Latinas. However, this effect also disappears once controls for human capital are taken into account. So, contrary to the glass ceiling hypothesis, there is no evidence that group differences in employer benefits increase with movement up the authority hierarchy net of education, total work experience, total work experience squared, prior job specific experience, and job tenure.

Effects of a white male supervisor versus a non-white-male supervisor

Do the findings above vary according to whether a respondent reports to a white male supervisor versus a minority or female supervisor? To answer this question, the MCSUI sample was stratified by whether respondents report to a white male supervisor. That is, statistically, models were fitted separately for each scenario, controlling first for possible group differences in human capital (model 1) and group differences in human capital plus all other controls (model 2). If glass ceiling inequality is present, there should be evidence of increasing inequality between white men and other groups from supervisory authority to managerial control, and, in the strictest definition of glass ceiling inequality, this pattern should be most evident when employees report to a white male supervisor. Moreover, if glass escalator effects are present, inequity between white men and other groups should increase from low to high levels of authority in anomalous work settings, such as when minorities and women exercise authority over white men.

The first sets of results are straightforward and are presented without tables. Contrary to the glass ceiling hypothesis, there is no evidence of increasing group

TABLE 2
Group Differences in Retirement Benefits (Standard Errors in Parentheses)

Key Variables and Model Statistics (White Men as Comparison Group)	Ethnoracial and Gender Identity of Supervisor			
	Non-White Male Supervisor		White Male Supervisor	
	Human Capital Controls[a]	All Controls[b]	Human Capital Controls[a]	All Controls[b]
Worker	−0.851 (0.523)	−0.790 (0.559)	0.383 (0.342)	0.489 (0.389)
Manager	1.79 (1.147)	1.406 (1.178)	0.273 (0.410)	0.392 (0.459)
Black men	0.065 (0.579)	−0.005 (0.633)	−0.400 (0.509)	−0.730 (.599)
Black men × worker	0.567 (0.646)	0.674 (0.710)	0.872 (0.566)	1.219° (0.661)
Black men × manager	−3.570°°° (1.302)	−3.081°° (1.364)	0.737 (0.783)	1.165 (0.878)
Latino	−0.281 (0.603)	−0.348 (0.688)	0.444 (0.505)	0.224 (0.594)
Latino × worker	0.813 (0.659)	1.200 (0.736)	−0.484 (0.551)	−0.234 (0.633)
Latino × manager	−2.472°° (1.311)	−2.114 (1.372)	−0.373 (0.696)	−0.168 (0.780)
White women	0.356 (0.587)	0.765 (0.636)	0.135 (0.547)	0.209 (0.646)
White women × worker	0.075 (0.647)	−0.382 (0.703)	−0.187 (0.593)	−0.153 (0.687)
White women × manager	−2.469°° (1.260)	−2.331° (1.307)	0.755 (0.783)	0.778 (0.873)
Black women	−0.078 (0.526)	0.111 (0.569)	−0.171 (0.523)	−0.344 (0.598)
Black women × worker	0.491 (0.584)	0.429 (0.631)	0.312 (0.571)	0.440 (0.654)
Black women × manager	−2.112° (1.241)	−2.279° (1.282)	1.239 (1.062)	1.479 (1.142)
Latina	−0.065 (0.586)	0.394 (0.642)	−0.167 (0.782)	0.492 (0.890)
Latina × worker	0.327 (0.643)	0.240 (0.696)	0.233 (0.820)	−0.103 (0.910)
Latina × manager	−2.606°° (1.322)	−2.620°° (1.377)	−1.011 (1.405)	−0.444 (1.643)
Model χ^2 (df)	625.57 (22)	1,022.97 (45)	330.28 (22)	560.26 (45)

a. $\text{Log}[\text{Pr}(\text{Retirement Benefits}_n)/\text{Pr}(\text{Retirement Benefits}_{n-1})] = a + [\text{Group}] + [\text{Authority Level}] + [\text{Group} \times \text{Authority Level}] + [\text{years of school completed, total experience, total experience squared, previous work experience, job tenure}]$.
b. $\text{Log}[\text{Pr}(\text{Retirement Benefits}_n)/\text{Pr}(\text{Retirement Benefits}_{n-1})] = a + [\text{Group}] + [\text{Authority Level}] + [\text{Group} \times \text{Authority Level}] + [\text{years of school completed, total experience, total experience squared, previous work experience, job tenure, foreign-born, English speaking ability, age, marital status, child status, nonspousal adult in household, establishment size(logged), employment sector (public/private), socioeconomic index, occupational categories, percent female occupation, job complexity (face-to-face, phone, read, write, computer, math) + union status, and city of residence (Atlanta, Los Angeles, Boston)}]$.
°$p < .10$. °°$p < .05$. °°°$p < .01$ (two-tailed tests).

differences, relative to white men, in either scenario (whether employees have a white male or non-white male supervisor) for sick leave, personal health insurance, or family health insurance. However, when it comes to retirement benefits, a different story emerges. The results, reported in Table 2, show that black men, Latinos, white women, Latinas, and, marginally, black women each experience increasing inequality, relative to white men, with movement from supervisor to manager in jobs overseen by someone other than a white male superior net of human capital controls.

Consequently, in this type of setting, women and racial minorities with the same human capital as their white male counterparts have substantially lower probabilities of receiving retirement benefits from their employers. As we might expect, these findings are modified somewhat once all statistical controls are taken into account, rendering the effects for white women and black women marginally significant. To observe these patterns from a different perspective, consider the probabilities in Table 3. Table 3 shows that, all else being equal, white men at the supervisory and managerial level who report to women and minority superiors are far more likely than any other group, including white men who report to white male supervisors, to have retirement benefits—and the disparities increase with movement up the authority hierarchy, as the glass ceiling hypothesis predicts.

Summary and Discussion

In the United States, ethnoracial and gender disparities in workplace processes and outcomes remain formidable obstacles to the fulfillment of a truly meritocratic system of attainment. Using wages and employer-sponsored benefits as key dependent variables, this study sought to determine whether women and minorities confront a glass ceiling at work and whether white men experience glass escalator–like advantages when they are supervised by women and racial minorities. The main findings both corroborate and extend prior research. The wage results show that relative inequality between white men and other groups remains the same at each level of authority, but there is no evidence, even net of controls, that such generalized wage inequality increases with movement up the authority hierarchy. Thus, this finding is very consistent with prior cross-sectional (Baxter and Wright 2000) and longitudinal (Zeng 2011) tests of the glass ceiling hypothesis. However, the analysis of supervisor effects broadens our understanding regarding the employment context in which glass ceiling inequality may be most operative. The data show that when employees work in settings that require them to report to minority and female supervisors, all groups, except black men, experience increasing wage inequality, relative to white men, with movement up the authority hierarchy. This pattern is very consistent with prior quantitative evidence of glass escalator inequality favoring white men working outside their traditional work settings (Hultin 2003; Maume 1999, 2011) and a glass ceiling for women and racial minorities (Huffman 2004; Hutlin 2003; Maume 1999, 2011).

When it comes to employer benefits, group disparities coalesced around retirement benefits. The data show that group differences, which are especially large and consistent for Latinos and Latinas, relative to white men, are mainly a function of group disparities in human capital. Once these differences are taken into account, Latinos/Latin as have roughly the same probabilities as white men of receiving employer-provided benefits. When these inequalities are examined

TABLE 3

Likelihood of Having Employer-Sponsored Retirement Benefits among Employees Reporting and Not Reporting to a White Male Supervisor Net of Controls

	White Men		Black Men		Latinos		White Women		Black Women		Latinas	
	White Male Supervisor	Non-White Male Supervisor	White Male Supervisor	Non-White Male Supervisor	White Male Supervisor	Non-White Male Supervisor	White Male Supervisor	Non-White Male Supervisor	White Male Supervisor	Non-White Male Supervisor	White Male Supervisor	Non-White Male Supervisor
Manager	70	94	73	38	50	32	83	71	88	64	52	37
Supervisor	54	73	41	77	50	56	59	83	47	74	46	61
Worker	65	54	72	65	41	48	64	59	65	61	49	40

NOTE: Logit model: Retirement Plan = a + [Group] + [Authority Level] + [Group × Authority Level] + [years of school completed, total experience, total experience squared, previous work experience, job tenure, foreign born, English speaking ability, age, marital status, child status, nonspousal adult in household, establishment size(logged), employment sector (public/private), socioeconomic index, occupational categories, percent female occupation, job complexity (face-to-face, phone, read, write, computer, math), union status, city of survey (Atlanta, Los Angeles, Boston)]. If not supervised by a male superior, n = 1,305. If supervised by a male superior, n = 2,063.

in different job contexts—specifically whether an employee reports to a white male superior—evidence consistent with a glass escalator–type of advantage for white men emerges once again. In sum, not only do white male supervisors and managers who report to women and minorities earn substantially more than their white male counterparts who report to white male supervisors (and their female and minority counterparts), net of all important controls, but they also have a greater probability than these groups of receiving lucrative retirement benefits, thereby extending disparities into the post-labor-market years.

Among other things, the results reported here support the contention that, just like the glass ceiling, the glass escalator is gendered and racialized (Maume 1999; Wingfield 2009). That is, white men experience a double advantage based on the fact that they possess two socially valued statuses with regard to race (white) and gender (male) (Browne, Tigges, and Press 2001). However, contrary to Budig's (2002) claim, this advantage does not necessarily extend to all work settings.

What is behind the glass escalator effects favoring white men? Three explanations seem reasonable. First, women and minority supervisors may simply yield, wittingly or unwittingly, to the normative favor white men experience as employees relative to other groups. If, as Williams (1992, 263) argued, "men take their privilege with them when they enter predominantly female occupations; [and] this translates into an advantage in spite of their numerical rarity," then not only do white men take their privilege with them to settings where they are supervised by women and minorities, but the privilege is magnified in those contexts. Second, women and minority supervisors may cater to white male subordinates to bolster the perception that they are fair and unbiased and perhaps as a talisman to ward off any accusations of reverse discrimination. Third, women and minority supervisors may favor white male subordinates to increase their own status in the eyes of their white male peers and superiors. That is, just as some mentors are partial to their most promising protégés, women and minority mentors may take a special interest in white male protégés because they possess two socially valued statuses.

Of course, additional research is needed to adjudicate between these possibilities. More tests of the glass ceiling and glass escalator hypotheses under different employment contexts are warranted. In addition to analyses that include a consideration of the total compensation package employees receive, future inquiries should explore the extent to which white male advantage is present when white men report to specific ethnoracial and gender groups. Data limitations required combining women and minority supervisors into one group. However, reporting to a white female superior may yield different rewards for white men relative to reporting to a minority female or a minority male superior. Ideally, a longitudinal design that tracks the same individuals over the course of their careers would constitute a more direct test of the ideas presented here. Despite these limitations, this study supports the contention that glass ceilings and glass escalators are alive and well in the United States.

Appendix

Descriptive Statistics on Variables Used in Analysis by Race, Ethnicity, and Gender (Weighted Data to Correct for Oversampling)

Total (N = 3,480)	White Men	Black Men	Latinos	White Women	Black Women	Latinas
Money, power, benefits						
Wage (hourly)	15.9	12.9	9.6	12.7	10.9	8.2
Wage (logged hourly)	2.7	2.5	2.2	2.4	2.3	1.9
Manager (%)	19.6	14.6	11.2	11.1	7.0	5.7
Supervisor (%)	14.6	14.4	12.9	16.2	17.3	10.8
Worker (%)	65.8	71.1	75.8	72.6	75.6	83.4
Retirement benefits (%)	69.0	69.0	42.0	65.0	60.0	38.0
Sick leave (%)	75.0	71.0	52.0	71.0	66.0	46.0
Personal health insurance (%)	83.0	75.0	60.0	72.0	67.0	51.0
Family health insurance (%)	77.0	59.0	41.0	62.0	59.0	37.0
Individual factors						
Age (years)	38.0	35.9	34.2	38.1	36.5	35.1
Education (years)	14.7	13.8	10.7	13.9	13.7	11.0
Total work experience (years)	17.2	15.3	15.9	15.1	15.1	13.6
Total work experience squared	420	339	369	328	339	303
Prior job-specific experience (0:1)	.62	.50	.45	.58	.49	.39
Job tenure (mean)	6.9	6.2	4.6	6.5	6.5	4.9
No English (0:1)	0	0	.05	0	0	.08
Fair English (0:1)	0	0	.48	0	0	.43
Good English (0:1)	1	1	.32	1	1	.34
Foreign-born (%)	5.3	23.1	68.9	7.6	6.5	69.8
Family and household factors						
Married (%)	57.4	42.2	59.2	60.9	31.7	45.1
Children (%)	32.7	36.2	48.3	43.8	43.1	63.9
Nonspouse living in household (%)	31.9	43.8	56.8	24.4	35.0	53.0
Job and organizational factors						
Log organizational size (mean)	4.6	4.6	3.6	4.5	4.7	3.9
White male supervisor (%)	68.0	42.0	40.0	43.0	27.0	14.0
Occupational indicators						
Professional/technical (%)	56.0	30.4	14.1	48.8	33.0	17.7
Sales (%)	3.3	1.4	2.3	5.7	8.9	10.1
Clerical (%)	9.3	17.6	8.5	28.9	31.8	19.5
Service (%)	7.1	23.1	16.1	9.5	19.0	19.3

(continued)

Appendix (continued)

Total (N = 3,480)	White Men	Black Men	Latinos	White Women	Black Women	Latinas
Craft/repair (%)	24.3	27.5	59.0	7.1	7.3	33.4
% female occupation	34.3	37.2	27.9	64.5	66.9	62.4
Socioeconomic index score (mean)	58.3	47.8	37.5	54.1	47.8	38.2
Weekly job task						
Face-to-face (%)	61.9	67.8	45.2	74.1	73.3	52.2
Phone (%)	63.3	56.1	28.2	72.6	70.3	42.6
Read (%)	81.5	74.5	60.5	71.6	73.8	50.0
Write (%)	64.5	48.2	35.7	65.9	54.4	36.4
Computer (%)	69.5	48.1	23.1	72.1	56.5	34.3
Sector, union status, city of residence						
Government/public (%)	19.1	18.8	7.5	17.6	26.5	13.5
Union (%)	22.6	31.2	21.4	15.7	25.5	16.8
Atlanta (%)	15.9	29.1	1.4	19.4	33.9	1.7
Los Angeles (%)	45.9	59.1	94.2	39.4	53.9	94.2
Boston (%)	38.1	11.7	4.4	41.2	12.1	4.0

Notes

1. The MCSUI also sampled residents from Detroit and Asian Americans. I omitted Detroit from this study because questions related to key variables were not asked of Detroit residents. Asian Americans were also omitted due to small sample sizes.

2. Information about the MCSUI comes from Bobo et al. (1998/2000).

3. The indicator of workplace power is not without limitations. First, the measure does not include corporate-level employees in the executive suites, so, if anything, I have underestimated the degree of inequality across ethnoracial and gender groups. Also, authority as defined may not mean the same for all groups. A manager at McDonald's may not receive the same remuneration or benefits as a manager in a larger establishment. To address this possibility, I added controls to simulate workplace context, such as establishment size, employment sector, job complexity, and occupational location.

4. Indicators for industry classification were also added to models without any significant alteration to the findings reported below. Consequently, industry was deleted from the models to maintain parsimony.

5. The inflation rate between May 1994 (approximate end date of survey) and March 2011 was approximately 51.50 percent. The rate of inflation was calculated by taking the average wage for workers in May 1994 ($23,920) × .5150 (inflation rate) = $12,319 + $23,920 = $36,239.

6. Hourly wages below $4 and above $30 were recoded to these respective bottom and top values to minimize the statistical influence of outliers. There were thirty-three cases (or less than 1 percent of the sample) below $3 and forty-six cases (or 1.3% of the sample) above $30. The sample includes civilian, non-self-employed workers with a superior (N = 3,480).

7. Several OLS models were generated leading up to the full model shown in Figure 4. The findings were resilient regardless of controls.

8. In the full set of results based on the OLS estimation, the interaction terms, net of all controls, for Latinos and Latinas were negative and statistically significant at the .05 level, while the interaction terms for white women and black women were marginally significant at the .10 level and nonsignificant for black men.

References

Baxter, Janeen, and Erik O. Wright. 2000. The glass ceiling hypothesis: A comparative study of the United States, Sweden, and Australia. *Gender & Society* 14 (2): 275–94.

Bobo, Lawrence, James Johnson, Melvin Oliver, Reynolds Farley, Barry Bluestone, Irene Browne, Sheldon Danziger, Gary Green, Harry Holzer, Maria Krysan, Michael Massagli, and Camille Zubrinsky Charles. 1998/2000. Multi-City Study of Urban Inequality, 1992–1994: Atlanta, Boston, Detroit, and Los Angeles Household Survey Data [computer file]. 3rd ICPSR version. Atlanta, GA: Mathematica/Boston, MA: University of Massachusetts, Survey Research Laboratory/Ann Arbor, MI: University of Michigan, Detroit Area Study and Institute for Social Research, Survey Research Center/Los Angeles, CA: University of California, Survey Research Program [producers], 1998. Interuniversity Consortium for Political and Social Research [distributor], 2000.

Britton, Dana, and Christine L. Williams. 2000. Response to Baxter and Wright. *Gender & Society* 14 (6): 804–8.

Browne, Irene, Leann Tigges, and Julie Press. 2001. Inequality through labor markets, firms, and families: The intersection of gender and race-ethnicity across three cities. In *Urban inequality: Evidence from four cities*, eds. Alice O'Connor, Chris Tilly, and Lawrence Bobo, 372–406. New York, NY: Russell Sage Foundation.

Budig, Michelle J. 2002. Male advantage and the gender composition of jobs: Who rides the glass escalator? *Social Problems* 49 (2): 258–77.

Cotter, David, Joan Hermsen, Seth Ovadia, and Reeve Vanneman. 2001. The glass ceiling effect. *Social Forces* 80:655–82.

Dobbin, Frank, John Sutton, John Meyer, and W. Richard Scott. 1993. Equal opportunity law and the construction of internal labor markets. *American Journal of Sociology* 99:396–427.

Elliott, James R., and Ryan A. Smith. 2004. Race, gender and workplace power. *American Sociological Review* 69 (3): 365–86.

Federal Glass Ceiling Commission. 1995. *Good for business: Making full use of the nation's human resources*. Washington, DC: U.S. Department of Labor.

Huffman, Matt. 2004. Gender inequality across wage hierarchies. *Work and Occupations* 31 (3): 323–44.

Huffman, Matt, and Philip Cohen. 2004. Occupational segregation and the gender gap in workplace authority: National versus local labor markets. *Sociological Forum* 19 (1): 121–47.

Hultin, Mia. 2003. Some take the glass escalator, some hit the glass ceiling: Career consequences of occupational sex segregation. *Work and Occupations* 30:30–61.

Hymowitz, Carol, and Timothy Schellhardt. 24 March 1986. Why women can't seem to break the invisible barrier that blocks them from top jobs. *Wall Street Journal*, D1, D4–5.

Jackson, Jerlando F. L., and Elizabeth M. O'Callaghan. 2009. What do we know about glass ceiling effects? A taxonomy and critical review to inform higher education research. *Research in Higher Education* 50:460–82.

Jacobs, Jerry A. 1992. Women's entry into management: Trends in earnings, authority and values among salaried managers. *Administrative Science Quarterly* 37:282–301.

Kanter, Rosabeth M. 1977. *Men and women of the corporation*. 2nd ed. New York, NY: Basic Books.

Kluegel, James. 1978. The causes and cost of racial exclusion from job authority. *American Sociological Review* 43:285–301.

Kmec, Julie. 2003. Minority concentration and wages. *Social Problems* 50 (1): 38–59.

Maume, David, J. 1999. Glass ceilings and glass escalators: Occupational segregation and race and sex differences in managerial promotions. *Work and Occupations* 26 (4): 483–509.

Maume, David, J. 2004. Is the glass ceiling a unique form of inequality? Evidence from a random-effects model of managerial attainment. *Work and Occupations* 31 (2): 250–74.

Maume, David, J. 2011. Meet the new boss . . . same as the old boss? Female supervisors and subordinate career prospects. *Social Science Research* 40:287–98.

McGuire, Gail M., and Barbara F. Reskin. 1993. Authority hierarchies at work: The impacts of race and sex. *Gender & Society* 7:487–506.

Morgan, Laurie A. 1998. Glass ceiling effect or cohort effect? A longitudinal study of the gender salary gap for engineers, 1982–1989. *American Sociological Review* 63 (4): 479–93.

Morrison, Ann M., and Mary Ann Von Glinow. 1990. Women and minorities in management. *American Psychologist* 45:200–208.

Paulin, Geoffrey D., and Elizabeth M. Dietz. August 1995. Health insurance coverage for families with children. *Monthly Labor Review* 118:13–23.

Penner, Rudy G. 2008. Measuring personal savings: A tale of American profligacy. Retirement Policy Program Brief 21. Washington, DC: The Urban Institute.

Reskin, Barbara F., and Debra B. McBrier. 2000. Why not ascription? Organizations' employment of male and female managers. *American Sociological Review* 65:210–33.

Reskin, Barbara F., and Catherine Ross. 1992. Authority and earnings among managers: The continuing significance of sex. *Work and Occupations* 19:342–65.

Robinson, Robert, and Jonathan Kelley. 1979. Class as conceived by Marx and Dahrendorf: Effects of income inequality in the United States and Great Britain. *American Sociological Review* 44:38–58.

Smith, Ryan A. 1997. Race, income, and authority at work: A cross-temporal analysis of black and white men, 1972–1994. *Social Problems* 44:19–37.

Smith, Ryan A. 2002. Race, gender and authority in the workplace: Theory and research. *Annual Review of Sociology* 28:509–42.

Smith, Ryan A. n.d. Power at work: The persistence of race, ethnic, and gender inequality. Unpublished manuscript.

Snyder, Karrie A., and Adam I. Green. 2008. Revisiting the glass escalator in a female dominated occupation. *Social Problems* 55 (2): 271–99.

Williams, Christine L. 1992. The glass escalator: Hidden advantages for men in the "female" professions. *Social Problems* 39 (3): 253–66.

Williams, Christine L. 1995. *Still a man's world: Men who do "women's work."* Berkeley, CA: University of California Press.

Wilson, George. 1997. Payoffs to power: Racial differences in the determinants of job authority. *Social Problems* 44:38–54.

Wingfield, Adia H. 2009. Racializing the glass escalator: Reconsidering men's experiences with women's work. *Gender & Society* 23 (1): 5–26.

Wolf, Wendy C., and Neil Fligstein. 1979. Sexual stratification: Differences in power in the work setting. *Social Forces* 58 (1): 94–107.

Wright, Erik O., Janeen Baxter, and Gunn E. Birkelund. 1995. The gender gap in workplace authority: A cross-national study. *American Sociological Review* 60:407–35.

Yoder, Janice. 1991. Rethinking tokenism: Looking beyond numbers. *Gender & Society* 5 (2): 178–92.

Zeng, Zhen. 2011. The myth of the glass ceiling: Evidence from a stock-flow analysis of authority attainment. *Social Science Research* 40:312–25.

Do Female Top Managers Help Women to Advance? A Panel Study Using EEO-1 Records

By
FIDAN ANA KURTULUS
and
DONALD
TOMASKOVIC-DEVEY

The goal of this study is to examine whether women in the highest levels of firms' management ranks help to reduce barriers to women's advancement in the workplace. Using a panel of more than twenty thousand firms during 1990 to 2003 from the U.S. Equal Employment Opportunity Commission, the authors explore the influence of women in top management on subsequent female representation in lower-level managerial positions in U.S. firms. Key findings show that an increase in the share of female top managers is associated with subsequent increases in the share of women in midlevel management positions within firms, and this result is robust to controlling for firm size, workforce composition, federal contractor status, firm fixed effects, year fixed effects, and industry-specific trends. The authors also find that the positive influence of women in top leadership positions on managerial gender diversity diminishes over time, suggesting that women at the top play a positive but transitory role in women's career advancement.

Keywords: female managers; gender; diversity; race; discrimination; mentoring; promotions; hiring; retention

Despite great advances in labor force participation and declines in both pay gaps and occupational segregation, women in the

Fidan Ana Kurtulus is an assistant professor in the Department of Economics at the University of Massachusetts, Amherst. She has conducted research on various topics in labor economics, including workplace diversity, affirmative action in employment, compensation systems, employee ownership, and participatory workplace practices.

Donald Tomaskovic-Devey is a professor in and chair of the Department of Sociology at the University of Massachusetts, Amherst. He is currently doing research on long-term trends in workplace gender and race segregation as well as developing theory and empirical models on the labor process and workplace inequality.

NOTE: The authors are grateful for helpful comments and suggestions from Doug Anderton, Michael Ash, Lee Badgett, Jed DeVaro, Ron Ehrenberg, Nancy Folbre, Richard Freeman, Jonathan Leonard, Lisa Saunders, Sheryl Skaggs, Peter Skott, Emma Stephens, and participants of the 2009 Annual Meetings of the Society of Labor Economists and the 2009 Annual Meetings of the Eastern Economic Association.

DOI: 10.1177/0002716211418445

United States remain underrepresented in managerial positions (Rothstein 2001; Blau, Ferber, and Winkler 2006, 181; Reskin and Bielby 2005). While women have made up around 45 percent of employment in large U.S. firms since the early 1990s, the proportion of women in managerial occupations was only 29 percent in 1990, although this figure has been steadily increasing, with 34 percent of management positions held by women in 2003.[1] The goal of this study is to empirically examine whether women in the highest levels of management at firms help to reduce barriers to advancement in the workplace faced by other women.

It is often argued that women in top leadership positions serve to improve women's recruitment and promotion to managerial positions by mentoring women in lower-level jobs, acting as positive role models, and enhancing hiring and retention of women at the firm. However, theories about whether gender diversity at high levels of firms' hierarchies helps women to advance have largely been based on anecdotal evidence and general observation due to the dearth of appropriate datasets conducive to an empirical analysis of this topic. The few empirical studies that have examined the influence of women in top company leadership on subsequent managerial gender diversity have primarily been based on small samples of firms or workers involved in limited tasks and often lack a longitudinal component.

This article uses a unique panel of more than twenty thousand large private-sector firms across all industries and states during 1990 to 2003, obtained from the U.S. Equal Employment Opportunity Commission, to study the influence of female top managers on the subsequent representation of women in midlevel management positions in U.S. firms and how this relationship varies with firm characteristics such as industry and federal contractor status. The Equal Employment Opportunity Commission EEO-1 data provide a unique opportunity to conduct a large-scale examination of this topic, which until now has been confined mainly to empirical studies limited in size and generalizability.

In addition to using a sample much larger in size and scope than previous studies, our study is also the first to exploit panel methods to identify the influence of female top managers on subsequent managerial gender diversity, allowing us to derive more precise estimates of this relationship. Though detecting the influence of female top managers is difficult in the absence of exogenous variation in female representation in the highest ranks of firm hierarchies, in our panel regressions we are able to control for numerous sources of heterogeneity that threaten the identification of the female top managers effect, including time-varying observed firm heterogeneity, time-invariant unobserved firm heterogeneity, and industry-specific and economy-wide trends that may additionally affect the evolution of female managerial representation at firms.

Our key findings show that an increase in the share of female top managers is associated with subsequent increases in the share of women in midlevel management, and this result is robust to controlling for firm size, workforce composition, federal contractor status, firm fixed effects, year fixed effects, and industry-specific time trends. Furthermore, although the influence of women in top management positions is strongest among white women, black, Hispanic, and Asian women in top management also have a positive influence on subsequent increases in black, Hispanic, and Asian women in midlevel management, respectively. Moreover, the influence of women in top management positions is stronger among federal contractors and in firms with larger female labor forces. We also find that the positive influence of female top managers on managerial gender diversity diminishes over time. These results suggest that women in the highest leadership positions play a positive but transitory role in women's career advancement in U.S. firms.

Mechanisms

Why might we expect greater representation of women in top leadership positions to lead to subsequent increases in managerial gender diversity at a firm? One potential mechanism is mentoring (Athey, Avery, and Zemsky 2000). Female managers may act as mentors to female employees in lower ranks of the firm's hierarchy, actively training them in firm-specific human capital and skills necessary to succeed at the firm, thereby improving the likelihood that they will get promoted to top managerial positions—an advantage male employees have long benefited from, given historically male-dominated management at firms (Kanter 1977; Ibarra 1993; Noe 1988).

Furthermore, if it is the case that female employees are given less favorable performance evaluations by male supervisors than by female supervisors—either because of gender discrimination in supervisor evaluations (both taste-based and statistical discrimination) or because women perform worse when working under male managers than under female managers—and are thus less likely to be promoted to higher positions (Tsui and O'Reilly 1989; Giuliano, Leonard, and Levine 2006), then women employees would be more likely to be promoted in firms with a greater share of women at the top.

There have been a few empirical studies examining the relationship between the share of women in top management and internal promotions of women employees within firms, and the overall evidence is mixed. In his sample of 149 U.S. law schools, Chused (1988) found that female law professors were more likely to be granted tenure in faculties with a higher proportion of tenured women than in faculties with a very low proportion of tenured women. Using data on managerial workers at 333 savings and loan banks in California, Cohen, Broschak, and Haveman (1998) found that women were more likely to be promoted into a managerial job when a higher proportion of women were already there. On the other hand, Blau and DeVaro (2007) found no evidence of this in their cross-section of 1,772 urban establishments in Atlanta, Boston, Detroit, and Los Angeles from the Multi-City Study of Urban Inequality, and Rothstein (1997) found no evidence of differences in subjective perceptions of future promotion probabilities based on supervisor gender among young workers in the National Longitudinal Survey of Youth.

Another channel through which women in top leadership may play an influential role in increasing subsequent managerial gender diversity at a firm is by recruiting highly qualified women from other firms to managerial positions. For example, in their sample of 333 California savings and loan banks, Cohen, Broschak, and Haveman (1998) found increased external recruitment of female managers when there were more preexisting female managers. Company executives often socialize with executives from other firms, and these networks are commonly divided along gender lines. So it is likely that female top managers will be more knowledgeable than male top managers about women at outside firms who may be suitable for a managerial opening at their firm. In other words, women top managers can improve female recruitment using their female networks and informing women outside the firm of managerial job opportunities.

In addition to recruiting qualified females directly to the managerial positions of a firm, women in the top leadership may increase the recruitment of women to lower-level nonmanagerial positions, thereby increasing the likelihood of female internal promotions to managerial positions. A limited number of studies have documented greater external hiring of female nonmanagerial employees when management was composed of a higher female share (Carrington and Troske 1995, 1998). Huffman, Cohen, and Pearlman (2010) use EEO-1 data to show that increased female representation in management is associated with declines in nonmanagerial sex segregation in establishments.

Apart from increasing the probability of female promotions through increasing the proportion of female nonmanagers, women managers may utilize their female networks to recruit higher-quality female nonmanagers, which will also lead to higher internal promotions to managerial positions for a given proportion of female nonmanagers at the firm.

In addition to improved female recruitment, women in top leadership roles can facilitate growth in female managerial representation through improving retention of both existing female nonmanagers and managers. For instance, Giuliano, Leonard, and Levine (2006) found that female employees demonstrated lower quit rates working under female supervisors than under male supervisors at a large U.S. retail chain.

The above mechanisms are ways in which female top managers may actively increase the subsequent share of women in midlevel management positions at a firm. However, female top managers may also indirectly improve gender diversity in the managerial ranks of a firm.

First, women who have attained visibility in top positions of the corporate hierarchy may weaken traditional stereotypes claiming female managers are less capable than male managers, thereby weakening a formidable barrier to the advancement of women in the workplace (Blau, Ferber, and Winkler 2006, 179–91). This can make it more difficult for discriminatory employers to implement taste-based discrimination in hiring and promotion of women to managerial positions (Becker 1957). It can also lower statistical discrimination in hiring and promotion of women to managerial positions (Phelps 1972; Arrow 1973; Aigner and Cain 1977). Theories of statistical and taste-based discrimination also suggest that discriminatory employers will be less likely to hire women into jobs that have long promotion ladders or occupations that lead to eventual company management, so the weakening of stereotypes regarding women's ability to effectively manage are also likely to reduce discrimination of this form. Furthermore, theories of the signaling role of promotions suggest that the improved information regarding female managerial abilities, due to a greater salience of women in top leadership positions in the labor market, will increase the likelihood that a woman will be promoted to a managerial job from a lower level since the promoting firm will be less concerned about revealing information about the productivity of the promoted female to competing firms (Milgrom and Oster 1987; DeVaro and Waldman 2009).

Second, female top managers can act as role models to female employees at lower levels of a firm's hierarchy without actually mentoring them. In a series of qualitative interviews and questionnaires of attorneys at U.S. law firms, Ely (1994) found that female junior associates at firms with few female senior partners were less likely to view senior women as role models than those at firms with many senior women. Furthermore, the presence of a large share of female top managers can serve as a signal to lower-level female managerial employees at a firm that rising through the firm's ranks is feasible and hence can motivate lower-level female employees to put forth more effort in hopes of eventually attaining promotion to top management ranks. The presence of a large share of female top managers may also serve as an external signal that the firm provides a hospitable environment for women to succeed and attain the high wages associated with those positions, and this may attract highly qualified female applicants to both managerial and nonmanagerial openings. The gender gap in wages among both managers and nonmanagers has been shown to be lower in firms with more women at the highest levels (Bell 2005; Hultin and Szulkin 1999; Shenhav and Haberfeld 1992), and this lower gender gap is also likely to attract highly qualified female applicants.

Data and Methodology

The firm-level data we use in our empirical analyses come from confidential annual EEO-1 reports from 1990 to 2003 that have been collected by the U.S. Equal Employment Opportunity Commission as mandated by Title VII of the U.S. Civil Rights Act of 1964. The EEO-1 reports describe the occupation, race, and gender composition of employees across all U.S. private-sector firms with one hundred or more employees and private-sector federal contractors with fifty or more employees. We have records on more than twenty thousand firms over the

1990 to 2003 period. A great advantage of these data is their longitudinal nature, allowing us to follow firms over time and thereby enabling us to use panel regression methods to control for unobserved attributes of firms that may be correlated with female managerial representation and to derive sharper econometric estimates of the effects being studied. Firms are observed for 7.1 years on average. Finally, to our knowledge, the EEO-1 records constitute the only available cross-firm database with information on employee gender and race composition by occupational category at a firm.

EEO-1 reports contain employment counts at each firm by gender of five racial or ethnic groups (white, black, Hispanic, Asian or Pacific Islander, and American Indian or Alaskan Native) distributed across the following nine occupational categories: managers and officers, professionals, technicians, sales workers, office and clerical workers, craft workers, operatives, laborers, and service workers. Specifically, those in the managers and officers category are defined as administrative and managerial personnel who set broad policies, exercise overall responsibility for execution of these policies, and direct individual departments or special phases of the firm's operations. Examples of jobs in the managers and officers category include executives, plant managers, department managers, superintendents, and managing supervisors. Within this occupational category, we are able to distinguish between top managers working at firm headquarters with control over broad firm policy and firmwide visibility and middle managers working at the firm's nonheadquarter establishments.[2]

When filing their EEO-1 forms, firms are instructed not to include in their reports temporary or casual employees hired for a specified period of time or for the duration of a specified job but to include leased employees as well as both part-time and full-time employees. Robinson et al. (2005) compared employment covered in the EEO-1 data to employment estimates from the U.S. Bureau of Labor Statistics and reported EEO-1 coverage to be about 40 percent of all U.S. private-sector employment throughout the 1990s, with higher proportions in industries composed of larger firms such as manufacturing and transportation. The EEO-1 reports also include information on the firm's industry and geographic location, whether the firm is a federal contractor, and whether the firm is a multi-establishment organization.

We estimate fixed effects regressions of the relationship between the share of female top-level managers at a given firm in the past and the share of female midlevel managers in the future using the following model (equation 1):

$$\textit{\%Female Mid Manager}_{i,t} = \sum_{j=0}^{n} \alpha_j \textit{\%Female Top Manager}_{i,t-j} + X'_{i,t}\beta + \theta_i + \lambda_t + \textit{Industry}_i * t + \varepsilon_{i,t}$$

for specifications with incrementally more lags of % Female Top Manager on the right-hand side, that is, $n = \{0,1,2,3,4,5\}$. Here, $X_{i,t}$ is a vector that includes a constant term and an array of time-varying firm i year t controls, defined below. θ_i is a firm fixed effect, λ_t is a year fixed effect, and $\textit{Industry}_i * t$ represents industry-specific time trends (dummy variables indicating firm i's industry interacted with a linear time trend).

Our goal in this article is to estimate the influence of female top managers on subsequent female representation in middle management at a firm net of economy-wide and firm-specific factors that may also be influencing the evolution of female representation in midlevel management. Including firm fixed effects in equation 1 allows us to control for time-invariant unobserved firm attributes that may influence the future share of women in middle management, such as stable human resource policies. Furthermore, we include year fixed effects to control for any economy-wide shocks and general trends affecting the evolution of female managerial representation symmetrically across all firms. However, there may also be factors influencing the share of female midlevel managers that vary within a firm and a firm's industry over time that would bias our estimates of the influence of female top managers on subsequent female representation in midlevel management if such factors did not change at a national level uniformly and get picked up by the year fixed effects in our model. We would therefore like to additionally control for such firm-specific and industry-specific factors that may also be serving to increase the share of female middle managers at the firm over time. A very flexible way to do this is to incorporate firm-specific trends ($\theta_i * t$) into equation 1, but this is not feasible given the large number of firms in our sample. Instead, we incorporate interactions of industry dummies with a linear time trend to account for industry-specific trends in the prevalence of women in midlevel management positions. For example, many firms in a particular line of business or industry may react to a high-profile gender discrimination lawsuit against a similar firm by enacting a policy that increases the share of females in midlevel management positions over a period of time. Including industry-specific time trends allows us to control for such phenomena so that we can get more accurate estimates of the firm-level influence of female top managers on the subsequent representation of female middle managers net of any industry trends toward higher levels of managerial gender diversity.

Our study is the first to exploit panel methods to investigate the role that women in top leadership positions at firms play in increasing overall managerial gender diversity. One previous study, Cohen, Broschak, and Haveman (1998), analyzed 333 California savings and loan banks and found that both external hiring and upward mobility by women into management was facilitated by preexisting female managers; however, despite having collected yearly data on managers at these banks over the period 1975 to 1987, they pooled all observations across all years and banks and estimated logistic regressions of the probability of a managerial job being filled by a woman, given the current composition of employment at the bank, without accounting for any worker, firm, or year fixed effects. Our regressions, on the other hand, control for numerous sources of unobserved heterogeneity to more precisely quantify the influence of female top managers on the subsequent representation of women in firms' midlevel management ranks. Furthermore, the Cohen, Broschak, and Haveman (1998) study is both geographically and industry specific and so leaves open the question of the generality of this phenomenon, while our study is based on a longitudinal sample of more than twenty thousand firms covering a much broader geographic and industry scope.[3]

Even after accounting for firm fixed effects, year fixed effects, and industry-specific trends, there may still remain differences across firms in factors such as firm culture or diversity policies that vary over time within firms and that influence the evolution of female managerial representation at the firm, biasing our estimates of the effect of female top managers on subsequent managerial gender diversity. To alleviate this potential source of bias, we additionally control for a set of observable time-varying firm characteristics that are likely to be correlated with unobservable factors such as firm culture or the intensity with which diversity policies are implemented and that are likely to influence the extent to which women in top managerial positions can help to reduce barriers to advancement in the workplace faced by other women.

Previous research has shown that firms with formalized human resource practices, such as formal job titles, vacancy postings, and standardized employee evaluations, have lower occupational segregation, lower wage gaps, and higher female access to jobs at the top of their hierarchies (Elvira and Graham 2002; Konrad and Linnehan 1995; Reskin and McBrier 2000) and that the formalization of human resource practices is correlated with organizational size and complexity (Marsden, Cook, and Kalleberg 1996). We therefore control for firm size.

It is reasonable to expect that gender diversity in the nonmanagerial ranks at a firm may influence the extent to which female top managers can attract more women into midlevel management positions in the future. The most obvious reason for this is that the greater the percentage of women in nonmanagerial positions, the greater the probability that women will be promoted from lower levels to midlevel managerial positions. It is also possible that when women have a large share of employment at a firm, the firm may be more likely to promote women to midlevel managerial positions to motivate its lower-level female employees. Furthermore, there might be less resistance to increasing the share of women in management overall when there are many nonmanagerial women at a firm. Reskin and McBrier (2000), in their analysis of 516 employers from the 1991 National Organizations Study, showed that the higher women's share of jobs in an establishment, the higher the proportion of female managers. In their analysis of EEOC private-sector data, Stainback and Tomaskovic-Devey (2009) also found women's representation in management to be closely linked to their representation in nonmanagerial occupations. In a series of experimental studies on cognitive psychological processes and unconscious biases reviewed in Valian (1998, 139-44), women's performance ratings were more negative than men's when women composed smaller percentages within teams. We therefore also include in our regressions a control for the share of nonmanagerial employees at a firm who are women.

It is also reasonable to expect that firms that actively implement race diversity policies are more likely to give high priority to implementing gender diversity programs as well. We therefore also include as controls the share of black and Hispanic employees at a firm to account for idiosyncratic variation across firms in the implementation intensity of managerial gender diversity policies.

Furthermore, our models control for the share of employees who are managers to account for the difficulty of attaining managerial positions at a firm.

We also control for federal contractor status in all of our regression analyses. Firms with government contracts are subject to compliance reviews by the Office of Federal Contract Compliance Programs (OFCCP), with penalties for non-compliance ranging from revocation of current government contracts to suspension of the right to bid on future contracts. Firms that are government contractors may therefore be more likely to implement their diversity programs with greater intensity. They are also required to take affirmative action in recruiting and promoting women and minorities as mandated by Executive Order No. 11246 of 1965. In his analysis of EEO-1 records for the period 1974 to 1980, Leonard (1984a, 1984b, 1986) found that federal contractors increased the employment shares of women and minorities significantly faster than noncontractors and that the occupational advancement of minority groups into skilled white-collar work was more rapid within contracting than noncontracting establishments. Ashenfelter and Heckman (1976) used EEO-1 records for the period 1966 to 1970 to show that employment of black males relative to white males increased more rapidly in firms with government contracts than in firms without contracts, and Heckman and Wolpin (1976) found a similar result based on their analysis of EEO-1 records of firms in the Chicago metropolitan area for the period 1970 to 1973. Brown (1982) also concluded, from a review of the literature, that the employment shares of protected groups increased more rapidly among contractors than noncontractors. Konrad and Linnehan (1995) found that being a government contractor was positively associated with management attitudes about the importance of the company reputation in the area of equal employment opportunity and also positively associated with the percentage of women in high-level management and the percentage of female employees. Kalev and Dobbin (2006) found that OFCCP compliance reviews had a positive but declining effect on white female and black access to managerial jobs since the 1970s.

Table 1 presents detailed definitions and summary statistics for the variables used in our empirical analysis. Figure 1 shows trends in the percentage of women, female managers, female top managers, female middle managers, and female nonmanagers over the years 1990 to 2003.

Empirical Analysis

Influence of female top managers on female middle managers

To determine whether female top managers have a positive influence on subsequent midlevel female managerial representation, we estimate fixed effects regressions of the share of female top managers at firm i in year t on the share of female middle managers at firm i in year t and in the previous five years ($t - 1$, $t - 2, t - 3, t - 4$, and $t - 5$) and the full set of controls including firm size, whether

TABLE 1
Variable Definitions and Descriptive Statistics

Variable	Definition	Mean	SD	N
% female manager	Percentage of managers at the firm who are female	0.318	0.225	121,467
% female top manager	Percentage of top managers at firm headquarters who are female	0.303	0.212	121,467
% female mid manager	Percentage of middle managers at non-headquarter establishments who are female	0.322	0.283	121,467
Lnsize	Ln (number of employees at the firm)	6.403	1.361	121,467
Fed	Dummy variable equaling 1 if the firm is a federal contractor, 0 otherwise	0.492	0.499	121,467
% black	Percentage of employees at the firm who are black	0.108	0.127	121,467
% Hispanic	Percentage of employees at the firm who are Hispanic	0.089	0.133	121,467
% female nonmanager	Percentage of nonmanagerial employ-ees at the firm who are female	0.470	0.253	121,467
% manager	Percentage of employees at the firm who are managers	0.132	0.077	121,467
Year dummies (1990–2003)	Dummy variables indicating year (1990–2003)			121,467
Industry-specific time trends (9)	Interactions of a linear time trend with industry dummies (agriculture, min-ing, construction, manufacturing, transportation, wholesale, retail, finance, service)			121,467

NOTE: Based on the sample of $N = 121,467$ firm-years used in the baseline regression model presented in the last column of Table 2.

the firm is a federal contractor, the share of employees at the firm who are black or Hispanic, the share of nonmanagerial employees at the firm who are female, the share of management at the firm, year dummies, and industry-specific trends. The estimates are reported in Table 2. As seen in columns 1 through 6 of Table 2, the coefficient estimates are remarkably stable as we incrementally add older lags of the shares of top female managers to the right-hand side of the empirical specification. The estimates reveal a positive relationship between the share of female top managers at the firm in the past and the share of women in midlevel management in the future. Focusing on the specification in the last column with concurrent and five lags of female top manager shares and the full set of firm controls, year indicators, and industry-specific trends, we see that the coefficient on the concurrent percentage of female midlevel managers is 0.017

FIGURE 1

Percentage of Females, Female Managers, Female Top Managers, Female Middle
Managers, and Female Nonmanagers, All Industries, 1990–2003

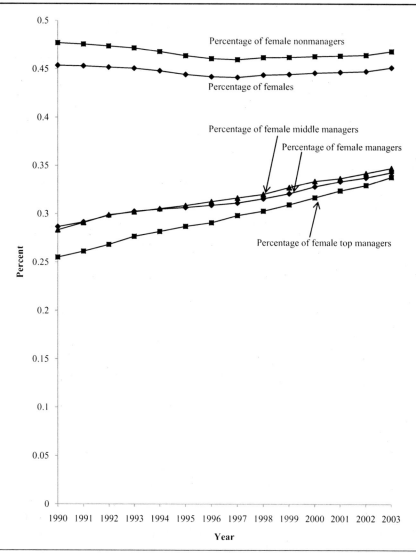

SOURCE: U.S. Equal Employment Opportunity Commission EEO-1 Reports.

and statistically significant at the 1 percent level. The coefficient on the percent-age of female middle managers in year $t - 1$ is even larger, 0.024, and significant. The coefficients on older lags are also positive and significant and gradually become smaller in magnitude.[4] Note that another way to interpret the results in

TABLE 2
Relationship between Percentage of Female Middle Managers and Lagged Percentage of Female Top Managers (Fixed Effects Estimates)

	Dependent Variable: % Female Mid Manager					
	1	2	3	4	5	6
% female top manager	.025°°°	.016°°°	.016°°°	.016°°°	.017°°°	.017°°°
	(.006)	(.006)	(.006)	(.006)	(.006)	(.006)
% female top manager_Lag1		.031°°°	.023°°°	.023°°°	.024°°°	.024°°°
		(.005)	(.005)	(.005)	(.005)	(.005)
% female top manager_Lag2			.023°°°	.019°°°	.019°°°	.020°°°
			(.005)	(.005)	(.005)	(.005)
% female top manager_Lag3				.013°°°	.009°°	.009°°
				(.005)	(.005)	(.005)
% female top manager_Lag4					.013°°°	.011°°
					(.004)	(.004)
% female top manager_Lag5						.008°
						(.004)
Lnsize	.016°°°	.016°°°	.016°°°	.016°°°	.016°°°	.016°°°
	(.002)	(.002)	(.002)	(.002)	(.002)	(.002)
Fed	−.003°°	−.003°°	−.003°°	−.003°°	−.003°°	−.003°°
	(.001)	(.001)	(.001)	(.001)	(.001)	(.001)
% black	.061°°°	.061°°°	.061°°°	.061°°°	.061°°°	.061°°°
	(.019)	(.019)	(.019)	(.019)	(.019)	(.019)
% Hispanic	.029	.029	.029	.030	.030	.030
	(.020)	(.020)	(.020)	(.020)	(.020)	(.020)
% female nonmanager	.159°°°	.159°°°	.158°°°	.158°°°	.158°°°	.158°°°
	(.018)	(.018)	(.018)	(.018)	(.018)	(.018)
% manager	.250°°°	.248°°°	.247°°°	.247°°°	.247°°°	.247°°°
	(.025)	(.025)	(.025)	(.025)	(.025)	(.025)
Year dummies	Yes	Yes	Yes	Yes	Yes	Yes
Industry-specific trends	Yes	Yes	Yes	Yes	Yes	Yes
Constant	.066°°°	.060°°°	.057°°°	.054°°°	.052°°°	.050°°°
	(.017)	(.017)	(.017)	(.017)	(.017)	(.017)
Observations	121,467	121,467	121,467	121,467	121,467	121,467
Number of firms	22,885	22,885	22,885	22,885	22,885	22,885
Adjusted R-squared	.019	.020	.020	.021	.021	.021

NOTE: Robust standard errors in parentheses.
°$p < .1$. °°$p < .05$. °°°$p < .01$.

the last column of Table 2 is that a 1 percentage point increase in the share of women in top-level management this year is associated with a 0.017 percentage point increase in the share of female middle managers in the same year, a 0.024

percentage point increase in the next year, a 0.020 percentage point increase two years later, a 0.009 percentage point increase three years later, a 0.011 percentage point increase four years later, and a 0.008 percentage point increase five years later. These amount to a six-year cumulative increase of 0.088 percentage points in the share of female middle managers.[5]

We infer from these results that women in top management have the greatest impact on women's advancement to midlevel managerial ranks in firms after one year, but the effect gradually weakens in later years. A possible explanation for the diminishing effect is that women may exit the firm to take up better jobs elsewhere after several years of serving in midlevel managerial positions, and the positions they vacate are statistically more likely to be filled by men. As seen in Table 1, the probability that a midlevel managerial position will be filled by a man is more than 70 percent. We conclude that female top managers help women to advance, but the positive impact of an increase in the share of female top managers slowly tapers off over the years.[6]

Race of female managers

A potential objection to the results presented above is that the revealed positive effect of female top managers may represent only a white female manager effect. This, however, turns out not to be the case. Despite the fact that the incidence of nonwhite female top managers is much lower than the incidence of white female top managers in any given year during 1990 to 2003 (Table 3), our within-race estimates of equation 1 (that is, fixed effects regressions of the share of female middle managers of a particular race on the concurrent and lagged shares of female top managers of that race) with the full set of firm controls, year indicators, and industry-specific trends, illustrated in Table 4, indicate that black, Hispanic, and Asian female top managers in fact have a positive and statistically significant influence on expanding the subsequent representation of black, Hispanic, and Asian women in middle management, just as white female top managers have on expanding the subsequent representation of white women in middle management. As seen in Table 4, panel B, a 1 percentage point increase in the share of black female top managers at a firm is associated with a statistically significant 0.022 percentage point increase in the share of black female middle managers in the following year and a 0.034 percentage point increase in the share of black female middle managers after five years. As seen in panels C and D, a 1 percentage point increase in the share of Hispanic female top managers is associated with a 0.027 percentage point increase in the share of Hispanic female middle managers after two years and a 1 percentage point increase in the share of Asian female top managers is associated with a 0.016 percentage point increase in the share of Asian female middle managers after five years. Note that the estimated relationships between the contemporaneous shares of minority female top managers and middle managers are generally negative, probably because an expansion in minority female top managers is likely to be due to promotion of minority women from middle management ranks (thus

TABLE 3
Percentage of Female Top Managers and Female Middle Managers,
Means by Race and Year

Panel A: Percentage of female top managers

Year	% Female Top Manager	% White Female Top Manager	% Black Female Top Manager	% Hispanic Female Top Manager	% Asian Female Top Manager	% Native American Female Top Manager
1990	.255	.233	.010	.006	.004	.001
1991	.261	.239	.010	.007	.005	.001
1992	.268	.244	.011	.007	.005	.001
1993	.277	.251	.012	.007	.006	.001
1994	.282	.255	.012	.007	.006	.001
1995	.287	.259	.013	.008	.006	.001
1996	.291	.262	.014	.008	.007	.001
1997	.298	.267	.014	.009	.007	.001
1998	.303	.271	.015	.009	.007	.001
1999	.310	.273	.017	.010	.008	.001
2000	.317	.279	.017	.011	.009	.001
2001	.324	.285	.017	.012	.009	.001
2002	.330	.290	.017	.012	.009	.001
2003	.338	.297	.018	.012	.010	.001

Panel B: Percentage of female middle managers

Year	% Female Mid Manager	% White Female Mid Manager	% Black Female Mid Manager	% Hispanic Female Mid Manager	% Asian Female Mid Manager	% Native American Female Mid Manager
1990	.283	.252	.015	.010	.004	.001
1991	.291	.258	.017	.010	.005	.001
1992	.299	.266	.017	.010	.005	.001
1993	.302	.269	.017	.010	.005	.001
1994	.305	.270	.018	.011	.005	.001
1995	.309	.269	.021	.012	.005	.001
1996	.313	.274	.020	.012	.006	.001
1997	.317	.275	.021	.013	.006	.001
1998	.320	.277	.022	.013	.006	.001
1999	.327	.281	.024	.015	.007	.002
2000	.334	.285	.025	.016	.007	.002
2001	.337	.286	.026	.017	.008	.001
2002	.342	.289	.027	.017	.007	.001
2003	.348	.295	.026	.018	.008	.002

TABLE 4
Within-Race Relationships between the Percentage of Female Middle Managers and
Lagged Percentage of Female Top Managers (Fixed Effects Estimates)

Panel A: White Women	Dependent Variable: % White Female Mid Manager
% white female top manager	.004 (.006)
% white female top manager_Lag1	.024°°° (.005)
% white female top manager_Lag2	.027°°° (.005)
% white female top manager_Lag3	.012°°° (.005)
% white female top manager_Lag4	.005 (.004)
% white female top manager_Lag5	.003 (.005)
Constant	.088°°° (.017)
Observations	123,050
Number of firms	23,045
Adjusted R-squared	.012

Panel B: Black Women	Dependent Variable: % Black Female Mid Manager
% black female top manager	−.077°°° (.026)
% black female top manager_Lag1	.022° (.012)
% black female top manager_Lag2	.011 (.010)
% black female top manager_Lag3	.005 (.012)
% black female top manager_Lag4	.002 (.011)
% black female top manager_Lag5	.034°° (.014)
Constant	−.020°°° (.005)
Observations	123,050
Number of firms	23,045
Adjusted R-squared	.036

Panel C: Hispanic Women	Dependent Variable: % Hispanic Female Mid Manager
% Hispanic female top manager	−.059°°° (.016)
% Hispanic female top manager_Lag1	.007 (.013)
% Hispanic female top manager_Lag2	.027° (.016)
% Hispanic female top manager_Lag3	.016 (.012)
% Hispanic female top manager_Lag4	.006 (.016)
% Hispanic female top manager_Lag5	−.005 (.014)
Constant	−.010°° (.004)
Observations	123,050
Number of firms	23,045
Adjusted R-squared	.022

(continued)

TABLE 4 (CONTINUED)

Panel D: Asian Women	Dependent Variable: % Asian Female Mid Manager
% Asian female top manager	−.044°° (.018)
% Asian female top manager_Lag1	.021 (.013)
% Asian female top manager_Lag2	.011 (.010)
% Asian female top manager_Lag3	−.002 (.014)
% Asian female top manager_Lag4	.011 (.010)
% Asian female top manager_Lag5	.016° (.009)
Constant	−.003 (.002)
Observations	123,050
Number of firms	23,045
Adjusted R-squared	.005

Panel E: Native American Women	Dependent Variable: % NatAm Female Mid Manager
% Native American female top manager	.022 (.060)
% Native American female top manager_Lag1	−.006 (.023)
% Native American female top manager_Lag2	.032 (.041)
% Native American female top manager_Lag3	.006 (.023)
% Native American female top manager_Lag4	−.006 (.030)
% Native American female top manager_Lag5	.019 (.020)
Constant	.002 (.001)
Observations	123,050
Number of firms	23,045
Adjusted R-squared	.001

NOTE: All models include the full set of firm controls and year dummies as listed in the last column of Table 2. Robust standard errors in parentheses.
°$p < .1.$ °°$p < .05.$ °°°$p < .01.$

shrinking their middle management share in the contemporaneous period). Although the relationship between black, Hispanic, and Asian women in top management and subsequent increases in black, Hispanic, and Asian women in middle management is quite a bit smaller than the relationship between white female top managers and subsequent increases in white female middle management revealed in panel A, there are clear effects for black, Hispanic, and Asian women, indicating that the average effects revealed earlier in the article were not merely a white female manager phenomenon.[7,8]

Federal contractor status

As explained earlier, firms with federal contracts are required to take affirmative action in recruiting and promoting women and minorities and are subject to

OFCCP reviews. Previous empirical work has found that the increase in employment shares and occupational advancement of protected groups was more rapid among federal contractors than noncontractors during the initial years of the civil rights movement. Given these regulatory pressures, it is reasonable to suspect that women in top leadership roles may be better able to expand managerial gender diversity at firms with government contracts in comparison to noncontractors. We test this hypothesis by augmenting the most controlled regression specification presented in the last columns of Table 2 with interactions of the current and lagged shares of female top managers with current federal contractor status.[9]

The estimates from this model are presented in Table 5, with the lower panel showing the marginal effects of women top managers at firms holding federal contracts versus noncontractors. It is interesting to note that among noncontractors, the influence of female top managers can be characterized as more of a short-term phenomenon, with most of the statistically significant female top manager effects concentrated in the current and early periods; while with federal contractors there are more sustained, longer-term effects as indicated by the fact that the coefficients on later lags (lags one, two, three, and four) are also strongly statistically significant. This suggests that affirmative action extends the persistence of the positive effect of women in top leadership. Moreover, we also see in the lower panel of Table 5 that the six-year cumulative effect of female top managers is slightly larger among contractors, providing further support for the idea that female top managers are better able to expand female managerial representation at firms with government contracts in comparison to noncontractors.

Industry

A unique advantage of the EEO-1 data is that they include firms across all industries of the United States. Since women's representation, gender norms, and occupational segregation by gender vary a great deal across industries, the positive influence of women in top leadership is likely to be more intense for certain industries than for others. We explore this idea in Table 6 by restricting the regression analysis to samples consisting of firms in each of the following industries: agriculture, mining, construction, manufacturing, transportation, wholesale trade, retail trade, finance, and the service industry. There is considerable variation in the impact of female top managers on subsequent female representation in midlevel management. Focusing on the six-year cumulative effect, firms in the construction, manufacturing, finance, and wholesale trade industries tend to exhibit the largest benefits to female top managers. Interestingly, some of these are also industries in which women have historically been underrepresented relative to men and therefore where the benefits of female managers on increasing recruitment, retention, and promotion of women may be expected to be large. On the other hand, firms in the agriculture and mining industries exhibit the weakest effects.

TABLE 5
How the Relationship between Percentage of Female Middle Managers and Lagged
Percentage of Female Top Managers Varies with Federal Contractor Status
(Fixed Effects Estimates)

Panel A: Regression Estimates

	Dependent Variable: % Female Mid Manager
% female top manager	.025°°° (.008)
% female top manager_Lag1	.018°°° (.006)
% female top manager_Lag2	.019°°° (.006)
% female top manager_Lag3	.005 (.006)
% female top manager_Lag4	.006 (.006)
% female top manager_Lag5	.012° (.006)
% female top manager*Fed	−.019° (.010)
% female top manager_Lag1*Fed	.014 (.009)
% female top manager_Lag2*Fed	.000 (.009)
% female top manager_Lag3*Fed	.010 (.008)
% female top manager_Lag4*Fed	.012 (.008)
% female top manager_Lag5*Fed	−.010 (.008)
Constant	.051°°° (.017)
Observations	121,467
Number of firms	22,885
Adjusted R-squared	.021

Panel B: Implied Marginal Effects

	Implied Effect on % Female Mid Manager	
	For Fed = 0 Firms	For Fed = 1 Firms
% female top manager	.025°°° (.008)	.007 (.007)
% female top manager_Lag1	.018°°° (.006)	.032°°° (.007)
% female top manager_Lag2	.019°°° (.006)	.019°°° (.006)
% female top manager_Lag3	.005 (.006)	.015°° (.006)
% female top manager_Lag4	.006 (.006)	.017°°° (.006)
% female top manager_Lag5	.012° (.006)	.002 (.006)
Six-year Cumulative Effect	.085°°° (.014)	.091°°° (.013)
(Six-year effect for fed = 1 firms) − (Six-year effect for fed = 0 firms)	.007 (.007)	

NOTE: The model includes the full set of firm controls, year dummies, and industry-specific
trends as listed in the last column of Table 2. Robust standard errors in parentheses.
°$p < .1$. °°$p < .05$. °°°$p < .01$.

TABLE 6

How the Relationship between Percentage of Female Middle Managers and Lagged Percentage of Female Top Managers Varies by Industry (Fixed Effects Regressions by Industry)

	Dependent Variable: % Female Mid Manager								
	Agriculture	Mining	Construction	Manufacturing	Transportation	Wholesale	Retail	Finance	Service
% female top manager	-.087	.032	.067°°	.000	.006	-.024	.010	-.007	.044°°°
	(.077)	(.036)	(.028)	(.012)	(.020)	(.016)	(.013)	(.014)	(.012)
% female top manager_Lag1	-.067	.002	.066°°	.007	.012	.054°°°	.014	.050°°°	.023°°
	(.064)	(.024)	(.026)	(.009)	(.018)	(.013)	(.011)	(.011)	(.009)
% female top manager_Lag2	-.064	-.002	.001	.022°°	.031°	.020	.021°°	.006	.022°°
	(.048)	(.020)	(.026)	(.009)	(.019)	(.012)	(.011)	(.010)	(.009)
% female top manager_Lag3	.014	-.031	.031	.028°°	-.001	-.000	-.003	.017°	.003
	(.043)	(.026)	(.020)	(.011)	(.019)	(.013)	(.010)	(.009)	(.009)
% female top manager_Lag4	.144	.010	-.003	.010	-.013	.035°°°	-.003	.024°°	.007
	(.110)	(.023)	(.020)	(.009)	(.019)	(.013)	(.010)	(.010)	(.008)
% female top manager_Lag5	.181	.022	-.009	.020°°	.000	.007	-.003	.007	.04
	(.118)	(.025)	(.029)	(.009)	(.016)	(.014)	(.010)	(.010)	(.008)
Constant	-.489°°°	-.140°°	.061	-.106°°°	-.066	-.106°°	.052	.208°°°	.214°°°
	(.183)	(.054)	(.060)	(.028)	(.048)	(.042)	(.062)	(.060)	(.039)
Six-year cumulative effect	.122	.033	.153°°	.087°°°	.036	.092°°°	.036	.097°°°	.103°°°
	(.206)	(.055)	(.068)	(.028)	(.047)	(.036)	(.030)	(.030)	(.026)
Observations	735	1,114	2,921	34,293	6,912	11,061	12,374	18,496	33,561
Adjusted R-squared	.093	.069	.047	.024	.028	.034	.060	.028	.010
Number of firms	129	198	562	6,235	1,324	1,999	2,339	3,491	6,608

NOTE: Each model includes the full set of firm controls, year dummies, and industry-specific trends as listed in the last column of Table 2. Robust standard errors in parentheses.
°$p < .1$. °°$p < .05$. °°°$p < .01$.

Nonmanagerial gender diversity

It is reasonable to expect that gender diversity in the nonmanagerial ranks at a firm may influence the extent to which female top managers can attract more women into midlevel managerial positions in the future. This may be because the greater the percentage of women in nonmanagerial positions, the greater the probability that women will be promoted from lower levels to middle management positions; or because when women have a large share of employment at a firm, the firm may be more likely to promote women to management ranks to motivate its lower-level female employees; or because there may be less resistance to increasing managerial gender diversity when there are many nonmanagerial women at the firm. We test the hypothesis that gender diversity in firms' nonmanagerial ranks may influence the extent to which female top managers can attract more women into midlevel managerial positions by including interactions of the share of nonmanagerial employees who are female with the current and lagged shares of female top managers in the baseline regression of the share of female middle managers on the current and lagged shares of female top managers. Estimates from this regression are presented in Table 7, with the lower panel showing the implied marginal effects of the share of female top managers on subsequent female midlevel managerial representation computed at different shares of female nonmanagerial workers at a firm. Reading across rows in the lower panel, we see that the short-term benefits of female top managers (current and first lag) are increasing with the share of female nonmanagers at a firm, suggesting that indeed female top managers can more effectively diversify management ranks when women's overall firm presence is larger. Similarly, the six-year cumulative effect of women in top leadership is increasing with the share of nonmanagerial women. On the other hand, the longer-term benefits of female top managers (lags two, three, four, and five) are either decreasing with the share of female nonmanagers or not statistically significant.

Discussion and Conclusion

Using a unique panel of more than twenty thousand large private-sector firms across all industries and states during 1990 to 2003 from the U.S. Equal Employment Opportunity Commission, we show that female top managers have a positive influence on expanding the subsequent representation of women in the lower-level managerial ranks of U.S. firms, and this result is robust to controlling for firm size, workforce composition, federal contractor status, firm fixed effects, year fixed effects, and industry-specific time trends. Furthermore, the influence of female top managers on gender diversity in lower levels of management diminishes over time. Our findings collectively suggest that women in top management play a positive but transitory role in the advancement of women within U.S. firms.

We additionally uncover interesting differences in the effect of female top managers on the evolution of managerial gender diversity by managerial race,

TABLE 7

How the Relationship between Percentage of Female Middle Managers and Lagged Percentage of Female Top Managers Varies by Percentage of Female Nonmanagers (Fixed Effects Estimates)

Panel A: Regression Estimates

	Dependent Variable: % Female Mid Manager
% female top manager	.014 (.010)
% female top manager_Lag1	.014 (.009)
% female top manager_Lag2	.030*** (.008)
% female top manager_Lag3	.011 (.008)
% female top manager_Lag4	.007 (.008)
% female top manager_Lag5	.003 (.009)
% female top manager*% female nonmanager	.006 (.021)
% female top manager_Lag1*% female nonmanager	.018 (.018)
% female top manager_Lag2*% female nonmanager	-.019 (.017)
% female top manager_Lag3*% female nonmanager	-.003 (.016)
% female top manager_Lag4*% female nonmanager	.006 (.015)
% female top manager_Lag5*% female nonmanager	.009 (.016)
Constant	.052*** (.017)
Observations	121,467
Number of firms	22,885
Adjusted R-squared	.021

NOTE: The model includes the full set of firm controls, year dummies, and industry-specific trends as listed in the last column of Table 2. Robust standard errors in parentheses.
*$p < .1$. **$p < .05$. ***$p < .01$.

(continued)

TABLE 7 (CONTINUED)

Panel B: Implied Marginal Effects

	Implied Effect on % Female Mid Manager at Different Values of % Female Nonmanager						
% Female Non-manager=	.05	.10	.25	.50	.75	.90	.95
% female top manager	.014	.014*	.016**	.017***	.019**	.019*	.020
	(.010)	(.009)	(.007)	(.006)	(.009)	(.012)	(.013)
% female top manager_Lag1	.015	.016**	.019***	.024***	.028***	.031***	.032***
	(.008)	(.007)	(.005)	(.005)	(.007)	(.009)	(.010)
% female top manager_Lag2	.029***	.028***	.025***	.020***	.015**	.013	.012
	(.008)	(.007)	(.005)	(.004)	(.007)	(.009)	(.010)
% female top manager_Lag3	.011	.011	.010*	.009**	.009	.008	.008
	(.007)	(.007)	(.005)	(.004)	(.007)	(.009)	(.009)
% female top manager_Lag4	.008	.008	.009*	.010**	.012**	.013*	.013
	(.007)	(.007)	(.005)	(.004)	(.006)	(.008)	(.008)
% female top manager_Lag5	.003	.004	.005	.007*	.010	.011	.011
	(.008)	(.007)	(.006)	(.004)	(.006)	(.008)	(.009)
Six-year cumulative effect	.080***	.081***	.083***	.088***	.092***	.095***	.095***
	(.020)	(.018)	(.014)	(.013)	(.018)	(.024)	(.025)

federal contractor status, industry, and the proportion of female nonmanagers already working at a firm. For example, the positive effect of women in top leadership positions is found to be more persistent at firms holding federal contracts, and therefore bound by affirmative action obligations, than among noncontractors. Furthermore, although the influence of women in top management positions is strongest among white women, black, Hispanic, and Asian women in top management also have a positive influence on subsequent increases in black, Hispanic, and Asian women in midlevel management, respectively.

Our analysis reveals that an increase in the share of women in top leadership leads to subsequent further growth in managerial gender diversity at firms—but how does the initial increase in the share of female top managers come about? What are the exogenous influences that begin this process? Our analysis does not address how women can make initial inroads into top management that will lead to further increases in managerial gender diversity but points to the potential importance of external intervention (e.g., lawsuits, positive and negative press coverage) and government regulation in bringing about such initial inroads for women in top levels of company hierarchies. As Athey, Avery, and Zemsky (2000, 765) point out, a firm may have multiple steady states for female managerial representation, whereby temporary affirmative action policies may have a long-term impact on the evolution of diversity at the firm by moving the firm to a steady state characterized by greater female managerial representation.

Future work might involve a formal analysis of the mechanisms through which women in top leadership positions expand managerial gender diversity. A limitation of the EEO-1 database is that it does not contain information on promotions, hiring, turnover, or mentoring of female employees relative to men, preventing us from determining which of these different channels of influence are the predominant mechanisms underlying our main results. It would be useful to investigate the relative strengths of these various mechanisms using more detailed datasets in future research.

Notes

1. These figures are based on data from the U.S. Equal Employment Opportunity Commission EEO-1 files. Nationally representative data from the U.S. Bureau of Labor Statistics confirm these trends: Current Population Survey estimates of the share of employed women age 16 and older was steady around 45 percent during the 1990s, while the share of employed women in management occupations in private-sector firms (of all sizes) rose steadily from 33 percent in 1990 to 36 percent in 2003.

2. An example of a firm's establishment is a store branch of a retail chain.

3. Because Cohen, Broschak, and Haveman (1998) did not provide marginal effects, we are not able to compare the magnitudes of our estimates to theirs.

4. The coefficient on the contemporaneous share of female top managers is likely smaller than the $t-1$ coefficient because an expansion in the share of top managers will be in part due to promotion of women from middle management ranks (thus shrinking women's middle management share in the contemporaneous period).

5. We also estimated models with the lagged versions of the time-varying firm control variables; the estimates of the coefficients on the main independent variables remain nearly identical to those reported in Table 2. This is also true for all of the models in the remainder of the article. These results are available from the authors.

6. Our focus is on regressions of the share of female middle managers on the share of female top managers rather than the other way around, since, as we have argued throughout the article, the channels of influence are most likely to flow from higher levels to lower levels in a firm's hierarchy through mechanisms such as mentoring of lower-level employees and hiring and retention. However, we also explored the reverse specification by estimating analogous fixed effects regressions of the share of female top managers on the share of female middle managers. The estimated coefficients on the contemporaneous and lagged shares of female middle managers were either statistically indistinguishable from zero or considerably smaller than the estimates from our main specifications discussed above, showing that the direction of influence is from top management to middle management and not the other way around. These results are available from the authors.

7. We also estimated cross-race regressions of the influence of white women in top management on minority women in middle management. For black and Hispanic women, the influence was weakly positive; for Asian and Native American women, the impact was essentially zero.

8. Additionally including a control variable for the percentage of nonmanagerial workers belonging to the relevant race does not change the regression estimates very much.

9. We also estimated models in which the interaction terms were with one period lagged federal contractor status, five-year lagged federal contractor status, federal contractor status concurrent with the lag of the share of female managers, and an indicator of whether the firm was a federal contractor in each of the previous five years. The results are very similar to those reported here and are available from the authors.

References

Aigner, Dennis J., and Glen G. Cain. 1977. Statistical theories of discrimination in labor markets. *Industrial and Labor Relations Review* 30 (2): 175–87.

Arrow, Kenneth. 1973. The theory of discrimination. In *Discrimination in labor markets*, eds. Orley A. Ashenfelter and Albert Rees. Princeton, NJ: Princeton University Press.

Ashenfelter, Orley, and James Heckman. 1976. Measuring the effect of an anti-discrimination program. In *Evaluating the labor market effects of social programs*, eds. Orley Ashenfelter and James Blum. Princeton, NJ: Princeton University, Industrial Relations Section.

Athey, Susan, Christopher Avery, and Peter Zemsky. 2000. Mentoring and diversity. *American Economic Review* 90 (4): 765–86.

Becker, Gary S. 1957. *The economics of discrimination*. Chicago, IL: University of Chicago Press.

Bell, Linda A. 2005. Women-led firms and the gender gap in top executive jobs. Institute for the Study of Labor (IZA) Working Paper, Bonn, Germany.

Blau, Francine D., and Jed L. DeVaro. 2007. New evidence on gender differences in promotion rates: An empirical analysis of a sample of new hires. *Industrial Relations* 46 (3): 511–50.

Blau, Francine D., Marianne Ferber, and Anne Winkler. 2006. *The economics of women, men, and work*. 5th ed. New York, NY: Prentice Hall.

Brown, Charles. 1982. The federal attack on labor market discrimination: The mouse that roared? In *Research in labor economics*, vol. 5., ed. Ronald G. Ehrenberg, 11–68. Greenwich, CT: JAI.

Carrington, William J., and Kenneth R. Troske. 1995. Gender segregation in small firms. *Journal of Human Resources* 30 (3): 505–33.

Carrington, William J., and Kenneth R. Troske. 1998. Sex segregation in U.S. manufacturing. *Industrial and Labor Relations Review* 51 (3): 445–64.

Chused, Richard H. 1988. The hiring and retention of minorities and women on American law school faculties. *University of Pennsylvania Law Review* 137 (2): 537–69.

Cohen, Lisa E., Joseph P. Broschak, and Heather Haveman. 1998. And then there were more? The effect of organizational sex composition on the hiring and promotion of managers. *American Sociological Review* 63:711–27.

DeVaro, Jed L., and Michael Waldman. 2009. The signaling role of promotions: Further theory and empirical evidence. Cornell University Working Paper, Ithaca, NY.

Elvira, Marta E., and Mary E. Graham. 2002. Not just a formality: Pay systems and sex-related earnings effects. *Organization Science* 13:601–17.

Ely, Robin J. 1994. The effects of organizational demographics and social identity on relationships among professional women. *Administrative Science Quarterly* 39:203–38.

Giuliano, Laura, Jonathan Leonard, and David I. Levine. 2006. Do race, gender, and age differences affect manager-employee relations? An analysis of quits, dismissals, and promotions at a large retail firm. Institute for Research on Labor and Employment Working Paper, University of California, Berkeley, CA.

Heckman, James J., and Kenneth I. Wolpin. 1976. Does the contract compliance program work? An analysis of Chicago data. *Industrial and Labor Relations Review* 29 (4): 544–64.

Huffman, Matt L., Philip N. Cohen, and Jessica Pearlman. 2010. Engendering change: Organizational dynamics and workplace gender desegregation, 1975–2005. *Administrative Science Quarterly* 55:255–77.

Hultin, Mia, and Ryszard Szulkin. 1999. Wages and unequal access to organization power: An empirical test of gender discrimination. *Administrative Science Quarterly* 44:453–72.

Ibarra, Herminia 1993. Personal networks of women and minorities in management: A conceptual framework. *Academy of Management Review* 18:46–87.

Kalev, Alexandra, and Frank Dobbin. 2006. Enforcement of civil rights law in private workplaces: The effects of compliance reviews and lawsuits over time. *Law & Social Inquiry* 31:855–903.

Kanter, Rosabeth. M. 1977. *Men and women of the corporation.* New York, NY: Basic Books.

Konrad, Alison M., and Frank Linnehan. 1995. Formalized HRM structure: Coordinating equal employment opportunity or concealing organizational practice? *Academy of Management Journal* 38:787–820.

Leonard, Jonathan S. 1984a. Anti-discrimination or reverse discrimination: The impact of changing demographics, Title VII and affirmative action on productivity. *Journal of Human Resources* 19:145–74.

Leonard, Jonathan S. 1984b. Employment and occupational advance under affirmative action. *Review of Economics and Statistics* 66:377–85.

Leonard, Jonathan S. 1986. The effectiveness of equal employment law and affirmative action regulation. In *Research in labor economics*, vol. 8., ed Ronald G. Ehrenberg, 318–50, Greenwich, CT: JAI.

Marsden, Peter V., Cynthia R. Cook, and Arne L. Kalleberg. 1996. Bureaucratic structures for coordination and control. In *Organizations in America: Analyzing their structures and human resource practices*, eds. Arne L. Kalleberg, David Knoke, Peter V. Marsden, and Joe L. Spaeth, 69–86. Thousand Oaks, CA: Sage.

Milgrom, Paul, and Sharon Oster. 1987. Job discrimination, market forces, and the invisibility hypothesis. *Quarterly Journal of Economics* 102:453–76.

Noe, Raymond A. 1988. Women and mentoring: A review and research agenda. *Academy of Management Review* 13:65–78.

Phelps, Edmund S. 1972. The statistical theory of racism and sexism. *American Economic Review* 62 (4): 659–61.

Reskin, Barbara F., and Denise D. Bielby. 2005. A sociological perspective on gender and career outcomes. *Journal of Economic Perspectives* 19 (1): 71–86.

Reskin, Barbara F., and Debra Branch McBrier. 2000. Why not ascription? Organizations, employment of male and female managers. *American Sociological Review* 65:210–33.

Robinson, Corre L., Tiffany Taylor, Donald Tomaskovic-Devey, Catherine Zimmer, and Matthew Irwin. 2005. Studying race or ethnic and sex segregation at the establishment level: Methodological issues and substantive opportunities using EEO-1 reports. *Work and Occupations* 32:5–38.

Rothstein, Donna S. 1997. Supervisor gender and labor market outcomes. In *Gender and family issues in the workplace*, eds. Francine D. Blau and Ronald G. Ehrenberg. New York, NY: Russell Sage Foundation.

Rothstein, Donna S. 2001. Supervisory status and upper-level supervisory responsibilities: Evidence from the NLSY79. *Industrial and Labor Relations Review* 54 (3): 663–80.

Shenhav, Yehouda, and Yitchak Haberfeld. 1992. Organizational demography and inequality. *Social Forces* 71:123–43.

Stainback, Kevin, and Donald Tomaskovic-Devey. 2009. Intersections of power and privilege: Long-term trends in managerial representation. *American Sociological Review* 74:800–820.

Tsui, Anne S., and Charles A. O'Reilly III. 1989. Beyond simple demographic effects: The importance of relational demography in superior-subordinate dyads. *Academy of Management Journal* 32 (2): 402–23.

Valian, Virginia. 1998. *Why so slow? The advancement of women.* Cambridge, MA: MIT Press..

Minorities in Management: Effects on Income Inequality, Working Conditions, and Subordinate Career Prospects among Men

By
DAVID MAUME

Scholars differ on whether the increase in minority managers represents real or vacuous progress toward the elimination of racial bias in the labor market. This study uses the National Study of the Changing Workforce to examine racial differences in work outcomes across the authority divide. On balance, this study finds more support for the pessimistic view of the minority presence in management, in that racial wage inequality is as large among supervisors as among non-supervisors, and minority supervisors get less challenging job assignments and are more vulnerable to layoffs than white supervisors. Among subordinates, this study finds support for "bottom-up ascription" processes, in that minority workers who report to a minority boss earn less despite being more committed workers. The article concludes with a brief discussion of the implications of these findings and the need for further research on minorities in management.

Keywords: race; management; labor markets; inequality; organizations

As minority groups increasingly enter the ranks of management, some scholars claim that racial discrimination in the labor market is a vestige of the past (Brown et al. 2003). Others are more pessimistic, arguing that minority managers are concentrated in lower-paying service industries, often exercising authority over other minorities who themselves occupy devalued positions within firms (see, e.g., Elliott and Smith 2001).

David Maume is a professor of sociology at the University of Cincinnati, where he studies the work-family nexus and racial and gender inequality in the labor market. His recent papers have appeared in Social Science Research, Gender & Society, *and the* American Sociological Review.

NOTE: This research was supported by grants from the National Institute of Child Health and Human Development (R03-HD42411-01A1) and the Charles Phelps Taft Research Center at the University of Cincinnati. I thank Julie Kmec, Matt Huffman, Ryan Smith, and George Wilson for their comments on earlier drafts of this article.

DOI: 10.1177/0002716211420230

Given the importance of this question, it is surprising that there is study of the effects of minorities in management positions. Organizationa iorists and industrial psychologists have extensively researched how women in management positions affect workplace dynamics and firm performance (for a review, see Powell and Graves 2003), whereas sociologists have shown that firm and labor market factors determine minority representation in management (for a review, see Stainback, Tomaskovic-Devey, and Skaggs 2010). Generally lacking, however, are studies of how minority status affects the wages and working conditions among managers and the subordinates who report to them.

Although understanding the processes governing minority access to management positions is crucial to an assessment of the persistence of racial inequality in the labor market, it is also important to assess how minorities as a group fare when some of their members attain positions giving them the opportunity to reduce inequality. Thus, this study asks not only whether the jobs of minority and majority managers are similar but also whether minority bosses influence the job and career prospects of subordinates, and minority subordinates in particular. As I show in the review below, these questions have not been addressed in prior studies of minorities in management. Thus, by examining the influence of race on the job assignments and rewards of managers and nonmanagers alike, this study provides an answer to the larger question of whether diversity in managerial ranks represents real or vacuous progress toward eliminating racial bias in the labor market.

Background

Whereas diversity is associated with improved firm performance (Herring 2008), it has also long been known that senior managers tend to promote junior colleagues with similar backgrounds and worldviews, thereby reproducing the dominance of white men in management (Kanter 1977). For this reason, recent research has analyzed the political, economic, and organizational determinants of minority access to managerial positions.

Access to management

Minorities steadily increased their presence in management after the passage of 1960s-era antidiscrimination legislation. Drawing on employer reports to the Equal Employment Opportunity Commission (EEOC; the federal agency charged with monitoring and combating discrimination in the labor market), Stainback and Tomaskovic-Devey (2009, 802) showed that the proportion of all managers who were white men declined from 91 percent in 1966 to 57 percent in 2000; by comparison, there were virtually no African American managers in 1966, whereas in 2000, one in fourteen managers was African American. These figures imply that white men lost managerial jobs over time, but this was not necessarily the case in a growing economy. Indeed, Stainback and Tomaskovic-Devey's analysis revealed that white men retained their advantaged positions in "old" goods-producing industries, whereas African Americans and white women rapidly increased their managerial presence in the growing (but lower-paying) personal and social service industries.

Nevertheless, political and legal pressure on firms was instrumental in diversifying the ranks of management. For example, Edelman (1990) showed that in response to EEOC lawsuits and affirmative action regulations, firms created human resource departments charged with ensuring compliance with antidiscrimination legislation, and these "responsibility structures" worked to increase the number of African Americans in management (Kalev, Dobbin, and Kelly 2006). Similarly, Skaggs (2009) found that supermarkets, industry-wide, increased their hiring and promotion of black managers a year after a discrimination lawsuit had been filed against an employer and in jurisdictions with more minority federal judges sitting on the circuit court.

Collins (1997) puts a human face on these findings in her interviews with black corporate executives, many of whom were the highest-ranking African Americans in their respective Fortune 500 firms. In looking back over their careers, many acknowledged that they were hired in response to the racial unrest of the 1960s. Some were hired into human relations departments and charged with ensuring compliance with affirmative action regulations and EEOC mandates. Others were hired as vice presidents of community and public relations, acting as liaisons to African American communities and charged with developing products for black customers or recruiting black employees into the firm. Although Collins's informants earned comfortable salaries, they had been placed in "racialized jobs" that responded to the concerns of African Americans, as opposed to whites who worked in jobs with wider constituencies (e.g., sales, operations, marketing, and financing). As a result, by the end of their careers, African Americans were more limited than whites in how high they could rise within the firm, and they grew resentful as others were groomed to be CEOs of their respective firms (see Cose 1993). Moreover, many black executives sensed that their jobs could be eliminated in cost-cutting measures if the government relaxed its oversight of firms' compliance with antidiscrimination legislation (see Leonard 1984). Of course, for lower-placed middle managers and semiprofessionals (e.g., social workers, counselors, corrections officers, etc.), government expansion in the postwar era employed African Americans in middle-class jobs, and efforts to shrink the size of government would directly threaten their livelihoods (Collins 1983; W. J. Wilson 1980).

Effects of minorities in management

The discussion above begins to highlight the difference between optimistic and pessimistic interpretations of an increased minority presence in management. On one hand, minorities have made demonstrable progress in entering managerial jobs that are among the most rewarding and prestigious in the economy

(Stainback and Tomaskovic-Devey 2009). On the other hand, there is some evidence that in response to government pressure, firms reclassified some clerical and administrative jobs as managerial jobs (Jacobs 1992; J. Smith and Welch 1984) and created new managerial jobs filled by blacks to respond to African American demands for equality (Collins 1997). This pessimistic view is further supported by mobility studies showing that minorities lag behind white men in receiving promotions to top managerial jobs (Maume 1999) and that it is in government, not the private sector, where rates of minority ascendance to managerial jobs is most rapid (G. Wilson, Sakura-Lemessy, and West 1999). Furthermore, when minorities do get promoted into management, they typically manage minority subordinates who are themselves poorly paid and immobile (Elliott and Smith 2001; R. Smith and Elliott 2002; Tomaskovic-Devey 1993).

The degree of similarity in the managerial jobs minorities and whites hold is the main point of contention between those who are optimistic that a decline in racial inequality is evidenced by the growth in minority managers and those who are pessimistic about such a conclusion. Thus, the first aim of this study is to assess whether reaching managerial jobs matters for minorities, specifically by comparing the size of the racial wage residual between managers and nonmanagers. If minority managers hold jobs that are as rewarding as those of white managers, then the racial wage residual should be lower among managers than among nonmanagers—a finding that would support the optimistic view of minorities in management. Whereas Jacobs (1992) assessed the degree of similarity in managerial jobs held by men and women, I am unaware of a study that makes this assessment by race.

Another approach in assessing the effects of minorities in management would be to determine if, among managers, minorities differ from whites in the responsibility, freedom, job security, and interpersonal relations characterizing their jobs. The pessimistic view suggests that minorities are given less challenging and more unstable managerial jobs, and that in interpersonal encounters they are often reminded of their differences with majority managers (Collins 1997; Cose 1993; Kanter 1977). If so, then minority managers will differ significantly from their white counterparts in holding lower-quality and devalued managerial jobs. Of course, if minority managers hold jobs that resemble those of whites, then the evidence would support the optimistic view of minorities in management.

Some scholars suggest that another way minority managers are devalued is by their placement over minority workgroups. After majority groups reserve the best jobs for themselves (Reskin, McBrier, and Kmec 1999; Tomaskovic-Devey 1993), the challenge for the organization is obtaining desired work behavior and commitment from those who occupy devalued and immobile jobs. To solve this problem, organizations engage in "bottom-up ascription," that is, placing minority superiors in charge of minority-dominated workgroups (Elliott and Smith 2001; R. Smith and Elliott 2002). Not only does this signal a firm's compliance with external legal pressures to diversify the ranks of management, but it also creates the impression among minority subordinates that via hard work, commitment, and loyalty to their employers, they too can advance to supervisory positions.

Given these considerations, a second aim of this study is to assess whether having a minority manager matters for the rewards, experiences, and career prospects of minority subordinates. A pessimistic view of minorities in management is that they are powerless to affect the careers of minority subordinates, providing no more career support or mentoring to minority subordinates than white supervisors provide to white subordinates. Furthermore, because minority workers are devalued within the firm, they are paid less than whites irrespective of the minority status of their immediate superior. Such findings would suggest that minority managers are mere "cogs in the machine" whose role is to provide a symbolic image of potential mobility to minority subordinates, who otherwise occupy low-paying and dissatisfying jobs.

A more optimistic view of minorities in management would suggest that they act as "change agents," taking an active role in advancing the careers of minority subordinates. One study shows that when given the opportunity, minority supervisors tend to promote minority subordinates (e.g., see Elliott and Smith 2004). Furthermore, bonds between minority supervisors and subordinates may be strengthened by shared discrimination experiences (e.g., see Cose 1993), and supervisors may not want subordinates to face the same career obstacles that they did. If so, then minority supervisors may seek to advance the careers of minority subordinates by providing job-related advice, support, and mentoring and by ensuring that they are paid similarly to whites. Some attempts have been made to assess whether female managers advance the careers of female subordinates (Cohen and Huffman 2007; Maume 2011; Stainback and Kwon this volume), but no one has yet made this assessment with regard to minorities in management.

Data

Sample

The data used in this study are from the 1997 and 2002 National Study of the Changing Workforce (NSCW) surveys, both of which are representative samples of the employed civilian labor force (for details on the design and implementation of the NSCW, see Bond et al. 2003). For theoretical and practical reasons, two restrictions were placed on the composition of the sample. First, from a total of 5,687 wage and salary workers, the sample is limited to adults ages 18 to 64 who worked full time ($N = 4,535$), on the grounds that these workers are fully committed to career pursuits (although the full-time restriction will be relaxed when analyzing subordinate work outcomes; see below). Second, including women in the analytic sample would complicate attempts to assess race effects on minorities in management, given that race and gender are distinct axes of inequality (Tomaskovic-Devey 1993). The most conservative estimate of the effects of minorities in management would be to contrast the rewards and job experiences of minority men with those of white men, and for this reason only men (N = 2,245) are included in the analytic sample (see Maume [2011] for an analysis of the effects of female supervisors on the career prospects of subordinates).

Who is a minority? Who is a manager?

The NSCW asked whether respondents identified themselves as Hispanic and also asked them to identify their race as either "white," "black," or "other." Preliminary cross-tabulations indicated that most Hispanics saw themselves as members of a minority group (i.e., nearly 8 in 10 Hispanics claimed to be other, and only a handful of whites identified as Hispanic). Furthermore, when blacks and Hispanics were contrasted with non-Hispanic whites on outcome measures, the effects of these separate statuses were often similar in direction and magnitude but nonsignificant (likely because of small subgroup sample sizes). For the sake of parsimony, then, blacks and Hispanics are scored 1 on a binary measure of *minority* (non-Hispanic white men compose the reference group).

Regarding managerial status, the NSCW asked respondents to report on their usual duties and kind of work they did, and responses were classified using the 1990 standard occupation codes (SOC) developed by the Census Bureau. But by convention, the Census Bureau defines "executives and managers" as largely consisting of professionals (e.g., business executives, financiers, lawyers, etc.) who have substantial control over a firm's fiscal and human resources (Maume 1999). On one hand, this is advantageous in that minorities in census-defined managerial occupations hold the most prestigious and rewarding jobs in the economy. On the other hand, many white-collar jobs (e.g., technical, sales, and clerical jobs) as well as blue-collar and service jobs require incumbents to supervise, evaluate, and reward the work of subordinates, but these jobs are often classified by their relevant job category rather than as managerial. To capture these individuals, the NSCW asked respondents if "supervising other people is a major part of your job"; those who answered affirmatively were defined as supervisors. A cross-tabulation of managerial and supervisory statuses showed that seven in ten managers supervised others, but only one in four supervisors was a manager. Thus, the analyses below distinguish between those in census-defined managerial occupations and self-reported supervisors.

Measures

Most of the measures described below were included in both the 1997 and 2002 surveys, but some were asked only in the 2002 survey. The appendix provides descriptive statistics on all measures used in the analyses.

Outcomes for managers

The most basic job reward is annual pay (including bonuses and overtime pay) in the year of the survey. After inflating the 1997 salary to 2002 dollars, the natural log of annual income was calculated to correct for its rightward skew. Approximately one in twelve respondents refused to divulge his earnings and was assigned the mean value on income; a binary measure was created to control for mean assignment.

The working conditions of managers were assessed by a series of composite indices. Except when noted, all component items were measured on a five-point Likert scale, and preliminary factor analyses confirmed that individual items tapped a single underlying construct (all composite indices had acceptable alpha reliabilities of between .6 and .8). First, the *high-pressure job* index was calculated as the mean of three items assessing the need to work fast, hard, and under tight deadlines. Second, the *job autonomy* index was constructed as the mean of four items asking about the respondent's freedom to decide what to do on the job and when to take breaks, responsibility for deciding how the work is done, and ability to have "a lot of say" in what work gets done. Third, *being disrespected* on the job was assessed as the mean of two items asking about "having to do things on the job that go against my conscience" and "being treated with respect" on the job (reverse-coded). Finally, because of extreme skew on the component items, the *job insecurity* index was assessed by a count of answering affirmatively that they had been previously laid off because work was slow and saying it was "very likely" that they would lose their job and need to find another one.

Outcomes for subordinates

Testing the argument that minority managers oversee devalued minority subordinates requires information on the race of the immediate supervisor, the superior's work-related behavior, and subordinates' reactions to their work situations. First, subordinates were asked whether their supervisor was of the same racial or ethnic background, enabling the construction of a binary measure for reporting to a *minority supervisor*. Second, subordinates' *annual income* (logged) was calculated in the same manner described above. Third, the subordinate's perceived *advancement opportunities* were measured by a single item ("How would you rate your own chance to advance in your organization"; responses ranged from 1 = *poor* to 4 = *excellent*). Fourth, the *supervisor's job support* index was calculated as the mean of four Likert items tapping supervisors' keeping subordinates informed about job matters, having realistic expectations of job performance, recognizing when work is done well, and being understanding and supportive about problems at work. Finally, *organizational commitment* was calculated as the mean of two standardized items assessing how loyal the respondent was to his employer and whether he worked harder than he had to for the benefit of the company.

Individual controls

Besides race, the analytic models include a continuous control for *years of completed education* and binary controls for *being single* and/or a *parent*, living in the *South*, and *sample year* (1 = 2002; 0 = 1997). In addition, the models included controls for *years of pre-employer work experience* (indicative of the accumulation of general skills) and *years of tenure with the employer* (tapping the stock of firm-specific skills as well as employment rights and benefits conferred by seniority); years of pre-employer work experience was calculated by subtracting employer tenure from years worked full time since age 18. To capture potential nonlinearities in their relationships with the outcome measures, squared terms for experience and tenure were entered into all analytic models but were significant and retained only in the models of annual income.

Job-related controls

Prior studies show that minority presence in management is higher in government and social services as well as in those firms that created human resource departments to monitor compliance with antidiscrimination laws and affirmative action (Edelman 1990; Stainback and Tomaskovic-Devey 2009; G. Wilson 1997). Thus, the models include a binary control for working in *government or the nonprofit sector* (with the private sector serving as the reference category). Although the NSCW lacks information on the formalization and implementation of human resources policies in response to EEOC oversight (e.g., codified job descriptions, posting of job openings, formal written evaluations of employees' job performance, etc.), the NSCW does have a measure of *firm size* (an ordinal scale, ranging from 1 = *under 25 employees* to 10 = *10,000+employees*), which is a strong correlate of firms' creation of bureaucratic structures and procedures to ensure due process (Marsden 1996).

A key measure in testing for bottom-up ascription processes is the *racial composition of subordinates' coworkers*. This was assessed by the question "About what percentage of your coworkers are people from your racial, ethnic, or national background?" This measure (available only in the 2002 survey) has ordinal responses ranging from 1 = *100 percent of coworkers* to 6 = *0 percent of coworkers*; at the maximum value on this measure, the respondent is a racial token in his workgroup. In addition, the bottom-up ascription argument suggests that minorities are given managerial authority over devalued workers, a key indicant of which is the strength of their job attachment; thus the analytic models of subordinate outcomes will include a binary control for *working part time*. Finally, it is possible that subordinates' opinions about their bosses and their own career prospects may be affected by whether they exercise authority on the job; thus, the models of subordinate outcomes include additional binary controls for exercising *supervisory authority* over other workers (self-reported by respondents) and holding a *managerial occupation* (as defined by census occupation codes).

TABLE 1

Unstandardized OLS Effect of Minority Status on Annual Salary (Log), by Supervisor/
Manager Status, Full-Time Employees, Men Ages 18 to 64, 1997 and 2002 NSCW

| | Defined by Census Occupation | | | | Defined by Self-Report | | | |
| | Nonmanagers | | Managers | | Nonsupervisors | | Supervisors | |
	b	N	b	N	b	N	b	N
1. All men	−.123°°	1,825	−.041	337	−.128°°	1,272	−.119°°	904
2. By industrial sector[a]								
Private/for-profit sector	−.125°°	1,371	−.087	246	−.142°°	989	−.108°°	630
Public/nonprofit sector	−.068	413	−.083	87	−.042	251	−.062	259
3. By firm size[a]								
Fewer than 100 employees	−.139°°	656	−.145°°	104	−.199°°	438	−.069	322
100+ employees	−.118°°	1,149	−.020	233	−.086°°	818	−.144°°	577

NOTE: Models control for education, pre-employer experience, experience squared, employer tenure, tenure squared, married, parent, Southern resident, sample year, and income assignment. In panel 1, the models explained between 26 percent and 33 percent of the variation in pay (for nonmanagers and supervisors, respectively; r-squared values were slightly higher in the panel 2 and 3 models due to smaller sample sizes.
a. The sum of subgroups may be less than the total N in panel 1 because of missing data.
°°$p < .05$.

Results

Pay inequality and the managerial divide

I first consider racial pay inequality, comparing across the authority divide. Table 1 presents unstandardized coefficients from an ordinary least squares (OLS) regression analysis and can be interpreted as the proportionate decrement in minority men's earnings relative to white men. The results suggest that empirical support for the optimistic or pessimistic views of minorities in management depends on how authority status is defined.

When census occupational codes are used to distinguish managers from non-managers, the results tend to support the optimistic perspective that when minorities ascend to privileged managerial positions they are paid similarly to white male managers. That is, in panel 1, minority nonmanagers earn 12.3 percent less than white nonmanagers, but among managers the minority pay gap shrinks to 4.1 percent and is no longer statistically significant. Furthermore, this pattern of results is replicated in large firms (panel 3). Firms with 100+ employees are required to report to the EEOC on the diversity of their payrolls, and among these employers the racial pay gap declined from 11.8 percent among nonmanagers to a nonsignificant 2 percent among managers (similar results were observed when two other thresholds for large firm size were defined—250+ employees and 500+ employees).

In smaller firms, however, black managers earn 14.5 percent less than white managers, which is slightly higher than the 13.9 percent racial pay gap among nonmanagers employed in small firms. The pattern of results is less clear by sector (panel 2). The 12.5 percent racial difference in pay among nonmanagers in the private sector is the only residual that reaches statistical significance; the remaining racial pay gaps are insignificant, although hardly trivial.

When the authority divide is defined by self-reported supervisory status, the findings tend to support the pessimistic view of minorities in management. That is, among all men (panel 1), the minority wage residual barely declines when workers exercise supervisory authority (11.9 percent) compared with nonsupervisors (12.8 percent). Similarly, minority wage gaps are sizable and significant among private-sector nonsupervisors (14.2 percent) and supervisors (10.8 percent) alike. Yet similar to census-defined managers, minority nonsupervisors and supervisors are paid more similarly to their white counterparts when employed in the public sector.

In contrast to the declining pay gap across the managerial divide among large-firm employees, the minority wage gap increases across the supervisory divide in large firms (panel 3). That is, in firms of 100 or more employees, minority supervisors earn 14.4 percent less than white supervisors—a pay gap that is two-thirds larger than the minority pay gap among nonsupervisors. The differing results in panel 3 for large-firm employees (i.e., the pay gap increases across the authority divide for supervisors, but decreases for managers) likely stem from the fact that census-defined managers are professionals employed at the apex of their employers' hierarchies, whereas supervisors are more likely to be middle managers in large firms. As other research shows, it is in large firms where job titles proliferate (Baron, Davis-Blake, and Bielby 1986; Marsden 1996), and it is more difficult to codify skills requirements and define successful job performance (and thus set pay levels) among middle managers than among line workers (Baron, Davis-Blake, and Bielby 1986; Kanter 1977). Thus, despite the presence of human resources policies and government oversight of their implementation, supervisors tend to proliferate in large firms, and the difficulty in evaluating their performance allows organizational biases against minority supervisors to be reflected in pay scales (McGuire and Reskin 1993; Reskin, McBrier, and Kmec 1999). By contrast, pay gaps are smaller among managers employed in large firms because minority managers are fewer in number and bias against them is more easily detected by the human resource practices implemented in large firms (Kalev, Dobbin, and Kelly 2006).

Informal human resource practices and visibility in small firms may also explain why minority supervisors are paid only 6.9 percent less than white supervisors (a difference that is not significant), in contrast to the 19.9 percent pay gap among nonsupervisors. That is, lacking internal labor markets to motivate subordinates, a supervisor's personality and charisma become even more important in motivating subordinates to work hard on behalf of the firm (Edwards 1979), and minorities who can effectively manage work groups are paid similarly to white supervisors in smaller firms.

TABLE 2
Standardized OLS Effect of Minority Status on Working Conditions of Full-Time
Supervisors and Managers, Men Ages 18 to 64, 1997 and 2002 NSCW

	Census-Defined: Managers	Self-Reported: Supervisors
1. High-pressure job[a]	−.15°°	−.10°°
2. Job autonomy[b]	.07	−.07°°
3. Job insecurity[c]	.04	.08°°
4. Disrespected on job[d]	.00	.08°°

NOTE: $N = 332$ and 885 managers and supervisors, respectively. Models control for education, pre-employer experience, employer tenure, married, parents, Southern resident, firm size, government/nonprofit sector, and sample year. R-squared values ranged from a low of .04 in predicting being disrespected on the job among supervisors to a high of .11 in predicting job insecurity among managers.
a. Job requires respondent to work hard, fast, and under tight deadlines.
b. Respondent has freedom to decide what to do on the job, is responsible for how work gets done, has a lot of say in what work gets done, and decides when to take breaks.
c. Respondent has been temporarily laid off or had hours cut when work was slow and expects to lose job and search for new job.
d. Respondent is disrespected at work and has to do things that go against conscience.
°°$p < .05$.

Working conditions of managers and supervisors

Additional evidence for adjudicating between the optimistic and pessimistic views of minorities in management may be found in comparing the jobs held by minorities and whites who exercise authority. Table 2 presents standardized OLS effects of minority status on the working conditions of managers and supervisors.

As was the case above regarding the pay gap, it appears that support for the optimistic and pessimistic views of minorities in management depends on how managerial authority is defined. That is, in three of four outcomes, minority managers (as defined by census criteria) are similar to white managers, specifically in regard to exercising autonomy on the job, feeling insecure about their jobs, and being disrespected on the job. The only case in which minority and white managers significantly differ is the former reporting less pressure on the job in the form of working fast, hard, and under tight deadlines ($B = -.15$). Whereas some view having a high-pressure job as stressful (e.g., Karasek 1979), Kanter (1977) argued that fast-paced and pressure-packed jobs offer individuals the chance to display their talents. In other words, challenging jobs may be visible jobs, offering incumbents a chance to signal their suitability for promotion based on successful performance in a demanding job, and on this dimension, minorities lag behind whites in placement in high-pressure jobs (among managers and supervisors alike).

Stronger support for the pessimistic view is found in the significant minority residuals for the remaining working conditions that typify supervisory jobs. For example, compared with white supervisors, minority supervisors exercise less autonomy on the job ($B = -.07$). Not only does job autonomy tend to lead to better psychic adjustment to the demands of one's job (Karasek 1979), but making decisions and organizing the flow of one's work and the work of others is another way to display one's talent and skills (Kanter 1977). These results suggest that minorities are more likely to be placed in jobs that restrict their decision-making abilities, thus limiting their chances to demonstrate to their own superiors that they would make good leaders of the firm. Similarly, several analysts claim that more so than whites, minority supervisors are placed in positions that are more vulnerable to the ebb and flow of the market, and they must suppress their minority identities to further their careers in white-dominated firms (Collins 1997, 1983; Cose 1993). The results in lines 3 and 4 of Table 2 are consistent with these arguments; that is, compared with white supervisors, minority supervisors are more insecure in their jobs and more disrespected by others at work.

To summarize the findings thus far, the optimistic view of minorities in management receives its strongest support among those who reach upper-echelon management positions, as defined by the Census Bureau. Upon doing so, minority managers earn salaries that more closely approach those of their white counterparts; their reported levels of job autonomy, security, and getting respect from others also approach those of their white counterparts. But lower down in the occupational hierarchy where supervisors are found, compared with their white counterparts, minority supervisors are paid less and placed in less demanding jobs, with less autonomy and less job security and where they are more disrespected by others—findings that support the pessimistic view of minorities in management.

Racial segregation of subordinates and minority supervisors

The bottom-up ascription argument posits that a minority-dominated workgroup is likely to report to a minority supervisor. I evaluated this proposition in a multivariate logistic regression model using the controls shown in Tables 1 and 2 (including dummy controls for whether the worker is part time, supervises others, and/or holds a managerial occupation). The predictor variable of interest in this analysis is an ordinal measure of the racial composition of coworkers (available only in the 2002 survey). Because the results were straightforward, they are briefly described (rather than shown in a table) here. In race-stratified models, for whites and minorities alike, the odds of reporting to a minority manager significantly increase as one's coworkers are increasingly composed of minorities. These results confirm a basic tenet of the bottom-up ascription argument: namely, that minority supervisors tend to exercise authority over minority workgroups.

TABLE 3

Standardized OLS Effects of Having a Minority Supervisor and Racial Composition of
Coworkers on the Experiences and Career Prospects of Subordinates, by Minority Status,
Men Ages 18 to 64, 2002 NSCW

	Whites	Minorities
1. Supervisor support index[a]		
Minority supervisor	−.02	.02
Race atypical coworkers	−.03	−.16°°
2. Organizational commitment[b]		
Minority supervisor	.01	.16°°
Race atypical coworkers	−.01	.02
3. Advancement opportunities[c]		
Minority supervisor	.05	.14°
Race atypical coworkers	.02	−.01
4. Annual pay (log)		
Minority supervisor	−.05	−.21°°
Race atypical coworkers	.02	−.03

NOTE: $N = 949$ and 248 whites and minorities, respectively. Models control for education,
pre-employer experience, employer tenure, married, parent, Southern resident, government
sector, firm size, supervises others, managerial occupation, and works full time. In panels 1 to
3, r-squared values ranged from .03 to .06 among whites and from .10 to .16 among minorities;
in panel 4, the models explained 37 percent and 40 percent of the variation in pay among
whites and minorities, respectively.
a. Boss keeps respondent informed about work matters, has realistic expectations, recognizes
work well done, and is supportive when problems arise.
b. Respondent is loyal to employer and will work harder than he has to for firm's success.
c. Chance to advance within organization (1 = *poor*; 4 = *excellent*).
°$p < .10.$ °°$p < .05.$

Minority supervisors and subordinate
job experiences and career prospects

Table 3 shows the partial standardized effects of reporting to a minority supervisor
and the racial composition of the workgroup on subordinates' work experiences
and career prospects, by minority status. Among whites, in all cases the racial
composition of the workgroup and the minority status of the immediate supervisor
have no effect on their job experiences and rewards.

Among minorities, however, the results unequivocally support the pessimistic view of minorities in management and, in particular, that bottom-up ascription processes motivate the matching of minority supervisors with minority

subordinates. Panel 1 shows that minority subordinates in white-dominated workgroups report receiving significantly lower support from their immediate superior ($B = -.16$)—a result that might be anticipated from research on gender tokenism (Kanter 1977). Yet when minority subordinates report to a minority supervisor, they get no more job-related support than they would from a white supervisor. Furthermore, minority subordinates show more loyalty toward and work harder for their employers when they report to a minority supervisor (panel 2), and they are marginally more likely to expect a promotion when their boss is a minority (panel 3). These results must be viewed in the context, however, that minority subordinates get lower pay when reporting to minority supervisors (panel 4). Social closure perspectives on workplace dynamics suggest that minorities are devalued within organizations (Tomaskovic-Devey 1993), and they are assigned minority bosses to make the symbolic promise that via hard work and commitment, they too can advance to the ranks of management (Elliott and Smith 2001). The results in Table 3 show that when reporting to a minority boss, minority subordinates receive lower pay, yet are more committed to their employers and more likely to expect to receive a promotion—results that are consistent with the reasons for and the effects of firms practicing bottom-up ascription when placing minorities in management positions.

Summary and Discussion

Scholars have rightly analyzed trends in and determinants of minority access to managerial positions, but lacking is an understanding of the effects of such access on pay inequality, working conditions, and career prospects among supervisors and subordinates. Progress has been made in eliminating race as a criterion for entry into management, but if this represents real progress, the race gap in managerial rewards and working conditions should narrow, and minority subordinates should describe their jobs and career prospects in more optimistic terms when reporting to a minority boss. This study tested these propositions with recent surveys of the labor force, finding that support for the optimistic or pessimistic views of minorities in management depended on minority managers' placement in firms' hierarchies.

The strongest support for the optimistic view of minorities in management was found in analyses using census criteria to distinguish between managers and nonmanagers. In these analyses, the minority pay gap declined across the authority divide and was negligible in the public sector and in large organizations. Furthermore, among census-defined managers, minorities and whites reported similar levels of autonomy, job security, and respectful treatment from colleagues. The Census Bureau's definition of managers as professionals who exercise authority tends to identify those at the apex of the occupational hierarchy, where their relatively few numbers and high visibility within organizations makes it more difficult for employers to make job assignments and set pay levels based on race.

Below the upper echelon of managers are layers of middle and lower managers, where many technical, clerical, sales, and skilled blue-collar workers exercise supervisory authority over subordinates. The pessimistic view of minorities in management is that these positions are "glorified" administrative jobs that involve many of the same duties as the jobs occupied by those they are supervising (Jacobs 1992) and that minorities are often tapped to fill these supervisory roles to ensure the firm's compliance with federal mandates on affirmative action and equal opportunity laws (Elliott and Smith 2004, 2001). When comparing supervisors and nonsupervisors, the findings support the pessimistic view of minorities in management. That is, minority wage residuals are nearly as large among supervisors as among nonsupervisors, and in large firms (where greater occupational differentiation increases the potential to differentially assign workers to jobs based on minority status), the minority pay gap was larger among supervisors than among nonsupervisors. Furthermore, among those with supervisory authority, minorities were assigned to less challenging and more insecure jobs, given less autonomy, and shown less respect at work.

From the point of view of subordinates, the results more strongly support the pessimistic view and, in particular, the argument that firms practice bottom-up ascription when tapping minorities to manage other minorities. That is, because of lingering racial bias on the part of white superiors and coworkers, minorities tend to concentrate at the bottom of the queue of desirable workers and hold devalued jobs within the firm. Yet to obtain desired behavior and commitment from devalued workers, minorities are assigned as supervisors, offering subordinates the hope that via hard work they too can ascend to managerial positions within the firm. Thus, subordinates in minority-dominated workgroups tended to report to a minority supervisor, and in such cases minority subordinates were more committed to the organization and more likely to expect to receive a promotion despite earning lower pay than their white coworkers. These results suggest that minority bosses are not necessarily "change agents" who can foster the careers of minority subordinates but are more likely to be "cogs in the machine," whose role it is to ensure the commitment of subordinates to the firm even as they are paid less than whites.

On balance, then, the findings of this study support those who are skeptical about the degree of progress minorities have made in reaching the most rewarding and prestigious jobs in the American economy. These findings resonate with Tilly's (1998) contention that even after the state intervenes in the operations of the labor market with the aim of reducing inequality, privileged actors find new ways to sustain old distinctions. Bottom-up ascription appears to be one particularly effective way in which minorities are allowed to enter the ranks of management but in a way that does not threaten the status of white men. By placing minority supervisors over devalued minority subordinates, white men are freer to monopolize the more rewarding management positions within the firm. The findings reported here suggest that minority supervisors are aware of their devalued status, reporting that their supervisory jobs are less challenging and more constraining than those of white supervisors, and they continue to lag behind the pay of their white counterparts. What is needed now is further study of whether minority supervisors have the means and the inclination to collectively push for stronger measures to combat labor market inequality, or whether they will seek individual remedies (e.g., disengagement, turnover) to their unequal treatment by their employers.

There are several avenues for further research that address the limitations of this study. First, this study examined control over workers, but managers also control fiscal resources, such as by deciding which products and services to offer and how to market new and existing products, arranging financing for existing operations and planned expansions, and so on. Comparing minorities with whites on the degree of control each has over the full range of important decisions made within the firm would provide additional evidence on how highly placed minority bosses are in the organizational hierarchy relative to white managers.

Second, the cross-sectional design of this study necessarily suggests that longitudinal analyses will be valuable in shedding light on the antecedents and effects of minority representation in management. For example, this study implied that because they receive less challenging and more circumscribed job assignments, the careers of minority supervisors would be stunted compared with whites placed in more challenging and autonomous jobs. With longitudinal data, cohorts of managers could be compared on initial placement, success or failure in revenue-enhancing projects, mentoring subordinates, and so forth. Although social scientists have studied race differences in career trajectories over time, there is a need for more focused analyses of managers and their effects on subordinates' careers, given that there are now more minorities in the ranks of management.

Third, longitudinal data would also further test some of the key mechanisms of bottom-up ascription and how these processes unfold over time. That is, do the satisfaction and commitment of coworkers vary by whether a minority manager is hired from outside the firm or promoted from the pool of subordinates? If minority supervisors are placed in authority positions over devalued minority subordinates, are minority bosses at risk of leaving the firm, or are they rewarded handsomely enough to ensure that they remain with the firm? If a minority supervisor symbolizes potential mobility to minority subordinates, do minority subordinates increasingly disengage from their work or leave the firm when they grasp fully that their careers have plateaued? These are but some of the questions that need answers before we have a complete understanding of the effects on bosses and subordinates of increased minority representation in management.

Appendix
Descriptive Statistics on Variables Used in Analyses, Men Ages 18 to 64

	Min	Max	Mean	SD
Dependent variables				
Annual pay (logged)	8.29	13.82	10.67	0.61
High-pressure job[a]	1.00	5.00	3.88	0.91
Job autonomy[a]	1.00	5.00	4.11	0.86
Disrespected on job[a]	1.00	5.00	1.72	0.90
Job insecurity[a]	0.00	2.00	0.48	0.60
Reports to minority superior[b]	0.00	1.00	0.17	0.37
Advancement opportunities[b]	1.00	4.00	2.66	1.02
Supervisor job-related support[b]	1.00	5.00	4.36	0.80
Organizational commitment[b]	−3.46	1.07	−0.06	0.82
Individual controls				
Nonwhite	0.00	1.00	0.24	0.42
Years of education	9.00	20.00	13.66	2.88
Married	0.00	1.00	0.70	0.46
Parent	0.00	1.00	0.48	0.50
Southern resident	0.00	1.00	0.43	0.49
Surveyed in 2002	0.00	1.00	0.46	0.50
Pre-employer experience	9.00	63.23	31.12	9.96
Experience squared	81.00	3998.12	1067.88	698.00
Employer tenure	0.00	45.15	7.93	2.72
Tenure squared	0.00	2038.52	56.23	9.83
Pay is missing	0.00	1.00	0.08	0.27
Workplace context				
Government/nonprofit sector	0.00	1.00	0.31	0.46
Firm size	1.00	10.00	5.72	3.35
Race composition of coworkers[b]	1.00	6.00	2.77	1.35
Works part time[b]	0.00	1.00	0.09	0.28
Managerial occupation[b]	0.00	1.00	0.13	0.34
Self-reported supervisor[b]	0.00	1.00	0.43	0.49

a. Supervisors or managers only, 1997 and 2002 NSCW (see Table 2).
b. Subordinate workers surveyed only in 2002 NSCW (see Table 3).

References

Baron, James N., Alison Davis-Blake, and William T Bielby. 1986. The structure of opportunity: How promotion ladders vary within and among organizations. *Administrative Science Quarterly* 31: 248–73.

Bond, James T., Cindy Thompson, Ellen Galinsky, and David Prottas. 2003. *Highlights of the 2002 National Study of the Changing Workforce.* New York, NY: Families and Work Institute.

Brown, Michael K., Martin Carnoy, Elliott Currie, Troy Duster, David B. Oppenheimer, Marjorie Schultz, and David Wellman. 2003. *Whitewashing race: The myth of a color-blind society.* Berkeley: University of California Press.

Cohen, Philip N., and Matt L. Huffman. 2007. Working for the woman? Female managers and the gender wage gap. *American Sociological Review* 72:681–704.

Collins, Sharon M. 1983. The making of the black middle class. *Social Problems* 30:369–82.

Collins, Sharon M. 1997. *Black corporate executives.* Philadelphia, PA: Temple University Press.

Cose, Ellis. 1993. *The rage of a privileged class.* New York, NY: HarperCollins.

Edelman, Lauren B. 1990. Legal environments and organizational governance: The expansion of due process in the American workplace. *American Journal of Sociology* 95:1401–40.

Edwards, Richard C. 1979. *Contested terrain.* New York, NY: Basic Books.

Elliott, James R., and Ryan A. Smith. 2001. Ethnic matching of supervisors to subordinate work groups: Findings of bottom-up ascription and social closure. *Social Problems* 48:258–76.

Elliott, James R., and Ryan A. Smith. 2004. Race, gender, and workplace power. *American Sociological Review* 69:365–86.

Herring, Cedric. 2008. Does diversity pay? Race, gender, and the business case for diversity. *American Sociological Review* 74:208–24.

Jacobs, Jerry A. 1992. Women's entry into management: Trends in earnings, authority, and values among salaried managers. *Administrative Science Quarterly* 37:282–302.

Kalev, Alexandra, Frank Dobbin, and Erin Kelly. 2006. Best practices or best guesses: Assessing the efficacy of corporate affirmative action and diversity policies. *American Sociological Review* 71:589–617.

Kanter, Rosabeth Moss. 1977. *Men and women of the corporation.* New York, NY: Basic Books.

Karasek, Robert A. 1979. Job demands, job decision latitude, and mental strain: Implications for job redesign. *Administrative Science Quarterly* 24:285–308.

Leonard, Jonathan S. 1984. The impact of affirmative action on employment. *Journal of Labor Economics* 2:439–64.

Marsden, Peter V. 1996. The staffing process: Recruitment and selection methods. In *Organizations in America: Analyzing their structures and human resource practices*, eds. Arne K. Kalleberg, David Knoke, Peter V. Marsden, and Joseph L. Spaeth, 113–56. Thousand Oaks, CA: Sage.

Maume, David J. 1999. Glass ceilings and glass escalators: Occupational segregation and race and sex differences in managerial promotions. *Work and Occupations* 26:483–509.

Maume, David J. 2011. Meet the new boss . . . same as the old boss? Female supervisors and subordinate career prospects. *Social Science Research* 40:287–98.

McGuire, Gail M., and Barbara F. Reskin. 1993. Authority hierarchies at work: The impacts of race and sex. *Gender & Society* 7:487–506.

Powell, Gary N., and Laura M. Graves. 2003. *Women and men in management.* Thousand Oaks, CA: Sage.

Reskin, Barbara F., Deborah Branch McBrier, and Julie A. Kmec. 1999. The determinants and consequences of workplace sex and race composition. *Annual Review of Sociology* 25:335–61.

Skaggs, Sheryl. 2009. Legal-political pressures and African American access to managerial jobs. *American Sociological Review* 74:225–44.

Smith, James P., and Finis Welch. 1984. Affirmative action and labor markets. *Journal of Labor Economics* 2:269–301.

Smith, Ryan A., and James R. Elliott. 2002. Does ethnic concentration affect employees' access to authority? An examination of contemporary urban labor markets. *Social Forces* 81:255–79.

Stainback, Kevin, and Soyoung Kwon. 2011. Female leaders, organizational power, and sex segregation. *The Annals of the American Academy of Political and Social Science* (this volume).

Stainback, Kevin, and Donald Tomaskovic-Devey. 2009. Intersections of power and privilege: Long-term trends in managerial representation. *American Sociological Review* 74:800–820.

Stainback, Kevin, Donald Tomaskovic-Devey, and Sheryl Skaggs. 2010. Organizational approaches to inequality: Inertia, relative power, and environments. *Annual Review of Sociology* 36:225–47.

Tilly, Charles. 1998. *Durable inequality.* Berkeley: University of California Press.

Tomaskovic-Devey, Donald T. 1993. *Gender and racial inequality at work: The sources and consequences of job segregation*. Ithaca, NY: ILR Press.

Wilson, George. 1997. Payoffs to power among males in the middle class: Has race declined in significance? *Sociological Quarterly* 38:607–22.

Wilson, George, Ian Sakura-Lemessy, and Jonathan West. 1999. Reaching the top: Racial differences in mobility paths to upper-tier occupations. *Work and Occupations* 26:165–86.

Wilson, William Julius. 1980. *The declining significance of race*. 2nd ed. Chicago, IL: University of Chicago Press.

Female Leaders, Organizational Power, and Sex Segregation

By
KEVIN STAINBACK
and
SOYOUNG KWON

A large body of research has examined the organizational factors that promote women's access to positions of workplace authority. Fewer studies explore how women's access to these positions influences gender inequality among subordinates. Utilizing a 2005 national sample of South Korean organizations, this article examines whether having women in managerial and supervisory roles is associated with lower levels of workplace sex segregation. In other words, do female leaders function as "agents of change," or are they merely "cogs in the machine"? The findings indicate that women's representation in managerial positions is associated with lower levels of sex segregation. Women's representation among supervisory positions, however, is associated with higher levels of sex segregation. The results, in general, suggest that women in higher levels of organizational power may be important catalysts for change, while women in supervisory positions may be a manifestation of institutionalized inequality. The authors conclude with implications for theory and future research.

Keywords: workplace inequality; employment segregation; sex; gender; management

Theories of workplace inequality often emphasize men's overrepresentation in positions of organizational power as a key factor

Kevin Stainback is an assistant professor of sociology at Purdue University. His research examines gender and racial inequality in work organizations. His recent publications have appeared in the Annual Review of Sociology, *the* American Sociological Review, *and* Social Forces.

Soyoung Kwon is a graduate student in the Department of Sociology at Purdue University. Her research interests include social stratification and inequality, health, work and organizations, and quantitative research methods. She is currently working on her dissertation, which examines changing patterns of health disparities during China's market reform.

NOTE: This research was supported, in part, by a grant from the National Science Foundation (SES-1061430). We would like to thank Matt Huffman, Alexandra Kalev, and Donald Tomaskovic-Devey for comments and suggestions on previous versions of this article.

DOI: 10.1177/0002716211421868

in the re-creation of gender inequality, because it is assumed that their decisions regarding the allocation of organizational resources (e.g., jobs, wages) will benefit men and disadvantage women (Bielby 2000; Reskin 2000). By implication, researchers have become increasingly interested in identifying the factors that promote women into positions of organizational power, because it is widely believed that increasing women's access to decision-making roles may be a crucial factor in alleviating gender inequalities among subordinates (e.g., Cotter et al. 1997; Ely 1995; Nelson and Bridges 1999).

Scholars have highlighted three discrimination processes by which organizational decision-makers generate inequality. Petersen and colleagues (e.g., Petersen and Graham 1995; Petersen and Saporta 2004) have labeled these as allocative discrimination (the sorting of men and women into jobs of different quality), within-job discrimination (women receiving fewer pecuniary benefits than men working in the same job and workplace), and valuative discrimination (work performed by women receiving less compensation than work performed by men net of necessary education and skill requirements). Because many theories of gender discrimination conceptualize men's overrepresentation in positions of organizational power as a fundamental cause of gender inequality at work (Kanter 1977; Reskin 1988; Tomaskovic-Devey 1993), logical questions that emerge are: What happens when women attain positions of organizational power and decision-making? Do women in positions of organizational power reduce gender-linked inequality?

Despite a substantial body of research that seeks to discover the factors that promote or deny women's access to organizational power (e.g., Cotter, Hermsen, and Vanneman 2001; Elliott and Smith 2004; Gorman and Kmec 2009; Hirsh 2009; Huffman and Cohen 2004; Kalev, Dobbin, and Kelly 2006; Maume 2004; Purcell, Macarthur, and Samblanet 2010; Reskin and McBrier 2000; Skaggs 2008; Stainback and Tomaskovic-Devey 2009), fewer studies have examined whether women's access to these positions serves to challenge gender inequality among subordinates or maintain the status quo. There is, however, a recent and rapidly expanding literature addressing the influence of women in positions of organizational power (e.g., business owners, corporate leaders, managers, supervisors) on various inequality outcomes, including the male-female earnings gap (Cardoso and Winter-Ebmer 2010; Cohen and Huffman 2007; Hultin and Szulkin 1999, 2003; Penner and Toro-Tulla 2010; Penner, Toro-Tulla, and Huffman 2010), access to authority positions (Cohen, Broschak, and Havemen 1998; Skaggs, Stainback, and Duncan n.d.), sex segregation (Huffman, Cohen, and Pearlman 2010), and hiring (Gorman 2005, 2006). Recent research has also explored the effects of female supervisors on subordinates' receipt of social support (Maume 2011) and reported experiences of sexual harassment and discrimination (Chamberlain et al. 2008; Stainback, Ratliff, and Roscigno 2011). Paradoxically, the results of this growing area of research provide mixed evidence as to whether women's access to organizational power helps, hinders, or has no effect on gender inequality among subordinates.

This article contributes to the growing body of research examining the effects of women in positions of authority on gender inequality among subordinates, using a unique organization-level dataset of South Korean workplaces. Although previous research examining this topic has explored various national contexts (e.g., Sweden, Portugal, and the United States), this is the first study to explore the effects of female managers and supervisors on gender inequality among subordinates in South Korea. This provides an important comparative case for previous studies examining U.S. and European contexts.

We borrow from Cohen and Huffman's (2007) conceptualization of female managers and supervisors as either "change agents" or "cogs in the machine" to test alternative views of the effects of women in management on sex segregation. Understanding the factors that may reduce sex segregation is critical given the well-known association between segregation and wages (Cohen and Huffman 2003; Cotter et al. 1995; Levanon, England, and Allison 2009), promotion opportunities (Hultin and Szulkin 2003; Maume 1999), and segmented authority roles (Cohen, Huffman, and Knauer 2009; Elliott and Smith 2001, 2004; Stainback and Tomaskovic-Devey 2009). In this article, we address two core research questions. First, does women's representation in positions with general workplace authority (managers/supervisors) influence sex segregation among nonmanagerial workforces? Second, does women's representation within hierarchical authority matter?

Gender in Context: The Case of South Korea

Over the past few decades, South Korea has developed rapidly into a key player in the contemporary global economy. Although the Korean economy has fundamentally changed in recent years, women's and men's opportunities in that society continue to be shaped by strong patriarchal values steeped in tradition and Confucian ideology. As Kim (2005, 676) notes, "Women have been required to follow the Confucian virtues of subordination, endurance, and restriction from participation in social activities, and they are regarded as inferior to men in social status." Despite the strength of traditional Confucian ideology, the status of women in the labor market has gradually improved since the passage of laws designed to reduce gender inequality in the economic and political spheres of society, including the Equal Employment Opportunity Act (1987) and the Gender Discrimination Prevention and Relief Act (1999).

Women's labor force participation rate in South Korea reached 50.2 percent in 2005, which ranked it 26th among 177 countries. By comparison, women's labor force participation rate in the United States in 2005 was 59.6 percent, ranking it 12th (United Nations Development Program 2005). The female/male income ratio is only 40 percent in South Korea, compared to 63 percent in the United States (United Nations Development Program 2005). Indicators of women's access to valuable positions in the economy also suggest that South

Korea lags behind the United States in gender equality. Women are 8 percent of all legislators, senior officials, and managers in South Korea and 39 percent of all professional and technical workers. These percentages are noticeably lower than women's share in the United States, at 42 percent and 56 percent, respectively (United Nations Development Program 2005). Since much of the existing workplace gender inequality research examines countries that tend to exhibit greater gender equality (e.g., Sweden, the United States), exploring South Korea provides a unique opportunity to understand how gender dynamics operate in a less egalitarian national context than previously studied.

Women's Access to Organizational Power and Gender Inequality among Subordinates

Female leaders as "agents of change"

Because men are overrepresented in positions of organizational power, it is assumed that they will reproduce unequal opportunities between female and male subordinates. Theories of gender inequality have suggested that bias processes, such as in-group preference and stereotyping (Gorman 2005; Kanter 1977) as well as out-group exclusion (Roscigno 2007; Tomaskovic-Devey 1993), are the primary mechanisms reproducing male advantage in the workplace. As such, women's access to organizational power may be critical in reducing gender inequality.

Cohen and Huffman (2007, 682) note that if change is to be expected, women in leadership roles must have the "motivation and power" to help female subordinates. Previous research has suggested several interrelated reasons why women in positions of organizational power may benefit female subordinates, including (1) in-group preference in hiring, promotion, and wage-setting decisions (Gorman 2005, 2006); (2) increased access to career-enhancing social networks and mentoring opportunities (Brass 1985; Ibarra 1993; Konrad, Kramer, and Erkut 2008); and (3) declines in gender stereotyping with increases in women's representation in higher-level positions (Ely 1994; Konrad, Kramer, and Erkut 2008).

The work of Hultin and Szulkin (1999, 2003) provides empirical support consistent with the "agents of change" perspective. In their 1999 study, they examined a cross-sectional Swedish employee-employer matched dataset and found that, ceteris paribus, women's wages tend to be higher in workplaces with a greater number of women in leadership positions compared to workplaces with a greater number of men in these positions. They also demonstrated that these effects were stronger when decision-making was decentralized. Their follow-up study in 2003 examined an extraordinarily rich dataset of Swedish workplaces that included all workers within each establishment. This study provided even greater support for the effects of females in managerial and supervisory roles on reducing the male-female wage gap. Further analyses separating the effects of percent female managers and percent female supervisors among blue-collar workers provided interesting results. Among blue-collar workers, they found that female representation in supervisory positions, but not managerial jobs, reduced the gender wage gap. They suggested that this effect is the result of homophily processes between female supervisors and female subordinates that increase social interaction and promote closer relationships.

Other studies also find empirical support for women's access to organizational power. Cardoso and Winter-Ebmer (2010) performed a longitudinal analysis using a unique employer-employee (all employees) matched dataset of male- and female-led firms in two industries (manufacturing and services) to examine the wages of female subordinates and the gender wage gap in female-led firms in Portugal. They found that female-led firms provide higher wages to women compared to male-led firms and that the gender wage gap is also lower in female-led firms.

A cross-sectional study conducted by Cohen and Huffman (2007), using occupation-industry cells to approximate jobs within local labor markets in the United States, found that women's representation in managerial jobs reduced the male-female earnings gap. The effect was particularly pronounced with increased female representation in higher-level managerial positions. Although their study did not use organization-level data, other research corroborates their general finding that having women in higher-level managerial positions erodes gender workplace inequality (Cohen, Broschak, and Haveman 1998; Skaggs, Stainback, and Duncan n.d.).

Studies that specifically examine the effects of female leadership on sex segregation tend to find a beneficial effect as well. For example, in a study of public-sector California state agencies, Baron, Mittman, and Newman (1991) found that women's presence in managerial positions reduced sex segregation over time. The most comprehensive study of female leadership and sex segregation to date was conducted by Huffman, Cohen, and Pearlman (2010). They estimate time series models utilizing confidential data collected annually by the U.S. Equal Employment Opportunity Commission (EEOC) from medium to large private-sector U.S. firms from 1975 to 2005. What is important is that they demonstrate that as women's representation in managerial jobs increases within these work-places, sex segregation among nonmanagerial workers declines. Another set of studies examining the effects of female college administrators on sex segregation also finds support for the agents of change perspective in that these administrators promote sex integration (Kulis 1997; Pfeffer, Davis-Blake, and Julius 1995).

With respect to experiential inequalities, Stainback, Ratliff, and Roscigno (2011) found that having a female supervisor reduces women's reported experiences of workplace discrimination by 40 percent compared to women working for male supervisors, while having a female supervisor had no effect on men's reports of sex discrimination. Hence, female managers may function as "change agents" by reducing gender inequality and protecting female subordinates from workplace discrimination.

Female leaders as "cogs in the machine"

In contrast to the "agents of change" expectation, other research suggests that women may have no influence on gender workplace inequality. The key assumption outlined by Cohen and Huffman (2007) with regard to why women in positions of organizational power should promote change is that they have both the "motivation and power" to help female subordinates. However, female leaders' motivation to assist female subordinates may be leveled for fear of being seen as sympathetic to women or not being a team player. For example, Maume (2011, 289) suggests it could be the case that "supervisory women are either not powerful enough to affect the careers of their subordinates or they have been selected to their managerial positions *because* they identify with powerful men at the apex of firms, a selection process that comes at the expense of female subordinates." In this sense, female leaders may seek to distance themselves from female subordinates and issues closely related to female subordinates such as work-family and equal employment opportunity. Rather than improve women's opportunities in the workplace, female leaders may further institutionalize gender inequality among subordinates.

Recent research by Penner and colleagues finds support for the "cogs in the machine" perspective. Penner and Toro-Tulla (2010) examined the effects of female business owners on the gender wage gap using a 1992 sample of small businesses. Their findings indicate that the gender wage gap does not differ across female- and male-owned firms. In another study, Penner, Toro-Tulla, and Huffman (2010) examined data collected from a large grocery retailer and found that women in managerial jobs and store manager positions had no effect on the gender wage gap among nonmanagerial workers. Drawing from expectation states theory, they suggest that female managers' ability to lessen gender inequality for female subordinates may be constrained by the larger cultural system of gender.

Finally, Maume's (2011) recent study provides additional evidence that female leaders may operate as "cogs in the machine." Analyzing a national survey of U.S. workers, he finds that men report receiving more work-related support from female supervisors than do women. Furthermore, his analysis also reveals that compared to women, men working for female supervisors also tend to report greater expectations for upward mobility in the workplace. These findings suggest that women may not automatically have the motivation to help female subordinates. In fact, the career-related support provided to men may further exacerbate gender inequality in the future.

Alternative explanations: Organizational policy, structure, and environment

In addition to the potential effects of women in positions of organizational power on reducing gender inequality outlined in the "agents of change" and "cogs in the machine" perspectives, there are a host of organizational characteristics that may also influence sex segregation suggested by previous theories and research (see Kalev, Dobbin, and Kelly 2006; Reskin and McBrier 2000; for reviews, see Reskin, McBrier, and Kmec 1999; Stainback, Tomaskovic-Devey, and Skaggs 2010). As such, we control for a host of organizational characteristics in our statistical estimates, including measures of various organizational policies, structures, and environments that may influence sex segregation.

Methods

Data

This study utilizes the 2005 Korean Workplace Panel Survey (KWPS), a nationally representative sample of establishments in the Republic of Korea collected by the Korea Labor Institute (KLI) in 2006.[1] The KWPS is a stratified sample of private- and public-sector establishments with thirty or more employees. Of the workplaces sampled, 3,916 were in the private sector and 400 in the public sector. The survey was completed in 1,905 workplaces from the sample. After excluding sample organizations that were ineligible (those with fewer than thirty employees in 2005), the response rate was 53.6 percent (50.1 percent in the private sector and 88.4 percent in the public sector). After excluding missing cases on the analytic variables and omitting establishments with either only one manager or one supervisor, the final sample size for our study was 1,596.

The survey data were collected through face-to-face interviews conducted with multiple organizational members, including human resource and industrial relations managers, using computer-assisted personal interviewing (CAPI). Survey questions asked about workplace demographics, organizational finances, and various policies and practices in place during the previous year (2005). To enhance reliability, the organizations were contacted in advance and mailed materials regarding the information that would be collected during the interview (e.g., financial data, demographic composition of workers).

Measurement

Dependent variable. Sex segregation is measured with the index of dissimilarity (D). Because we are interested in estimating the effect of female managers/supervisors on the sex segregation of nonmanagerial workers, the index is computed within workplaces across eight nonmanagerial occupational categories: professionals, technicians, clerks, service workers, sales workers, skilled agricultural and fishery workers, production workers, and laborers. The index of dissimilarity is calculated as follows:

$$\left(1/2 \sum_{i=1\,to\,8} | M_i - F_i | \right) \times 100,$$

where M_i and F_i are the proportion of men and women in the ith occupational category, respectively. These eight occupational gender distributions are then summed within each establishment. The index ranges from 0 (indicating complete integration) to 100 (total segregation). The index can be interpreted as the percentage of women or men that would have to change jobs to create a gender-integrated workforce. As such, negative regression coefficients indicate integration effects, while positive coefficients indicate segregation effects.

Independent variables. The key independent variables in this study are women's representation in positions of organizational power. The KWPS data contain a measure that distinguishes between women's and men's representation in managerial and nonmanagerial positions. Following the work of Hultin and Szulkin (1999, 2003), our first measure is the percentage of women in all positions of authority, irrespective of hierarchical level. Hence, the measure includes the percentage of women in all positions classified as managerial or supervisory.

The survey item also makes hierarchical distinctions within the managerial ranks. To examine whether women's positions in managerial hierarchies matter for gender inequality among subordinates, we make a further distinction between *managers* (including executives, general managers, deputy general managers, managers)—positions that generally entail routine decision-making responsibilities and are granted substantial organizational power—and *supervisors* (including deputy managers and plant officers who fill supervisory roles)—positions that hold substantially less organizational power. These two measures of hierarchical authority are calculated as the percentage of women in managerial and supervisory positions respectively. The measures are moderately correlated with each other ($r = .545$).

We also estimate models with quadratic terms for percent female managers and percent female supervisors because previous research has shown a nonlinear association between percent female managers and sex segregation (Huffman, Cohen, and Pearlman 2010). Variable descriptions, means, and standard deviations are provided in Table 1.

Control variables. Previous research suggests that sex segregation is likely to be affected by organizational factors, including formal policies, structures, and environments (e.g., see Kalev, Dobbin, and Kelly 2006; Reskin and McBrier 2000; Tomaskovic-Devey et al. 2006). We control for a variety of these characteristics in our statistical estimates to reduce the likelihood of identifying spurious effects between our focal associations.

Some research has shown that formalization of the human resource function reduces gender-linked inequality (Elvira and Graham 2002; Konrad and Linnehan 1995; Reskin and McBrier 2000; but see Huffman and Velasco 1997; Kmec 2005). Although we do not have data on the policies and practices governing the allocation of jobs, the data do contain indicators of formalization and gender egalitarianism, including formal gender antidiscrimination policy, family-friendly

TABLE 1
Variable Descriptions, Means, and Standard Deviations

Variable	Description	Mean	Standard Deviation
Sex segregation (nonmanagerial)	Index of dissimilarity (D) calculated for the eight nonmanagerial occupational categories observed in the data	47.65	138.82
Female leadership			
Percent female managers/ supervisors	Percentage of managerial/supervisory categories, including executive, general managers, deputy general manager, managers, deputy managers, and plant officers	32.06	166.37
Percent female managers	The four highest managerial categories, including executive, general managers, deputy general manager, and managers	6.68	55.18
Percent female supervisors	Deputy managers and plant officers who fill supervisory roles	20.55	102.51
Organizational policy and structure			
EEO for gender discrimination	Gender discrimination policy (1 = yes; no = 0)	0.32	
Family-friendly policies	Number of family policy provisions	2.63	8.36
Human resource management (HRM) office	Formal office (1 = yes; no = 0)	0.37	
Total employment (ln)	Total number of employees	4.33	3.40
Organization age	2005–establishment founding year	15.61	54.86
Unionized workplace	Unionized (1 = yes; 0 = no)	0.17	1.68
Occupational heterogeneity (nonmanagers)	Heterogeneity index	42.08	92.61
Environmental pressures			
Competition	How intense is competition? *Not at all intense* (coded 1) to *very intense* (coded 5)	3.92	4.16
Downsizing	10 percent or more employment reduction in past year (1 = yes; 0 = no)	0.15	1.58
Public sector	Public sector (1 = yes; 0 = no)	0.01	

NOTE: Descriptive statistics are weighted. $N = 1,596$.

policies, a human resource management office, and organizational size. A binary variable is included indicating whether an organization has a formal *gender anti-discrimination policy* (coded 1 for yes, 0 for no). The family-friendly policies variable is a count of ten formal *family-friendly policies* (e.g., maternity leave, on-site childcare, lactation rooms). A binary variable is included for the presence of a *human resource management office*. *Organizational size* is the natural logarithm of the total employment.

We also include controls for organizational age and unionization. As Stinchcombe (1965) noted, the structures of organizations are imprinted with technological and cultural aspects of their environments at the time of founding. From this perspective, older organizations are likely to exhibit higher levels of sex segregation. *Organization age* is measured as the year in which the survey was conducted (2005) minus establishment founding year. *Age squared* is also included to account for potential nonlinear effects. *Unionization* is measured with a binary variable coded 1 for unionized workplaces and 0 otherwise.

An *occupational heterogeneity index* is incorporated to account for measurement error associated with our dependent variable. The index of dissimilarity (D) is influenced by the distribution of workers across the eight nonmanagerial occupational categories. In organizations where people are more evenly distributed across these eight categories, observed segregation will tend to be higher than organizations in which employment is primarily in just a few categories. Hence, measurement error in our segregation index is dependent on the degree to which the eight occupational categories match divisions of labor within workplaces. The KWPS data will accurately measure *between* occupation segregation; however, they are likely to underestimate *within* occupation job segregation. The extent to which these occupational categories match actual divisions of labor will vary across workplaces, and therefore measurement error will also vary (e.g., see Stainback, Robinson, and Tomaskovic-Devey 2005; Tomaskovic-Devey et al. 2006). We adjust for this source of measurement error by controlling for observed workplace occupational heterogeneity using the Gibbs-Martin Heterogeneity index:

$$1 - \sum_{i=1 to 8}^{N} p_i^2,$$

where p_i is the proportion of total employment in each of the eight workplace occupations squared and summed.

Finally, we include measures of environmental pressures—market competition, downsizing, sector, and industry. Market competition is presumed to push organizations to operate in the most efficient manner possible. Therefore, organizations that continue to discriminate against women will be less competitive as a result of paying a wage premium for male workers and failing to hire the most productive female workers (Becker 1971). Previous research has shown that market pressures may encourage sex integration (McTague, Stainback, and

Tomaskovic-Devey 2009; Reskin and McBrier 2000). *Market competition* is measured with a survey item that asked, "How intense is competition in the Korean market for your workplace's main good/product or service?" The Likert item response categories ranged from *very intense* (coded 1) to *not at all intense* (coded 5). The item was reverse coded so that higher values indicate greater market competition.

Recent research has also suggested that organizations that experience downsizing may have lower sex segregation because in the process of becoming "lean and mean," they often eliminate feminized departments (Haveman, Broschak, and Cohen 2009; Kalev n.d.). *Downsizing* is incorporated into our statistical models with a binary variable coded 1 for workplaces that have experienced a 10 percent or more decrease in the size of its workforce within the past year.[2]

Institutional theory suggests that the public sector is more likely to conform to legal mandates issued by the state than private-sector firms because (1) they are directly interconnected to the federal government and (2) adherence to institutional rules is an indicator of performance for public-sector firms (e.g., DiMaggio and Powell 1983). As a result of the passage of federal laws making gender discrimination illegal in South Korea (the Equal Employment Opportunity Act 1987 and the Gender Discrimination Prevention and Relief Act 1999), we suspect that the public sector may have more quickly integrated its workforce than the private sector. *Public sector* is a binary variable coded 1 for public sector organizations and 0 otherwise.

Finally, because of the well-established relationship between industry and sex segregation (McTague, Stainback, and Tomaskovic-Devey 2009; Tomaskovic-Devey et al. 2006), we control for *industry* at the two-digit classification level with an industry fixed effect. The industry fixed effect coefficients absorb all between-industry variation.

Results

Table 2 provides the results from three ordinary least squares regression models. Model 1 includes the percentage of women in all positions of organizational power and controls for organizational characteristics. Model 2 estimates the effects of female managers and female supervisors separately to determine whether women's position in the organizational power structure affects sex segregation among subordinate workers. Model 3 tests for the potential nonlinear effects of female leadership on sex segregation.

Model 1 estimates the effect of percent female managers/supervisors on sex segregation. The effect is not statistically significant ($b = .025$), controlling for organizational characteristics. The notion that having women anywhere in the organizational power structure benefits all women does not receive empirical support in this model.

TABLE 2
The Effects of Female Leadership on Sex Segregation

	Model 1	Model 2	Model 3
Female leadership			
Percent female managers/ supervisors	.025 (.020)		
Percent female managers		$-.187^{***}$ (.068)	$-.616^{****}$ (.138)
Percent female managers squared			$.008^{***}$ (.002)
Percent female supervisors		$.066^{*}$ (.035)	$-.281^{****}$ (.083)
Percent female supervisors squared			$.005^{****}$ (.001)
Organizational policy and structure			
Gender discrimination policy	-2.844^{**} (1.373)	-2.849^{**} (1.369)	-3.045^{**} (1.352)
Family-friendly policies	$-.207$ (.354)	$-.216$ (.354)	$-.404$ (.351)
Human resource management office	.368 (1.420)	.382 (1.418)	.275 (1.400)
Total employment (ln)	-1.259^{*} (.712)	-1.324^{*} (.703)	-1.176^{*} (.694)
Organizational age	$-.110$ (.107)	$-.113$ (.107)	$-.084$ (.105)
Organizational age squared	.000 (.001)	.000 (.001)	.000 (.001)
Unionized workplace	3.620^{**} (1.716)	3.504^{**} (1.718)	2.847^{*} (1.698)
Occupational heterogeneity	$.505^{****}$ (.033)	$.506^{****}$ (.034)	$.504^{****}$ (.033)
Environmental pressures			
Competition	-1.282^{*} (.690)	-1.330^{*} (.688)	-1.190^{*} (.680)
Downsizing	-3.363^{*} (2.037)	-3.533^{*} (2.034)	-3.550^{*} (2.007)
Public sector	-4.612^{*} (2.727)	-4.959^{*} (2.726)	-4.950^{*} (2.691)
Adjusted R^2	.3275	.3305	.3492

NOTE: Unstandardized metric coefficients with standard errors in parentheses. Models contain fixed effects for industry. $N = 1,596$.
$^{*}p < .10$. $^{**}p < .05$. $^{***}p < .01$. $^{****}p < .001$ (two-tailed test).

Model 2 separates the effects of female managers and female supervisors. What is interesting is that the coefficients exhibit opposite signs. The effect of women in managerial jobs is associated with lower levels of sex segregation ($b = -.187$, $p < .01$). As women's managerial representation increases, segregation declines. Although marginally significant ($.05 < p < .10$), women in supervisory positions are associated with higher levels of sex segregation ($b = .066$). Taken together, this suggests that women in higher-level decision-making roles have beneficial effects on workplace sex integration. However, the resegregating effects of percent female supervisors is likely to be related to the process of bottom-up ascription, where women supervisors often find themselves in low-level leadership roles supervising other women (Elliott and Smith 2001; Stainback and Tomaskovic-Devey 2009).

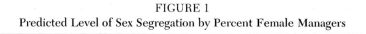

FIGURE 1
Predicted Level of Sex Segregation by Percent Female Managers

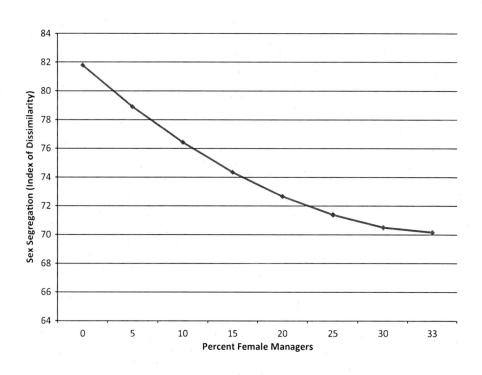

Model 3 provides estimates with the quadratic terms for percent female managers and percent female supervisors to test for nonlinearity. All four coefficients are statistically significant ($p < .05$). The negative coefficient for percent female managers and positive coefficient for percent female managers squared indicate that female managers have the effect of reducing sex segregation among subordinates at a decreasing rate. The nature of the association is depicted in Figure 1.

Predicted segregation values are displayed in Figure 1 and represent the effects of percent female managers (x-axis) on sex segregation (y-axis) at the 5th and 95th percentile (0 percent managers and 33.3 percent managers, respectively), while holding all other variables at their sample means with the exception of the index of heterogeneity. To adjust for measurement error associated with the distribution of workers across the eight occupational categories, the index of heterogeneity is multiplied by its theoretical maximum (80.83). In general, the presence of female managers is associated with lower levels of sex segregation at lower levels of managerial representation, but the effect essentially levels off

FIGURE 2
Predicted Level of Sex Segregation by Percent Female Supervisors

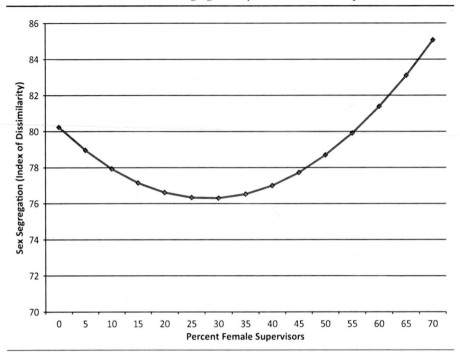

once women occupy approximately 30 percent of the managerial jobs. This finding provides support for the "agents of change" perspective and is consistent with the findings of Huffman, Cohen, and Pearlman (2010).

The predicted relationship between female supervisors and sex segregation is depicted in Figure 2. The figure represents the effects of percent female supervisors at the 5th and 95th percentile. In model 2, estimating the linear effect of female supervisors, we found that female supervisors are associated with greater sex segregation. The nonlinear models, however, provide an interesting result. Female supervisors appear to have beneficial effects on alleviating sex segregation until they reach approximately 30 to 35 percent of supervisors. Once this threshold is reached, women's presence in supervisory roles is associated with greater segregation. Although the "agents of change" perspective suggests that the presence of women in managerial and supervisory positions is likely to reduce gender inequality through top-down processes, this finding suggests a bottom-up process whereby women gain access to supervisory positions directing the work of female subordinates (Elliott and Smith 2001, 2004). In effect, sex-segregated employment generates sex-segregated supervisory roles.

Although organizational characteristics were included as control variables in our statistical estimates, a couple of significant findings are worth noting. On average, sex segregation is lower in organizations with a formal antidiscrimination policy and in larger workplaces. Unionized workplaces tend to have higher levels of sex segregation compared to nonunionized workplaces. All three of the environmental pressure variables are marginally significant ($p < .10$). The results indicate that organizations embedded in more competitive environments have lower levels of sex segregation. The findings also suggest that organizations that have experienced downsizing within the past year tend to be less segregated than firms that have not experienced downsizing. This finding is consistent with recent research that suggests that downsizing may lead to the elimination of feminized departments and jobs (Haveman, Broschak, and Cohen 2009; Kalev n.d.). Finally, consistent with institutional theory expectations, organizations in the public sector have less sex segregation on average compared to private-sector workplaces.

Conclusion

Although some previous research suggests that increasing women's access to organizational power may curtail gender-linked inequality within workplaces (Cohen and Huffman 2007; Cotter et al. 1997; Hultin and Szulkin 1999), few studies to date have explored this topic with regard to sex segregation. Drawing from Cohen and Huffman's (2007) framework conceptualizing women in positions of organizational power as either "change agents" or "cogs in the machine," we examine the question, Do women in managerial and supervisory positions reduce sex segregation among subordinates?

Theoretically, the "agents of change" perspective suggests that women's representation in managerial jobs is likely to reduce gender inequality among subordinates by reducing bias processes responsible for recasting male advantage (in-group preference, stereotypes) and increasing women's access to career-enhancing social networks and mentoring opportunities with female managers and supervisors (Cohen and Huffman 2007; Hultin and Szulkin 1999, 2003). In contrast, the "cogs in the machine" perspective suggests that female managers and supervisors are unlikely to affect gender inequality among subordinates because they are severely constrained by the larger cultural system of gender (see Maume 2011; Penner and Toro-Tulla 2010; Penner, Toro-Tulla, and Huffman 2010). From this perspective, status beliefs about men's competence and abilities may lead both male and female decision-makers to contribute to gender inequality among subordinates. In addition, female managers and supervisors may also avoid appearing sympathetic to female subordinates in an effort to maintain career-enhancing ties to powerful men in the organization (Maume 2011).

Utilizing a representative dataset of South Korean organizations, our findings provide some support for the "agents of change" perspective. We find that organizations with a larger percentage of women in managerial jobs tend to have lower observed levels of sex segregation. This result is consistent with the recent work of Huffman and colleagues (2010) and suggests the importance of integrating managerial hierarchies for reducing gender inequality among subordinates. The policy implications of this finding are important because they suggest that promoting women's access to higher-level managerial positions may be crucial for eradicating workplace gender inequality. Because women account for less than 7 percent of managers in South Korea, specific policies should be developed and implemented to increase women's access to these positions.

Our analyses of the effects of female supervisors on sex segregation provide mixed results. At lower levels of representation, female supervisors are associated with lower levels of sex segregation consistent with the "agents of change" expectation. However, once women occupy approximately 30 percent of supervisory positions, sex segregation begins to rise with increases in female representation among supervisors. This resegregation effect could be the result of supervisors' in-group preferences for same-sex subordinates; however, we believe the effect is more consistent with a bottom-up ascription explanation—women are most likely to find themselves in supervisory roles directing female workers (Elliott and Smith 2001, 2004). Of course, our cross-sectional data cannot adjudicate between these two explanations.

A limitation of this study is that it relies on cross-sectional data. Although our theoretical framework is dynamic, we can only observe static associations. As with all cross-sectional studies, statistical relationships between core theoretical variables can be established, but temporal order is dependent on theoretical expectations. Future studies utilizing panel data will be valuable for establishing causality.

Further research should more thoroughly interrogate the relationship between women's access to organizational power and inequality among subordinates, especially given inconsistent findings across studies. Researchers should seek to develop a better theoretical and empirical understanding of how hierarchy within authority structures matters and for which outcomes (e.g., segregation, wages, and career support). For example, Hultin and Szulkin's (2003) finding that female supervisors may be more important for reducing the gender wage gap than managers differs sharply from our results. We believe that these differences may be related to the different outcomes examined, although, admittedly, we cannot rule out potential differences in national context. While the wage gap and segregation are two important indicators of inequality, the process governing allocation may be quite different. For example, supervisors may influence the wage gap through the formal evaluation of subordinates. Allocation to jobs themselves, however, is unlikely to be the decision of supervisors. Hiring and promotion decisions are likely being made by managers. From this standpoint, the allocation of women and men into jobs is made largely by managers, not supervisors. Following this logic, it seems reasonable to expect that women at different levels of organizational power may have unique effects on different gender inequality outcomes. Future research should seek to (1) more precisely specify which organizational actors are making which decisions affecting gender inequalities and (2) identify the organizational contexts that enhance female managers' ability to reduce gender inequality.

Notes

1. More information about these data can be located on the Korea Labor Institute's website at www .kli.re.kr/wps.

2. We also estimated models with downsizing defined as a 15 percent decrease in employment. Our substantive findings did not change.

References

Baron, James N., Brian S. Mittman, and Andrew E. Newman. 1991. Targets of opportunity: Organizational and environmental determinants of gender integration within the California civil service, 1979–1985. *American Journal of Sociology* 96 (6): 1362–401.

Becker, Gary. 1971. *The economics of discrimination.* Chicago, IL: University of Chicago Press.

Bielby, William T. 2000. Minimizing workplace gender and racial bias. *Contemporary Sociology* 29:120–29.

Brass, Daniel J. 1985. Men's and women's networks: A study of interaction patterns and influence in an organization. *Academy of Management Journal* 28 (2): 327–43.

Cardoso, Ana Rute, and Rudolf Winter-Ebmer. 2010. Female-led firms and gender wage policies. *Industrial and Labor Relations Review* 64 (1): 143–63.

Chamberlain, Lindsey Joyce, Martha Crowley, Daniel Tope, and Randy Hodson. 2008. Sexual harassment in organizational context. *Work and Occupations* 35 (3): 262–95.

Cohen, Lisa E., Joseph P. Broschak, and Heather A. Haveman. 1998. And then there were more? The effect of organizational sex composition on hiring and promotion. *American Sociological Review* 63 (5): 711–27.

Cohen, Philip N., and Matt L. Huffman. 2003. Occupational segregation and the devaluation of women's work across U.S. labor markets. *Social Forces* 81 (2): 881–907.

Cohen, Philip N., and Matt L. Huffman. 2007. Working for the woman? Female managers and the gender wage gap. *American Sociological Review* 72 (2): 681–704.

Cohen, Philip N., Matt L. Huffman, and Stephanie Knauer. 2009. Stalled progress? Gender segregation and wage inequality among American managers, 1980–2000. *Work and Occupations* 36 (4): 318–42.

Cotter, David A., JoAnn M. DeFiore, Joan M. Hermsen, Brenda M. Kowalewski, and Reeve Vanneman. 1995. Occupational gender segregation and the earnings gap: Changes in the 1980s. *Social Science Research* 24 (4): 439–54.

Cotter, David A., JoAnn M. DeFiore, Joan M. Hermsen, Brenda Marsteller Kowalewski, and Reeve Vanneman. 1997. All women benefit: The macro-level effect of occupational segregation on gender earnings equality. *American Sociological Review* 62:714–34.

Cotter, David A., Joan M. Hermsen, and Reeve Vanneman. 2001. Women's work and working women: The demand for female labor. *Gender & Society* 15 (3): 429–52.

DiMaggio, Paul J., and Walter W. Powell. 1983. The iron cage revisited: Institutional isomorphism and collective rationality in organizational fields. *American Sociological Review* 48:147–60.

Elliott, James R., and Ryan A. Smith. 2001. Ethnic matching of supervisors to subordinate work groups: Findings on bottom-up ascription and social closure. *Social Problems* 48 (2): 258–76.

Elliott, James R., and Ryan A. Smith. 2004. Race, gender and workplace power. *American Sociological Review* 69 (3): 365–86.

Elvira, Marta, and Mary Graham. 2002. Not just a formality: Pay system formalization and gender earnings effects. *Organization Science* 13 (6): 601–17.

Ely, Robin J. 1994. The effects of organizational demographics and social identity on relationships among professional women. *Administrative Science Quarterly* 39 (2): 203–38.

Ely, Robin J. 1995. The power in demography: Women's social constructions of gender identity at work. *Academy of Management Journal* 38 (3): 589–634.

Gorman, Elizabeth H. 2005. Gender stereotypes, same-gender preferences, and organizational variation in the hiring of women: Evidence from law firms. *American Sociological Review* 70 (4): 702–28.

Gorman, Elizabeth H. 2006. Work uncertainty and the promotion of professional women: The case of law firm partnership. *Social Forces* 85:865–90.

Gorman, Elizabeth H., and Julie A. Kmec. 2009. Hierarchical rank and women's organizational mobility: Glass ceilings in corporate law firms. *American Journal of Sociology* 114 (5): 1428–74.

Haveman, Heather A., Joseph P. Broschak, and Lisa E. Cohen. 2009. Good times, bad times: The effects of organizational dynamics on the careers of male and female managers. In *Research in the sociology of work*, vol. 18, ed. Nina Bandelj, 119–48. Bingley, UK: Emerald Publishing Group.

Hirsh, C. Elizabeth. 2009. The strength of weak enforcement: The impact of discrimination charges on sex and race segregation in the workplace. *American Sociological Review* 74 (2): 245–71.

Huffman, Matt L., and Philip N. Cohen. 2004. Occupational segregation and the gender gap in workplace authority: National versus local labor markets. *Sociological Forum* 19:121–47.

Huffman, Matt L., Philip N. Cohen, and Jessica Pearlman. 2010. Engendering change: Organizational dynamics and workplace gender segregation, 1975–2005. *Administrative Science Quarterly* 55 (2): 255–77.

Huffman, Matt L., and Steven C. Velasco. 1997. When more is less: Sex composition, organizations, and earnings in U.S. firms. *Work and Occupations* 24 (2): 214–44.

Hultin, Mia, and Ryszard Szulkin. 1999. Wages and unequal access to organizational power. *Administrative Science Quarterly* 44 (3): 453–72.

Hultin, Mia, and Ryszard Szulkin. 2003. Mechanisms of inequality: Unequal access to organizational power and the gender wage gap. *European Sociological Review* 19 (2): 143–59.

Ibarra, Hermenia. 1993. Personal networks of women and minorities in management: A conceptual framework. *Academy of Management Review* 18 (1): 56–87.

Kalev, Alexandra. n.d. How you downsize is who you downsize: Structural vulnerability and accountability in layoffs. Tel Aviv University, Department of Sociology Working Paper, Tel Aviv, Israel.

Kalev, Alexandra, Frank Dobbin, and Erin Kelly. 2006. Best practices or best guesses: Assessing the effectiveness of corporate affirmative action and diversity policies. *American Sociological Review* 71 (4): 589–617.

Kanter, Rosabeth Moss. 1977. *Men and women of the corporation*. New York, NY: Basic Books.

Kim, Sangmook. 2005. Gender differences in the job satisfaction of public employees: A study of Seoul metropolitan government, Korea. *Sex Roles* 52:667–81.

Kmec, Julie A. 2005. Setting occupational sex segregation in motion: Demand-side explanations of sex traditional employment. *Work and Occupations* 32:322–54.

Konrad, Alison M., Vicki Kramer, and Sumru Erkut. 2008. Critical mass: The impact of three or more women on corporate boards. *Organizational Dynamics* 37:145–64.

Konrad, Alison M., and Frank Linnehan. 1995. Formalized HRM structure: Coordinating equal employment opportunity or concealing organizational practice? *Academy of Management Journal* 38 (3): 787–820.

Kulis, Stephen. 1997. Gender segregation among college and university employees. *Sociology of Education* 70 (2): 151–73.

Levanon, Asaf, Paula England, and Paul D. Allison. 2009. Occupational feminization and pay: Assessing causal dynamics using 1950–2000 census data. *Social Forces* 88 (2): 865–92.

Maume, David J. 1999. Occupational segregation and the career mobility of white men and women. *Social Forces* 77:1433–59.

Maume, David J. 2004. Is the glass ceiling a unique form of inequality? Evidence from a random-effects model of managerial attainment. *Work and Occupations* 31 (2): 250–74.

Maume, David J. 2011. Meet the new boss . . . same as the old boss? Female supervisors and subordinate career prospects. *Social Science Research* 20:287–98.

McTague, Tricia, Kevin Stainback, and Donald Tomaskovic-Devey. 2009. An organizational approach to race and sex desegregation in United States workplaces. *Social Forces* 87 (3): 1499–528.

Nelson, Robert L., and William P. Bridges. 1999. *Legalizing gender inequality: Courts, markets, and unequal pay for women in America*. New York, NY: Cambridge University Press.

Penner, Andrew M., and Harold J. Toro-Tulla. 2010. Women in power and gender wage inequality: The case of small businesses. In *Research in the sociology of work: Gender and sexuality in the workplace*, eds. Christine L. Williams and Kirsten Dellinger, 83–105. Bingley, UK: Emerald Publishing Group.

Penner, Andrew M., Harold J. Toro-Tulla, and Matt L. Huffman. 2010. Do women managers ameliorate gender differences in wages? Evidence from a large grocery retailer. Paper presented at the meeting of the International Sociological Association Research Committee on Social Stratification and Mobility (RC28), May, Haifa, Israel.

Petersen, Trond, and Laurie Graham. 1995. Separate and unequal: Occupation establishment sex segregation and the gender wage gap. *American Journal of Sociology* 101 (2): 329–65.

Petersen, Trond, and Ishak Saporta. 2004. The opportunity structure for discrimination. *American Journal of Sociology* 109 (4): 852–901.

Pfeffer, Jeffrey, Alison Davis-Blake, and Daniel J. Julius. 1995. AA officer salaries and managerial diversity: Efficiency wages or status? *Industrial Relations* 34 (1): 73–94.

Purcell, David, Kelly Rhea Macarthur, and Sarah Samblanet. 2010. Gender and the class ceiling at work. *Sociology Compass* 4 (9): 705–17.

Reskin, Barbara F. 1988. Bringing the men back in: Sex differentiation and the devaluation of women's work. *Gender & Society* 2:58–81.

Reskin, Barbara F. 2000. The proximate causes of employment discrimination. *Contemporary Sociology* 29:319–28.

Reskin, Barbara F., and Debra B. McBrier. 2000. Why ascription? Organizations' employment of male and female managers. *American Sociological Review* 65 (2): 210–33.

Reskin, Barbara F., Debra Branch McBrier, and Julie A. Kmec. 1999. The determinants and consequences of workplace sex and race composition. *Annual Review of Sociology* 25:335–61.

Roscigno, Vincent. 2007. *The face of discrimination: How race and gender impact work and home lives*. New York, NY: Rowman & Littlefield.

Skaggs, Sheryl. 2008. Producing change or bagging opportunity? The effects of discrimination litigation on women in supermarket management. *American Journal of Sociology* 113 (4): 1148–83.

Skaggs, Sheryl, Kevin Stainback, and Phyllis Duncan. n.d. Shaking things up or business as usual? The influence of female corporate executives and board of directors on women's managerial representation. Unpublished manuscript.

Stainback, Kevin, Thomas Ratliff, and Vincent J. Roscigno. 2011. The organizational context of sex discrimination: Sex composition, workplace culture, and relative power. *Social Forces* 89 (4): 1165–88.

Stainback , Kevin, Corre L. Robinson, and Donald Tomaskovic-Devey. 2005. Race and workplace integration: A "politically mediated" process? *American Behavioral Scientist* 48 (9): 1200–1228.

Stainback, Kevin, and Donald Tomaskovic-Devey. 2009. Intersections of power and privilege: Long-term trends in managerial representation. *American Sociological Review* 74 (5): 800–820.

Stainback, Kevin, Donald Tomaskovic-Devey, and Sheryl Skaggs. 2010. Organizational approaches to inequality: Inertia, relative power, and environments. *Annual Review of Sociology* 36:225–47.

Stinchcombe, Arthur L. 1965. Social structure and organizations. In *Handbook of organizations*, ed. James G. March, 142–93. Chicago, IL: Rand McNally.

Tomaskovic-Devey, Donald. 1993. *Gender and racial inequality at work: The sources and consequences of job segregation*. Ithaca, NY: Industrial and Labor Relations Press.

Tomaskovic-Devey, Donald, Catherine Zimmer, Kevin Stainback, Corre L. Robinson, Tiffany Taylor, and Tricia McTague. 2006. Documenting desegregation: Segregation in American workplaces by race, ethnicity, and sex, 1966–2003. *American Sociological Review* 71:565–88.

United Nations Development Program (UNDP). 2005. *Human development report*. New York, NY: UNDP. Available from http://hdr.undp.org/report (accessed 4 April 2011).

Checking the Pulse of Diversity among Health Care Professionals: An Analysis of West Coast Hospitals

By
SHERYL L. SKAGGS
and
JULIE A. KMEC

What factors are associated with variation in the racial/ethnic composition of hospital health care professionals? Institutional theories suggest that organizations react to external environmental and internal structural pressures for the racial/ethnic integration of workers. Using an institutional framework, we bring to bear new insight into how hospitals respond to such pressure for diversity. Models estimated with original data from 328 U.S. West Coast hospitals provide evidence that establishment size and a hospital's minority patient base promote diversity among health care professionals. The state legal environment is also associated with the racial/ethnic composition of professional hospital workers, indicating the importance of fair employment laws and court decisions in signaling expectations about workplace diversity. Last, the findings show that factors within hospitals' competitive and internal environments have positive consequences for diversity among health care professionals. We discuss implications for our findings, especially in the context of health care worker shortages and ongoing health care reform.

Keywords: organizational diversity; professions; occupations; health care industry

The U.S. health care workforce is expanding, but it remains the domain of white workers; African Americans, Hispanic Americans, and Native Americans account for roughly only 10 percent of the physician workforce (Council on Graduate Medical Education [COGME] 2005; Saha and Shipman 2008). The absence of minority professionals in the health care field represents more than an uneven distribution of workers along race/ethnic lines; it is also an important factor contributing to racial and ethnic

NOTE: This research was supported by Washington State University New Faculty Seed Grant 148-02-06E-2480-9912. An earlier version of this article was presented at the 2010 American Sociological Association Annual Meeting in Atlanta, Georgia. The authors thank Bliss Cartwright and Patrick Ronald Edwards at the Equal Employment Opportunity Commission's Office of Research for supplying supplemental data and statistical coding files.

DOI: 10.1177/0002716211421869

disparities in access to health care, diagnosis, and treatment (U.S. Department of Health and Human Services [DHHS] 2009, iii; Agency for Healthcare Research and Quality [AHRQ] 2000).[1] Minority patients tend to prefer and more closely identify with health care professionals with whom they share a racial/ethnic background (see Saha et al. 1999; Cooper-Patrick et al. 1999). Hence, in the absence of a diverse workforce, patients may avoid or put off necessary treatment, recommended screenings, and other preventive health care measures.

In addition, minority health care professionals may increase access to health care for racial/ethnic minority populations. Compared to their white counterparts, racial/ethnic minority health care professionals are more likely to serve minority populations and enter primary care and practice in health profession shortage areas (see Saha et al. 2008; COGME 2005). For example, in 2009, African American physicians in California were five times more likely than their white peers to practice in predominantly African American communities (see DHHS 2009, 9). Nationally, African American physicians composed only 4 percent of the health care workforce in 2005, yet they served more than one-fifth of African American patients (see COGME 2005).

The diversification of health care providers along racial/ethnic lines may provide a partial solution to the persistent health disparities of race and ethnic minorities. Agencies ranging from the American Medical Association (2009) to the DHHS (2009) agree that racial/ethnic minority health care providers fill a critical void for minority patients. If the benefits of the current health care reform are to reach the growing minority population in the United States, scholars must understand the factors that lead to racial/ethnic diversity among health care professionals. To this end, this article sheds light on key mechanisms in an organization's institutional, legal, competitive, and internal environment alleged to be at work in shaping racial/ethnic minority representation among health care professionals employed in hospitals.[2] Specifically, we examine the impact of factors such as organizational size, managerial workforce demographics, state location, and patient demographic composition. To do so, we draw on an original dataset of more than three hundred hospital establishments in the western

Sheryl L. Skaggs is an associate professor of sociology and public policy at the University of Texas at Dallas. Her research primarily focuses on workplace diversity among racial/ ethnic minorities and women. Her research has been published in the American Sociological Review, American Journal of Sociology, Sociological Forum, Research in Political Sociology, *and* Work and Occupations. *Currently, she is studying the influence of female members of the board of directors and executives on gender diversity within Fortune 500 firms.*

Julie A. Kmec is an associate professor of sociology at Washington State University. Her research agenda focuses broadly on gender and race inequality in work organizations. She has pursued research on job gender segregation, the glass ceiling, gender and work effort, and caregiving penalties at work. Most recently, she is pursuing a study of how human resource practices influence work organizations. Her work has appeared in Work and Occupations, Gender & Society, American Journal of Sociology, *and* Social Science Research.

United States, which includes the racial/ethnic composition of hospital professionals as annually reported to the Equal Employment Opportunity Commission (EEOC).

We developed an institutional framework to explain how organizations—namely, hospitals—react to external environmental and internal structural pressures for professional racial/ethnic integration (Stainback, Robinson, and Tomaskovic-Devey 2005; Scott 2003). Our research question is straightforward: what factors are associated with variation in the racial/ethnic composition of hospitals' health care professional workers? Our contribution is to bring to bear new insights into how workplaces situated within a long-standing core service industry respond to pressures for increased racial/ethnic diversity among an essential group of workers.[3] As health care reform has become an increasingly important topic, we believe that improved racial/ethnic matching of professionals to patients is a critical factor in providing greater access to disadvantaged groups. Without sufficient attention to diversity within health care facilities, policy efforts are likely to be limited. To this end, we theoretically distinguish four areas linked to professional worker racial/ethnic composition and show that to varying degrees, pressures from hospitals' institutional, legal, competitive, and internal environments shape health care professional diversity.

Theoretical Background

The health care industry has been the target of attempts to racially/ethnically diversify for more than a decade. The 1998 Presidential Initiative on Race and Health was the first national commitment to eliminate health disparities between whites and racial/ethnic minorities. Since the initiative, the American Medical Association, the Joint Commission on the Accreditation of Hospitals, the Kaiser Family Foundation, the DHHS, the AHRQ, and the Institute of Medicine at the National Academy of Sciences, among others, have commissioned reports documenting the disparity and advising the health care industry on how to eliminate it. Among the solutions from these reports was a call for the racial/ethnic diversification of health care workers who serve minority populations. Hospitals—a primary employer of health care professionals—are clearly under pressure to alter their workforce composition.

Demographic change in the health care field is also timely. As states implement health care reform, providers within this industry may soon be in a position to reform their practices. Part of this may include the revision of hiring and retention policies that target racial and ethnic minorities. At the same time, the currently debated national health plan provides access to insurance for more individuals, which will undoubtedly increase the demand for health care professionals. To meet these demands, health care providers will need to broaden their labor pool. Indeed, President Obama's Economic Recovery Act of 2009 allotted $500 million to pay for the training of future health care workers (White House 2009).

Using hospitals to study organizational response to external environmental and internal structural pressures for professional racial/ethnic integration is appropriate for three additional reasons. First, although no industry is recession-proof, demand remains high for health care professionals, particularly in an aging society. Thus, it is expected that recruitment and hiring of qualified candidates, along with efforts to increase workforce diversity, will remain a priority within the health care industry. With high demand for their services, hospitals are not greatly affected by downturns in the economy that subsequently reduce pressure for diversity (see King, Knight, and Hebl 2010). Second, employment within the health care and social service industries (of which hospitals are a part) is projected to increase by more than 4 million by 2016, making it one of the fastest-growing industries in the country (U.S. Bureau of Labor Statistics 2007). Consequently, hospital hiring will continue to grow at a steady rate over the next decade. Third, the health care and social assistance industry is the third largest employer in the United States, offering about 12 percent of all private-sector jobs (U.S. Bureau of Labor Statistics 2007). Thus, the prominence of the health care industry and hospital care in particular, along with an increasingly diverse population, demands a diverse workforce, and health care professionals provide a strong basis for examining professional diversity within this organizational context.

External Pressures for Racial/Ethnic Workforce Diversity

Organizations are located within and responsive to their environmental contexts (Scott 2002; for a review, see Stainback, Skaggs, and Tomaskovic-Devey 2010). Institutional theorists argue that organizations are embedded within a context of legal rules and normative practices that shape their structures, routines, and practices (DiMaggio and Powell 1983; Meyer and Rowan 1977), which, in turn, influence their demographic composition. Organizations' environmental forces push them toward similarity in form and structure so that over time, policies and practices across fields or industries become increasingly homogeneous, reflecting a set of institutional expectations and rules (see DiMaggio and Powell 1983). The similarity in structure, routine, and practice among organizations stems from the tendency to gain and maintain legitimacy among industry peers as well as from the legal, political, and public spheres (Suchman 1995).

While an organization's demographic composition is the result of a variety of factors, such as labor supply, employment practices, and political pressures, external pressures influence variation in the racial/ethnic composition of its professional workforce. That is, whom an organization employs is the result of organizational response to expectations, rules, and practices in the institutional (industry) environment. In the sections that follow, we discuss pressures for health care professional diversification stemming from organizations' external institutionalized, legal, and competitive environments.

Institutional environment

Institutional theory suggests that the normative environment within an industry will influence the internal organization of work, including policies and practices that shape workforce demographic composition. As Stainback, Skaggs, and Tomaskovic-Devey (2010) suggested, workforce diversity tends to reflect a more general set of established norms rather than a specific set of mandates from more powerful entities outside of institutional fields (e.g., oversight agencies, courts). We anticipate that several key factors within the external environment will influence hospital racial and ethnic diversity among health care professionals.

Establishment size. Previous research has demonstrated the importance of organizational size in shaping workforce composition. Size shapes workforce demographics in two particular ways. First, large organizations have more jobs and a greater number of hierarchical layers than smaller ones. As job opportunities expand, employers are likely to cast a broader net to fill positions, particularly when labor is in high demand, as in the case of health care professionals. Second, and more important, large organizations tend to be more visible than smaller ones. This visibility subjects them to greater public (Salancik 1979; Suchman 1995; see also Huffman 1999) and government scrutiny. With growing societal and business expectations for employment diversity (see Herring 2009), large organizations are likely to increase the racial/ethnic composition of their workforce as a way to signal their compliance with social norms about diversity to the public, other organizations, and the government. Furthermore, increased visibility often corresponds with greater pressures from government regulatory agencies to comply with civil rights laws (Edelman 1992). Thus, large hospitals may take proactive steps in the employment process to attract, employ, and retain a diverse professional workforce. We subsequently predict:

Hypothesis 1: The larger the hospital, the more racially/ethnically diverse its health care professional workforce.

Patient demographic composition. Customers place demands on organizations to act in ways consistent with their needs and preferences. In hospitals, patients may exert an above-average level of control over whom a hospital hires since patients report improved care when they share the same race/ethnicity as their health care providers (Collins et al. 2002; Cooper-Patrick et al. 1999), greater adherence to prescribed treatments (Cooper-Patrick et al. 1999), and a general preference for being cared for by demographically similar providers (Gray and Stoddard 1997; LaVeist and Nuru-Jeter 2002; LaVeist and Carroll 2002). As a result, hospitals with a racially diverse patient base may have an incentive to employ racial/ethnic minority health care workers, especially if satisfied patients return to the hospital for their elective medical needs. This leads to the following hypothesis:

Hypothesis 2: A racially/ethnically diverse patient base will be associated with a more racially/ethnically diverse health care professional workforce.

Legal Environment

The laws governing organizations and how they recruit workers—and the threat of sanction for law violations—are likely to impact the racial/ethnic composition of a hospital's health care professional workforce. Below we identify several sources of legal pressure that may increase employment diversity among hospitals.

State location. Since states provide the legal environment in which organizations operate, it is likely that the level of pressure to promote employment diversity, particularly among vital professionals, will vary by state location. Some state climates are more conducive to equity than others. For instance, Beggs (1995) found employment equality among racial and gender groups to be higher in states with strong support for equal opportunity. Similarly, a study by Sutton and his colleagues (1994) showed adoption rates of due-process governance to be higher in California, a state with progressive judicial and legislative histories, than in states with historically more conservative legal and judicial environments.

The three states in our sample—California, Oregon, and Washington—have different state-level regulation and laws governing equal employment. Washington and California have each adopted legislation prohibiting government agencies from granting preferential treatment to any individual or group on the basis of race, gender, color, ethnicity, or national origin in the operation of public employment (Washington State Department of Personnel 2004; California Fair Employment and Housing Commission 2009); Oregon has no such policies. All three states have policies that address comparable worth/gender pay equity for state employees (Nelson and Bridges 1999). However, California has very specific state-level laws that are designed to provide protections to female and minority workers who have historically been disadvantaged (California Fair Employment and Housing Commission 2009). Sutton and colleagues (1994) noted that California's progressive environment has yielded a legal environment favorable toward workers. In light of these state-level differences, we predict:

Hypothesis 3: Hospitals located in California will have a more racially/ethnically diverse health care professional workforce than Washington and Oregon hospitals.

Competitive environment

Organizational competition may influence the racial/ethnic composition of a hospital's professional workforce. Becker (1975) has argued that status-based discrimination should be eliminated in competitive markets; discriminating organizations cannot survive if they are willing to hire only white workers at a higher wage than nonwhite workers. That said, we might expect to see a more diverse workforce in competitive markets.

Establishment competition. A greater concentration of hospitals in a given geographic area means greater competition for an already small pool of available minority health care professionals. Such competition might compel hospitals to implement hiring and recruitment strategies that attract minority applicants. Likewise, a competitive environment may encourage hospitals to implement strategies to retain minority employees once they are hired. Consequently, we hypothesize:

Hypothesis 4: The greater the competition for a health care professional work-force, the more racially/ethnically diverse a hospital's professional workforce.

Internal Pressures for Racial/Ethnic Workforce Diversity

Internal pressures are also responsible for shaping organizational demographic composition. In this section, we discuss two internal organizational structures that are presumed to affect the demographic composition of an organization's workforce: (1) managerial racial/ethnic diversity and (2) nurse unions.

Managerial racial/ethnic composition. The racial/ethnic makeup of an organization's managerial ranks may shape the diversity of its professional workforce. Although we know of no study specifically examining this type of relationship, or the effects of managerial diversity on an establishment's racial/ethnic workforce composition more generally, researchers have found a connection between the share of women managers and gender integration. In particular, findings from a study by Huffman, Cohen, and Pearlman (2010) show that the greater the share of female managers, the greater the gender integration of nonmanagerial workers over time. While these researchers were unable to identify a mechanism whereby female managers increased gender integration, one possibility is that the presence of women in high-level positions not only creates opportunities for similar others at lower levels through hiring, recruitment, and promotions but also has the effect of reducing discriminatory practices that keep women out of management. Similarly, it may be the case that minority managers reduce barriers—either perceived or real—to the employment and retention of minority workers, particularly those in professional positions who are more similar in status. We argue that because managers make many of the hiring decisions, especially at the higher levels, diversity within the top ranks will have a trickle-down effect on the racial/ethnic diversity for professionals. We hypothesize that:

Hypothesis 5: The more racially/ethnically diverse a hospital's managerial workforce, the more diverse its health care professional workforce.

Nurse unions. Registered nursing is the largest occupation in hospitals (American Association of Colleges of Nursing 2004), and in recent times, hospitals in the three states we examine, similar to those in much of the nation, are facing significant nursing shortages (Healthcare Personnel Shortage Task Force 2002; Oregon Center for Nursing 2005; American Society of Registered Nurses 2007). In response, health care labor unions have developed strategic plans to alleviate labor shortages (Washington State Strategic Plan for Nursing 2002; Healthcare Personnel Shortage Task Force 2002; Lawton 2002). In fact, one of the foremost priorities of the Washington State Nurses Association is to address the nursing shortage (Washington State Nurses Association 2004). A key component of unions' strategic response to labor shortages involves the recruitment and hiring of a diverse health care workforce. Accordingly, unions representing registered nurses, particularly in a time of labor shortage, likely exert pressure on hospitals to create greater diversity within their workforce. Therefore:

Hypothesis 6: The presence of a nurse union in a hospital will be positively associated with racial/ethnic diversity among health care professionals.

Additional Factors Affecting Professional Racial/Ethnic Composition

We examine several additional factors that may affect organizations' workforce demographic composition.

Urban location. Based on several key factors, we anticipate that differences in diversity of health care professionals exist between rural and urban hospitals. In general, rural hospitals tend to experience greater difficulty than urban facilities in recruiting and retaining health care professionals due to such factors as lower salaries, fewer career opportunities, limited resources, and higher workloads (Rural Assistance Center 2009). Furthermore, because physicians and other health care professionals are typically trained and educated in urban areas, they are likely to be attracted to the cultural and social life of urban areas. These factors, combined with the fact that racial/ethnic minority populations tend to be larger in urban settings, suggest a potential gap in the diversity of minority health care professionals within rural and urban hospitals.

Health system membership. Affiliation with a health system, one that coordinates health coverage and operates multiple hospitals or clinics, indicates interconnectedness and a shared governing structure with other hospitals. The interconnectedness of a health system might be linked to the racial/ethnic composition of the professional workforce because linked hospitals may be able to share the cost of implementing affirmative action plans, an equal employment office/manager, or an equal opportunity policy, all of which are linked to minority recruitment.

Organization type. Distinctions between types of hospital organizations may also affect diversity of health care professionals. For example, it could be argued that the racial/ethnic composition of health care professionals is more diverse among general hospitals than their specialty counterparts. At least part of this difference may reflect variation in career opportunities, with general hospitals offering a wider range of departments and greater resources associated with these departments. On the other hand, with the growth of specialty hospitals, particularly those in financially lucrative areas, such as cardiac and orthopedic care (Tynan et al. 2009), general hospitals may be viewed as less attractive to minority health care professionals who seek to quickly recoup educational costs. Similarly, teaching hospitals could be viewed as an attractive option for minority health care professionals who seek extensive career opportunities within some of the most advanced medical facilities. Teaching hospitals have long been recognized as the source of specialized medical care involving cutting-edge treatments and surgeries (American Association of Medical Colleges 2009). They not only serve as training centers for many new physicians and health care professionals but continually strive to increase knowledge through research and development of new life-saving treatments. Conversely, given that teaching hospitals represent a much smaller percentage of medical facilities than their nonteaching counterparts and often provide medical care to the millions of Americans without health insurance (American Association of Medical Colleges 2009), they may attract a less diverse labor pool.

Sector. The sector in which hospitals operate may be related to the demographic composition of its health care professionals. Nonprofit hospitals are the most common type of facilities in the United States. In general, nonprofit organizations are often marked by bureaucratic operating procedures (Grodsky and Pager 2001) and well-developed affirmative action procedures that have been found to increase the employment of racial/ethnic minorities (see Harper and Reskin 2005; Kalev, Dobbin, and Kelly 2006). Nonprofits are also more publicly visible and subject to greater pressures to implement fair employment practices than are private-sector organizations (Meyer and Scott 1983; Dobbin et al. 1988; Kelly and Dobbin 1999). What is more, compared to for-profit hospitals, the public may judge nonprofits more by their activities and policies than their economic performance and expect nonprofits to provide employment opportunities for racial/ethnic minorities (see Dobbin et al. 1988; Marsden, Cook, and Knoke 1994).

Organizational age. The literature on organizational founding suggests that internal practices and policies are often shaped by factors within a firm's external institutional environment such as local or regional social and cultural norms, laws, and even standard business practices (Stinchcombe 1965). Because internal structures, particularly those related to recruitment, hiring, and promotions, are often difficult to change once established, organizations founded in the pre–civil rights era are likely to have informal, and even some formal, policies that are less consistent with antidiscrimination legislation than those organizations founded since the 1970s. Thus, we expect that younger hospitals will have greater diversity and will more closely reflect progressive social norms and attitudes about fair employment opportunities.

Data and Methods

Our primary data come from hospitals located in three Western states—California (CA), Oregon (OR), and Washington (WA)—that filed an annual EEO-1 report in 2005. Under an Intergovernmental Personnel Act agreement with the EEOC, the authors obtained access to a list of EEO-1 reporting hospitals in these states. Annually, private employers with one hundred or more employees or federal contractors with fifty or more employees (or first-tier federal subcontractors involving agreements worth $50,000) are required to file an EEO-1 report describing the racial/ethnic and gender composition of employees in nine of the establishment's occupational categories. The EEOC uses these reports to ensure employer compliance with federal laws prohibiting employment discrimination. We supplemented the EEO-1 data with establishment-level data collected through Internet searches and telephone calls to hospitals (see the appendix for sources of data).

We selected these three states because they differ in terms of the population's racial/ethnic composition and, as a result, have different levels of an available racial/ethnic minority health care labor pool. In 2000, 13 percent of Oregon's population was nonwhite (U.S. Census Bureau 2005a), 18 percent of Washington's population was nonwhite (U.S. Census Bureau 2005b), and roughly 40 percent of California's population was nonwhite (U.S. Census Bureau 2009).

The final sample consists of 328 hospitals. Analyses for this study are conducted at the *establishment* level and so allow for the examination of racial/ethnic diversity of health care professionals across individual worksites. Such detail would be lost with organizational-level analyses.[4] So, although practices and policies may be relatively uniform across organizationally linked hospital facilities, factors within a hospital's local environment, including state laws and local labor market characteristics, may create significant variation in health care professional segregation.

Before proceeding with the analyses, it is necessary to mention data-related caveats. First, the sample represents hospitals in a limited geographical area. Thus, our intent is not to draw inferences about the racial/ethnic composition of hospital health care professionals across the entire industry. It is possible that the racial/ethnic composition patterns we observe differ in regions with more or less diverse labor pools, different local racial/ethnic composition, or different state regulations governing employment. Second, we lack data on the race/ethnicity of actual job applicants. We know of no publicly available multiestablishment data-set that includes characteristics of job applicants, especially those who applied and were not hired. Consequently, our measures of labor supply will provide conservative estimates of the actual number of minority applicants. Despite these limitations, the data at hand are well suited for testing theories of environmental influences on race/ethnic workforce diversity. This study is also among the first to use EEO-1 reports that accurately capture the demographic composition of employees much more precisely than self-reports of demographic composition in other surveys (Robinson et al. 2005).

Measures

Dependent variable

Our outcome of interest is the log odds that hospital health care professionals are nonwhite. Odds are calculated as the proportion of professionals from that group divided by the proportion not from that group (proportion/[1 − proportion]). We calculated these measures from the yearly EEO-1 reports filed by hospitals. Professional workers in hospitals include dietitians and nutritionists, optometrists, pharmacists, physicians and surgeons, physician assistants, podiatrists, registered nurses, audiologists, occupational therapists, physical therapists, radiation therapists, recreational therapists, respiratory therapists, speech-language pathologists, all other therapists, and all other health diagnosing and treating practitioners (EEOC 2009).

Independent variables

We measure our predictor variables at the establishment level. Data sources are listed in the appendix.

Institutional environment. Hospital size is measured as the number of beds in a facility, a typical industry indicator of size. To capture potential differences in hospital professional workforce diversity, based on customer or patient demand, we include a measure of the *minority patient base* calculated as the African American, Hispanic, Asian, and Native American population in a particular hospital service area (HSA) divided by the corresponding total population in the hospital's zip code. Following the EEOC (2005), we obtained HSA data from the Dartmouth Atlas of Healthcare (2003), which classifies health care markets according to an established zip code scheme. We used zip codes from the 2000 U.S. Census to create matches between HSAs and California, Washington, and Oregon population data.

Legal environment. Models include a set of dichotomous variables denoting hospital state location, coded 1 if the hospital is located in Oregon or Washington (California is the reference category).

Competitive environment. Hospital *competition* is a variable denoting the number of hospitals within twenty miles of the sampled hospital, top-coded to 2.

Internal pressures for diversity. We measure *managerial racial/ethnic composition* as the percentage of racial/ethnic minorities in managerial occupations in the hospital. We also include a dichotomous variable indicating the presence of a *nurse union.* The effects of this measure are of particular interest given that registered nurses represent the largest group of hospital employees (American Association of Colleges of Nursing 2004).

Controls. Models include a dichotomous variable noting whether a hospital is located in an *urban* area (rural is the reference category, coded 0). Following industry practice, a hospital is urban if it is located within twenty-five miles of another hospital in an area with a population of at least thirty thousand. To capture the contextual influence of membership in a *health system,* we include a continuous measure indicating the number of hospitals that are members of a particular health care system (e.g., Group Health Cooperative, Providence Health System). If a hospital was not part of a health system, we coded this variable 0. We also control for *hospital classification* based on the primary specialty and purpose of the facility. Given the small number of specialty facilities, including acute care, children's, psychiatric, urgent, trauma, naval, and respiratory, we collapsed these classifications into one group. Comparisons are then made between general hospitals, coded 1, and specialty hospitals, coded 0. We also include a dichotomous measure to examine potential differences in racial and ethnic diversity among health care professionals in *teaching* (coded 1) and nonteaching hospitals (coded 0). A dichotomous variable is included measuring hospital sector, coded 1 if a hospital is nonprofit (i.e., a community-based nonprofit hospital with no stockholders whose profits are reinvested into the hospital) and 0 if either a for-profit or government (state- or county-run) hospital. Due to the small number of government-run hospitals in our sample ($n = 11$), we combined all publicly funded facilities (i.e., district, county, state/federal) with for-profit hospitals. Finally, a measure of organizational *age* (in years) is included and calculated by subtracting the founding year from the study year (2002). The natural logarithm of hospital age is used for the primary analysis to create a more uniform distribution of the measure. This is particularly appropriate given the relatively large standard deviation of 29 years.[5]

Method of Analysis

Because our outcome—the log odds that hospital professionals are nonwhite—ranges from 0 to 1, we estimate logistic regression models. Tests verify that

TABLE 1
Descriptive Statistics

Variables	Mean/Percentage	Range
Dependent variables		
Minority health care professional	33.35% (24.18)	0.00–96
Minority health care professional logit	–1.182 (2.098)	–9.21–3.11
Institutional environment		
Hospital size (number of beds)	203.10 (132.36)	20.00–875.00
Minority patients	39.42% (26.10)	0.00–97.34
Legal environment		
California	84.76%	Dichotomous
Oregon	4.27%	Dichotomous
Washington	10.98%	Dichotomous
Competitive environment		
Competition	1.72 (0.57)	0.00–2.00
Internal environment		
Percent minority managers	20.65% (17.93)	0–90.90
Nurse union	30.18%	Dichotomous
Controls		
Urban	88.11%	Dichotomous
Health care system	8.35 (11.01)	0.00–33.00
General hospital	82.93%	Dichotomous
Teaching hospital	13.41%	Dichotomous
Nonprofit	73.48%	Dichotomous
Age	60.21 (29.34)	5.00–144.00
N = 328		

NOTE: Standard deviations in parentheses.

multicollinearity is not a problem in models. To facilitate coefficient interpretation, we transformed unstandardized beta coefficients to odds ratios with the formula $(e\beta – 1) \times 100$. Odds ratios of 1 reflect total racial/ethnic workplace equality among health care professionals. Values less than 1 denote underrepresentation of minority professionals, and although rare, values greater than 1 indicate that health care professionals are more likely to be minority than white.

Results

Table 1 displays descriptive statistics for the 328 hospitals examined. On average, racial and ethnic minorities compose 33 percent of hospitals' health care professional workforce. The average hospital examined has 203 beds, with a range

TABLE 2
Logistic Regression Predicting Minority Health Care Professional Representation

Variables	Coefficient	Odds Ratio	Standard Error
Institutional environment			
Size (ln # beds)	0.292°°	1.339	0.106
Minority patients	0.018°°°	1.018	0.003
Legal environment			
Oregon	−0.181	0.834	0.350
Washington	−0.759°°	0.468	0.255
Competitive environment			
Competition	0.330°	1.391	0.153
Internal environment			
Racial/ethnic managers	0.049°°°	1.050	0.005
Nurse union	0.440°°	1.553	0.153
Controls			
Urban	0.548°	1.730	0.253
Health care system	−0.0002	0.999	0.006
General hospital	0.969°°°	2.635	0.181
Teaching hospital	0.217	1.242	0.192
Nonprofit	−0.088	0.916	0.151
Age (ln)	−0.297°	0.743	0.122
Intercept = −5.097°°°			
Adjusted R^2 = .742			
F = 73.32°°°			

°p < .05. °°p < .01. °°°p < .001.

between 20 and 875. On average, hospitals in the sample have a patient base that is 39 percent minority, with values ranging from 0 to 97 percent minority. Approximately 85 percent of hospitals in our sample are located in California; a much smaller percentage are located in Washington and Oregon (11 and 4 percent, respectively). On average, the hospitals in our sample compete with two other facilities within a twenty-mile area. Roughly 30 percent of hospitals have a nurse union. On average, racial and ethnic minorities compose 21 percent of managerial workers in hospitals. Roughly 88 percent of the sampled hospitals are located in urban areas. Only around 13 percent are classified as teaching institutions, while about 80 percent are classified as general hospitals. Hospitals in the sample are part of a health care system of ownership with approximately eight other hospitals. Just over 73 percent of hospitals in our sample are classified as nonprofit organizations. Finally, hospitals in the sample are, on average, 60 years old.

Results of our primary analysis are presented in Table 2. First, we find that among the three institutional factors examined, hospital size and minority patient base have a significant and positive influence on the racial/ethnic composition of hospitals' health care professional workforce. Increased hospital size (as measured by number of beds) is associated with increased net odds that a health care professional is a racial/ethnic minority. The percent minority of a hospital's patient base is also significantly related to health care professional worker racial/ethnic diversity, although the effect is quite small; for every 1 percent increase in a hospital's minority patient base, it experiences a roughly 2 percent increase in the net odds that a health care professional is a racial/ethnic minority.

An organization's legal environment, captured by variation in state-level fair employment legislation, appears to matter, at least in part, for hospital health care professional diversity. We find that diversity is greater in California than in Washington; however, there is no significant difference between California and Oregon hospitals. The results show that hospitals located in Washington are less than half as likely to have minority professionals as California hospitals included in our sample. We also find a positive association between hospital competition and minority representation among health care professionals; a unit increase in competition (having one or two or more hospitals within a twenty-mile area) increases the net odds of minorities in professional health care positions by 39 percent.

The results also reveal that internal pressures matter for promoting greater diversity among health care professionals. In particular, we find that the coefficient for managerial diversity is significant, although the effect is small; a 1 percent point increase in nonwhites' share of managerial positions is associated with a roughly 5 percent increase in the net odds that a health care professional is a racial/ethnic minority. Our findings also show that professional health care diversity is approximately 1.6 times greater in hospitals with a nurse union than in facilities without this form of internal pressure. Controls for both urban location and type of hospital based on specialty have a positive effect on minority representation among health care professionals. Specifically, we find that the odds a racial/ethnic minority is in a professional position are 1.7 times greater at urban compared to rural hospitals. Furthermore, the results indicate that the odds a minority is in a professional position when employed in general hospitals are more than two and a half times greater compared to the odds at specialty hospitals. However, we find no evidence of variation in professional workforce diversity between teaching and nonteaching hospitals, or between facilities that are part of a health care system and those that are independently owned. The results further reveal no difference between the demographic composition of minority health care professionals in nonprofit and other hospital types. However, we find that the older a hospital, the lower the net odds of employing minority health care professionals.

Discussion and Conclusions

We examined the influence of a set of external institutional, legal, and competitive factors and internal pressures expected to increase hospital racial/ethnic diversity among health care professionals. Previous research suggests that organizations respond to such demands as a way to maintain legitimacy within institutional fields or industries. The findings of this study indicate that hospital size, patient diversity, geographic location (including state and urban location), market competition, establishment managerial minority representation, nurse unionization, and hospital specialty increase the racial/ethnic diversity of health care professionals.

We argued that larger hospitals, because of their greater visibility and more extensive jobs structures, would provide more employment opportunities for nonwhite health care professionals. The results of this study support our prediction; increased size has a net positive effect on diversity among professionals. We suspect that because large hospitals experience greater scrutiny from the public and government regulatory agencies, they have developed practices and established human resource supports that expand recruitment and retention of minority professionals. It is also likely that large hospitals provide more attractive benefits and employment opportunities that help to recruit and retain minority professionals. Less important seems to be the influence of a hospital's minority patient base. We find only a negligible positive effect for this measure, which suggests that hospitals may pay only minimal attention to the matching of demographic characteristics between health care professionals and patients. This is somewhat surprising given evidence from the literature indicating a greater need and demand to provide minority patients, particularly those with limited English language skills, with health care professionals who can close cultural and language gaps. It could be that such matches are more important for physicians in private practices, because of long-term patient-doctor relationships, than in hospitals, where patients predominantly seek treatment for acute illnesses or those that require only limited care.

The results of our study show that the legal environment matters, particularly in relation to hospitals' state location. Although we predicted that Oregon hospitals would be significantly less likely to hire racial/ethnic minority professionals than California hospitals, we find no evidence of this. It is possible that the small number of Oregon hospitals in our sample obscures significant differences within this legal context. However, as predicted, we find that California hospitals are more likely to hire racial/ethnic minority professionals than are those located in the state of Washington. We believe this is largely a factor of the extensive fair employment legislation established in California. While Washington and Oregon have clearly established laws that address both gender and race/ethnicity-based discrimination, California's laws not only exceed those of many states throughout the United States, but the courts within this state have tended to take a strong stance against employment discrimination (CCH Legal Database 2011). In general, this suggests the importance of the legal environment, broadly defined, in regulating and promoting employment equality.

We initially hypothesized that hospitals operating in more locally competitive markets would have greater racial/ethnic professional diversity. Our findings support this prediction and show a substantial advantage for minority health care professionals as local competition increases. Consistent with the literature, we suspect that having more hospitals with which to compete not only increases opportunities for minorities in a given area but also improves working conditions, pay, and benefits. This is particularly likely as hospitals attempt to attract the highest-quality professionals and respond to public demands for fair employment opportunities.

In regard to hospitals' internal environment, our results show a significant effect of diversity among hospital managers on the racial/ethnic composition of health care professionals. We predicted that greater diversity in upper-level positions might influence the racial/ethnic composition of health care professionals as managers look to their same-race networks to recruit and hire workers. While the overall effect in our study is relatively small, it may be that having more minority managers affects diversity among professionals by signaling a hospital's commitment to fair employment practices and policies, which are likely to reduce perceived or real discrimination (see Elliott and Smith 2001). The analyses also provide support for our hypothesis that predicted a positive relationship between nurse unionization and diversity among health care professionals. We suspect that although nurse unions may largely seek to improve working conditions, they also place some emphasis on hospital recruiting and retention strategies that may increase the racial/ethnic diversity of all health care professionals.

Last, our results point to a significant difference in the racial/ethnic composition of health care professionals between urban and rural hospitals and between general and specialty facilities. Hospitals located in urban areas not only have the advantage of expanded cultural and social experiences but also tend to have a more diverse labor pool than do those in rural areas. These factors, along with the generally higher pay, expanded career opportunities, and lower workload demands, are likely to make urban hospitals attractive to a wider range of workers. Likewise, general hospitals—the majority of hospitals in our sample—may draw a wider labor pool through increased job opportunities for a wide range of health care professionals. We also find that the age of a hospital has a significant effect on the diversity of health care professionals. Older hospitals employ fewer racial/ethnic minority professionals than their more recently established counterparts. The implication of this is that founding period matters by shaping the types of internal practices and policies that either discourage or ignore issues of discrimination. Newer hospitals are likely to reflect more progressive public views about fair employment opportunities and may even be pressured to adopt comprehensive and restrictive policies that promote workplace equality. We suspect that both of these processes operate, at least to some degree, to shape diversity not only among health care professionals, but also among the more general hospital workforce.

Our findings are relevant to policy-makers concerned with laws governing the workplace. In particular, our findings indicating differences in diversity among health care professionals by state location illuminate the role that the legal environment plays in shaping fair employment opportunities in this workplace context and for organizational-level processes more generally (see also Beggs 1995; Skaggs 2009). Policy-makers must pay closer attention to how state laws, regulations, and court decisions influence diversity both within and across workplaces.

Second, our findings with regard to patient demographics suggest policy-makers should pay close attention to the importance of demographic matching between patients and health care providers. As the minority population in the United States continues to grow, so will demands for quality health care and health care providers within these racial/ethnic groups. Given this, policy-makers should note that institutional pressures may not be the best way to increase professional diversity. If improved health care quality and increased preventive care are truly issues at the forefront of policy, hospital administrators and private-practice practitioners must be mindful of creating strategies that will address the common demographic mismatches between health care professionals and patients.

Third, policy-makers should also take note of the positive relationship between minority managers and racial/ethnic minority health care professionals. This finding suggests that one pathway to increased racial/ethnic diversity among hospital professionals may be through establishing policies and guidelines that increase managerial diversity, perhaps by enforcing best practices (see Kalev, Dobbin, and Kelly 2006).

Our findings also have implications for scholarly research. First, the use of establishment-level data in this study has provided an opportunity to explore how external and internal organizational factors influence workplace diversity. Rarely are such data available, yet as we have demonstrated, an organization's reaction to internal and external pressures has real implications for the demographic composition of high-status professional workers. Second, the results related to market competition also have implications for how researchers think about diversity and workplace practices. This seems particularly relevant in an economy where competitive forces play a major role in the birth and death of organizations. Understanding how organizations respond to these types of external forces is likely to shape theory about organizational resource sharing and dependency as well as research in the areas of diversity and organizational profits.

This study also highlights the importance of understanding how managers influence key decisions related to workforce diversity. Our results suggest that managers from diverse racial/ethnic backgrounds may not only be invested in increasing their professional workforce and better able to accomplish this through social network ties to other minorities, but they may also ensure that equal opportunity policies are established and enforced. Future research should consider *how* managers shape internal fair employment policies and the extent to which numerical representation plays a role in carrying out these policies.

As with any research, this study has some limitations worth noting. The first involves the absence of data on the share of minority applicants to health care professional positions. If student diversity within medical and professional schools is limited, then this, in turn, has strong implications for the diversity of hospital applicant pools. Second, it has been more than a year since the passage of the Affordable Care Act, and states continue to debate the implementation of the law. In this uncertain legal environment, pressures for diversifying the health care workforce may come second to pressures for compliance with the law. The act also changes the relationship between health care providers and health insurers, yet we are not able to speak to how, if at all, insurance companies exert pressure for diversity on hospitals. Finally, the act increased patients' rights. As time passes, hospitals may see increasing pressures for diversity from minority patients. Given the cross-sectional nature of our data, we are unable to capture this possible change. Limitations aside, this article is among the first to demonstrate, with the most accurate demographic data available, what shapes workforce diversity in the United States' crucial health care industry.

Appendix A
Data Sources

Variable	Source
Racial/ethnic minorities in health care professional occupations	EEO-1 reports
Sector (public versus private)	Various hospital websites
Hospital size (# beds)	Various hospital websites
Minority patient base	Dartmouth Atlas of Healthcare (2003)
Hospital competition	Location and address matches using the MapQuest website
Nurse union	State nursing associations (e.g., Washington State Nurses Association, Oregon Nurses Association, California Nurses Association)
Racial/ethnic minorities in managerial occupations	EEO-1 reports
Urban location	State hospital directories (e.g., Washington State Department of Health, Oregon Office of Rural Health, California Rural Hospitals)
Membership in health care system	Various hospital websites
Hospital type	Hospital Soup website
Age	Various hospital websites

Notes

1. About 30 percent of Hispanic and 20 percent of black Americans lack a usual source of health care, compared with less than 16 percent of whites. Meanwhile, 16 percent of African Americans and 13 percent of Hispanic Americans rely on hospitals or clinics for their usual source of care, compared with 8 percent of white Americans (Agency for Healthcare Research and Quality 2000).

2. Hospital health care professionals include dietitians and nutritionists, optometrists, pharmacists, physicians and surgeons, physician assistants, podiatrists, registered nurses, audiologists, occupational therapists, physical therapists, radiation therapists, recreational therapists, respiratory therapists, speech-language pathologists, all other therapists, and all other health diagnosing and treating practitioners.

3. Throughout the text, we use the terms "racial/ethnic diversity" and "diversity" interchangeably.

4. An *establishment* refers to the specific place where workers carry out job tasks, while an *organization* refers to the parent company that encompasses all affiliated worksites.

5. Although not shown, we also tested separate models with a control for racial/ethnic minority representation in the local (county) and state labor markets. Because these measures are highly correlated with a hospital's minority patient base, we opted, based on theoretical importance, to include only the institutional measure of minority patient base.

References

Agency for Healthcare Research and Quality (AHRQ). 2000. Addressing racial and ethnic disparities in health care fact sheet. Rockville, MD: AHRQ. Available from www.ahrq.gov/research/disparit.htm.

American Association of Colleges of Nursing. 2004. AACN fact sheet. Available from www.aacn.nche.edu/Media/FactSheets/aacnfact.htm (accessed October 18, 2004).

American Association of Medical Colleges. 2009. Teaching hospitals. Available from www.aamc.org/teachinghospitals.htm (accessed December 30, 2009).

American Medical Association. 2009. Report on racial and ethnic disparities in health care. Available from www.ama-assn.org (accessed November 1, 2009).

American Society of Registered Nurses. 2007. California forecasts nursing shortage of 12,000 by 2014. Available from www.prlog.org (accessed November 10, 2009).

Becker, Gary. 1975. *Human capital.* New York, NY: National Bureau of Economic Research.

Beggs, John. 1995. The institutional environment: Implications for race and gender inequality in the U.S. labor market. *American Sociological Review* 60 (4): 612–33.

California Fair Employment and Housing Commission. 2009. The Fair Employment and Housing Act. Code Section 12960-12976. Available from www.fehc.ca.gov/act/pdf/FEHA_Outline.pdf (accessed December 30, 2009).

CCH Legal Database. 2011. Available from www.cch.com.

Collins, Karen Scott, Dora L. Hughes, Michelle M. Doty, Brett L. Ives, Jennifer N. Edwards, and Katie Tenney. 2002. *Diverse communities, common concerns: Assessing healthcare quality for minority Americans.* New York, NY: The Commonwealth Fund.

Cooper-Patrick, Lisa, Joseph J. Gallo, Junius J. Gonzales, Hong T. Vu, Neil R. Powe, Christine Nelson, and Daniel E. Ford. 1999. Race, gender and partnership in the physician-patient relationship. *Journal of the American Medical Association* 282:583–89.

Council on Graduate Medical Education (COGME). 2005. *Minorities in medicine: An ethnic and cultural challenge for physician training, an update.* COGME Seventeenth Report. Washington, DC: U.S. Department of Health and Human Services.

Dartmouth Atlas of Healthcare. 2003. 2003 zip code to HSA to HRR crosswalk file. Available from www.dartmouthatlas.org/faq.php (accessed July 6, 2005).

DiMaggio, Paul J., and Walter W. Powell. 1983. The iron cage revisited: Institutional isomorphism and collective rationality in organizational fields. *American Sociological Review* 48 (2): 147–60.

Dobbin, Frank R., Lauren B. Edelman, John W. Meyer, W. Richard Scott, and Ann Swidler. 1988. The expansion of due process in organizations. In *Institutional patterns and organizations: Culture and environment*, ed. Lynne G. Zucker, 71–98. Cambridge, MA: Ballinger.

Edelman, Lauren. 1992. Legal ambiguity and symbolic structures: Organizational mediation of civil rights law. *American Journal of Sociology* 97:1531–76.

Elliott, James R., and Ryan A. Smith. 2001. Ethnic matching of supervisors to subordinate work groups: Findings on "bottom-up" ascription and social closure. *Social Problems* 48:258–76.

Equal Employment Opportunity Commission (EEOC). 2005. The healthcare industry: Employment and the population they serve. Unpublished manuscript.

Equal Employment Opportunity Commission (EEOC). 2009. EEO-1 job classification guide. Available from www.eeoc.gov/eeo1survey/jobclassguide.html (accessed November 1, 2009).

Gray, Bradley, and Jeffrey J. Stoddard. 1997. Physician-patient pairing: Does racial and ethnic congruity influence selection of a regular physician? *Journal of Community Health* 22:247–59.

Grodsky, Eric, and Devah Pager. 2001. The structure of disadvantage: Individual and occupational determinants of the black-white wage gap. *American Sociological Review* 66 (4): 542–67.

Harper, Shannon, and Barbara F. Reskin. 2005. Affirmative action at school and work. *Annual Review of Sociology* 31:357–79.

Healthcare Personnel Shortage Task Force. 2002. Who will care for you? WA hospitals face a personnel crisis. Available from www.healthcarepersonnel.org/publications.htm (accessed November 15, 2004).

Herring, Cedric. 2009. Does diversity pay? Race, gender, and the business case for diversity. *American Sociological Review* 74:208–24.

Huffman, Matt L. 1999. Who's in charge? Organizational influences on women's representation in managerial positions. *Social Science Quarterly* 80:738–56.

Huffman, Matt L., Philip Cohen, and Jessica Pearlman. 2010. Engendering change: Organizational dynamics and workplace gender desegregation, 1975–2005. *Administrative Science Quarterly* 55:255–77.

Kalev, Alexandra, Frank Dobbin, and Erin A. Kelly. 2006. Best practices or best guesses? Assessing the efficacy of corporate affirmative action and diversity policies. *American Sociological Review* 71:589–617.

Kelly, Erin A., and Frank Dobbin. 1999. Civil rights law at work: Sex discrimination and the rise of maternity leave policies. *American Journal of Sociology* 105 (2): 455–92.

King, Eden B., Jennifer L. Knight, and Michelle R. Hebl. 2010. The influence of economic conditions on aspects of stigmatization. *Journal of Social Issues* 66:446–60.

LaVeist, Thomas A., and Tamyra Carroll. 2002. Race of physician and satisfaction with care among African American patients. *Journal of the National Medical Association* 94:937–43.

LaVeist, Thomas A., and Amani Nuru-Jeter. 2002. Is doctor-patient race concordance associated with greater satisfaction with care? *Journal of Health and Social Behavior* 43:296–306.

Lawton, Wendy. 2002. Hey, fellas: Operation tries to get guys into nursing. *The Oregonian*.

Marsden, Peter V., Cynthia V. Cook, and David Knoke. 1994. Measuring organizational structures and their environments. *American Behavioral Scientist* 37:891–910.

Meyer, John W., and Brian Rowan. 1977. Institutionalized organizations: Formal structure as myth and ceremony. *American Journal of Sociology* 83 (2): 340–63.

Meyer, John W., and Richard Scott. 1983. *Organizational environments: Ritual and rationality.* Beverly Hills, CA: Sage.

Nelson, Robert L., and William P. Bridges. 1999. *Legalizing gender inequality: Courts, markets, and unequal pay for women in America.* New York, NY: Cambridge University Press.

Oregon Center for Nursing. 2005. Oregon's nursing shortage: A public health crisis in the making. Available from www.oregon-centerfornursing.org/about/shortage.html (accessed February 15, 2005).

Robinson, Corre L., Tiffany Taylor, Donald Tomaskovic-Devey, Cathy Zimmer, and Matthew Irvin. 2005. Studying race and sex segregation at the establishment level: Methodological concerns and substantive opportunities in the use of EEO-1 data. *Work and Occupations* 32:5–38.

Rural Assistance Center. 2009. Why is there a health care workforce shortage problem in rural areas? Available from www.raconline.org (accessed December 30, 2009).

Saha, Somnath, Gretchen Guiton, Paul F. Wimmers, and LuAnn Wilkerson. 2008. Student body racial and ethnic composition and diversity-related outcomes in U.S. medical schools. *Journal of the American Medical Association* 300:1135–45.

Saha, Somnath, Miriam Komaromy, Thomas D. Koepsell, and Andrew B. Bindman. 1999. Patient-physician racial concordance and the perceived quality and use of healthcare. *Archives of Internal Medicine* 159:997–1004.

Saha, Somnath, and Scott A. Shipman. 2008. Race-neutral versus race-conscious workforce policy to improve access to care. *Health Affairs* 27:234–45.

Salancik, Gerald R. 1979. Interorganizational dependence and responsiveness to affirmative action: The case of women and defense contractors. *Academy of Management Journal* 22:375–94.

Scott, W. Richard. 2002. Organizations and the natural environment: Evolving models. In *Organizations, policy, and the natural environment: Institutional and strategic perspectives*, eds. Andrew Hoffman and Marc Ventresca, 453–64. Stanford, CA: Stanford University Press.

Scott, W. Richard. 2003. *Organizations: Rational, natural, and open systems*. 5th ed. Upper Saddle River, NJ: Prentice Hall.

Skaggs, Sheryl. 2009. Legal-political pressures and African American access to managerial jobs. *American Sociological Review* 74:225–44.

Stainback, Kevin, Corre Robinson, and Donald Tomaskovic-Devey. 2005. Race and workplace integration: A politically mediated process? *American Behavioral Scientist* 48:1200–29.

Stainback, Kevin, Sheryl L. Skaggs, and Donald Tomaskovic-Devey. 2010. Organizations and inequality: Inertia, relative power, and environments. *Annual Review of Sociology* 36:225–47.

Stinchcombe, Arthur L. 1965. Social structure and organizations. In *Handbook of organizations*, ed. James G. March, 142–93. Chicago, IL: Rand McNally.

Suchman, Mark C. 1995. Managing legitimacy: Strategic and institutional approaches. *Academy of Management Review* 20:571–610.

Sutton, Robert, Frank Dobbin, John W. Meyer, and W. Richard Scott. 1994. The legalization of the workplace. *American Journal of Sociology* 99:944–71.

Tynan, Ann, Elizabeth November, Joanna Lauer, Hoangmai H. Pham, and Peter Cram. 2009. General hospitals, specialty hospitals and financially vulnerable patients. *Research Brief, Center for Studying Health System Change* 11:1–8.

U.S. Bureau of Labor Statistics. 2007. Industry outlook. Available from www.bls.gov (accessed December 14, 2009).

U.S. Census Bureau. 2005a. Oregon quick facts. Available from http://quickfacts.cens-us.gov/qfd/states/41000.html (accessed August 20, 2005).

U.S. Census Bureau. 2005b. Washington quick facts. Available from http://quickfacts.cens-us.gov/qfd/states/53000.html (accessed August 20, 2005).

U.S. Census Bureau. 2009. DP-1 profile of general demographic characteristics: 2000 California. Available from http://factfinder.census.gov (accessed November 2, 2009).

U.S. Department of Health and Human Services (DHHS). 2009. *Ensuring that health care reform will meet the health care needs of minority communities and eliminate disparities*. Washington, DC: DHHS. Available from www.diversityconnection.org/diversityconnection/membership/ACMH_HealthCareAccessReport_October2009.pdf (accessed November 1, 2009).

Washington State Department of Personnel. 2004. Washington voters approve initiative banning affirmative action. Available from http://hr.dop.wa.gov/help-academy/resource/arrafact.htm (accessed January 29, 2004).

Washington State Nurses Association. 2004. Facilities with which WSNA has a current labor relations agreement. Available from www.ws-na.org/snas/wa/labor/facility.htm (accessed September 10, 2004).

Washington State Strategic Plan for Nursing. 2002. Ensuring a future nursing workforce. Available from www.wsna.org (accessed 14 December 2004).

White House. 2009. Health care: The president's plan. Available from www.whitehouse.gov (accessed November 24, 2009).

The Gender Gap in Executive Compensation: The Role of Female Directors and Chief Executive Officers

By
TAEKJIN SHIN

While many studies have explored the issue of women's representation among top management, little is known about the gender gap in compensation among those who reached the top. Using data on 7,711 executives at 831 U.S. firms, this study investigates social-psychological factors that explain the gender gap in executive compensation. Consistent with theories on social identity and demographic similarity effects, the gender gap in executive pay is smaller when a greater number of women sit on the compensation committee of the board, which is the group responsible for setting executive compensation. However, the presence of a female chief executive officer (CEO) is not associated with the compensation of female non-CEO executives working under the female boss. The findings highlight the need to study women's representation on corporate boards.

Keywords: gender; executive compensation; board of directors; compensation committee; chief executive officer; CEO

More than two decades after a *Wall Street Journal* article coined the term "glass ceiling" to describe the barriers to women's advancement at the top levels of corporations, women's representation among top management remains very low. According to a 2010 report, women constitute only 2 percent of chief executive officers (CEOs), 14 percent of top executives, and 16 percent of directors at Fortune 500 companies (Catalyst 2010). While the persistent underrepresentation of women at the very top has drawn much attention from academics, policymakers, and the public alike (e.g., Eagly and Carli 2007; *The Economist* 2005; Gorman and Kmec 2009; Oakley 2000), much less is known about how female top managers are

Taekjin Shin is an assistant professor at the School of Labor and Employment Relations at the University of Illinois at Urbana-Champaign. His research interests concern executive compensation, corporate governance, economic sociology, and wage inequality. He is currently studying the institutional explanation for the rise in executive compensation and the linkage between corporate downsizing and executive compensation.

DOI: 10.1177/0002716211421119

evaluated and rewarded once they achieve the top position. Are female top executives who break the glass ceiling rewarded the same as are their male counterparts? If gender disparities exist even at the very top, what explains the gap?

The issue of evaluation and compensation is inherently related to the issue of representation and access to top positions. The same kinds of social, cultural, and institutional barriers that keep women from climbing up the corporate hierarchy may also affect women who gain access to the top positions, making it more difficult for female managers to succeed in their positions. This is not just an issue for the few women who are currently in the top positions. Gender disparities and discrimination at the top may further hinder women's access to the top jobs and may discourage women at lower levels of the corporate hierarchy from aspiring to reach top management. Thus, the issue of gender disparities in compensation among top management is an important gap in our understanding of gender inequality in management.

In recent years, the compensation of corporate executives has become a highly contentious issue in the United States. In an era of stagnant wages, corporate downsizing, and high unemployment, excessive CEO compensation has received much attention from the public and has highlighted issues of fairness and equity (e.g., Colvin 2001; Kaplan 2008; Walsh 2008). While the public debate has centered on the issue of whether CEOs are overpaid, little attention has been paid to female executives, who may be significantly underpaid relative to their male counterparts. Studying gender inequality in the context of executive compensation complements the existing discussion about income inequality.

From a methodological point of view, studying executive compensation provides several advantages to the investigation of the gender gap in pay. One of the biggest challenges in studying the gender gap in pay has been the task of isolating the pure effect of gender while controlling for all other factors that may affect pay. Since top executive managers constitute a relatively homogeneous group, any differences between male and female executives can be largely attributed to gender discrimination. Another methodological advantage concerns the availability of rich information about employers and their employees. The conventional approach in the literature is to rely on data from a large-scale household survey, which lacks information about employers, or the case study of a single organization. Neither approach is based on information about a large number of employers matched with their employees. Studying executive compensation has a clear advantage in this regard. All publicly traded companies in the United States are required to disclose details on the compensation of their top executives as well as other accounting and finance information in their filings with the Securities and Exchange Commission (SEC). Many other details about top executives (e.g., career history) are also publicly available and easily linked to company-level data.

While many studies have examined the individual-level determinants (e.g., human capital) and economic factors (e.g., employer size) that affect the gender gap in pay (see Blau and Kahn [2000] and Leicht [2008] for reviews), this article focuses on social-psychological factors at the group level. Drawing from theories of social

ınizational demography, and women in leadership, this article formu-
ıses that explain the social-psychological sources of the gender gap
....ι compensation. Specifically, I hypothesize that the gender gap in pay
is smaller when there is a greater proportion of female directors on the compensation committee or board of directors responsible for monitoring and evaluating
management. I also predict that the gender pay gap is smaller when the company
has a female CEO, who may function as a role model or mentor for other female
executives and send out a positive signal to other constituencies (including male
executives and male directors) about the value of female executive talent, thereby
increasing the compensation of female non-CEO executives working under the
female CEO.

These hypotheses are tested using compensation data from 7,711 executives who
managed 831 firms during the period from 1998 to 2005. Consistent with the
hypothesis, female executives at firms where the compensation committee has a
greater proportion of women receive significantly greater compensation than female
executives at firms where the compensation committee has a smaller proportion of
women. However, there is no support for the hypothesis that the presence of a
female CEO is positively associated with the compensation of female non-CEOs
working under the female CEO. The findings imply that rather than having a female
leader in top management, having greater female representation on the board of
directors can generate a greater, more positive impact on female executives' compensation, thereby reducing the gender pay gap among top management.

Explaining the Gender Gap in Executive Compensation

While researchers have examined the gender wage gap in a variety of contexts,
few have systematically analyzed the gender gap in executive compensation.
A group of studies have explored the economic determinants of executive compensation, primarily by estimating regression models predicting the amount of
executive pay (Bertrand and Hallock 2001; Muñoz-Bullón 2010; Renner, Rives,
and Bowlin 2002). These studies provide two important findings: first, there exists
a significant pay gap between male and female executives, and second, some but
not all of the gap can be explained by economic factors at the individual or firm
level. For example, Bertrand and Hallock (2001) analyzed compensation data
from 1992 to 1997 and found that female executives were paid 45 percent less
than male executives. A large part of this gap was explained by characteristics
of the firms (e.g., firm size) and executives (e.g., job title, age, and tenure at the
company). Compared to male executives, female executives tended to manage
smaller companies and were less likely to hold the title of CEO, chair, or president. Female executives were also younger and had lower seniority in the companies (Bertrand and Hallock 2001). Muñoz-Bullón (2010) and Renner, Rives, and
Bowlin (2002) found that an unexplained gender gap in executive pay exists in the
performance-based components of compensation packages.

In addition to the amount of pay, the sensitivity of pay to company performance has been frequently studied in the mainstream literature on executive compensation (see Devers et al. [2007] and Finkelstein, Hambrick, and Cannella [2009] for reviews). Kulich et al. (2010) examined gender differences in the sensitivity of executive pay to firm performance using data from the United Kingdom and found that the compensation of male executives is more sensitive to firm performance than that of female executives. Based on this finding, Kulich et al. argued that compared to male executives, female executives are evaluated less favorably and receive lower compensation for the same level of performance as their male counterparts.

While existing studies on the gender gap in executive compensation provide descriptive information and valuable insights, the present study advances our knowledge in this topic by more directly incorporating social-psychological explanations into the analysis. To develop testable hypotheses, it is important to understand the process of setting executive compensation. The compensation packages of top executive managers are designed by the board of directors, which is legally responsible for monitoring, rewarding, and, if necessary, dismissing top executives. The board of directors is typically divided into several specialized committees. Virtually all publicly held companies in the United States have a compensation committee that is responsible for the design of the executive compensation packages (Ellig 2007).

Although the fiduciary duty of the board mandates that directors engage in arm's-length bargaining with executives to negotiate the most efficient contract to align managerial incentives with shareholder interest, there is ample evidence that board members in general and compensation committee members in particular are subject to various social, psychological, and political influences that thwart the arm's-length bargaining process (Bebchuk and Fried 2004; Devers et al. 2007; Finkelstein, Hambrick, and Cannella 2009). For example, executives with greater authority are paid more than those with less authority, controlling for other determinants of compensation (Main, O'Reilly, and Wade 1995; Wade, O'Reilly, and Chandratat 1990). More relevant to the present article, there is evidence that demographic similarities between CEOs and the board members affect CEO compensation. Westphal and Zajac (1995) found that demographic similarities between the CEO and the board were associated with greater CEO compensation; however, their measures of demographic similarity were not based on gender but on age, educational level, functional background, and insider/ outsider status. Young and Buchholtz (2002) examined whether the sensitivity of CEO pay to firm performance varies by demographic similarities between the CEO and the compensation committee members, hypothesizing that compensation committee members who are more dissimilar to the CEO tie the CEO's pay more closely to firm performance. Contrary to their prediction, a gender similarity between the CEO and the compensation committee was not related to sensitivity of CEO pay to performance, although dissimilarity in company tenure was positively associated with pay-performance sensitivity.

For the present study, theories on social identity, organizational demography, and women in leadership provide useful resources for developing testable hypotheses. Social identity theory suggests that people have a tendency to evaluate the competencies of in-group members more positively than those of out-group members (Tajfel 1982; Tajfel and Turner 1979; Hogg and Terry 2000). Board members may categorize executive managers into in- or out-group members based on perceived attributes, such as gender, with executives perceived to be in-group members more favorably evaluated than out-group executives. The implication is that male directors evaluate male executives more favorably than they evaluate female executives, resulting in higher pay for men than for women. Conversely, female directors evaluate female executives more favorably than they evaluate male executives, reducing the gender gap in pay. While this prediction concerns the process at the level of the evaluator-evaluatee (i.e., director-manager) dyad, the same logic can be applied when we consider the demographic composition of the group—either the board of directors or compensation committee. A greater proportion of female directors on the board or compensation committee should be associated with a more favorable evaluation of and higher pay for female (i.e., in-group) executives.

Organizational demography provides additional support for this hypothesis. Theoretically rooted in social identity theory, organizational demography proposes that the demographic characteristics of organizations, such as composition and segregation, in terms of gender, race, age, or organizational tenure, shape people's attitude about others as well as work relationships, which may in turn affect performance evaluation (Pfeffer 1983; Tsui and O'Reilly 1989). A demographic similarity in gender between an executive and the board of directors would facilitate mutual liking and attraction, which should be related to higher compensation for the executive. Based on these perspectives, the following hypothesis is tested:

Hypothesis 1: The gender gap in executive compensation is smaller when a greater proportion of women are on the compensation committee.

While the above hypothesis considers the demographic composition of the board members, the demographic profile of top management also matters. Women's representation at the very top of the corporate hierarchy may benefit the career success of other women in the organization. Women in senior executive positions may provide support for other female executives by serving as a mentor or role model, even without an explicit mentoring relationship (Ely 1994; Sealy and Singh 2010). Female mentors can be particularly crucial for female managers because they can protect the protégés from gender discrimination and provide legitimacy for female leadership (Ragins 1989). The presence of a female top executive can also be a proxy for the organization's unobserved cultural and institutional characteristics, such as female-friendliness, affirmative action policies, or an egalitarian culture. More specifically, female CEOs can be the most influential figures impacting the career success of other women in the organization. The CEO is the most visible and powerful decision-maker in an organization. Thus, the appointment of a female CEO may be beneficial to other female executives by providing legitimacy to female leadership, which may dilute the board members' stereotypical view of female leaders and contribute to a more favorable evaluation of female executives. These beneficial effects of female CEOs may result in relatively higher compensation for female executives working under female bosses. Therefore, I propose the following hypothesis on the female CEO's presence and the gender gap in compensation among non-CEO executives:

Hypothesis 2: Among non-CEO executives, the gender gap in executive compensation is smaller when the CEO is a woman.

Data and Methods

Sample

The compensation data come from Standard and Poor's (S&P) ExecuComp database. From this database, 1,367 companies included in the S&P 1500 index (S&P 500, S&P MidCap 400, and S&P SmallCap 600) in 1998 were selected. These companies were actively traded on one of the two largest U.S. stock markets—the New York Stock Exchange and the NASDAQ—and are representative of the population of publicly held companies. The present study traces these firms and their executives for the period of 1998 to 2005.

Among these firms, 831 companies that had a fiscal year end of December were selected to match the timing of accounting measures across the sample. More than half (61 percent) of the firms in the ExecuComp database had a fiscal year end of December. September was the second most frequently chosen fiscal year end, constituting 5 percent of the S&P 1500 firms in the ExecuComp database. The results of two-sample t-tests showed that firms with December as the fiscal year end were significantly bigger (in total sales) than the other firms, but there was no significant difference in firm performance (measured by return on assets [ROA], return on equity [ROE], and one-year total shareholder returns) between the two groups.

For each firm in the sample, ExecuComp provides compensation data for the five highest-paid executives in the company, including the CEO. The 831 firms in the sample include 7,827 executives who managed these companies for at least one year during 1998 to 2005. Six executives had affiliations with multiple firms in a given year. An additional 110 executives switched firms during the study period and therefore had multiple firm affiliations during the study period. After deleting such cases, the final sample included 7,711 executives (472 female [6 percent] and 7,239 male [94 percent]). The panel data include 27,643 executive-years, which are the unit of analysis.

Variables

The main dependent variable is the amount of total compensation awarded to each executive. ExecuComp provides this measure, which includes annual salary, bonuses, restricted stock grants, stock options (using the Black-Scholes method), and other long-term incentive pay. Logarithms of this value are used in the regression analysis to address outliers.

Gender is coded as a binary variable with the value equal to 1 for women and 0 for men. The ExecuComp database identifies the gender of each executive. To test hypothesis 1, the proportion of female members on the compensation committee as well as on the board of directors was calculated. Information about boards of directors comes from the RiskMetrics Directors Database, and any missing values were supplemented by information collected from the manual coding of proxy statements filed at the SEC. Hypothesis 2 was tested using a binary variable for the presence of a female CEO.

The regression models control for many variables at the individual manager and firm levels. At the individual level, executives who are also members of the board are identified. Such individuals are expected to have a greater influence on the board or at least to have more interpersonal interactions with the board members, which should positively contribute to the compensation awards. Executive job titles are categorized into eleven groups: CEO, chief finance officer (CFO), chief operating officer (COO), president, chair, vice chair, executive vice president (EVP), senior vice president (SVP), corporate counsel, corporate secretary, and all others. All other titles constitute the omitted reference category. Job titles were identified in ExecuComp and supplemented by a manual search of proxy statements and various biographic databases such as *Who's Who in Finance and Industry*, *Dun & Bradstreet Reference Book of Corporate Managements*, and the *International Directory of Company Histories* as well as company websites.

While economic theories (e.g., human capital theory) consider age and company tenure as key determinants of wages and compensation, information on executives' age and tenure is largely missing in ExecuComp: 53 percent of all observations have missing values for age, and nearly 63 percent have missing values for tenure. In the present study, the executive age and tenure variables are supplemented by hand-collected information from various biographic databases as well as proxy statements. This is done for a subsample of executives managing firms with at least one female executive present. More details are below.

Firm-level determinants of executive compensation include firm size and performance. In the present study, firm size is measured by the logarithm of total sales. Firm performance is measured in both accounting and market terms: ROA and one-year total shareholder returns.

While the hypothesis testing examines the gender composition of the compensation committee (and the board of directors), other characteristics of the compensation committee and the board may also affect compensation. CEOs typically have significant influence on the process of nominating directors, and the norms of reciprocity (Gouldner 1960) would suggest that directors appointed by the CEO may have a sense of indebtedness and obligation to the CEO. Such psychological tendency can make directors reluctant to object to increases in CEO compensation (Main, O'Reilly, and Wade 1995). The present study uses two measures of such an effect: the proportion of the compensation committee members appointed after the arrival of the CEO and the proportion of board members appointed after the arrival of the CEO.

Another important characteristic of the board is independence. Many scholars have hypothesized that board members who are more independent from the management act as more vigilant monitors, prevent excessive compensation awards, and more closely tie compensation to performance (Devers et al. 2007; Finkelstein, Hambrick, and Cannella 2009). The present study uses a typical measure of board independence: the proportion of board members who are outsiders. An outsider is defined as a board member who is not a current or former employee of the company; does not provide any professional services to the company (or the employer does not); and is not a major customer of the company, a recipient of charitable funds, an interlocking director, or a family member of a director or executive of the company. The U.S. Internal Revenue Code Section 162(m) requires that to qualify for a tax deduction, performance-based pay must be set by a compensation committee composed solely of outsiders (Ellig 2007), so virtually all compensation committee members are outsiders. Therefore, this study measures the proportion of outsiders only on the board, not on the compensation committee. In addition, dummy variables for year and two-digit standard industrial classifications (SIC) are included in all regression models. All dollar values, including compensation measures, are adjusted for inflation.

Analysis

The models are estimated using a random-effects regression with robust standard errors. Fixed-effects models cannot be estimated because variables that do not change over time, such as executive's gender, cannot be included in fixed-effects models. In random-effects models, information from both within and between observations is used to estimate the coefficients, so time-invariant variables such as gender can be included in the models. To check the robustness of the findings, alternative estimation techniques were used, including ordinary least squares (OLS), a generalized linear model (GLM) with one-year autocorrelation (Hardin and Hilbe 2007), and a three-level hierarchical linear model (HLM) with random intercepts (Raudenbush and Bryk 2001). Since the results are substantively similar across the various techniques, I present random-effects models as main results.

Results

Table 1 presents the descriptive statistics of the variables included in the analysis. Male executives receive greater compensation than female executives,

TABLE 1
Descriptive Statistics

	All Managers			Female Managers			Male Managers			Gender Difference
	Mean	SD	N	Mean	SD	N	Mean	SD	N	p-value
Ln(compensation)	7.258	1.067	26,851	6.926	0.975	1,324	7.275	1.069	25,527	.000***
Proportion women on compensation committee	0.102	0.154	24,774	0.134	0.176	1,341	0.101	0.152	23,433	.000***
Proportion women on the board	0.100	0.085	25,063	0.131	0.103	1,359	0.098	0.084	23,704	.000***
Executive is a director	0.347	0.476	27,643	0.147	0.354	1,378	0.358	0.479	26,265	.000***
CEO	0.218	0.413	27,643	0.065	0.246	1,378	0.226	0.418	26,265	.000***
COO	0.069	0.254	27,643	0.052	0.221	1,378	0.070	0.255	26,265	.003***
CFO	0.140	0.347	27,643	0.180	0.384	1,378	0.138	0.345	26,265	.000***
Chair	0.162	0.368	27,643	0.018	0.134	1,378	0.170	0.375	26,265	.000***
Vice chair	0.035	0.184	27,643	0.024	0.153	1,378	0.036	0.185	26,265	.007***
President	0.218	0.413	27,643	0.128	0.335	1,378	0.223	0.416	26,265	.000***
EVP	0.147	0.354	27,643	0.207	0.405	1,378	0.144	0.351	26,265	.000***
SVP	0.111	0.314	27,643	0.197	0.398	1,378	0.107	0.309	26,265	.000***
Counsel	0.046	0.208	27,643	0.093	0.290	1,378	0.043	0.203	26,265	.000***
Secretary	0.046	0.210	27,643	0.115	0.319	1,378	0.042	0.202	26,265	.000***
Ln(sales)	7.460	1.545	27,543	7.351	1.574	1,373	7.466	1.543	26,170	.008***
ROA	0.044	0.125	27,543	0.050	0.077	1,373	0.044	0.127	26,170	.006***
Total shareholder returns	1.153	71.811	27,393	0.174	0.469	1,361	1.204	73.664	26,032	.024**
Proportion of compensation committee members appointed by CEO	0.370	0.379	24,307	0.341	0.370	1,336	0.371	0.380	22,971	.004***
Proportion of directors appointed by CEO	0.372	0.309	24,567	0.349	0.300	1,353	0.374	0.310	23,214	.004***
Proportion of outside directors	0.680	0.164	25,063	0.695	0.168	1,359	0.680	0.164	23,704	.001***

**p < .05. ***p < .01.

TABLE 2
Regression Models Predicting
Total Compensation for Executive Managers

	Model 1	Model 2	Model 3	Model 4	Model 5	Model 6
Female	−.163°°°	−.237°°°	−.210°°°	−.185°°°	−.207°°°	−.129°°°
	(.032)	(.049)	(.042)	(.038)	(.039)	(.026)
Proportion women on comp. comm.	−.036		−.051	−.032	−.028	−.062°
	(.059)		(.072)	(.085)	(.042)	(.037)
Proportion women on comp. comm. × Female	.264°°		.330°°	.389°°°	.247°	.342°°°
	(.105)		(.159)	(.146)	(.143)	(.108)
Proportion women on the board		.112				
		(.137)				
Proportion women on the board × Female		.829°°°				
		(.269)				
Executive is a director	.273°°°	.271°°°	.242°°°	.266°°°	.246°°°	.293°°°
	(.023)	(.023)	(.026)	(.028)	(.024)	(.015)
CEO	.514°°°	.513°°°	.400°°°	.564°°°	.554°°°	.540°°°
	(.028)	(.028)	(.031)	(.032)	(.031)	(.019)
COO	.234°°°	.234°°°	.187°°°	.290°°°	.264°°°	.264°°°
	(.024)	(.024)	(.027)	(.031)	(.027)	(.018)
CFO	.074°°°	.074°°°	.066°°°	.079°°°	.063°°°	.091°°°
	(.015)	(.015)	(.019)	(.015)	(.020)	(.014)
Chair	.209°°°	.209°°°	.194°°°	.237°°°	.204°°°	.196°°°
	(.026)	(.025)	(.029)	(.032)	(.030)	(.018)
Vice chair	.122°°°	.122°°°	.123°°°	.209°°°	.113°°°	.117°°°
	(.032)	(.032)	(.040)	(.041)	(.035)	(.026)
President	.103°°°	.102°°°	.142°°°	.145°°°	.093°°°	.130°°°
	(.016)	(.016)	(.019)	(.020)	(.019)	(.013)
EVP	.070°°°	.070°°°	.056°°°	.097°°°	.056°°°	.068°°°
	(.019)	(.019)	(.021)	(.026)	(.019)	(.014)
SVP	−.012	−.013	−.026	−.021	−.056°°°	−.029°
	(.021)	(.021)	(.022)	(.029)	(.020)	(.016)
Counsel	−.032	−.033	−.018	−.068°	−.045	−.060°°
	(.029)	(.029)	(.035)	(.035)	(.037)	(.026)
Secretary	−.074°°	−.072°°	−.059	−.069°	−.061	−.054°°
	(.033)	(.033)	(.041)	(.038)	(.040)	(.026)
Ln(sales)	.399°°°	.397°°°	.376°°°	.402°°°	.394°°°	.382°°°
	(.013)	(.013)	(.015)	(.014)	(.007)	(.009)
ROA	.060	.059	−0.062	.009	.142°	.074°°
	(.095)	(.096)	(.078)	(.094)	(.075)	(.035)
Total shareholder returns	.079°°°	.079°°°	.164°°°	.119°°°	.069°°°	.061°°°
	(.016)	(.016)	(.020)	(.023)	(.010)	(.008)

(continued)

TABLE 2 (continued)

	Model 1	Model 2	Model 3	Model 4	Model 5	Model 6
Proportion of comp. comm. members appointed by CEO	.019 (.048)	.019 (.048)	−0.006 (.055)	.015 (.075)	.072°° (.033)	.005 (.029)
Proportion of directors appointed by CEO	.072 (.059)	.072 (.059)	.124° (.067)	.115 (.093)	.015 (.041)	.064° (.035)
Proportion of outside directors	.262°°° (.074)	.248°°° (.074)	.280°°° (.082)	.392°°° (.101)	.321°°° (.046)	.200°°° (.039)
Constant	3.596°°° (.122)	3.597°°° (.122)	4.420°°° (.143)	3.429°°° (.127)	3.581°°° (.083)	3.748°°° (.458)
N	23,528	23,528	16,035	23,528	19,086	23,528

NOTE: Robust standard errors are in the parentheses.
°$p < .10.$ °°$p < .05.$ °°°$p < .01$ (two-tailed test).

and the difference is statistically significant. In real dollar terms, men are paid $1,443,607 (in 2000 dollars) on average, while women receive $1,018,107 (in 2000 dollars) on average, or 42 percent less than men. There are gender differences in all other variables as well. Female executives tend to manage firms with greater proportions of females on the compensation committee and board as compared with men. Female managers are less likely than male managers to be a board member. Women are far less represented in higher-ranking positions such as CEO, COO, chair, and president and are more likely to hold positions such as EVP, SVP, counsel, and secretary. Women tend to manage smaller companies. Other studies have documented these differences, attributing them to the main sources of the gender gap in pay (Bertrand and Hallock 2001; Muñoz-Bullón 2010). In addition, Table 1 shows that firms with women executives have smaller proportions of compensation committee members and board members who were appointed by the CEO and a greater proportion of outside directors.

Table 2 shows the results of the random-effects regression models predicting the amount of total compensation (in logarithm). All models in this study include dummy variables for year and two-digit industry, which are not presented in the tables. In all models, coefficients for the female dummy variable demonstrate a significant gender gap in pay. Model 1 suggests that women are paid about 16 percent less than men after controlling for individual- and firm-level factors included in the model. The coefficient for the proportion of female directors on the compensation committee is negative but not significant, suggesting that the compensation of male executives is not significantly lower when there is a greater representation of women on the compensation committee than when women's representation is smaller. The interaction term between the female indicator variable and the proportion of women on the compensation committee is used to test hypothesis 1, which predicted that the gender gap in executive compensation

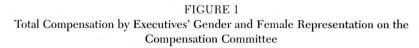

FIGURE 1
Total Compensation by Executives' Gender and Female Representation on the
Compensation Committee

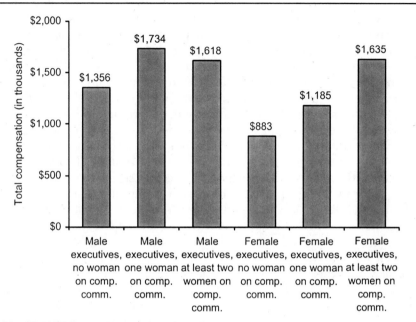

is smaller when there are more women on the compensation committee. The inter-action term is positive and significant at the 5 percent level, providing support for hypothesis 1.

To illustrate this effect in real dollar terms, Figure 1 shows a comparison of the predicted values of total compensation for men and women separately based on the level of female representation on the compensation committee. For male executives, compensation does not vary systematically by the level of female rep-resentation. For women, however, compensation rises when more women are on the compensation committee. Female executives in a firm where the compensation committee does not include female members receive $883,000 on average. Adding one woman on the committee increases female executives' pay by $302,000, mak-ing the average $1,185,000—equivalent to a 34 percent increase. Having at least two women on the committee increases the pay of female executives by another $450,000. This makes the average pay $1,635,000, which is an additional 38 percent increase. For firms with at least two women on the compensation committee, the gender gap in pay seems to disappear. Indeed, when the regression model (model 1) is estimated only for executives at firms with at least two women on the compensation committee, the coefficient on the female dummy variable becomes insignificant (results available from the author).

To check the robustness of the findings, models 2 through 6 use alternative measures and estimation techniques. Instead of the proportion of women on the compensation committee, model 2 uses the proportion of women on the board of directors. The results are substantively similar; women's representation on the board is positively associated with the compensation of women but not that of men. In model 3, all independent variables are lagged by one year. The results remain substantially the same. The next three models (models 4 through 6) use alternative estimating techniques: OLS with robust standard errors (model 4), GLM with one-year autocorrelation (model 5), and a three-level HLM with random intercepts (model 6). Model 6 exploits the nested structure of the data. The data have repeated observations for each year nested within executive managers, which in turn are nested within firms. Executives at the same firm constitute a top management team and share many firm-level attributes. The random intercept model estimates a randomly varying intercept assigned to each firm, rather than requiring all managers across all firms to share a fixed constant (Raudenbush and Bryk 2001). Regardless of the estimating technique, the substantive finding remains the same. Female representation on the compensation committee is positively associated with the compensation of female managers.

Certain job titles (CEO, COO, CFO, chair, vice chair, president, and EVP) are associated with higher compensation, while corporate secretaries tend to earn less than managers with all other job titles. As seen in Table 1, women are significantly underrepresented in high-paying jobs (except for EVP) but are overrepresented among secretaries. Consistent with other studies, executive compensation is positively associated with firm size (measured in sales) and firm performance (measured in total shareholder returns). The proportions of directors and compensation committee members appointed by the CEO are not significantly related to executive compensation. Having a greater proportion of outside directors is positively associated with compensation.

Hypothesis 2 predicted that the gender gap in executive compensation would be smaller when the CEO is a woman. To test this, the sample was restricted to non-CEOs. Table 3 presents the random-effects regression results. In model 1, the interaction term between the female indicator and the presence of a female CEO is not significant, although the direction of the effect is consistent with the hypothesis. The interaction between female executive and female representation on the compensation committee is still positive and significant, further supporting hypothesis 1. Model 2 uses one-year lagged independent variables. The interaction term between female and female CEO is still insignificant.

The impact of female CEOs on other executives may depend on their tenure as CEO. Newly appointed CEOs simply do not have time to provide direct support to other women or to prove their own competency to those skeptical about female leadership. For this reason, model 3 controls for the CEO's tenure in the position. The interaction between female variable and female CEO variable remains insignificant. Finally, model 4 excludes all cases where the CEO is relatively new, defined here as those with less than two years as CEO. Again, the results do not

TABLE 3
Random-Effects Regression Models Predicting Total
Compensation for Non-CEO Executive Managers

	Model 1	Model 2	Model 3	Model 4
Female	−.166***	−.197***	−.165***	−.174***
	(.033)	(.040)	(.032)	(.034)
Proportion women on comp. comm.	−.042	−.003	−.044	−.035
	(.061)	(.075)	(.061)	(.067)
Proportion women on comp. comm. × Female	.264**	.297**	.263**	.284**
	(.109)	(.148)	(.109)	(.126)
Female CEO	−.001	−.025	−.006	−.052
	(.093)	(.139)	(.092)	(.150)
Female CEO × Female	.148	−.039	.149	.164
	(.117)	(.177)	(.116)	(.147)
Executive is a director	.231***	.166***	.233***	.229***
	(.025)	(.028)	(.025)	(.027)
COO	.219***	.141***	.219***	.231***
	(.024)	(.030)	(.024)	(.026)
CFO	.081***	.079***	.080***	.081***
	(.015)	(.019)	(.015)	(.017)
Chair	.297***	.239***	.294***	.226***
	(.047)	(.052)	(.047)	(.056)
Vice chair	.159***	.168***	.158***	.186***
	(.035)	(.042)	(.036)	(.036)
President	.158***	.172***	.158***	.166***
	(.023)	(.026)	(.023)	(.024)
EVP	.080***	.062***	.080***	.096***
	(.020)	(.023)	(.020)	(.023)
SVP	−.001	−.017	−.002	.004
	(.022)	(.022)	(.022)	(.024)
Counsel	−.023	−.013	−.024	−.046
	(.029)	(.035)	(.030)	(.033)
Secretary	−.072**	−.045	−.073**	−.054
	(.033)	(.041)	(.033)	(.036)
Ln(sales)	.392***	.369***	.391***	.387***
	(.014)	(.016)	(.014)	(.015)
ROA	−.004	−.098	−.002	−.036
	(.090)	(.102)	(.091)	(.071)
Total shareholder returns	.067***	.153***	.067***	.077***
	(.015)	(.021)	(.015)	(.019)
Proportion of compensation committee members appointed by CEO	.023	−.012	.030	.030
	(.047)	(.055)	(.047)	(.050)

(continued)

TABLE 3 (continued)

	Model 1	Model 2	Model 3	Model 4
Proportion of directors appointed by CEO	.032	.099	.084	.113
	(.057)	(.066)	(.065)	(.077)
Proportion of outside directors	.267°°°	.250°°°	.257°°°	.278°°°
	(.073)	(.081)	(.074)	(.079)
CEO tenure			−.004	−.005°
			(.003)	(.003)
Constant	3.633°°°	4.203°°°	3.655°°°	3.560°°°
	(.122)	(.144)	(.124)	(.132)
N	18,327	11,781	18,327	14,711

NOTE: Robust standard errors are in the parentheses.
$°p < .10.$ $°°p < .05.$ $°°°p < .01$ (two-tailed test).

support hypothesis 2. The other estimating techniques (OLS, GLM, and HLM) also fail to support hypothesis 2 (results available from the author).

One limitation of the ExecuComp data is that information on executives' age and tenure is often missing. As a remedy, this study added hand-collected information about age and tenure for a subsample of firms with at least one female executive. Three hundred and thirty firms (40 percent of the firms in the main sample) had at least one female executive, which means that 60 percent of the firms in the main sample did not have a woman among the top five executives. Firms with at least one female executive have a total of 2,273 executive managers: 472 women and 1,801 men. After adding hand-collected information about age and tenure, the percentage of missing values is reduced from 53 percent to 7 percent for the age variable and from 63 percent to 10 percent for the tenure variable. Besides reducing the number of missing values, this approach has an added benefit of restricting the sample to a presumably more homogeneous set of firms. Companies that have at least one female top executive can be considered different—in terms of organizational culture, policies, or other unobservable characteristics—from a majority of other firms that do not have any female top executives. Restricting the sample to a homogeneous set of firms reduces the impact of unobserved heterogeneities that can bias the estimation. Table 4 presents the results of the random-effects models. Models 1 to 4 test hypothesis 1. Model 1 here is identical to model 1 presented in Table 2. Models 2 to 4 add age and tenure variables, in both linear and squared terms. Consistent with hypothesis 1, the interaction terms between the female dummy variable and the proportion of women on the compensation committee are positive and significant in all models. Interestingly, the age and tenure variables are not significant.

Models 5 to 8 in Table 4 test hypothesis 2 using the non-CEO sample. The data do not support the hypothesis, as the interaction terms between female and

TABLE 4

Random-Effects Regression Models Predicting Total
Compensation for Executives at Firms with at Least One Female Executive

	All Managers				Non-CEOs Only			
	Model 1	Model 2	Model 3	Model 4	Model 5	Model 6	Model 7	Model 8
Female	-.126***	-.134***	-.127***	-.132***	-.118***	-.124***	-.121***	-.123***
	(.026)	(.028)	(.027)	(.028)	(.026)	(.027)	(.026)	(.027)
Proportion women on comp. comm.	-.031	-.035	-.025	-.032	-.063	-.070	-.052	-.064
	(.112)	(.114)	(.113)	(.114)	(.112)	(.115)	(.112)	(.115)
Proportion women on comp. comm. × Female	.241***	.258***	.252***	.259***	.243***	.264***	.255***	.269***
	(.085)	(.087)	(.089)	(.091)	(.092)	(.095)	(.097)	(.099)
Female CEO					.045	.049	.040	.043
					(.110)	(.111)	(.111)	(.111)
Female CEO × Female					.096	.086	.113	.102
					(.117)	(.117)	(.117)	(.117)
Executive is a director	.296***	.307***	.306***	.313***	.238***	.247***	.247***	.251***
	(.048)	(.049)	(.049)	(.049)	(.045)	(.046)	(.046)	(.046)
CEO	.503***	.500***	.513***	.508***				
	(.068)	(.068)	(.069)	(.069)				
COO	.199***	.196***	.229***	.222***	.173***	.173***	.200***	.194***
	(.053)	(.054)	(.054)	(.055)	(.051)	(.052)	(.052)	(.053)
CFO	.106***	.102***	.105***	.100***	.109***	.106***	.109***	.105***
	(.024)	(.024)	(.024)	(.024)	(.024)	(.024)	(.024)	(.024)
Chair	.258***	.271***	.261***	.275***	.382***	.402***	.385***	.402***
	(.057)	(.058)	(.058)	(.058)	(.100)	(.103)	(.101)	(.105)
Vice chair	.136**	.142**	.152**	.156**	.167**	.172***	.184***	.187***
	(.067)	(.067)	(.068)	(.068)	(.065)	(.065)	(.065)	(.065)
President	.173***	.164***	.161***	.156***	.276***	.265***	.273***	.270***
	(.041)	(.041)	(.042)	(.043)	(.053)	(.053)	(.054)	(.055)
EVP	.051	.050	.058	.055	.075*	.074*	.084**	.082**
	(.042)	(.042)	(.039)	(.039)	(.043)	(.043)	(.040)	(.040)
SVP	.011	.013	.013	.013	.036	.039	.040	.041
	(.042)	(.042)	(.041)	(.042)	(.044)	(.045)	(.044)	(.044)

(continued)

TABLE 4 (continued)

	All Managers				Non-CEOs Only			
	Model 1	Model 2	Model 3	Model 4	Model 5	Model 6	Model 7	Model 8
Counsel	-.055	-.046	-.060	-.050	-.053	-.048	-.055	-.049
	(.048)	(.047)	(.049)	(.048)	(.047)	(.047)	(.049)	(.049)
Secretary	-.123°°	-.124°°	-.110°°	-.113°°	-.120°°	-.121°°	-.111°°	-.112°°
	(.050)	(.050)	(.051)	(.051)	(.050)	(.050)	(.052)	(.052)
Ln(sales)	.381°°°	.381°°°	.376°°°	.376°°°	.364°°°	.364°°°	.355°°°	.356°°°
	(.023)	(.023)	(.023)	(.024)	(.023)	(.024)	(.023)	(.024)
ROA	.555°	.555°	.524°	.519°	.437	.431	.404	.394
	(.291)	(.296)	(.299)	(.304)	(.305)	(.312)	(.312)	(.319)
Total shareholder returns	.039	.038	.043	.040	.027	.027	.028	.026
	(.035)	(.035)	(.036)	(.036)	(.032)	(.032)	(.033)	(.033)
Proportion of comp. comm. members appointed by CEO	.025	.018	.041	.040	.044	.032	.062	.057
	(.108)	(.106)	(.109)	(.109)	(.104)	(.102)	(.104)	(.103)
Proportion of directors appointed by CEO	.001	.017	-.020	-.010	-.069	-.049	-.094	-.081
	(.127)	(.126)	(.129)	(.128)	(.123)	(.121)	(.124)	(.123)
Proportion of outside directors	.252°	.258°	.252°	.256°	.258°	.264°°	.263°°	.268°°
	(.137)	(.136)	(.136)	(.136)	(.133)	(.131)	(.128)	(.128)
Age		-.005		-.004		-.005		-.005
		(.016)		(.016)		(.017)		(.018)
Age²		.000		.000		.000		.000
		(.000)		(.000)		(.000)		(.000)
Tenure			-.003	-.002			-.001	-.001
			(.002)	(.002)			(.003)	(.003)
Tenure²			.000	.000			.000	.000
			(.000)	(.000)			(.000)	(.000)
Constant	3.492°°°	3.674°°°	3.491°°°	3.630°°°	3.623°°°	3.771°°°	3.621°°°	3.762°°°
	(.191)	(.497)	(.191)	(.498)	(.187)	(.529)	(.186)	(.535)
N	5,128	5,080	4,909	4,870	4,000	3,952	3,814	3,775

NOTE: Robust standard errors are in the parentheses.
°p < .10. °°p < .05. °°°p < .01 (two-tailed test).

274

female CEO are not significant in any specification, while the interaction is significant between female and female representation on the compensation committee. Overall, the results from the subsample further support the findings: the compensation of female executives is significantly higher when more women are on the compensation committee, but the compensation is unrelated to the presence of a female CEO.

Discussions and Conclusion

Drawing from social identity theory, organizational demography, and theories about women in leadership, hypotheses were developed in this study regarding the effects of social-psychological factors on the gender gap in executive compensation. Theories about in-group bias and a demographic similarity effect suggest that women serving on the compensation committee are likely to evaluate female executives' leadership and competence more favorably, thereby granting greater compensation packages to female executives as compared with the men on the compensation committee. The empirical analysis supports this hypothesis. As the proportion of women on the compensation committee increases, the gender gap in executive compensation narrows. At firms with at least two women on the compensation committee, there is virtually no gender gap in executive pay. On average, the compensation committee has four members, so having two women on the compensation committee means having a gender-balanced committee. Few firms (10 percent in the sample) have such a level of female representation. A majority of the firms (81 percent in the sample) have an all-male compensation committee.

The findings about the compensation committee are consistent with social identity theory's predictions about in-group bias and a demographic similarity effect. Women evaluate other women more favorably compared with men's evaluation of women, but do women evaluate men less favorably than they evaluate women? This can be checked from the main effect of the compensation committee composition. In all models, the coefficients for the main effect indicate that the proportion of women on the compensation committee is not significantly associated with the compensation of male executives, with the exception of the results from HLM (model 6 in Table 2), where the main effect is marginally significant ($p = .09$). The gender composition of the compensation committee does not significantly affect the compensation of men, as Figure 1 also suggests. The implication is that the effect of in-group bias and demographic similarity is not gender neutral. A status difference between men and women may be the key dimension, where the higher-status group (i.e., men) is evaluated more favorably on average than the lower-status group (i.e., women), even if individuals with higher status are out-group members from the perspective of female directors (Berger, Rosenholtz, and Zelditch 1980; Oldmeadow et al. 2003). A simple account of in-group bias and demographic similarity cannot fully explain the nuanced differences in gender inequality.

This study demonstrates the link between female directors on the board and the gender gap in executive compensation. If women's representation on the compensation committee and board of directors is crucial in narrowing the gender inequality in corporate leadership, how do we bring more women to the compensation committee and the board? In the sample used in this study, compensation committees had on average 0.4 women, and the boards had an average of one female director. Most of these women are tokens in male-dominated boardrooms (Kanter 1977). A recent study shows that there is no gender difference in assignment to compensation committees: once on the board, women are as likely as men to sit on compensation committees (Peterson and Philpot 2007). This suggests that the real question is how to increase the number of women joining boards of directors.

While there has been a large amount of research on women's representation in top management, research on women's representation on the board of directors is needed. Such research will help us to understand the barriers female managers face in reaching the boardroom and public policies that can help companies to increase female representation on the board. A possible policy intervention is to impose a mandatory quota that would force companies to appoint a certain proportion of women to their boards. The experience in European countries is illustrative. In 2005, Norway required that the boards of publicly held companies be at least 40 percent women, and France and Spain recently committed to the same quota (*The Economist* 2010). More research about the impact of such quotas and challenges in implementing such measures is needed.

In the current study, I also hypothesized that the presence of a female top decision-maker contributes to the career success of other female managers working under her through the development of actual mentorship relationships or by providing a positive role model that weakens stereotypical views of women's leadership and strengthens women's professional self-image. Such benefits of a female leader at the very top should lead to a narrowing of the gender gap in pay. However, the data do not support this hypothesis. In many alternative models, the presence of a female CEO is not associated with an increase in the compensation of female executives.

Why is there no linkage between the presence of female CEOs and executive compensation for women? One possibility is that many female CEOs may not be available for active mentoring relationships. For top managers who need to juggle demanding job requirements and performance pressures, developing effective mentoring relationships may be a challenge. Rather than acting as a supportive mentor, some female CEOs might be subject to what is called "queen bee syndrome" (Staines, Jayaratne, and Tavris 1974; Mavin 2008), which describes highly successful women who are rewarded by men for denigrating other women and keeping other women from achieving success. If relationships between female executives are more competitive than supportive, female managers may perceive their female bosses more as competitors than as positive role models.

Another possible explanation for the lack of linkage between the presence of female CEOs and executive compensation is based on the facts that the compensation of female CEOs is, on average, lower than that of their male counterparts and that the compensation of non-CEOs is usually set relative to CEO compensation so that there is a certain ratio between ranks (Carpenter and Sanders 2002). Therefore, lower pay for the CEO may trickle down to other executives and suppress other executives' compensation. This may offset any positive effect of having a female CEO on non-CEOs' compensation.

To summarize, this study documented a significant gender gap in executive compensation and sought to find social-psychological explanations for this gap. The longitudinal analysis of compensation data suggests that the gender pay gap varies significantly depending on the gender composition of the board of directors or the compensation committee but is not dependent on the gender of the CEO. Specifically, the gender pay gap is significantly smaller as women's representation on the board of directors or the compensation committee increases. However, the presence of a female CEO does not affect the compensation of female executives working under the female CEO. While much research effort has been devoted to the issue of women's representation among top management, a financial impact of having a female CEO on other female executives is not found. The present findings highlight the need for future research on women's representation on the board of directors. Public policy efforts that aim to reduce gender inequality in management should focus more on providing support for women to gain requisite industry experience and helping companies find qualified women for the boards.

References

Bebchuk, Lucian, and Jesse M. Fried. 2004. *Pay without performance: The unfulfilled promise of executive compensation*. Cambridge, MA: Harvard University Press.

Berger, Joseph, Susan J. Rosenholtz, and Morris Zelditch. 1980. Status organizing processes. *Annual Review of Sociology* 6:479–508.

Bertrand, Marianne, and Kevin F. Hallock. 2001. The gender gap in top corporate jobs. *Industrial and Labor Relations Review* 55 (1): 3–21.

Blau, Francine D., and Lawrence M. Kahn. 2000. Gender differences in pay. *Journal of Economic Perspectives* 14 (4): 75–99.

Carpenter, Mason A., and W. M. Gerard Sanders. 2002. Top management team compensation: The missing link between CEO pay and firm performance? *Strategic Management Journal* 23:367–75.

Catalyst. 2010. *2010 Catalyst census: Fortune 500 women executive officers and top earners*. New York, NY: Catalyst.

Colvin, Geoffrey. 25 June 2001. The great CEO pay heist. *Fortune*.

Devers, Cynthia E., Albert A. Cannella, Gregory P. Reilly, and Michele E. Yoder. 2007. Executive compensation: A multidisciplinary review of recent developments. *Journal of Management* 33 (6): 1016–72.

Eagly, Alice H., and Linda L. Carli. September 2007. Women and the labyrinth of leadership. *Harvard Business Review*, 63–71.

The Economist. 23 July 2005. The conundrum of the glass ceiling.

The Economist. 11 March 2010. Skirting the issue.

Ellig, Bruce. 2007. *The complete guide to executive compensation*. 2nd ed. New York, NY: McGraw-Hill.

Ely, Robin J. 1994. The effects of organizational demographics and social identity on relationships among professional women. *Administrative Science Quarterly* 39:203–38.

Finkelstein, Sydney, Donald C. Hambrick, and Albert A. Cannella. 2009. *Strategic leadership: Theory and research on executives, top management teams, and boards.* New York, NY: Oxford University Press.

Gorman, Elizabeth H., and Julie A. Kmec. 2009. Hierarchical rank and women's organizational mobility: Glass ceilings in corporate law firms. *American Journal of Sociology* 5:1428–74.

Gouldner, Alvin W. 1960. The norm of reciprocity: A preliminary statement. *American Sociological Review* 23 (2): 161–78.

Hardin, James W., and Joseph M. Hilbe. 2007. *Generalized linear models and extensions.* College Station, TX: Stata.

Hogg, Michael A., and Deborah J. Terry. 2000. Social identity and self-categorization process in organizational contexts. *Academy of Management Review* 25 (1): 121–40.

Kanter, Rosabeth Moss. 1977. *Men and women of the corporation.* New York, NY: Basic Books.

Kaplan, Steven N. 2008. Are U.S. CEOs overpaid? *Academy of Management Perspectives* 22 (2): 5–20.

Kulich, Clara, Grzegorz Trojanowski, Michelle K. Ryan, S. Alexander Haslam, and Luc D. R. Renneboog. 2010. Who gets the carrot and who gets the stick? Evidence of gender disparities in executive remuneration. *Strategic Management Journal* 32 (3): 301–21.

Leicht, Kevin T. 2008. Broken down by race and gender? Sociological explanations of new sources of earnings inequality. *Annual Review of Sociology* 34:237–55.

Main, Brian G. M., Charles A. O'Reilly, and James Wade. 1995. The CEO, the board of directors and executive compensation: Economic and psychological perspectives. *Industrial and Corporate Change* 4 (2): 293–332.

Mavin, Sharon. 2008. Queen bees, wannabees, and afraid to bees: No more "best enemies" for women in management? *British Journal of Management* 19:S75–S84.

Muñoz-Bullón, Fernando. 2010. Gender-compensation differences among high-level executives in the United States. *Industrial Relations* 49 (3): 346–70.

Oakley, Judith G. 2000. Gender-based barriers to senior management positions: Understanding the scarcity of female CEOs. *Journal of Business Ethics* 27:321–34.

Oldmeadow, Julian A., Michael J. Platow, Margaret Foddy, and Donna Anderson. 2003. Self-categorization, status, and social influence. *Social Psychological Quarterly* 66 (2): 138–52.

Peterson, Craig, and James Philpot. 2007. Women's roles on U.S. Fortune 500 boards: Director expertise and committee memberships. *Journal of Business Ethics* 72 (2): 177–96.

Pfeffer, Jeffrey. 1983. Organizational demography. *Research in Organizational Behavior* 5:299–357.

Ragins, Belle Rose. 1989. Barriers to mentoring: The female manager's dilemma. *Human Relations* 42 (1): 1–22.

Raudenbush, Stephen W., and Anthony S. Bryk. 2001. *Hierarchical linear models: Applications and data analysis methods.* 2nd ed. Thousand Oaks, CA: Sage.

Renner, Celia, Janet M. Rives, and William F. Bowlin. 2002. The significance of gender in explaining senior executive pay variations: An exploratory study. *Journal of Managerial Issues* 14 (3): 331–45.

Sealy, Ruth H. V., and Val Singh. 2010. The importance of role models and demographic context for senior women's work identity development. *International Journal of Management Reviews* 12 (3): 284–300.

Staines, Graham L., Toby E. Jayaratne, and Carol Tavris. 1974. The queen bee syndrome. *Psychology Today* 7 (8): 55–60.

Tajfel, Henri. 1982. Social psychology of intergroup relations. *Annual Review of Psychology* 33:1–39.

Tajfel, Henri, and John C. Turner. 1979. An integrative theory of intergroup conflict. In *The social psychology of intergroup relations*, eds. William G. Austin and Stephen Worchel, 39–47. Monterey, CA: Brooks-Cole.

Tsui, Anne S., and Charles A. O'Reilly. 1989. Beyond simple demographic effects: The importance of relational demography in superior-subordinate dyads. *Academy of Management Journal* 32 (2): 402–23.

Wade, James, Charles A. O'Reilly, and Ike Chandratat. 1990. Golden parachutes: CEOs and the exercise of social influence. *Administrative Science Quarterly* 35 (4): 587–603.

Walsh, James P. 2008. CEO compensation and the responsibilities of the business scholar to society. *Academy of Management Perspectives* 22 (2): 5–20.

Westphal, James D., and Edward J. Zajac. 1995. Who shall govern? CEO/board power, demographic similarity, and new director selection. *Administrative Science Quarterly* 40:60–83.

Young, Michael N., and Ann K. Buchholtz. 2002. Firm performance and CEO pay: Relational demography as a moderator. *Journal of Managerial Issues* 14 (3): 296–313.